WINDOW ·3·
A USER'S GUIDE

About the Author

Michael Hearst trained initially on mainframe computers, specifically an ICL 1900, and then went on to work in industry for a number of years. Later he worked for a small software company when the IBM PC was launched. He went on to teach in further education for some time before becoming a journalist with one of the UK's leading computer magazines. Today he is a full-time writer and freelance journalist — his time is mainly spent in writing books and beta testing programs for major software companies.
He has had a number of books published on a range of software and hardware topics.

WINDOWS™ 3
A USER'S GUIDE

MICHAEL HEARST

Prentice Hall
New York London Toronto Sydney Tokyo Singapore

First published 1990 by
Prentice Hall International (UK) Ltd
66 Wood Lane End, Hemel Hempstead
Hertfordshire HP2 4RG
A division of
Simon & Schuster International Group

© Prentice Hall International (UK) Ltd, 1990

All rights reserved. No part of this publication may be reproduced, stored in a retrieval system or transmitted, in any form, or by any means, electronic, mechanical, photocopying, recording or otherwise, without prior permission, in writing, from the publisher.
For permission within the United States of America contact M&T Publishing Inc, 501 Galveston Drive, Redwood City, California 94063-9925.

NOTICE
The author and the publisher have used their best efforts to prepare the book, including the computer examples contained in it. The computer examples have been tested. The authors and the publisher make no warranty, implicit or explicit, about the documentation. The authors and the publisher will not be liable under any circumstances for any direct or indirect damages arising from any use, direct or indirect of the documentation or the computer examples contained in this book.

Typeset in New Century Schoolbook 10pt by
Phoenix Communications, Mountsorrel, Loughborough, Leics.

Printed and bound in Great Britain at Dotesios Printers Ltd, Trowbridge, Wiltshire.

Library of Congress Cataloging-in-Publication Data

Hearst, Michael.
    Windows 3: a user's guide/Michael Hearst.
    p.   cm.
    Includes bibliographical references (p.   ) and index.
    ISBN 0-13-605338-6
    1. Microsoft Windows (Computer programs) 2. MS-DOS (Computer operating system) I. Title.   II. Title: Windows three.
QA76.76.W56H4   1990
005.4 3-dc20

British Library Cataloguing in Publication Data

Hearst, Michael
  Windows 3: a user's guide.
  1. Microcomputer systems. Operating systems
  I. Title
  005.446
  ISBN 0-13-605338-6

1 2 3 4 5   94 93 92 91 90

For Pat Bitton,
Who has always had the Write Idea
and is the current Solitaire Champion.

Trademarks

Microsoft, MS-DOS, and the Microsoft logo are registered trademarks of Microsoft Corporation. Windows, Windows/286 and Windows/386 are trademarks of Microsoft Corporation.

8086, 8088, 80186, 80188, 80286, 80386SX, 80386, 80486 and Intel are trademarks of Intel Corporation.

Apple, LaserWriter and LaserWriter NTX are registered trademarks of Apple Corporation.

Corel Draw is a registered trademark of Corel Systems Corporation.

Hayes is a registered trademark of Hayes Microcomputer Products, Inc.

HP, Laserjet and PCL are registered trademarks of Hewlett-Packard Company.

IBM and IBM PC are registered trademarks of International Business Machines Corporation. IBM PC-AT and IBM PC-XT are trademarks of International Business Machines Corporation.

ITC and Zapf Dingbats are registered trademarks of International Typeface Corporation.

Laser 386 and Vtec are trademarks of Video Technology Computers Corporation.

Norton is a registered trademark of Peter Norton Computing, Inc.

PageMaker is a registered trademark of Aldus Corporation.

Paintbrush is a trademark of ZSoft Corporation.

PostScript is a registered trademark of Adobe Systems, Inc.

WordStar is a registered trademark of WordStar International Corporation.

Contents

Foreword 13

Notational Conventions 16

Assumptions 18

Terminology 19

Introduction 21
   A brief history of windows 22
   What's the point 24
   About this book 27

Chapter 1 Installing Windows 3

   Before you begin 29
   Open the box 29
   Running SETUP 31
   Allocating memory 34
   Installing a printer 37
   Setting up existing applications 38
   Summary 41

Chapter 2 System Resources

   Chips and more chips 43
   80386 Modes 47
   Disk Drives 49
   Memory Types 51
   MS-DOS Versions 53
   Getting the best you can 55
      The 80286 55
      The 80386SX 57
      The 80386 58
      The 80486 59
   Summary 60

Chapter 3 Starting Windows

Select a mode 61
Swapfile 62
Creating a swapfile 63
Windows layout 66
Dialogue boxes 71
System messages 72
Summary 78
Keyboard Summary 79

Chapter 4 Program Manager

Windows in use 81
Groups 89
Rearranging group contents 95
Adding things to groups 99
Deleting files from Groups 107
Creating a new Group 108
Menus 112
    File Menu 113
    Options Menu 115
    Windows Menu 116
    Control Box 117
Help 119
Program Manager Summary 121
Keyboard Summary 122

Chapter 5 Control Panel

Running the program 125
Color 128
Fonts 138
Pitch and Point 139
Fonts in Windows 141
Mouse 146
Desktop 148
Cursor Blink Rate 154
Icon Spacing 154
Sizing Grid 154
Border width 154

Network 155
Printers 155
International 165
Keyboard 174
Date/Time 174
Sound 174
386-Enhanced 174
Summary 176

Chapter 6 Setup

What is it? 177
Changing the settings 178
Adding programs 182
Problems with Setup 185
Summary 186
Keyboard Summary 187

Chapter 7 File Manager

What is it? 189
Basic actions 191
File Manager Menus 196
Summary 223
Keyboard Summary 224

Chapter 8 Print Manager

What is it? 227
Printing from Windows 230
Print Manager Menus 232
Problems with printing 235
Summary 237
Keyboard Summary 237

Chapter 9 Odds and Ends

Clipboard 239
Clipboard Summary 243
Clipboard Keyboard Summary 243
Task Switching 244
DOS Window 246

Chapter 10 Paintbrush

What is it? 249
Paintbrush Layout 250
File Menu 257
Edit Menu 262
View Menu 263
Text menus 266
Pick Menu 268
Options Menu 269
Paintbrush Tools 271
Summary 280
Keyboard Summary 280

Chapter 11 Write

What is it? 283
Cursor Keys 293
Changing Text 294
Summary 299
Keyboard Summary 300

Chapter 12 All the C's

Calculator 303
Calculator Summary 307
Calculator Keyboard Summary 307
Calendar 309
Calendar Menus 310
Calendar Summary 320

Calendar Keyboard Summary 320
Cardfile 323
Cardfile menus 324
Using the program 328
Cardfile Summary 333
Cardfile Keyboard Summary 334
Clock 335

Chapter 13 Games people play

Reversi 338
Reversi Summary 341
Reversi Keyboard Summary 341
Solitaire 342
Playing the game 344
Scoring 345
Let's Play 346
Solitaire Summary 350
Solitaire Keyboard Summary 351

Chapter 14 Notepad

What is it? 353
WIN.INI 370
Summary 370
Keyboard Summary 370

Chapter 15 Further Accessories

PIF Editor 373
PIF Editor Summary 379
PIF Editor Keyboard Summary 379
Recorder 381
Macro Tips 383
Creating a macro 383
Recorder Summary 385
Recorder Keyboard Summary 385
Terminal 387
Windows Layout 389

Terminal Summary 392
Terminal Keyboard Summary 392

Chapter 16 Problems in Windows

What problems? 395
Earlier Versions 396
MS-DOS Programs 397
Increasing Performance 398
General Problems 400

Appendices

1. Intel 8000 Series 403
2. ANSI Character Set 408

Glossary 411

Index 445

Foreword

I can remember the days when the only way to get information into a computer was using punched cards and tape. On the very first computer I ever used, an ICL 1900 series which had to be housed in a specially ventilated room, I had to learn how to decipher the cards manually, because the card punch did not have a facility to print an English translation. Happily those days are long gone. The computer industry has moved on at an exponential rate. The computer that I am writing this book on sits on one corner of my desk and has more computing power than that huge machine I first used. Similarly the method of entering information into the computer has changed dramatically. With the advent of friendly machines and operating systems, using a computer has never been easier.

Be all that as it may, many people are still intimidated by a blank screen. A computer is a tool, in exactly the same way as a hammer or a lawn-mower: it simply allows you to do certain things better and more efficiently that using something else - try hammering in nails with a half brick and you'll see what I mean. Equally try doing word processing with a typewriter - it is not possible, you must use a computer. There is this odd myth about computers - they are complex, frighteningly fast, super-human, and awkward to use, but this is only partially true. Yes, they are complex, but the complexities are hidden away and have little or no relevance to the user; they are fast, but speed is not everything; however, no machine is super-human: if anything a computer is merely an idiot savant - processing numbers at a rapid pace but the numbers mean nothing to it. (In fact the computer uses electrical currents, not numbers, which mean even less.)

It is when you come to the question of them being awkward to use that some level of truth applies. Any computer that runs under MS-DOS (the acronym means Microsoft Disk Operating System and it is the most popular and widespread computer operating system in the World) normally uses a system prompt, a thin flashing line. It is this which appears on the screen when you turn the computer on. All the prompt does is echo whatever you type on the keyboard, in exactly the same way that a typewriter echoes what you type onto the paper. However once you press the Enter or Return key the computer then begins to act on what you have typed, unlike a typewriter which simply scrolls the paper up one line. Whatever you have typed the computer assumes to be a command, i.e. something that will cause a result. It is only when it starts acting on that command that any problems will arise.

Nonetheless, Microsoft have long recognised that many people do not like the system prompt, and they developed an alternative called Windows. The technical term for Windows is a GUI, Graphical User Interface: in other words it gives you pretty pictures, called Icons, instead of a bare screen. The environment it creates is known as a WIMP environment. This acronym is short for Windows, Icons, Mouse and Pull-down menus, and this describes, very adroitly, exactly how Windows works. Instead of having to enter things from the keyboard, you simply point at the Icon, using the Mouse to activate it, then control the actions of the program using Pull-down menus. Each program normally runs in its own separate Window and you can switch from one to the other by simply clicking on it. At least that's the theory.

There have been three versions of Windows and each one has been a response to an improvement in the hardware available. The first version ran on the original PC and its cousins, i.e. those which used an 8088 or 8086 microchip. The next version was used mainly on 80286 machines. (There was a version for 80386 machines, called Windows/386, but not many people used it, preferring to use Windows/286 for a number of reasons.) The latest version is intended to run on 80386 machines and it is the best yet. In many ways Windows 3, as it is known, is what Windows always should have been. It is quick and easy to use, simple and intuitive.

This book is about learning to use and master Windows 3. It is intended principally for those people who are new to Windows, new to computing or both. The book will cover every aspect of the program and how it behaves on different machines, from the initial installation through to using the programs that are part of the Windows package. I have expressly written the book in a light, conversational style which is easy to read without getting bogged down in technical terms. Each time that a new term is mentioned it will be defined and explained so that you know what it is. The terms are also included in the Glossary at the back of the book. I hope you will enjoy reading it as much as I have enjoyed writing it.

Before we go any further, I must take some time to thank those people who have supported, encouraged and otherwise assisted with the production of this book. No book is the work of any one person: many people make contributions, suggestions, criticisms and they should all be acknowledged. Therefore I want to publicly thank them here.

> Michael Cash, my Editor, must be mentioned. He provided the initial impetus and encouragement that lead to this book.

Brian Iddon, at Microsoft, provided the software and gave a number of valuable tips and suggestions, some of which have been incorporated.

Gerry Kelly at ALR supplied the 80486 machine used for running Windows 3. A high performance machine that worked extremely well.

Tim Kay at Arche Technologies arranged for me to borrow his 386SX machine.

Michelle Mathews, at Text 100 (Microsoft's PR company in the U.K.) supplied a vast amount of background information and was always very pleasant whenever I rang her up for more details and data.

Bryan Betts, at MicroScope magazine, made a number of suggestions and he also helped check things out on various machines.

Malcolm Brown, at Star Micronics, helped out with the printer problems. He and his team are to be thanked for solving most of these.

Alan and Pat, David and Gill, at Phoenix Communications, had the unenviable task of turning the manuscript into Camera Ready Copy - a job they completed on time even though they kept getting interrupted by me wanting to make changes.

Michael Hearst

Notational Conventions

Throughout this book you will find mentioned certain keystrokes and actions that will produce specific effects. The following section details how these will appear.

Key Names and Labels

The names of the keys will appear in Bold type as they appear on the keyboard, e.g. **A**, **M**, **1**, **9**, **F3**, **F10**.

Key labels will also appear in Bold type, exactly as they appear on the keyboard, e.g. **Enter**, **Backspace**, **Del**, **Insert**, **Esc**, etc.

The cursor keys will be given according to their direction of operation, again in Bold, e.g. **Left**, **Right**, **Up** and **Down**. You can use either the actual cursor keys or those on the numeric keypad, providing you have the **Num Lock** turned off, as they both have the same effect.

Key Combinations and Sequences

Where it is necessary for you to press a number of keys together they will appear in the text joined by a hyphen, e.g. **Alt-Space** means you press the **Alt** key and the **Spacebar** at the same time, **Ctrl-F4** means you press **Ctrl** and the function key **F4** at the same time.

If the keys are to be pressed sequentially then they appear in bold but without a hyphen. Thus **Alt-Space C** means you press **Alt** and the **Spacebar** together, release them and then press **C**. **Ctrl Esc F4** means you press **Ctrl**, release it, press **Esc**, release and finally press **F4**.

Entering Commands

Throughout this book anything that you have to type verbatim, i.e. exactly as written, will appear in Bold small caps, e.g. **SETUP**, **WIN** or **WIN SOL**.

Where you are required to press **Enter** at the end of a command you will normally be told so. However, the phrase 'Enter something' means that you type the something and then press **Enter**. For example, 'enter **WIN**' means that at the system prompt you type **WIN** and then press **Enter** to activate Windows.

Anything that you have to supply as an adjunct to a command will appear in the same way as the command but enclosed in square brackets. For example, **Alt-F-S [filename]** means you press **Alt**, **F** and **S** all together and then supply a name, of your choice, as the **[filename]**.

Keyboard actions

Because this book makes extensive use of hands-on exercises using both the keyboard and the mouse, I have decided to use specific symbols for each one. Therefore wherever you can use the keyboard within an exercise the symbol on the left will appear.

Mouse Actions

Where you can use the Mouse to generate an action the symbol for the mouse will appear at the side of the text. Windows 3 has been purposely created to make using a Mouse the main option, however in many instances using the mouse and the keyboard together is faster and more precise. Thus you may find the words **Click-Alt F4** which means **Click** the left hand mouse button while pressing **Alt** at the same time, and then press **F4**.

Clicking simply means pressing one of the mouse buttons once. Unless it is otherwise mentioned the action always refers to the Left Hand Button. If you are left handed you can swap the mouse buttons around, see Chapter 5 for details.

Dragging means that you click on the subject, whether an Icon, a Window or a filename, and while still holding down the Mouse button move the Mouse so that the subject moves with you.

Pointing is moving the pointer on the screen, which normally appears as a white arrowhead and will follow the direction you move the mouse, until it touches the subject. In the case of files these will normally turn inverse, i.e. white letters on a black background.

Assumptions

This book makes a number of assumptions about certain things and is written to reflect those assumptions. They are:

Boot means, simply, to supply the machine with power so that it operates. Reboot means restarting the machine, either by pressing **Ctrl-Alt-Del** or turning the computer off and then on again. (Make sure you allow the disk to stop spinning before you restore the power if you do the latter.)

Ctrl refers to the Control key. On the majority of keyboards this is placed at the left hand bottom corner of the keyboard - on the same line that contains the spacebar. In many of the Windows menus you will see something like ^O, the ^ symbol refers to the **Ctrl** key and thus this sequence means that press **Ctrl-O**.

Hard disk means Drive-C, the disk that you would normally boot from. While it is possible to run Windows from a floppy disk it is so much hassle, even using high density disks, that it is just not worth it. To use Windows properly and effectively you absolutely must have a hard disk. Equally that hard disk must have between 5 Mb and 10 Mb spare capacity - you need nearly 4 Mb just to install Windows!

MS-DOS means MS-DOS or PC-DOS Version 3.2 or later. Wherever possible Windows has been tested with MS-DOS Versions 3.1, 3.2, 3.3 and 4.01.

Windows means Windows 3 and refers to the program as a whole. Where the word **window** appears, with no Upper Case initial, it refers to a window in which a program is running.

Terminology

Certain words and phrases will have specific meanings in this book. The following section details what these are.

Application Programs are, generally, those programs which have been supplied with Windows 3 and are included in the package. These programs have been specially written to take advantage of the way in which Windows 3 operates, especially in its use of memory and disk storage. Other Application Programs include, for example, Word for Windows, PageMaker, Excel and Ami Professional.

Copy means that you are duplicating something, e.g. a file or an Icon and so making a copy of it. The duplicate will be identical to the original. You should note that the normal MS-DOS rules about duplicate filenames and directory names apply under Windows, i.e. you cannot have two files or sub-directories of the same name in the same directory.

Cursor Keys are those keys that will cause the cursor to move in a specific direction. On all PC-AT keyboards these keys appear twice: once on the Numeric keypad, that group of 17 keys to the extreme right of the main keyboard and again as two blocks of keys between the Numeric keypad and the main keyboard. Both sets of keys produce identical effects - if you have the **Num Lock** turned Off. If the **Num Lock** is On then the keys on the Numeric Keypad produce the characters that are annotated on them.

Group means a collection of files that have been gathered together as a single entity. (We'll cover Groups more thoroughly later.) Windows 3 uses Groups very specifically and they all share a number of characteristics as well as the menus that appear on the Group window.

Icons are simply pictorial representations of things. Thus the MS-DOS Icon is shown as a monitor with DOS written on it, Paintbrush appears as a colourful palette, Clock appears as a clock face, and so on. Windows 3 will allow you to change the Icons that many programs use.

A **Menu** is a list of commands, options or items. Normally hidden away so that it cannot be seen, within Windows it will appear when you click on the menu name or when you press **Alt** and the key letter of the menu, always shown underlined, unlike on the Mac where you have to drag the menu open.

Modes refer to the different ways that Windows 3 can operate. Modes are primarily concerned with the type of processor chip used in the machine because they directly affect how Windows can operate. Thus on any machine that uses an 8086 chip, Windows can only run in **Real Mode**. On an 80286 based machine the program will normally run in **Standard Mode** - provided that there is sufficient memory available for it to do so. On machines based on the 80386SX, 80386 and 80486, Windows 3 can operate in **386-Enhanced Mode**, but to do so it must have at least 2 Mb of RAM spare, i.e. after everything else, like BUFFERS and SMARTDRV.SYS, has been allocated. This effectively means that you can really only use 386-Enhanced Mode if you have 4 Mb of RAM - contrary to what all the publicity says!

Move means, literally, what it says. Under Windows 3 you have the ability to pick up a file, directory, Icon or Group in one location and move it to another one in a single action. This is identical to copying the subject and then deleting it from the source location.

MS-DOS Programs refers to any program which is intended to be run under pure MS-DOS or PC-DOS, i.e. those programs which have not been designed to run under Windows of any version.

Selecting means marking an item, normally files, ready to be acted upon. Only after the item(s) have been selected do you initiate an action.

Introduction

Regardless of whether you like it or not, MS-DOS is the most widely used operating system in the World - the system is used on approximately 40 million computers worldwide. Dating from the early days of the PC, MS-DOS was originally created by a company called Seattle Computer Products, for what was then the new, 16-bit microchips being developed by Intel Corporation. Prior to this the only operating system readily available was CP/M. Unfortunately this was based on 8-bit technology and so something new was needed. Seattle Computer Products created just such a thing and called it Q-DOS. The company had neither the financial nor the human resources to develop the product further and so they sold the program, complete with the full development rights, to another small software company called Microsoft. At the time this company was well known for its programming languages.

Then IBM decided that it would create a new breed of computers, ones that would sit on a desktop and so could be used by anybody. They called the machine the Personal Computer. Because IBM wanted to build the machine very quickly they decided to make it from bits and pieces that were all readily available, off the shelf, that just needed to be put together. That's exactly what they did, but they then found that they had no operating system. The 8088 and 8086 chips were so new, at the time, that there was no operating system around that could handle the 16-bit processes. So there was IBM, with a machine all ready to go but no operating system. They approached Digital Research, the creators of CP/M, trying to get a 16-bit version of their operating system. But for some reason, that no-one now likes to recall, Digital Research politely declined to supply it. And there, waiting in the wings so to speak, was a young man from Seattle named Bill Gates.

He and his partner, Paul Allen, had taken the fledgling operating system, Q-DOS, and rewritten it, improved and otherwise enhanced it. Bill Gates sold the rights to use the operating system to IBM - note he didn't sell them the whole thing, just a licence to use it, and so the IBM PC was born. Since then Bill Gates, who personally owns 45% of Microsoft, has become the youngest dollar billionaire in the world, and Microsoft has gone from strength to strength. In 1981 when the PC was launched, MicroSoft employed less than 100 people at one site - today they employ over 4,000 people worldwide.

But MS-DOS has a big problem - it is very unfriendly, or apparently so. The operating system controls every aspect of the computer, not just the disk drives, and it does this without you, the user, even noticing. And that's the problem. When you turn on the computer, it runs through its in-built tests, loads the operating system, runs your tailoring files, the CONFIG.SYS and AUTOEXEC.BAT, and then sits there... waiting.... All you can see is a little cursor flashing away rhythmically on an otherwise blank screen. Not the most inspiring introduction to the joys of computing.

In addition the operating system has largely remained unchanged since its inception. Because it has to remain downwards compatible, which simply means that it must be able to run any software that was written for a previous version, it becomes limited in what it can do. Since the original IBM PC there have been enormous advances in the chip technology; firstly to the 80286, then the 80386 and now to 80486 - and the 80586 is due before the end of 1990. But MS-DOS still has to operate as if the computer was an 8086 - it cannot take advantage of the enhancements and improvements in the chip design and technology. So what can be done? The answer is to work around the problem.

Because they realised that many people are intimidated by the operating system, Microsoft developed a new product that used pictures instead. The system is called Windows and it is known as a GUI system. The acronym means Graphical User Interface and is simply technospeak for a system that uses images on screen rather than a system prompt. The User bit refers to you, and the Interface is the visual aspect of the program with which you interact. (There are probably more acronyms in the computer industry than anywhere else, and new ones are created almost every day.)

A brief history of Windows

Bill Gates, the co-founder of Microsoft, has often been heard to say that he would like to see "a PC in every business and one in every home". Pursuant to this dream is the concept underlying Windows. The system is designed to be easy and intuitive to use and to remove any latent fear that people might have with regard to computers. Because many people are intimidated by the system cursor on a bare machine, MicroSoft created the Windows environment.

Windows presents you with a series of Icons, essentially pictures, of programs, files, disks, etc. and you use a Mouse and Pull-down Menus to select and run the software that you want to use, hence the name WIMP environment. One major advantage of the system is that once you master Windows you essentially know how to use 80% of any software that has been designed to run under the environment. Because Windows provides a consistent interface for the software, there will be only minor differences between various packages - their overall performance and use will remain unchanged. The advantage of this is that it provides a consistency that is lacking under pure MS-DOS.

Microsoft launched the first version of Windows in November 1983. The program was an immediate success and a number of leading hardware manufacturers decided to bundle the software with their machines. At the same time various software companies latched on to the system as an ideal method of producing universally acceptable software. A new standard was born.

In July 1989, Microsoft launched Windows/286. Designed to run on the recently launched 80286 chip from Intel Corporation, the new version of Windows was a great improvement of the original. However because it had to be downwards compatible, i.e. capable of running software from the original version, Windows/286 could not take active advantage of the memory usage abilities of the new chip. However, the interface was a big improvement and it provided additional support for the new printers that were appearing, enhanced graphic resolutions and better machine configurations. At roughly the same period of time, Intel launched the 80386 microchip and Microsoft produced a version of Windows which was intended to be specific to that chip, called Windows/386. However, this was really only a 'tweaked' version of Windows/286 and as such it had no real advantages, with the result that many people never bothered moving up from Windows/286.

On May 22nd. 1990, Microsoft Corporation launched Windows 3 amidst a fanfare of publicity. The launch, which actually took place in New York, was broadcast by satellite around the U.S.A. and is rumoured to have cost over a million dollars. So what is so special as to warrant spending that kind of money? Windows 3 is a system so far advanced from the earlier versions that they might as well be two different products, for all that they look very similar. Windows 3 provides full and total support for the 80386 microchip and its ability to control memory. It is now possible to have full concurrency using Windows. This means that, providing you have sufficient memory, you can effectively run a number of programs as if each was running on a separate PC - all on one machine. This ability is limited only by the amount of RAM that is installed in the computer on which the system is being run. Windows 3 is what Windows always should have been and further demonstrates Microsoft's commitment to end users.

What's the point?

Windows 3 does much more than provide the end user, i.e. you, with a standardised interface: that is just the surface gloss. Beneath this colourful exterior the heart of the system has been radically changed. For example, Windows 3 is downwards compatible with previous versions of Windows only in a very limited sense. True the new program can run software from the earlier versions, but only in one particular way - in Real mode. Windows 3 is that rare thing in the computer industry - an upgrade that is so radically better than the original that it almost severs its connections with the earlier version.

Windows allows you to transfer images and text from one application to another with ease. Simply select the item you want in one application, copy it to the Clipboard, open the next application and paste the data into place. Because of the way in which Windows 3 works you can do this even from MS-DOS programs. Windows 3 allows you to open an MS-DOS window, effectively causing Windows to retreat into the memory, and operate the computer as if Windows wasn't there - though you do have to be careful about memory usage in such a case. You can then run any program as you would have done if you did not have Windows. When you have finished you simply enter **EXIT** and reinstate Windows onto the screen, fully operable and ready to go. (Fast software as opposed to fast food?)

When it comes to the actual hardware that the program is running on, Windows 3 really comes into its own. Windows 3 provides three different methods of operation, known as Modes, and these have a fundamental effect on how the computer works. Each mode is dependent on certain hardware parameters being present.

The modes are:

> **Real** which forces the chip, regardless of whether it is an 80286, 80386, 80386SX or 80486, to operate in an identical way to the 8086 chip that was the heart of the original IBM PC. This means that it can run standard MS-DOS software without any modifications to the programs. Any program running in Real mode can access a maximum of 1 Mb of RAM. If you are using software that was developed for an earlier version of Windows then the only way that you can use that software without encountering any problems is to use this mode. Windows 3 must be told to run in Real mode and you do so by entering **WIN/R**

from the system prompt, when you activate the Windows program. On any machine that has 1 Mb or less of RAM you can only run Windows 3 in Real mode.

Standard is fully compatible with the 80286 microchip Protected mode and it is in this mode that Windows 3 is normally likely to run on most machines. In this mode Windows has access to extended memory and it will allow you to switch between non-Windows programs - providing you have enough memory to do so. For example, one of the machines that this book is being written on is an 80386 AT with 2 Mb of RAM. Because 256 Kb is used for SMARTDRV.SYS and 768 Kb is used for a Ramdrive, which provides the print buffer for Windows, there is insufficient memory to allow switching between MS-DOS programs from within Windows. I can switch from Windows to MS-DOS and back again, but I cannot have two or more MS-DOS programs open at the same time. If I try to do so the machine locks up tight and needs to be rebooted. (Mind you, that could well be the machine's fault rather than Windows'.)

386-Enhanced is brand new and this is what makes Windows 3 so special. Put simply, it allows Windows 3 to operate on an 80386, 80386SX or 80486 chip in such a way that it simulates the Real mode of the 8086. It does this by using the Virtual Memory capabilities of these three chips which will allow programs, in this case Windows 3, to use more memory than is actually present. (It does so by using the hard disk as you will see later.) When in this mode Windows 3 can perform genuine multi-tasking of either specific Windows application and/or of MS-DOS programs. Each program operates independently of the others and each is allocated its own 1 Mb chunk of the available RAM. In essence this means that you can have a number of programs all running on the same machine, in tandem with and yet separate from each other, i.e. you can apparently have multiple PC's on the same machine.

Note, however, that if the machine possesses less than 4 Mb of RAM then the multi-tasking will be severely limited or even nonexistent. In a sense, the amount of RAM available will have a direct bearing on the number of programs that can be multi-tasked, as each one will require 1 Mb for its own use. Thus if you have 4 Mb you can have four programs running simultaneously, 8 Mb gives you eight and so on. (In fact you can do slightly better but the principle remains the same.) 386-

Enhanced mode will only operate by default if your system hardware matches the specification required of it, see below. However you can force the program to run in this mode on a machine with less than the optimum system resources, by entering **WIN/3** at the system prompt. The problem with this though, is that the program is very likely to run appreciably slower than if it was in Standard mode on the same machine.

Each mode places a limit on the minimum hardware requirements as follows:

To run in Real mode you can use any Intel based computer provided that it has a minimum of 640 Kb of RAM.

To run in Standard mode you need an 80286 or better plus a minimum of 1 Mb of RAM, after installing other devices like BUFFERS, though the more memory you have, the better.

For 386-Enhanced mode you must have an 80386, 80386SX or 80486 plus an absolute minimum of 2 Mb of free RAM although, again, more memory helps.

In addition, regardless of what mode you will be using, you must also have the following:

a) A hard disk with at least 5 Mb, and preferably 10 Mb, of free capacity.

b) At least one floppy drive.

c) A Mouse. You can use Windows without a Mouse but it's like trying to dig without a spade - possible but very exhausting and hasslesome.

d) If you want to use the Terminal program (the telecommunications linker) you must also have a Hayes compatible modem.

About this book

This book is intended to be a hands on tutorial guide to Windows 3. It will help you learn to use the Windows itself and every one of the bundled programs that come with the main package. Each and every program, its characteristics, mode of operation and method of use, will be described and explored in detail. At the end of each chapter I have included exercises and experiments that you can perform to help you get the best out of the software. In addition, each chapter ends with a complete reference guide to the program concerned.

This book has been written on four separate machines so that all eventualities will have been covered, especially the Windows installation. The machines used were as listed below, for each machine I have also given the Norton SI figures - these are purely by way of comparison.

a) A Samsung 80286-based AT, running at 10 MHz and fitted with 1 Mb of RAM. The machine has two 20 Mb MFM hard disks and a single 5.25" 1.2 Mb floppy drive. The SI figures are:

Computing Index (Relative to an IBM/XT)................. 11.2
Disk Index (Relative to an IBM/XT) 2.3
Overall Performance (Relative to an IBM/XT)............ 8.2

b) An Arche 80386SX-based AT running at 16 MHz and fitted with 8 Mb of RAM. The machine has a single 1.2 Gb SCSI hard disk and a single floppy drive. The Norton SI figures for the machine are:

Computing Index (Relative to an IBM/XT)................. 15.6
Disk Index (Relative to an IBM/XT) 8.4
Overall Performance (Relative to an IBM/XT).......... 13.2

The performance figure for the Hard disk on this machine is very misleading. A SCSI drive is phenomenally fast but Norton SI cannot interpret it properly. In actuality this hard disk is the fastest one fitted to any of the four machines, it has an access time that is less than half of that on the other machines and thus produced correspondingly high data handling times. Because of the way in which Windows works this machine actually produces the best performance of all four machines.

c) A Vtec Laser 80386-based AT running at 25 MHz and fitted with 2 Mb of RAM. The machine has a single 70 Mb RLL hard disk, two floppy drives; a 5.25" 1.2 Mb and a 3.5" 1.44 Mb. The Norton SI figures for this machines are:

Computing Index (Relative to an IBM/XT) 28.2
Disk Index (Relative to an IBM/XT) 8.9
Overall Performance (Relative to an IBM/XT) 21.7

d) An ALR 80486-based AT running at 20 MHz with 4 Mb of RAM and fitted with a 40 Mb ERLL hard disk. The Norton SI figures are:

Computing Index (Relative to an IBM/XT) 27.2
Disk Index (Relative to an IBM/XT) 5.6
Overall Performance (Relative to an IBM/XT) 21.3

Chapter 1

Installing Windows 3

Before you begin

There is a well documented problem with using Windows 3 on any machine that has a hard disk which is partitioned using the Disk Manager DMDRV.BIN program. It appears that the SMARTDRV.SYS program, which is a disk cache used by Windows, and DMDRV.BIN are in conflict at some level. In the worst cases recorded to date the File Allocation Table of the hard disk becomes damaged, as a result of which data will be lost from the hard disk. The problem can, apparently, occur with other third party hard disk utility software which produces disk partitions above the 32 Mb MS-DOS 3.30 limit.

Another problem occurs with hard disks that have more than 1024 cylinders on them. Again the damage can be substantial and far reaching.

As yet there is no easy answer available. However if your hard disk is partitioned using Disk Manager then it is suggested that you do not install SMARTDRV.SYS, see later, and so avoid the problem. Microsoft will soon be offering a updated version of SMARTDRV.SYS to all registered users - which is a good reason for filling in and returning the Registration Card.

On the plus side, many MS-DOS programs seem to work much faster when used from the Windows environment. In particular those that are heavily keyboard dependent, like word processors, seem to run about 50% faster. Don't ask why, I'm not sure. However I suspect it is because Windows has better control of the keyboard than MS-DOS itself has, and because you can vary the keyboard speed you get better results.

Open the box

Windows 3 is supplied on either 360 Kb or 1.2 Mb 5.25" floppies or on 720 Kb 3.5" disks and you have to specify which one you want when you purchase the product. When you open the box you will find a packet of disks in an envelope which is printed with the licence agreement, a manual, a run time version of Asymetrix Toolbook, and half a dozen bits of paper. Normally you probably wouldn't bother with the bits of paper but in this case I suggest you read them.

One sheet contains an impressive list of hardware that has been tested with Windows 3. Some of these are prefixed by an asterisk, which means that the machines concerned need to be dealt with in a specific way as part of the installation routine.

Another sheet gives a list of companies that have already begun production of, or have already released, Windows 3 compatible versions of their software. Even when this list first appeared, prior to the Windows 3 launch, it was out of date. At the last count (July 1990) there were well over 500 companies preparing Windows 3 based software and the number grows daily. Proof positive that Windows 3 is the most important software development of the decade.

However the most important piece of paper in the package is the Registration Card. It is vital that you fill this in and return it to Microsoft. Why? Well, registering software, any software, allows the manufacturer to gauge the public acceptance of the program and to build a picture of where the program is being used and by whom. From the user's point of view, filling in the registration card (and returning it) brings a range of privileges to make life easier. Registered users get advance notice of new products, better technical support, increased awareness of things and other benefits. Even if you have never registered a program in your life before you should register your copy of Windows 3.

One other very important point - read the licence agreement. Yes, I know it's full of legalese and is not suitable for reading at the breakfast table, but you should read it. You may be surprised to learn that you do not own the software! All you have is a licence to use the program on your computer - but Windows remains the property of Microsoft. This is not unusual, every software house has the same kind of clauses. You never own software, unless you write it yourself, you merely have permission to use it. The licence is printed on the envelope that contains the disks and once you open this, you have accepted the licensing restrictions and clauses.

When you open the envelope you will find either five 1.2 Mb 5.25" floppies or seven 720 Kb 3.5" ones. The 360 Kb 5.25" disks have to be specially ordered which implies that Microsoft intend that the program only be used on PC-AT machines, i.e. the ones with high density drives.

Running SETUP

Windows 3 will take about 20 to 30 minutes to install completely, depending on how many printers you include. You cannot interrupt the installation once it has begun. Either you are installing the software or you're not! You cannot go part way through the routine, stop it and then come back and carry on later - unless you want to leave the computer sitting there doing nothing while you go away, which is not a good idea.

Turn on your computer and, once it has booted up, enter **DIR**. The important point about this is that it will tell you how much free disk space you have available. To install Windows 3 you need to allow an absolute minimum of 5 Mb, that's 5,242,880 bytes. You can install it in less space than that but in the end it's not worth it - you must have sufficient room on your hard disk.

If you are updating from a previous version of Windows then I suggest that you rename the directory that contains the old files. If you don't have a utility that will allow this, you should create a new directory by entering **MD C:\WIN-OLD**. Then copy all the files from the old windows directory to the one you have just created by entering **COPY C:\WINDOWS*.* C:\WIN-OLD**, assuming that the old directory was named WINDOWS. Once the files have been copied enter **DEL WINDOWS** to delete the files from the original directory. Answer **Y** when prompted and all the files will be erased. Finally enter **RD WINDOWS** to remove the old directory.

Now, take the Windows 3 disk labelled Disk 1 and place it into the corresponding drive, usually Drive-A, and then enter **A:**, followed by **SETUP** once you are logged onto the drive.

After a short time you will be presented with a message bidding you welcome to Setup. From here you can press **F1** to activate the help with setup routine, which simply gives you various methods of using the program. Pressing **F3** will terminate the installation, both at this screen and at any time further on into the installation. To begin the installation proper just press **Enter**.

You will be asked to specify which drive and directory you want Windows 3 installed on and in. By default this is always **C:\WINDOWS** - hence the reason for renaming any directory containing an older version of Windows. If you want to use another drive, use the cursor keys to move back to the drive letter, delete it and then type the new drive designator.

If you want to use a different directory, erase the default and type your preference. To accept the Windows default, or your own choice, press **Enter** again and there will then be a delay while the setup program checks your system configuration.

This part of the program is quite perceptive. It will check all your system resources, from the monitor type through to the keyboard configuration, and present you with a list of what it finds. However, if you are installing the program on anything other than a computer configured to the American standard, the list will be wrong - but only in minor detail.

```
Windows Setup

     Setup has determined that your system includes the following hardware
     and software components. If your computer or network appears on the
     Hardware Compatibility List with an asterisk, press F1 for Help.

            Computer:        MS-DOS or PC-DOS System
            Display:         EGA
            Mouse:           No mouse or other pointing device
            Keyboard:        Enhanced 101 or 102 key US and Non US keyboards
            Keyboard Layout: US
            Language:        English (American)
            Network:         Network not installed

            No Changes:      The above list matches my computer.

     If all the items in the list are correct, press ENTER to indicate
     "No Changes." If you want to change any item in the list, press the
     UP or DOWN ARROW key to move the highlight to the item you want to
     change. Then press ENTER to see alternatives for that item.

     ENTER=Continue  F1=Help  F3=Exit
```

Windows Setup System Identification

For example, the Keyboard Layout section always says US - I've never seen it say anything else. While this might be true in the U.S.A. it is wrong for the U.K. The keyboard layout tells Windows what characters are produced by certain keys, for example, in the U.K. you want **Shift-3** to produce a Sterling Pound sign (£), whereas in the U.S. it normally produces a hash (#).

To change this setting, or any of the others, move the highlighter bar up using the cursor keys until it overlays the area you want to change. Once there press **Enter** to pop-up a menu of possible configurations. Select the one you want, again using the cursor keys, then press **Enter** again. You will be returned to the Setup screen with your choice now set as the new default. Once you have changed all the parameters you want or need to, pressing **Enter** will begin the actual installation.

The program creates the necessary directories on your hard disk and begins copying the files. After a while it will ask you to remove Disk 1 and replace it with Disk 2. Do so and press **Enter** to continue the process.

Suddenly the setup screen vanishes and you find yourself in a true GUI window, although you are not yet truly into Windows 3, a sort of proto-windows. At this point you cannot use the program for anything other than continuing the installation. A word of warning: Any memory resident program you may have loaded cannot now be activated. Trying to activate any such program may cause the machine to hang up completely.

The screen contains three pre-checked options:

> Set up Printers
> Set up Applications Already on Hard Disk
> Read on-line Documents

As this is the first time you are installing Windows, I suggest that you accept all three options by just pressing **Enter**. Alternatively you can deselect any option by clicking on it. You are better off doing all three things here, rather than having to do it later.

The installation continues with more files being copied and after a while you will be asked to remove Disk 2 and replace it with Disk 3. Do so and press **Enter** again or click on the button that says **OK** to continue the installation. Replace Disk 3 when asked in the same way. Setup continues to copy files until all the necessary ones, plus those device drivers you have selected (whether you knew it or not) on the previous screen have been installed.

The next stage is that Windows Setup needs to change your CONFIG.SYS and AUTOEXEC.BAT files. You can allow the program to do this for you, the fastest option, or you can review the changes before they are made, the best option because you can see what is going on. Alternatively you can make the changes later by having setup write the recommended files to the disk you for to modify later.

Click on the second option using the mouse, or if you prefer to use the keyboard press **Down**, and then press **Enter**. You will be presented with two windows, one above the other, the top one containing your current AUTOEXEC.BAT and the bottom one containing the suggested changes. The usual change at this point is to ensure that the WINDOWS directory is added to your PATH statement, or if you do not have such a thing then the program will create one for you. Press **Enter** to accept the changes and your original AUTOEXEC.BAT will be renamed to AUTOEXEC.OLD while the setup one will be written to your disk as AUTOEXEC.BAT.

Allocating memory

Next come the changes to the CONFIG.SYS and these depend on the type of machine you are using. Windows 3 is a memory hungry little beast and it needs enormous amounts of RAM to operate correctly, therefore it will hog as much of the available memory as possible.

For example, on the Samsung I had a Ramdrive of 320 Kb set up, but Windows reduced this to 128 Kb and took the remaining 192 Kb of RAM for itself. Equally there was no room for it to install SMARTDRV.SYS (which is supposed to be essential) so it didn't bother with it. It did replace the HIMEM.SYS device driver - the version supplied with Windows 3 differs from that supplied with previous versions and you must use the right one or the program will not work. You can use old versions of Windows with the new HIMEM.SYS but not vice versa. Setup is not very user friendly, the HIMEM.SYS file was copied into the Root of the hard disk and the CONFIG.SYS file amended accordingly with the line **DEVICE=C:\HIMEM.SYS**. However, I like to keep the Root directory as clean and file free as possible, but Setup has no provision for placing the device driver anywhere else. The result is that you have to move it yourself later and then manually change the CONFIG.SYS to accommodate the change. (We use the CONFIG.SYS and AUTOEXEC.BAT files as the examples for Notepad later because the program produces pure ASCII files.) The funny thing is that Setup stores SMARTDRV.SYS in the WINDOWS directory, so why can't it do the same thing with HIMEM.SYS?

The Arche 80386SX had more than enough memory available for SMARTDRV.SYS to be fully installed - after all 8 Mb should be enough for just about anything. The machine originally had all of the extended memory configured as a Ramdrive. Because the disk is a SCSI one (See Page 50) it uses its own built in disk cache and so there was no need for an external one. The original CONFIG.SYS looked like this:

```
FILES=30
BUFFERS=30
COUNTRY=044,,C:\DOS\COUNTRY.SYS
INSTALL  C:\DOS\SHARE.EXE
DEVICE=C:\WINDOWS\RAMDRIVE.SYS  7168  /E
```

The Windows Setup program added two lines, the first installing HIMEM.SYS and the second installing SMARTDRV.SYS with the parameters 2048 1024. In other words it took 2 Mb of the RAM for its own purposes and will allow a minimum cache of 1024 Kb. This speeds up Windows enormously. While the Arche machine is only a 16 MHz 80386SX, it has the greatest system resources of all the machines used for this book. This is the only one of the four machines that will allow Windows to run in 386-Enhanced mode by default - but for all that the program runs slower on this machine than it does on the Laser 80386.

On the Laser, there was enough memory for SMARTDRV.SYS to be installed, but only as a 256 Kb cache. But then it did something funny. The Laser 386 has 2 Mb of RAM and originally 1344 Kb of this was set up as a Ramdrive, because 64 Kb of the memory is used as a system cache. During the Windows 3 Setup, the program installed SMARTDRV.SYS using 256 Kb of the RAM and then reduced the amount of RAM allocated to the Ramdrive down to 256 Kb - but it ignored the remaining 832 Kb!

So I reinstated the Ramdrive with all 1088 Kb, the Windows allocation of 256 plus the unused bit. After rebooting, to activate the changes, Windows wouldn't run, in any mode, because there wasn't enough memory for it! Gradually by trial and error, which meant rebooting the machine after every change, I found that using a ramdrive of 768 Kb allowed sufficient memory for everything. But why didn't the Windows setup allow this much? I don't know and haven't been able to find out.

The CONFIG.SYS on the Laser 386 now looks like this:

```
FILES=30
BUFFERS=10
COUNTRY=044,,C:\DOS\COUNTRY.SYS
INSTALL  C:\DOS\SHARE.EXE
DEVICE=C:\DOS\HIMEM.SYS
DEVICE=C:\WINDOWS\SMARTDRV.SYS  256  256
DEVICE=C:\WINDOWS\RAMDRIVE.SYS  768  /E
```

The Files command, which specifies how many different files can be open at any one time, must be set to a minimum of eight for running

MS-DOS. Because I use WordStar, which is heavily file dependent, and PageMaker which is even more so, I have had to increase the number of files to 30. Each one above the minimum eight, uses an additional 48 bytes of RAM. Therefore the 30 files use up 1056 bytes or just over 1 Kb.

Each buffer takes up 528 bytes, therefore the 10 of them use 5280 bytes or just over 5 Kb. Notice that the number of Buffers is very small, in the normal course of events you would set the buffers to at least 20 and preferably 30, on an 80386 machine with a 70 Mb hard disk. But SMARTDRV.SYS takes over some of the activities of the buffers command, with the result that you can reduce the number of buffers to 10. Don't make it less than this or you will run into problems.

In the end the RAM on the Laser 386 is allocated as follows:

> System Disk Cache 64 Kb
> MS-DOS reserved area 640 Kb
> FILES 1 Kb
> BUFFERS 5 Kb
> HIMEM.SYS 64 Kb
> SMARTDRV.SYS 256 Kb
> RAMDRIVE 768 Kb

If you add that up you will find that only 1798 Kb of the RAM is allocated to various things, leaving 250 Kb unaccounted for. SMARTDRV.SYS automatically uses a minimum of an additional 17 Kb just by being there, but that still leaves 233 Kb of the memory unaccounted for. Where has it gone? I don't know, all I do know is that if I change any of the sizes mentioned above, Windows 3 will not run because there is not enough memory available for it. To be honest, I don't care - as long as everything works the way that I want it to!

On the ALR machine, which had 4 Mb of extended memory there were a lot of problems getting the machine to recognise that it had this much RAM in the first place. (The machine as loaned by ALR was brand new and had to be configured completely before it could be used.) Eventually, after a lot of messing about and numerous phone calls to ALR I did manage to get it to recognise the extra RAM. Only after that did I install Windows. As with the Arche machine, SMARTDRV.SYS took 2 Mb for itself and left 2 Mb for a Ramdrive. But the strange thing is that after expecting this machine to be the best in terms of performance, it was actually slower than either of the 386 machines.

Conclusion

Having played about with various memory configurations, RAM allocations and what have you, I found that Windows would run in Standard mode by default on both the Laser and the ALR machines but each would could be forced to run in 386-Enhanced mode by entering WIN/3 at the system prompt. In this mode the Laser ran Windows faster than the ALR machine, even though the latter uses a superior chip.

On the Samsung it ran in Real mode and it was impossible to get it to run in anything else. Using Windows 3 on the 80286, certainly on the one used for this book with its very limited resources, was a nonsense. It works, just, but the program is dreadfully slow, cumbersome, unwieldy and uncooperative. That's not to say that the Samsung 80286 is an inferior machine - it just doesn't work very well with Windows 3, because Windows needs so much more in terms of resources to run properly. I certainly would not recommend using Windows 3 on any 80286 based machine.

On the Arche 80386SX-based machine, Windows ran in 386-Enhanced mode by default, because there is so much RAM available, but the program actually ran visibly slower than on the 80386SX or the 80386. I'm still not sure why this was so but it did! It seems that Windows always runs slower in 386-Enhanced mode, regardless of the system resources available and the type of chip being used.

The fastest machine of the four when it came to running Windows, in any mode, was the Laser 80386 - which surprised me but also pleased me because this is my main machine.

Installing a printer

As the next stage of the installation, Setup allows you to install a printer. In actuality all it does is install the printer driver - you have to configure the printer separately. From here on the Setup acts as if you were in Windows proper - but be warned, you are not yet. The screen display shows a large box, covering almost half of the screen area, with a highlighter bar overlying the first name in the list of printers. Using the cursor keys move this highlighter to the printer type you want to install. In all probability you will have to install your printer as an emulation, unless you possess one of the mentioned printers. For example, my StarScript printer is not mentioned in the list of printers. But because it emulates, almost exactly, an Apple LaserWriter it can be installed as that.

It appears that Microsoft have rewritten a number of the printer drivers - I just wish they had told us. My StarScript, which is actually a Star Laser 8II with added PostScript emulation, used to run perfectly well under Windows/286 as an Apple LaserWriter NTX. So when I first installed Windows 3, I used that emulation for the printer. Result - complete hangup of the printer. It began throwing out error messages like there was no tomorrow. In the end, by trial and error, I found that it had to be installed as a plain Apple LaserWriter. Oddly enough, that emulation didn't work correctly running from Windows/286!

At this stage all you want to do is find the emulation you want and then press **Enter**. You may have to swap the disk, to #5, as part of the printer installation. If you want to install a second printer you can do so in exactly the same way. Finally click on the button marked **OK**. Using the keyboard press **Tab** until the **OK** key is highlighted and then press **Enter**.

Setting up existing applications

The next stage of the Setup is to allow Windows to configure itself so that you can run MS-DOS programs from within the Windows environment. The part of the program that does this is much faster than having to install applications by hand. You have three options:

    All Drives,
    PATH only, or
    Specific Drives

Which you select is entirely up to you and it will depend on how you want to use your computer. Once you select an option and click on OK the program searches through the chosen site trying to find files that have an extension of .EXE. It does not search for .COM files! As it searches you get a display telling you how much, in percentage terms, of your disk the program has searched. Once the search is finished the screen changes to display a list of the MS-DOS applications that have been found.

You now select which of these will be setup for use in Windows. Chances are that the program will have found many more applications than you will want to include and so you have to select specific ones by clicking on them. You can select as many as you want, each one will be highlighted in inverse video. Once your selection is complete click on **Add->**. Setup then creates specific PIF files for each application. (PIF stands for Program Information File and it is a special file that Windows needs in order to run MS-DOS programs. See the relevant chapter for full details.)

If you want to run Windows in place of the system prompt, then you should select everything that the program finds. However, because the Setup program only looks for .EXE files you will find that many of your current programs are not included, additionally, some programs you didn't know existed will be displayed. Windows 3 is actually designed to replace the system prompt but if you want to include all your programs and run them from within Windows you will have to install them separately. (We'll cover this later.)

Once you press **Enter**, or click on **OK**, Setup begins to create the program groups. A program group is, basically, a collection of programs that share certain attributes. The process is automatic and uninterruptable. You can change the groups later, but for now just let Setup get on with it.

Once the groups have been created Setup activates Windows Notepad and begins to displaying the .TXT files that have been installed. You can read these now - they contain a range of information that is not included in the manual, or leave them until later. Once you have finished reading a file press **Alt-Spacebar C** or **Alt-F4** to close the Notepad.

You now get a message telling you that Windows 3 has been installed and you are provided with three possible options:

> **Reboot** will perform a warm restart of your machine and activate the changes that have been made within the CONFIG.SYS and AUTOEXEC.BAT. As such this is the preferable option.

> **Restart Windows** will activate Windows proper. However, you may find that it does not work correctly or, even worse, not at all - especially if Setup has changed the memory allocations. This is the least preferable option.

Return to MS-DOS takes you out of the Setup program and drops you back to the system prompt. Personally, I used this one because I use Norton Format Recover to protect the files on my disk. By dropping out of Setup back to the system prompt, I was able to immediately update the Norton file. Additionally, I also compressed, or compacted, the disk (making all the files contiguous) because once you start Windows you need to add a huge file to your disk, as you will see, and it is better to compress the disk first.

Select whichever option you wish by clicking on it. Windows is now installed and ready for use but you will probably have to fiddle around with things first to get the optimum performance.

Summary

- There is a definite problem if you are using a hard disk partitioned with Disk Manager and you also want to use SMARTDRV.SYS.

- Read the Licence Agreement - it tells you your rights and obligations.

- Fill in and return the Registration card - it is more than worth your while.

- Remove any old version of Windows before installing Windows 3, ideally by renaming the old directory but you may have to physically move the old files. Don't delete the old version though because you may need it for some older Windows-based software until new versions of the software are released.

- Before you install Windows find out what hardware you are using. In particular what monitor type you are using and what kind of memory you have as this has a marked affect on Windows.

- Install your printer as part of the Setup, it's quicker and easier to do it here rather than later. However, you will need to know what printer yours emulates if it is not one of the named brands.

- Existing Windows applications may not run properly in Windows 3 if you use anything other than Real Mode. New versions of old Windows software is being released, make sure you get new copies if you want to use Windows 3 to advantage.

- When you have installed Windows return to the MS-DOS system prompt. From there organise your disk and compact the files before you reboot.

Chapter 2
System Resources

The purpose of this chapter is to examine some of the problems that you will encounter when running Windows 3 on different kinds of machines, but before we begin that let's have a look at computers in general and the resources, e.g. amount of memory, disk drives and what have you, that different machines have.

Chips and more chips

The original IBM PC, which after all is the machine that all other MS-DOS based machines are descended from, used the Intel 8088 chip as its main processor. This is really a cut-down version of the 8086, and it was introduced in 1978. IBM used the 8088 rather than the 8086 because it was cheaper and they thought that people would be disinclined to buy the more powerful and faster 8086. The original IBM PC, named the Model 5150-001 retailed at $1,355 in 1979, which in today's terms is worth around $4,000, and that is a fair amount of money and was even more then. IBM's dream was to create a machine that would be affordable by everyone, effectively creating a brand new market because prior to that time computers were big, bulky affairs that required specialised environments. It was an enormous and rather surprising risk that IBM took but it has paid off handsomely.

The 8088 has the same internal architecture, i.e. it does the same sort of thing as the 8086, but has only got an 8-bit data bus. This means that it is much slower in accessing data from disk or memory. It could, however, address up to a maximum of 1 Mb of RAM using a 20-bit address bus. The chip could run in only one way - Real mode. At the time this was no bad thing and alternative modes were just a gleam in the eyes of Intel's designers.

The original PC was a huge advance over existing computers. It was faster, more dynamic, better organised and, most important of all, small enough to sit on a desk. (Actually IBM had created a desk top computer prior to the Model 5150 but it was not a success and quickly vanished.) At the time of the launch of the PC, the machine used cassette tapes as its main storage medium and it had a very limited amount of memory.

(RAM chips have always been one of the most expensive elements of any computer and that is still true today.) However, within a very short space of time the cassettes were replaced by the first floppy disk drives.

These used single sided disks, which is really a misnomer because all disks are double sided - they are just not verified on both sides. These could hold 120 Kb which was at the time an enormous amount of data. Remember that the average program at that time was less than 64 Kb. Note that there were no hard disks, just floppies and tape cassettes. Memory capacity was low, by today's standards, but these machines were the effective start of the computer revolution.

Within a very short space of time a new PC arrived, this time based on the 8086. This was actually the first chip in the 8000 series created by Intel and it was developed by Intel in 1976 - unfortunately very few companies took it up at the time. The chip possesses a 16-bit data bus, which means it can access disk based data faster, but it was still limited in terms of addressing RAM. The 1 Mb maximum RAM usage limitation still applied however, although at the time this was not seen as a limitation. Again, the chip will run in only one way - Real mode.

Apart from the differences in the data bus size there is no real difference between the 8088 and the 8086, in fact the chips are virtually identical. However the larger bus on the 8086 means that it does tend to run slightly quicker because it can read and write the data faster. The original PC, using an 8088 chip, ran at 4.77 MHz, i.e. it could perform just under 5,000,000 operations per second, and this speed is used as the base measure against which all other chips are matched. It is still possible to purchase 8088 chips: they are very cheap and so they allow the construction of very basic, low level and low price machines. However the technology of the rest of the peripheral devices used in today's computers means that the 8088, or the 8086, actually act as a brake on the speed with which the computer can operate.

The next stage in the development of the personal computer was the XT, which stands for eXtended Technology. The only real difference between the PC and XT is that the latter uses Hard Disks. Apart from this there is no difference between the two types of machine. A hard disk is simply a collection of aluminium disks, today they are normally 3.5" in diameter, which have been coated with a magnetisable material. These platters, as they are called, are enclosed inside a sealed unit, along with the Read/Write heads and motor, to prevent dust and airborne particles from contaminating them.

A hard disk must have a controller card to operate it. The original standard for these was the ST-506/412 developed by Shugart Associates, or more properly by Allen Shugart himself. When IBM brought out the original XT they used a controller that matched this new standard, although the controller in their machines came from a company called XEBEC rather than the one available from Shugart Associates. But because the ST-506 was a standard, it meant that third party companies could produce hard disks and/or controller cards to that standard and be sure that they would work in the computers.

The IBM XT also had the equivalent of a new operating system, which was actually a rewritten version of the original. MS-DOS Version 2.0 had to be created to allow the computer to handle the hard disks. This is why you frequently see software which specifies that you must be using MS-DOS 2.0 or greater. The software is hard disk based and so needs the handling capabilities that Version 2.0 provides.

The next evolutionary step for personal computers came with the development of the 80286 chip. The 80286, launched in 1981, is special in a number of ways. The chip possesses a 16-bit data bus, can address up to 16 Mb of RAM using a 24-bit address bus, and finally it has a built-in real time clock. It is fully compatible with the earlier chips in the series and so any software written for the 8088 or the 8086 will run on an 80286. In order to do so the 80286 operates in two different modes - Real, which is identical to the 8086 and 8088, and Protected, which is specific to the 80286.

The 80286 was a major step forward because it brought an enormous amount of power and processing capability to the PC, so much so that the industry invented a new term for computers built around the chip - AT, short for Advanced Technology. The take-up of the chip has been enormous, so much so that it has supplanted the 8086 as the most widespread chip and a base level AT has become the most common entry level machine in the marketplace - although this has been changing over the past few months.

Theoretically the 80286 is capable of multi-tasking, i.e. it has the ability to do two or more things at the same time independently of each other. The problem is that the multi-tasking part does not work as well as it was expected to. In order to run the normal MS-DOS based programs the chip had to be in Real mode, but to use the multi-tasking you have to switch the chip into Protected mode. Unfortunately if you switch the chip in this way the system crashes and needs to be rebooted. OS/2, the tentative replacement for MS-DOS, was originally written to take account of this fact but the problems it created have led Microsoft to specify that in future to run OS/2 the user must have an 80386 based machine.

The result of all this is that the 80286 is actually used only as a fast 8086 and nobody really bothers with the multi-tasking ability. As such the chip can return a very impressive performance. Typically the 80286 will operate at two and a half times the speed of an 8086 when running identical software at the same clock speed, or 12 times faster than the original PC. (Curiously enough it can also run faster than a 25 MHz 80386 or produce speeds comparable with a 25 MHz 80486!) The fastest 80286 available from Intel is 12 MHz, although other chip manufacturers do provide faster versions. It is estimated that 40% of all the PC's and AT's sold in the past 12 months, i.e. to January 1990, were based around the 80286 chip. However its days are numbered with the advent of the next chip in the series.

Microsoft created Windows/286 specifically for the 80286 and the program is probably the most widespread GUI environment in the World, simply because there are so many 80286 based machines.

Most 80286 machines came complete with 1 or 2 Mb of RAM, a 40 Mb plus hard disk and a single floppy drive, usually 5.25" 1.2 Mb. The AT also used a new monitor specification - EGA, the acronym for Enhanced Graphics Adaptor, which was capable of producing more colours than anything previously seen. Windows/286 took advantage of this to produce bright and cheerful displays.

There is, by the way, an 80186 chip. It was introduced in 1982 and it is really just an enhanced version of the 8086. It has a 16-bit data bus and can address 1 Mb of RAM using a 20-bit address bus. It runs at a faster speed, normally around 10 MHz, although it is possible to get chips with a speed of 16 MHz. Its primary claim to fame is that it includes an on-board clock. Due to its internal architecture it can operate 25% faster than the 8086 - even when running at the same speed. There is also a cut down version of this chip, the 80188. Neither of these was taken up by the computer industry as a whole: after all the 80286 was released first, however a few machines based on the 80186 were developed but they soon faded away. Nowadays the 80186 is making a comeback as an embedded controller on the EISA (Extended Industry Standard Architecture) and MCA (Micro Channel Architecture) add-on cards. These are expansion cards that allow you to append additional hardware peripherals to your machine.

Then Intel produced the 80386. If the 80286 was a major step forward then the 80386 was a giant leap. A full 32-bit chip, it uses a 32-bit data bus, is capable of addressing a massive 4 Gigabytes (that is 4,096 Mb) of RAM using a 32-bit address bus, but most important of all, it is capable of true multi-tasking. Launched in 1985 but not commercially available in a computer until late 1986. The chip has a real time clock, which means that it is not dependent on the time in the battery backed RAM. Like the 80286 it can operate in Real or Protected Mode, and it can also use a third mode, which is specific to this chip - Virtual Real.

The 80386 is produced exclusively by Intel. Prior to its introduction, Intel had been prepared to allow other chip manufacturers to produce the 8000 series under licence but this does not apply to the 80386. (Not that this will make a great deal of difference because clone manufacturers will simply reverse engineer the chip. In other words, they will strip it layer by layer until they know what it contains and then build their own versions of the chip from the ground up. However, Intel have said that anyone who does will find themselves on the receiving end of a very large copyright infringement suit.)

The major difference between the 80286 and the 80386 is that the latter can multitask correctly. It can switch from one mode to the other without having to be rebooted. One major fault lies in its compatibility with the rest of the 8000 series. As a result of this, the chip cannot run standard MS-DOS software in Real mode, at the same speed, any faster than an 80286 can - in fact sometimes it will be slower than its earlier cousin!

80386 Modes

Real Mode forces the chip to operate in an identical way, albeit faster, than the original 8086 chip. In fact it makes the chip operate as an 80286. This means that it can run standard MS-DOS software without any modifications to the programs. Any program running in Real mode can only access 1 Mb of RAM.

Protected Mode is fully compatible with the 80286 Protected Mode, i.e. the mode that theoretically allows the chip to multitask.

Virtual Real Mode is new. It allows the chip to run with program memory protection but it simulates the Real mode of the 8086. In this mode the chip can perform genuine multi-tasking. Each standard MS-DOS program operates independently of the others and each is allocated its own 1 Mb chunk of the available RAM. In essence this means that you can have a number of programs all running on the same machine, in tandem with and yet separate from each other, i.e. you can apparently have multiple PC's on the same machine.

Note, however, that if the machine only possesses 1 Mb of RAM then the multi-tasking will be severely limited or even nonexistent. In a sense the amount of RAM available will have a direct bearing on the number of programs that can be multi-tasked as each one will require 1 Mb for its own use. Thus if you have 4 Mb you can have 4 programs running simultaneously, 8 Mb gives you 8 and so on. (In fact you can do slightly better than that but the principle remains the same.)

Windows 3 takes advantage of the way that the 80386 can use different modes of operation. Windows Real mode is identical to the chip's Real mode, Windows Standard mode uses the Protected mode, and 386-Enhanced uses Virtual Real mode.

Any AT based on the 80386 is a powerful machine and this is reflected by the storage media it uses. Most 80386 based machines will have a 70 Mb hard disk as a minimum, 120 Mb is commonplace and 320 Mb plus is not unusual. The machines will normally have 2 Mb of RAM as a minimum, more usually 4 Mb, and sometimes 8 Mb. High density floppy drives, either 5.25" 1.2 Mb, 3.5" 1.44 Mb or both is the norm. In addition the majority of these machines will use a VGA (Video Graphics Array) monitor that gives high definition and multiple colours.

Because the 80386 was so expensive, although it is much less so now due to market forces, and also because it had capabilities that could not be fully utilised, Intel produced a cut down version of the chip, the 80386SX. This chip bears the same relationship to the 80386 as the 8088 does to the 8086 - i.e. it has of the same internal architecture but its links with the rest of the machine are limited. The 80386SX has a 16-bit data bus, making data handling slower, and a 24-bit address bus which limits its maximum RAM usage to 16 Mb. However internally it can produce the same processing speeds as the 80386.

Due to its low price, machines based around this chip are fast becoming the most common entry level systems and are displacing the 80286 machines.

The latest chip in the series is the 80486. This chip will run 40% faster than the 80386 at the same clock speed with the result that a 25 MHz 80486 is faster than a 33 MHz 80386. In addition it has a built in co-processor. Prior to this chip, if you wanted to do a large amount of number crunching you had to purchase and fit a co-processor chip, designated by a 7 rather than a 6 at the end of the chip number, e.g. 80287 or 80387. However the 80486 has the co-processor already on board and so there is no need to fit additional chips.

As yet, mid-1990, there are very few 80486 based machines available and the few that are around are pitched at the high end of the market as Network Servers and the like. However it is likely that within 12 months such machines will have established themselves as the de facto standard of mid-level machines. Since the launch of the first 80486 machine the prices have continued to tumble. It is now possible to buy a 80486 computer for around $10,000 as opposed to $25,000 less than six months ago.

It is common knowledge that Intel are working on the 80586 and the 80686 chips, the former should be released by the end of 1990 and the latter within 9 to 12 twelve months of that. As to their capabilities - that is anyone's guess. The only thing that is certain is that both of these chips will have to possess a Real mode so that they can run standard MS-DOS software. In fact, these days this limitation is the one thing that is preventing the true evolution of the Intel 8000 series. If they could drop the requirement to run the old MS-DOS software they could produce real state of the art chips. But the MS-DOS program base is so vast that it is unlikely they will be able to do so.

Disk Drives

Windows 3 must have a hard disk to run from. The program simply cannot be run from a floppy disk, not even a high density one. At the very least you will need to allocate a minimum of 5 Mb of disk storage to hold all of the Windows files. The program doesn't care what kind of disk you are using, just so long as you have enough space. However, it has to be said that the faster your disk drive is the better Windows will work.

There are essentially four different types of disk drive systems:

> **MFM** which is short for Modified Frequency Modulation, uses an encoding system, i.e. the way that the data is recorded, that is very reliable and trustworthy. All MFM drives will usually have a maximum of 17 Sectors per Track and this limits the capacity of the disk. The only way to increase the capacity of MFM drives is to add more platters but as this means increasing the overall size of the drive, it is not very practicable. (MFM

encoding is also used for all floppy disk drives by the way, because it is so very reliable.)

RLL which is short for Run Length Limited, is the next development for hard disks. An RLL drive uses an alternative system of encoding which will allow it to have up to 27 Sectors per Track, although this may vary from 24 to 27, and the norm is for 26. RLL drives have much faster data transfer rates and are much more efficient in the way they operate. In essence an RLL drive has more than 50% greater capacity using the same size platters. You must never try and use an RLL drive with an MFM controller or vice versa - not unless you want to ruin the drive completely!

ESDI which is short for Enhanced Small Device Interface, was created in 1983 and was intended to work with both hard disks and tape drives. Its primary advantage is that the encoder/decoder is built into the drive unit itself, rather than being on the controller card, and this makes the drive very fast. An ESDI drive can have a transfer rate of up to 3 Mb per second although it is more normal to use values of about half that. Most ESDI drives use 34 Sectors per Track which is 30% better than RLL and 100% better than MFM drives, which means more capacity in the same space. Unfortunately ESDI drives tend to be expensive and so they are not often used.

SCSI which is short for Small Computer System Interface, pronounced Scuzzy, is not really a disk standard at all. Rather it is a standard for all peripherals which can be added to a personal computer. SCSI has been around for quite some time, nearly nine years, in one form or another. Originally it was developed by Shugart Associates who decided to develop an interface that would be capable of handling anything. The system they designed was called the Shugart Associates System Interface, SASI. The company then applied to the American National Standards Institute to have the device accepted as a standard. ANSI wanted changes, which were duly made, and then they also changed the name to Small Computer System Interface. At about the same time Shugart Associates changed their name to Shugart Corporation - any connection between the two sets of initials is, probably, purely coincidental!

SCSI is a system level interface which is, finally, beginning to be accepted by a number of computer manufacturers. The device was initially used almost exclusively by Apple for their

System Resources

machines and it is only now being used in IBM-compatible machines. It has recently been announced that IBM are adopting SCSI and future machines will use it. SCSI drives are very fast, which makes them ideal for disk intensive software like Windows.

The type of disk drive you are using does have an effect on how Windows operates, especially if you are using an 80286 machine. Many Windows applications constantly read to and write from the disk, especially those programs from third party manufacturers like PageMaker. In addition the printer spooler can use the disk as temporary storage, to hold files before they are actually sent to the printer, and this very effectively slows down Windows programs because the disk is trying to serve too many masters. However, a fast disk drive does help to alleviate this problem.

When Windows is running in 386-Enhanced mode it can simulate memory by using the hard disk and creating a swapfile, although actually you originate it. The swapfile is huge: it can be anything up to half the free space of your hard disk. Once the file has been created it remains on the hard disk until you remove it, although it does not appear when you enter **DIR** because it is a hidden, system file. (See Page 62.) Because Windows regards the swapfile as an extension of memory you can end up with a report which tells you that you have, for example, 8,096 Mb of free RAM. The advantage is that Windows runs much faster, however the type of disk being used does have a marked effect on the speed of the swapping.

With Windows running in Real or Standard mode, the program creates temporary application swapfiles, i.e. it doesn't use the swapfile mentioned above. Once you terminate Windows all these temporary files will be deleted.

Memory Types

RAM, Random Access Memory, is a fundamental part of the computer system, without it nothing will work. There are three kinds of memory available and which you use, and how you use them, will directly affect how Windows operates.

Conventional memory is found on every computer. As an absolute minimum they will have 256 Kb of RAM, although 512 Kb is the norm. The maximum amount of conventional memory that can be fitted to any computer is 640 Kb. MS-DOS uses this conventional memory for running, in fact the operating system itself uses a sizable chunk of it with the result that you may well find that you have a maximum free memory capacity of less than 550 Kb, even before you load any other programs - although this depends on which version of MS-DOS you are using. For example, Version 3.3 takes much less than Version 4.01.

Extended memory is that part of the RAM which extends above the 640 Kb limit. For example, most AT computers come complete with 2 Mb of RAM. 640 Kb of this is Conventional memory and the remaining 1408 Kb is Extended memory. You can also increase the amount of Extended memory by installing an add-on board into one of the vacant slots on the computer - although it has to be said that these tend to be expensive.

Expanded memory is different from the other two, in more senses than one. Such memory is always board mounted, so that it fits into an expansion slot, and it requires a special program so that the computer can use it. The majority of Expanded memory boards conform to a standard known as LIM, which is simply the initial letters of the three companies that developed the standard, namely Lotus, Intel and Microsoft. There are a number of variations on this standard, designated by numbers, so that you may have LIM 3.2 or LIM 4.0. One advantage of Expanded memory boards is that they can be configured so that they act as Extended memory, Expanded memory or both.

Windows 3 works best with Extended memory, although some Windows applications can work with Expanded memory. The amount of memory you have available has a direct effect on the way that Windows will operate.

- With less than 1 Mb of RAM, Windows can only run in Real mode, i.e. the slowest and least dynamic method of operation. Even if you machine is an 80286 it will still only run in Real mode if there is insufficient memory.

- With between 1 Mb and 2 Mb of RAM, Windows can run in either Real or Standard mode (on an 80286 machine) and by default it will run in the latter. However this depends on how the memory is allocated. If you have a number of memory resident programs loaded, and thus consuming memory, there may not be enough left for Windows to run in Standard mode - you must have at least 1 Mb of RAM free and available to run in Standard mode. Because the modes are downwards compatible, if you can run Standard mode you can also run in Real mode.

- With more than 2 Mb of RAM, the type of chip being used becomes the deciding factor. If you had an 80286 machine with 16 Mb of RAM, Windows will still only work in Standard mode - because that is all the chip is capable of. However, if you have an 80386 or 80386SX with even 2 Mb of RAM you can run Windows in 386-Enhanced mode. Note, this mode is only available on an 80386SX or better which allows Windows to run in any of the three modes.

MS-DOS Versions

Since its inception MS-DOS has been upgraded and improved a number of times. Generally these rewrites have been done to take account of new hardware advances but occasionally they are done to remove bugs which have been introduced into the operating system as the result of a previous rewrite. Traditionally, all computer software is sequentially numbered and this follows very strict rules. The Version number consists of two or three digits separated by a full stop, e.g. 1.0, 2.11, 3.21. The digit before the full stop is the actual Version number, while the remaining digits refer to the upgrade of that Version. The Version number changes only whenever there is a major rewrite of the software, adding extra capabilities or dramatic improvements. The rewrite digits change whenever a Version has to be debugged to correct minor errors. This ruling about Version numbers applies to all computer software, not just MS-DOS. The main MS-DOS versions were and are:

The original operating system, as used on the first IBM PC, was Version 1.0 and it did not last very long. With the advent of double sided floppy disk drives it was necessary to improve MS-DOS so that it could handle the new disks. However this was not a major rewrite and so was released as Version 1.10.

Version 2.0 came about as the result of the advent of hard disk drives - at the time of the release of the original PC, hard disk drives existed only for mainframe machines. In addition to improving the system so that it could support the hard disks the operating system was redesigned and improved to make it closer to the XENIX operating system, rather than remaining proximate to CP/M. This is why you will frequently see commercial software which says you must use MS-DOS 2.0 or higher.

Version 2.10 was created to allow support for half-height disk drives. The hardware configuration has a fundamental effect on how MS-DOS must operate and so changes from full height to half-height drives necessitated minor rewriting of the operating system. At the same time a number of bugs, which had become apparent in Version 2.0 were corrected. (Generally speaking any software labelled Version n.0 will contain some bugs - this is one of the laws of computing!)

Version 3.0 again came about because of a major hardware change. High capacity floppy disk drives had arrived, i.e. 1.44 Mb instead of 360 Kb, and so Microsoft took the opportunity to perform a major revision of the operating system. A number of the commands were completely rewritten, while others were merely improved.

Version 3.10 added support for a network, in this case MS-NET. Again a number of known bugs were corrected but the operating system did not fundamentally change, hence only the final two digits changed.

Version 3.2 provided support for the IBM Token ring network and the new 3.5-inch floppy disks. This is probably the most widely used version of MS-DOS in the world because it was supplied with the majority of machines sold during the great expansion of the market that occurred in the late 1980's, and there were an awful lot of computers sold during that time.

Version 3.21 corrected some more bugs but otherwise made no changes.

Version 3.30 was another minor rewrite. It provided support for the new high capacity 3.5-inch disks and allowed the machine to have and operate four serial ports - previous versions would only allow two. It also included a brand new command, FASTOPEN, and complete rewrites of many other commands. However, the basis of the operating system did not change, hence only the final two digits were changed.

Version 4.0 is the latest incarnation of MS-DOS. It includes some additional commands, enhanced device drivers and major rewrites of most of the commands - some of which now have additional features. One major benefit of this version is that it will allow you to have hard disk partitions which exceed 32 Mb. Because the standard size of hard disks is constantly increasing this is an important feature. Version 4.0 is noted for having a large number of bugs, some of which are highly problematical, and so Microsoft very quickly produced Version 4.01 - which is the one most people are using when they say they are using MS-DOS 4. One problem with MS-DOS 4 is that the core of the program is much larger than that is MS-DOS 3.3 and so you end up with less free RAM under this version.

MS-DOS 5 is due around the end of 1990 - according to the advance publicity - and one of its major benefits is that it will have a core much closer in size to MS-DOS 3.3. MS-DOS 5 will also include a host of other enhancements, amongst which are easier installation, a keyboard macro, command line editor, improved expanded memory manager (which will only take 6 Kb as against the 70 Kb that the one in MS-DOS 4 takes), and the program will be faster and more dynamic. In addition MS-DOS 5 will work better with Windows 3 and will incorporate some of the features that Windows 3 provides.

Getting the best you can

Right, now that we know all about system resources we can begin to do something with them and so optimise them for running Windows - hopefully. Let's look at the four different machines in turn.

The 80286

The Samsung 80286 has 1 Mb of RAM and is running under MS-DOS 3.30 and there are no memory resident programs. Windows 3 was installed according to the method outlined in the previous chapter, allowing the Setup program to make the changes it recommended. The resulting CONFIG.SYS now reads:

```
FILES=30
BUFFERS=30
COUNTRY=044,,\DOS\COUNTRY.SYS
DEVICE=C:\DOS\HIMEM.SYS
DEVICE=C:\WINDOWS\RAMDRIVE.SYS    128/E
DEVICE=C:\WINDOWS\EGA.SYS
```

The first four lines are identical to the original file because I moved the new HIMEM.SYS file into the DOS directory and overwrote the original version.

Line 5 creates the Ramdrive, albeit a very small one, using the new RAMDRIVE.SYS program supplied with Windows 3. If you want to use a Ramdrive with Windows then you must use the file supplied with the program - older versions of RAMDRIVE.SYS will not work correctly.

The final line is necessary if you are using an EGA monitor and you want to run MS-DOS programs from within the Windows environment.

Running CHKDSK now gives the report that there is 655,360 bytes of total memory, i.e. 640 Kb, (CHKDSK cannot see Extended memory) and of that there is 576,736 bytes free, i.e. 563 Kb. So everything should be alright.

Enter WIN to run Windows and the result is a complete system hangup, even the keyboard locks up, and the only way to unfreeze it is to press the reset button! Something is wrong somewhere. By trial and error, actually it was largely guesswork, I found that Windows was trying to run in Standard mode and there are not enough system resources to allow it to do so. Enter WIN/R, to run Windows in Real mode, and the program runs.

After rebooting the computer, I removed the Ramdrive and rebooted again to activate the new CONFIG.SYS. Entering WIN, which should allow Windows to run in Standard mode, still results in a complete hangup! (It was at this point that I began to tear my hair out.)

Theoretically, everything should be fine. There is sufficient base memory and enough free extended memory, so why won't the thing work? Windows has got to have the ability to access 30 Files, so that can't be changed. Try reducing the Buffers to 20. CHKDSK now reports 583,184 bytes free. Enter WIN again. Result: complete hangup! So that's no good. After playing around with various parameters for close on four hours, I wasn't able to solve the problem with the result that Windows 3 will only run in Real mode on this particular computer. So I recreated the original CONFIG.SYS file and left it at that.

Windows 3 does seem to have terrible problems running on 80286 machines. A friend of mine has such a machine with 4 Mb of Extended memory and after much playing around with memory allocations she can still barely get the program to run in Standard mode. Even then it runs so slowly that her only recourse is to run Windows in Real mode because it is so much faster. And she is not the only one who has had this problem, I don't know of anyone who has been able to use Standard mode properly on any 80286 machine.

The 80386SX

The Arche 16 MHz 80386SX came complete with 8 Mb of RAM. (This machine has the simplest and quickest way of upgrading RAM that I have ever seen. Just plug in the chips, run the system setup and that's it - the extra memory is there ready to be used. No messing about with pages or anything else, the machine does it all for you.) The machine was fitted with a 1.2 Gb SCSI drive, partitioned into two. Drive-C, which must be present, was limited to 32 Mb and the balance of the capacity went into one huge partition as Drive-D. The disk could have been partitioned into many more logical drives but MS-DOS 4 allows large partitions, there wasn't any point in doing so. Originally all of the extra extended memory was allocated to a single Ramdrive of just under 7 Mb but when Windows was installed this was changed by Setup. The changed CONFIG.SYS now reads:

```
FILES=30
BUFFERS=30
COUNTRY=044,,C:\DOS\COUNTRY.SYS
DEVICE=C:\DOS\HIMEM.SYS
DEVICE=C:\WINDOWS\SMARTDRV.SYS  2048  1024
DEVICE=C:\WINDOWS\RAMDRIVE.SYS  4096  /E
INSTALL  C:\DOS\SHARE.EXE
```

Note, that because of the two disk partitions the Ramdrive now becomes Drive-E. For a disk of this size the Buffers command is probably a bit low but allocating any more will use up base memory, that part below 1 Mb, and that's something that should be avoided. In the AUTOEXEC.BAT a new line was added saying **SET TEMP=E:**. This tells MS-DOS and Windows that temporary files are to be placed into the Ramdrive. The effect of this is to speed up Windows operational speed enormously, particularly when you are swapping data from one program to another.

By default Windows will run in 386-Enhanced mode on this machine. However, this is visibly slower than Standard mode on the Laser or the ALR. Slowing the program down, by entering **WIN/2** to run Windows in Standard mode, improves matters but then the slower chip speed seems to make a difference and it is still slower than the other machines. Thus, unless you are going to be using a lot of programs concurrently, or you are using a network, there seems to be little advantage in using this mode on this machine.

The 80386

On the Laser 80386 things are better. This machine has 2 Mb of RAM, a 60 Mb hard disk and is running under MS-DOS 4.01, again, there are no memory resident programs. Windows 3 was installed according to the method outlined in the previous chapter, allowing the Setup program to make the changes it recommended. The resulting CONFIG.SYS read:

```
FILES=30
BUFFERS=10
COUNTRY=044,,C:\DOS\COUNTRY.SYS
INSTALL  C:\DOS\SHARE.EXE
DEVICE=C:\DOS\HIMEM.SYS
DEVICE=C:\DOS\SMARTDRV.SYS  256  256
DEVICE=C:\DOS\RAMDRIVE.SYS  768  /E
```

The Buffers line was reduced because Setup installed SMARTDRV.SYS and if you use the disk cache you don't need to use as many buffers. The Install line allows MS-DOS to treat the hard disk as a single partition, i.e. it can access the entire hard disk, which is something made possible by MS-DOS 4. The final three lines came directly from the Windows Setup program.

Previously, i.e. before installing Windows 3, the Ramdrive was 1344 Kb and so it didn't seem to make any sense that it had been reduced by so much. Granted SMARTDRV was using 256 Kb, but what had happened to the other 832 Kb? So I increased the Ramdrive to take account of the missing memory. The result was that when I tried to run Windows I got an error message saying there was insufficient memory for Windows to run. After playing around with the Ramdrive size, and rebooting the computer every time, I finally found that a size of 768 Kb was the maximum I could have and still have everything work correctly.

By default, Windows runs in Standard mode on this machine. I can force it into 386-Enhanced mode by entering **WIN/3** but this causes problems. For one thing it is slower than if it is running in Standard mode - quite appreciably so, and for another I cannot run any MS-DOS program from within Windows as I should be able to. Every time I try to do so I get an error message telling me there is insufficient memory and that I should close an application to provide the necessary space. As there are no other applications open this is a bit pointless. The MS-DOS window works okay but none of the MS-DOS programs will. In Standard mode they all work perfectly well so I use that mode instead.

The 80486

The ALR 80486 machine had 4 Mb of Extended memory, all used as a Ramdrive, and a 40 Mb hard disk, partitioned as a single drive under MS-DOS 4. Once Windows was installed the resulting CONFIG.SYS was:

```
FILES=30
BUFFERS=30
COUNTRY=044,,C:\DOS\COUNTRY.SYS
INSTALL  C:\DOS\SHARE.EXE
DEVICE=C:\DOS\HIMEM.SYS
DEVICE=C:\DOS\SMARTDRV.SYS  2048  1024
DEVICE=C:\DOS\RAMDRIVE.SYS  1024  /E
```

Again the Ramdrive is used to store temporary files. Entering **WIN** at the system prompt runs Windows in Standard mode, although the program can be forced into 386-Enhanced mode by entering **WIN/3**. The same limitations as apply to the Laser, above, also applied to this machine.

Summary

- Your system resources have a definite effect on how Windows operates on your machine.

- Windows 3 must have an 80386SX or better to function in 386-Enhanced Mode. This mode is not available on 80286 machines.

- Conventional memory is that part of the RAM up to 640 Kb.

- Extended memory is that part of the RAM above the 640 Kb MS-DOS limit, which is installed in the machine. The more extended memory you have, the better Windows 3 will work.

- Expanded memory is board mounted and is intended to allow you to increase the amount of memory you have, quickly and easily. Memory boards must conform to the LIM standard to work with Windows 3.

- Neither the type of chip nor the type of disk interface you are using seems to make any really noticeable difference to Windows' performance but the amount of memory you have available does make a striking difference.

- The Windows Setup is not omnipotent, it does make mistakes when it allocates memory. You should always check this for yourself.

Chapter 3
Starting Windows

Select a mode

Having gone through the process of installing Windows and then playing around with allocating the system resources, you are now, finally, ready to run the Windows program itself. Windows can be run in three different ways, called modes, and which you chose depends on your system configuration and the type of microchip around which your computer is based.

Real mode is the most basic method. Essentially it means that your computer will be operating as if it were an 8086 machine - although it runs much faster. You will probably find that even if you are using an 80286, this is the only mode that is accessible to you. When running in real mode you are limited to using only those system resources that would be available under MS-DOS itself. In other words your use of RAM is limited to the Conventional memory and any Extended memory is best used as a Ramdrive. The same thing applies to Expanded memory - Windows will not use it properly.

Standard Mode will be the normal operating method on those machines which are based around the 80386SX or better. In this mode you can run MS-DOS programs as if Windows isn't there. Once you activate a non-Windows program, e.g. WordStar, Windows drops into the background and WordStar behaves as if it was running from under MS-DOS. But there is one very important difference. Printing from MS-DOS programs within Windows causes problems - basically you encounter memory limitation errors from Standard mode. I checked this with WordStar, Word Perfect, Logistix, PaintBrush, Harvard Graphics and a few others. With all of these programs the same error message occurred - of course it could be the machine, rather than the Windows environment, because using the print spooler requires memory which is somewhat limited on the Laser 80386 machine.

386-Enhanced mode is a real RAM hog and it only operates by default if you have at least 4 Mb of free RAM on an 80386SX or better. On the Arche 80386SX and the ALR 80486, 386-Enhanced mode works perfectly but on the other machines used for this book there are problems. On the

Laser 80386 this mode is much slower then Standard mode and constantly runs into memory problems. On the Samsung 80286 it will not work at all, even Standard mode won't work on that machine.

Windows will accept command line operands, in other words you can run Windows in specific modes, and automatically run Windows programs as part of the same command line. For example, entering **WIN SOL** will load Windows and then automatically run the Solitaire program. But the main reason for using the command line is to activate Windows within a specific mode. The command parameters are:

> **WIN/R** to run in Real mode
>
> **WIN/2** or **WIN/S** to run in Standard mode
>
> **WIN/3** to run in 386-Enhanced mode

If you enter just **WIN** then Windows will run in whatever default mode it is capable of, according to the system resources.

Once Windows has been loaded you can check which mode you are in by clicking on **Help** on the Menu Bar and then clicking on **About**. Alternatively press **Alt-H A**. A message box pops up telling you the mode you are in.

Swapfile

Windows 3 is unusual in that it can use your hard disk to simulate memory. You can create a special file on the disk called a swapfile. This is a hidden, system file and as such cannot normally be seen if you enter **DIR** from the system prompt. The important point about the swapfile is that there is no point in having one if you are running in anything other than 386-Enhanced mode. If you are using Standard mode for example, Windows creates temporary application swapfiles for any program you run as a matter of course.

A swapfile can be either temporary or permanent. When you start Windows in 386-Enhanced mode the program will search your hard disk trying to find a permanent file, if it cannot find one then it automatically creates a temporary one. When you close Windows the file will be erased.

A permanent swapfile on the other hand has to be created by you, via the Windows environment. The advantages of this are:

   a) The file is contiguous, i.e. it occupies sequential sectors, which makes writing to and loading from the file much faster.

   b) It ensures that Windows always has enough disk space available.

   c) It makes Windows run faster because the program can swap things from the memory to the disk.

   d) If you need the disk space back you can easily modify the file size or remove it altogether.

The only real disadvantages to using a permanent swapfile are that you cannot use one on a network, because it is a resource that everyone will try to access at the same time, or on a Ramdrive because that is impermanent. Of course it also reduces the amount of free space on your hard disk, but the advantages far outweigh this.

Creating a swapfile

Before you can create a permanent swapfile you must compress the hard disk - if you don't then there is no point in creating the swapfile because the file must be contiguous. To compact the disk you will need a utility like Norton Speed Disk or PC Tools Compress. Once the disk has been compacted you can create the swapfile using the following steps.

From the system prompt enter **WIN** - without any command line parameters because you want the program to run in its default mode.

Once Windows has loaded press **Alt-H A** to see what mode Windows operates in by default.

Click on **Help** and then on **About** in the menu that pops down.

64 *Windows 3 - A User's Guide*

You will get a message panel like this:

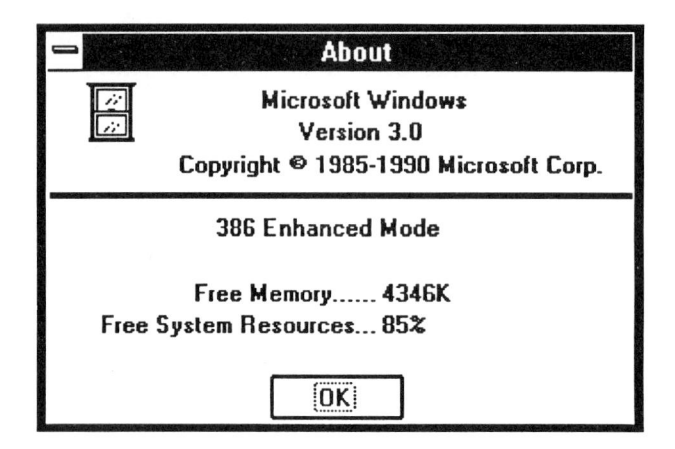

```
┌─────────────────────────────────────────┐
│ ─              About                    │
├─────────────────────────────────────────┤
│  ▨        Microsoft Windows             │
│           Version 3.0                   │
│     Copyright © 1985-1990 Microsoft Corp.│
├─────────────────────────────────────────┤
│           386 Enhanced Mode             │
│                                         │
│        Free Memory...... 4346K          │
│     Free System Resources... 85%        │
│                                         │
│              [  OK  ]                   │
└─────────────────────────────────────────┘
```

Windows Mode information

If the panel does not say 386-Enhanced mode then don't bother creating the swapfile because it is of no use to you.

Press **Enter** to close the message window.

Press **Alt-Space C** or **Alt-F4** to terminate Windows.

Click on the top left hand corner of the Program Manager window and then click on Close.

Once you are back at the system prompt enter **WIN/R** to run Windows in Real mode. You can only create or modify a swapfile when running in this mode! If you try to activate the swapfile program in any other mode you get an error message.

Press **Alt-F**, which opens the File menu, followed by **R** for Run and a dialogue box will appear.

Click on **File** in the Menu Bar and then again on **Run** to open the Dialogue box.

Now type **SWAPFILE** and press **Enter**. You will then get a message box appearing like this:

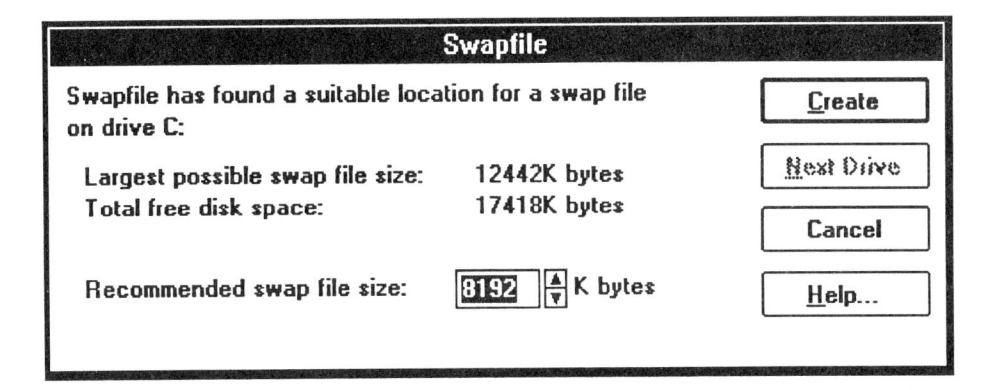

```
┌─────────────────────── Swapfile ───────────────────────┐
│ Swapfile has found a suitable location for a swap file    [ Create   ] │
│ on drive C:                                                             │
│                                                           [ Next Drive ]│
│   Largest possible swap file size:    12442K bytes                      │
│   Total free disk space:              17418K bytes        [ Cancel   ] │
│                                                                         │
│   Recommended swap file size:    [8192] ⇅ K bytes         [ Help...  ] │
└─────────────────────────────────────────────────────────┘
```

Swapfile message box

This tells you how much space is free on your disk and gives the size that is recommended for the swapfile. This size will never be more than 50% of the total available space. Equally the size specified will all be contiguous - hence the need to compact the disk first.

You can click on the arrows at the side of the proposed size to increase or decrease the swapfile size. Once it is a size you are happy with click on **OK** or press **Enter** and a final box appears telling you that the swapfile has been created.

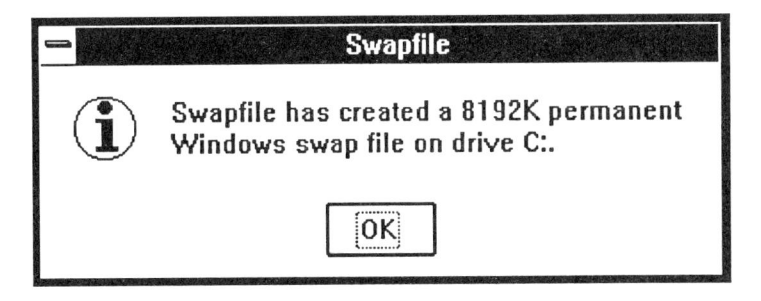

```
┌─────────────── Swapfile ───────────────┐
│                                         │
│  (i)  Swapfile has created a 8192K permanent │
│       Windows swap file on drive C:.         │
│                                         │
│              [ OK ]                     │
└─────────────────────────────────────────┘
```

Swapfile created

Click on **OK** or press **Enter** to remove the box from the screen.

Close Windows by pressing **Alt-F4** or by clicking on **File** and again on **Exit**.

When the message asking Close Windows appears press **Enter** and you will return to the system prompt. Now whenever you run Windows henceforth, you will be able to use this swapfile and Windows itself will run faster.

A word of warning: If you have two versions of Windows running on the same machine and you create a swapfile for one of them, then the other version cannot use this swapfile. Every time you try to run the second version you get an error message telling you that the swapfile is corrupt. In reality it isn't but the second version thinks it is.

I found this out by accident. Because I use Windows anyway I have the program installed on my computers as normal, using full colour, but to produce the illustrations used in this book I also have Windows installed in monochrome - so that I can capture the various screen shots that are necessary and they can be reproduced in this book and produce viable illustrations. When I tried to run the monochrome version in 386-Enhanced mode, and only then, I get an error message telling me the swapfile is damaged. Windows then runs in 386-Enhanced mode, after pressing any key to remove the message, but it creates a temporary swapfile rather than using the permanent one created for use with the colour version of Windows that I normally use. However, the swapfile is perfectly alright and the colour version of Windows runs without any problems. Therefore it seems that the swapfile is linked to the version of the program that created it but I have not been able to confirm this.

In other words, if you do install two versions of Windows and you run into the error message you can ignore it. Windows will run perfectly well using temporary swapfiles, albeit a bit slower.

Windows layout

Decide which mode you want Windows to run in and, from the system prompt enter the necessary command. Throughout the remainder of this book it is assumed, for brevity, that you will activate Windows using just **WIN**. However if you wish to use a specific mode then you will need to add the parameter for that mode.

Once the command has been issued and you have pressed **Enter**, Windows checks through your system resources before the program is actually run. It does this for two reasons:

> a) To make sure that the resources that were allocated as you installed the program still exist, e.g. you haven't changed the directory name without modifying the PATH statement, or something similar.

> b) To ensure that there is sufficient memory for the program to run. Windows is very memory hungry and you may well find that even having a small memory resident program loaded, which by the way will not normally work in the Windows environment, reduces the memory available by an amount sufficient for Windows not to run.

After a moment or several, depending on the computer configuration, the Windows 3 logo appears followed by Windows proper. The first time you run Windows this will consist of the Program manager window as shown below.

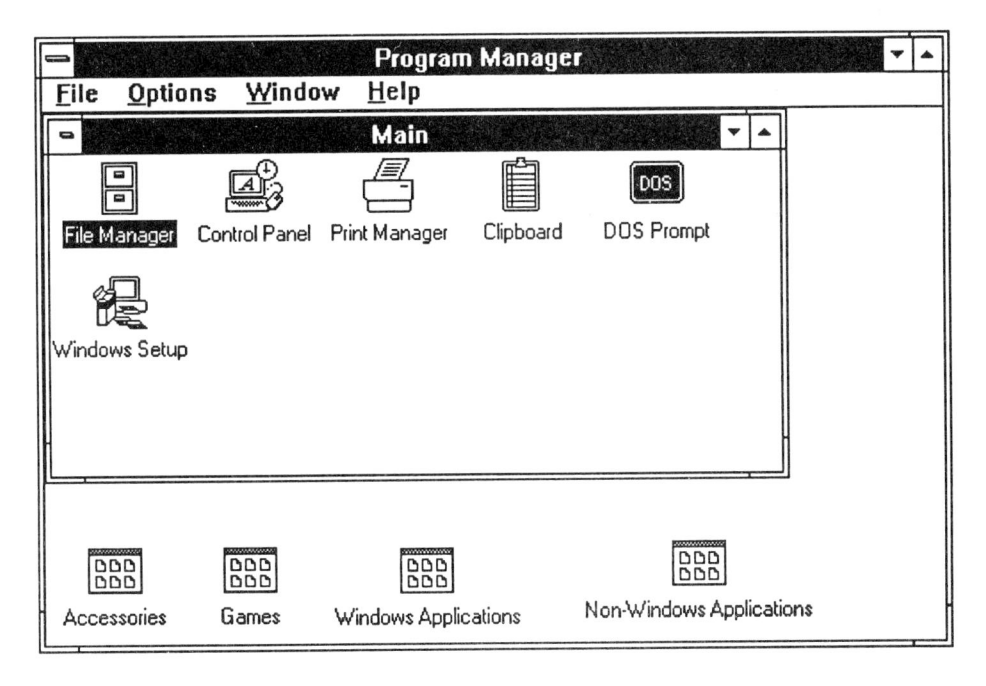

Windows first time

Before going any further let's examine the various features of Windows and how they are used.

On the screen is an open window containing a subsidiary window plus four icons. (Your screen layout may be very slightly different depending on what you installed originally.) The main window overlies the Background, which is effectively the whole usable area of the screen. By default the background is a dull grey on all monitors, however you can change this to any one of a vast range of colours, providing of course you are using a colour monitor. You can even incorporate graphics as the background if you so wish. (We'll cover all this in Chapter 5.) You cannot thereafter do anything with the background.

The main window consists of a number of sub-elements, most of which you can control to a greater or lesser extent. However before we get into doing that, let's continue with the descriptive detail.

- The window is surrounded by a **Border** which frames the entire window. Under the Windows default colours this is normally grey. You can enlarge a window by clicking on the border and then dragging it. If you click on any corner you will be able to drag the two sides of the window that are associated with that corner. For example, clicking on the left hand, bottom corner allows you to drag the base and the left hand side of the window at the same time.

- Inside the border, at the top left hand corner of the main window is a small box with a horizontal line within it. This is the **Control Box** and basically it allows you to control the major aspects of the window. Every window will normally have its own control box which contains the following commands:

    Restore is used to reinstate an icon or a window to its former size and position.

    Move allows you to move the window using the keyboard.

    Size allows you to change the size and shape of the window using the keyboard.

    Minimise is used to reduce a window to an icon.

    Maximise enlarges a window or an icon so that it fills the entire screen.

Close terminates Windows itself if used from the Program Manager, or it can be used to conclude specific windows and the programs they contain.

Switch To allows you to move directly to another window and/or program.

- Lying along the top of the window is the **Title Bar**, by default this is a hazy cyan colour. This simply contains the name of the program that is running within the window. You can move an open window, providing it is not maximised, by dragging the title bar. Move the pointer to the bar, click and hold the mouse button and then move the mouse. The open window will follow your movements. Note, there is liable to be a slight delay as the screen is refreshed, especially if you move the mouse rapidly, but this depends on the speed of the computer and the monitor.

- At the top right hand corner of the window, to the right of the Title Bar, are two boxes. The first contains a downwards pointing arrow. This is the **Minimise** switch. Clicking on this will reduce the window to an icon which will then appear at the bottom of the screen. Next to it is an upwards pointing arrow, the **Maximise** box. This will enlarge the window so that it fills the whole of the background area. Once it has done so the arrow changes to a double headed one, pointing up and down: clicking on it in this state will return the window to the size it was before it was enlarged.

- Immediately below the Title Bar is the **Menu Bar** containing four key words. These are the names of the various menus. Clicking on any word will open the appropriate menu from which you then select commands. If you open a menu inadvertently you can close it again by clicking anywhere on the screen outside the menu itself.

- Within the border, and below the Menu Bar, is the **Application Workspace**. This is shown as a very pale yellow or cream colour. It is within this area that subsidiary windows operate.

- Overlying the workspace is an open window, labelled **Main**. This is a **Group window** but it operates in the same way as ordinary windows. Note that it has its own Control Box, Title Bar, and Minimise and Maximise boxes. It does not, however, contain any Menu Bar. In this case, groups share the Menu Bar of the Program Manager and the commands the menus contain.

- Along the bottom of the main window, in the illustration above, are four **Icons** labelled, Accessories, Games, Windows Applications and Non-Windows Applications. These are **Group Icons** which are identifiable as such by the fact that they contain what looks like six pages with the top right hand corner of each folded over, plus a pale blue line along the top.

- Somewhere on the screen there will also be a white arrow. This is the **Mouse Pointer** and it is this that you use to manipulate the menus, icons and windows themselves. Any movement you make with the mouse will be reflected by the pointer, e.g. move the mouse left and the pointer moves to the left side of the screen. The pointer moves only when you move the mouse.

- There is another element of the windows environment which is not shown on the illustration, the **Scroll Bars**. These are Horizontal or Vertical lines which appear at the side of the window when the window contains more material that is being shown. You can have both scroll bars displayed at the same time if the window is too small in both directions. Each scroll bar terminates in a pair of arrows, pointing in opposite directions, and by clicking on these you can move the display to show the missing material. You can use the scroll bars to page through list boxes and text as follows:

    a) Clicking on the arrowheads will scroll the display one line at a time in the direction of the arrowhead you click on.

    b) Clicking on the scroll bar itself will page through the list or text one screenful at a time. The text will scroll according to whether you click above or below the marker - a square button on the scroll bar.

    c) You can drag the marker button along the scroll bar. As you do so the text in the list box moves with you. This facility is extremely useful if you are looking for something you know exists but can't be bothered searching for either one line or one screen at a time.

    d) In some list boxes, but not all unfortunately, you can click on any name in the list and then type the initial letter of the file you want. The list box will then automatically scroll to the first file it contains beginning with that letter. This facility tends to work only in those list boxes that allow for the loading of files, e.g. Windows Help, Corel Draw,

PageMaker. It rarely works in specific lists that provide options, e.g. the list of printers in Control Panel.

Dialogue boxes

A Dialogue Box is a small pop-up box that contains a list of options, which may be as few as two or as many as a dozen or so, from which you have to select the one you want. Usually there is a default option already selected and to accept this you simply press **Enter** or click on **OK**. To change the option you click on the one you want and this then becomes the default for that occasion.

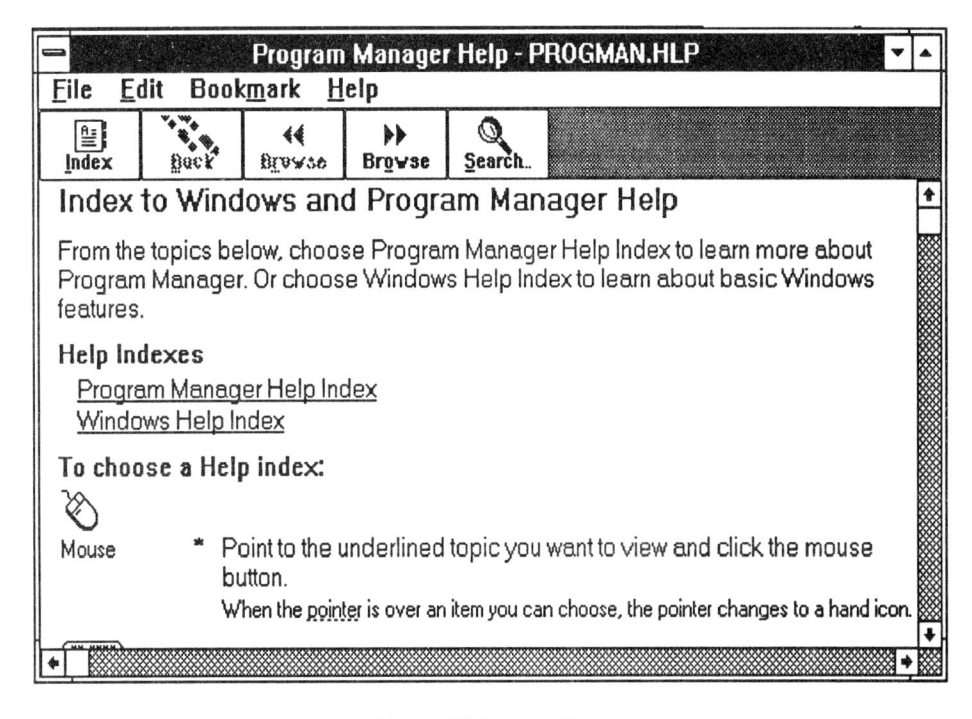

Help Dialogue Box

The layout of each dialogue box varies, depending on where it originated. The one shown above is the most complex of them all.

System messages

A System Message occurs, basically, when something has happened that should not, e.g. the printer runs out of paper. Windows then displays the message to tell you what has occurred, and it may also suggest possible methods of fixing the problem. A system message will pop-up over any existing application that you may be running because they take precedence over everything else.

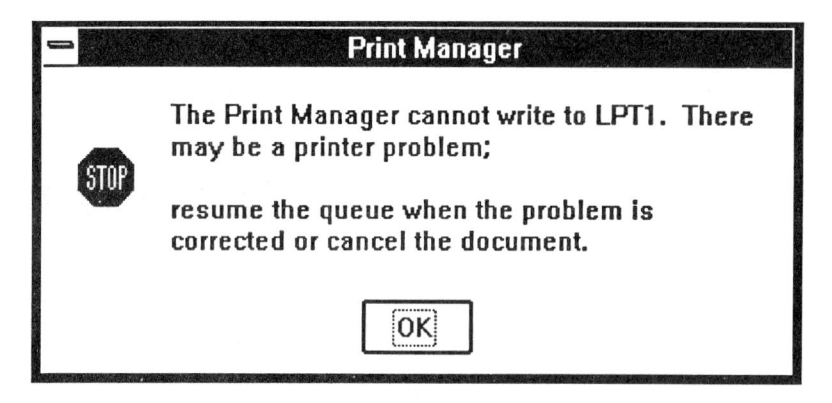

System Message

Exercise 3.1
The Window Dance

Moving windows is something that you may, on occasion want to be able to do. There are two ways to do so, one using the keyboard and the other using the mouse. Try each until you are happy with the process.

1) Press **Alt-Space** M. The pointer becomes a four-headed cross.

2) Press the **Right** key once. The window remains where it is but a framework appears that shifts slightly to the right. If you press **Enter** the window itself will now shift to occupy this position. If you do not press Enter then the frame remains visible.

3) Press the **Up** key twice and the framework moves towards the top of the background.

4) Press **Down** twice and the framework goes back down.

5) Press **Left** once and the framework returns to its original position.

> Notice that each time the framework moves by the same increment. This is built-in to the environment and you cannot move the framework by less than this amount using the keyboard.

6) Press and hold **Up**. The window will then move up against the background until it reaches the top of the screen and then keep right on going. Depending on your monitor, you may well find that the framework vanishes off the screen completely. Eventually it can go no further - at this point the computer may beep at you to inform you of this.

7) Press and hold **Left**. The framework moves as far to the left as it can go and again it may disappear from view.

8) Move the framework to the bottom right side of the screen. Note, you can only use the **Left, Right, Up** and **Down** keys. If you press anything else, other than **Enter**, then nothing happens.

9) Move the framework back so that it overlies the window. Press **Enter** to terminate the Move option.

1) Move the Pointer to the Title bar.

2) Click and hold the mouse button. The framework appears as you do so but it may not be visible.

3) Move the mouse in any direction you wish and the framework will follow your movements. Using the mouse it is difficult to make the entire framework disappear off screen - but then you don't want it to anyway!

4) Once you have the framework where you want it, release the button and the window will move to that position.

Exercise 3.2
Imagine that

Windows is particularly useful because it allows you to clear the main screen area, by reducing any window to an Icon, thus leaving it free for another window. Again you can do this using the keyboard or the mouse.

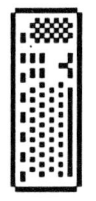

1) Press **Alt-Space N** and the window instantly shrinks to an Icon which will appear at the bottom left hand corner of the screen. Immediately below the icon will be the words Program Manager - thus telling you what the Icon represents. (A bit unnecessary here, perhaps, but when you have a number of icons on screen it is useful to know which is which.)

2) Press **Alt-Space R** or **Alt-Space Enter** to restore the icon to a window. (You can use the latter option because Restore is the highlighted option on the menu that appears.) It will reassume the same size and position it had before you iconised it.

Note that you cannot move the pointer using the cursor keys. If you press any of the cursor keys all that happens is that the highlighter, within the Main Group window, moves to another application.

1) Click on the **Minimise** box, the one containing the downwards pointing arrow to the right of the Title Bar. The window instantly becomes an icon.

2) Double click, i.e. press the mouse button twice in rapid succession, on the icon and the window is restored to its former position and size.

3) Click on the **Control Box**, to the left of the Title Bar, and a menu appears. Click on **Minimise**.

4) Double click on the icon again to restore the window.

You can, by the way, move the icons themselves around. You can position them anywhere on the screen, though any open window will mask them. Simply drag the icon to where you want it to be.

Exercise 3.3
A whole lot of window

There will be times when you want a window to be the maximum size possible, e.g. to provide better definition. Again there are two basic ways to do so.

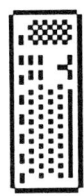

1) Press **Alt-Space X** and the window will enlarge to cover the whole of the background area. Any icons or other windows will be overlaid in the process.

2) Restore the window to the former size and position by pressing **Alt-Space R** or **Alt-Space Enter**.

1) Click on the Maximise button, at the extreme right hand edge of the Title Bar, and the window expands to fill the screen. Alternatively, double click on the Title Bar which has the same effect. The upwards pointing arrow now becomes double headed.

2) Click again in the same box and the window is restored to its former size and position.

3) Click on the Control Box and then on **Maximise**. The window expands.

4) Click on the Control box again and press **Enter**; or click on the Control Box and press **R**; or Click on the Control Box and then click on **Restore**. All three actions have the same result.

Exercise 3.4
All sizes and shapes

Any window can be altered to change the size and shape of it, other than just minimising and maximising it. This is much easier to do with the mouse but it is possible using the keyboard.

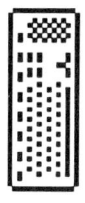

1) Press **Alt-Space S** - the pointer becomes a four-headed cross and the framework appears.

2) You now have to press one of the cursor keys. Whichever one you press will cause that side of the window to be acted upon. For example, pressing **Right** allows you to move the right hand side of the window, **Down** allows you to move the base of the window. For argument's sake, press **Right**.

3) Press **Left** and the framework moves slightly to the left. If you hold down the **Left** key you will find that there is a maximum amount that the framework will move. Position the framework so that it lies about halfway across the open window.

4) Now press **Up** and the pointer moves to the top right hand corner of the framework.

5) Pressing **Left** or **Right** will now move the top and the right hand side of the framework in unison. This time you will find that there is a minimum size to which the framework can be reduced. Pressing **Enter** will make the window assume the size of the framework.

Note that because you used the Size command you cannot Restore the window to its former size other than by resizing it, i.e. the Restore command does not apply.

1) Click and hold on the left hand side of the border.

2) Move the mouse to the right and the framework follows your action. Once you release the mouse button the window assumes the size of the framework.

3) Click and hold on the top left hand corner of the border. The pointer becomes a diagonal two headed arrow.

4) Move the mouse and the top and left hand side of the framework will be dragged along with it. Again, as you release the button the window assumes the size and shape of the framework.

Exercise 3.5
Ending it all

You should always terminate Windows before you turn off the computer, if only so that you can park the heads of the disk drives. Never try to park the heads from within Windows - you can do so but any temporary file created by a Windows program will still exist and this can cause problems later.

1) Press **Alt-Space C**; **Alt-F4**; or **Alt-F X** - all three have the same effect.

2) A dialogue box appears asking if you want to terminate windows. It also contains a small box with the words 'Save changes' beside it. This may or may not be checked, i.e. the box may contain a cross. If you close Windows with the option selected then the program will 'remember' everything that currently exists, and how it appears, in the environment and the next time you activate Windows that is how things will appear.

3) Press **Tab** until the 'Save Changes' command is outlined. Now press the **Spacebar** and you can toggle the selection, i.e. turn it off if it is on or vice versa. (I suggest that at this point you turn it off.)

4) Finally press **Enter** to active the closure and return to the system prompt.

1) Click on the Control Box and again on **Close**; or Click on **File**, in the Menu Bar, and then on **Exit** - both have the same effect.

2) You can change the 'Save Changes' option by simply clicking on it.

3) Press **Enter** or click on **OK** to close windows.

Note that if you have selected 'Save Changes' then your disk works away as the windows environment information is saved - this takes a number countable of seconds, depending on the type of disk you are using. Otherwise Windows just shuts down.

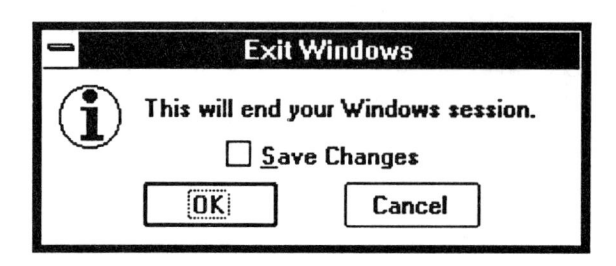

```
┌─ Exit Windows ──────────────────┐
│  (i)  This will end your Windows session. │
│           ☐ Save Changes        │
│        [ OK ]      [ Cancel ]   │
└─────────────────────────────────┘
```

Close Windows

Summary

- Real mode is the equivalent of running the computer as an 8086, albeit faster. To run Windows in Real mode enter **WIN/R** from the system prompt.

- Standard mode allows you to run MS-DOS programs easily and simply from Windows, but it needs an 80386SX or better to do so. To engage Standard mode from the system prompt enter **WIN/2** or **WIN/S**.

- 386-Enhanced mode will allow you to multitask several applications at the same time, each behaves as if it were running on its own 8086. Providing your machine is capable of it you can activate 386-Enhanced mode by entering **WIN/3** from the system prompt.

- A swapfile allows Windows to operate faster and more dynamically, but only when in 386-Enhanced mode. To create a swapfile you must activate Windows in Real mode, press **Alt-R** and then enter **SWAPFILE**.

- The border is the frame of the open window.

- The Control Box appears in every windowed application.

- Windows can be resized by clicking and dragging on the border.

- Windows can be moved by dragging the Title Bar.

- A dialogue box allows you to make choices and set new defaults.

- A system message provides notice of a fault and may give possible causes and cures.

Keyboard Summary

Alt-F C	Copy selected icon to another group.
Alt-F D	Delete selected icon or empty group window.
Alt-F M	Move the selected icon to another group.
Alt-F N	Create new group or add program to group
Alt-F O	Run the selected program.
Alt-F P	Activate group or icon properties dialogue box.
Alt-F R	Run any program by name.
Alt-F X	Terminate Windows.
Alt-F4	Terminate Windows and return to system prompt.
Alt-H A	Display copyright notice and check mode information.
Alt-H B	Activate Help skills information.
Alt-H C	Activate Help with commands.
Alt-H G	Activate Windows Glossary of terms.
Alt-H I	Activate Help index.
Alt-H K	Activate Help Keyboard information.
Alt-H P	Activate Help with procedures.
Alt-H U	Get help with using Help.
Alt-letter	Open selected menu.
Alt-O A	Toggle icon automatic arranging.
Alt-O M	Toggle Program Manager minimise on use.
Alt-Space C	Terminate Windows.
Alt-Space M	Move icon or window on screen.
Alt-Space N	Reduce window to an icon.
Alt-Space	Open Control Box.
Alt-Space R	Restore icon to previous size and position.
Alt-Space S	Change size of current window.
Alt-Space W	Activate Task Switching.
Alt-Space X	Enlarge icon or window to cover entire screen.
Alt-W C	Cascade open windows.

Alt-W Number	Switch to associated group.
Alt-W T	Tile open windows.
Ctrl-Esc	Activate Task Switching.
Ctrl-F4	Close active window, i.e. reduce it to an icon.
Ctrl-F6	Move between windows and icons.
Ctrl-Tab	Move between windows and icons.
Cursor Keys	Move highlighter within window or menu.
Del	Delete selected icon or empty group window.
Enter	Activate highlighted command or program.
Esc	Cancel current operation.
F1	Activate Main Help program.
Shift-F4	Tile windows.
Shift-F5	Cascade windows.
Shift-Tab	Move from one option to another in reverse order.
Space	Select the highlighted option.
Tab	Move from one option to another.

Chapter 4
Program Manager

Windows in use

Program Manager is the heart of the Windows 3 environment. It replaces the old MS-DOS Executive that was used in previous versions of Windows, and is much easier to use. By default, the Program Manager will be run whenever you activate Windows, although you can change this so that the File Manager (See Chapter 7 for details) will run by default instead. However, it is Program Manager which is intended to be used as the front end of the Windows environment and MicroSoft have put a lot of thought and work into getting it right. So just exactly what is it?

Program Manager is a social tool (using the word 'social' in its broadest sense) and it is used to organise the way that Windows handles programs and files. It is not a disk manager or utility, rather it is a request classifier which allows you to create groups of programs and files in such a way that the groups conform to your own preference. The Program Manager allows you to display the groups in a variety of ways, as sub-windows, as icons and/or as a combination of the two.There are no hard and fast rules about what goes into which group, or even about the number of groups that you should have. How you organise the groups and arrange the files within them is purely a matter of your own taste.

Once Program Manager is on the screen you can quickly and easily select which program you want to run, and by just double clicking on any program icon you can activate that program. As the selected program is being run, Program Manager slips into the background, ready for when it is needed again. To run any program just select it and press **Enter**, or using the mouse, double click on the program icon.

One thing that you must remember - you must return to the Program Manager to terminate Windows. You cannot close the Windows environment from any other position.

The Program Manager consists of a single window which contains a number of sub-windows. Each sub-window contains a Group of program files. When you install Windows 3 it will create a number of groups automatically for you but you can change these around to suit your own preference.

There is no apparent limit on the number of sub-windows or groups that you can have in Program Manager. As a test, I have just created, and subsequently deleted, an additional 60 groups, i.e. excluding the ones automatically created by Setup, without any problems. However it is really in your own interest to keep the number of groups to as few as possible. Why? Because each group will contain programs and/or document files and the more groups you create the smaller is the sub-window that they occupy, even keeping many of them as icons. The result is that you can end up with many group windows and you may not be able to see what they contain. Therefore the ideal is to keep the number of groups down as much as possible. Equally you should keep the number of files in each group to as few as necessary.

You can reduce any group window within the Program Manager to an icon, which allows you to have only specifically required windows open. Personally I prefer to have all the group windows visible at the same time without any of them being an icon.

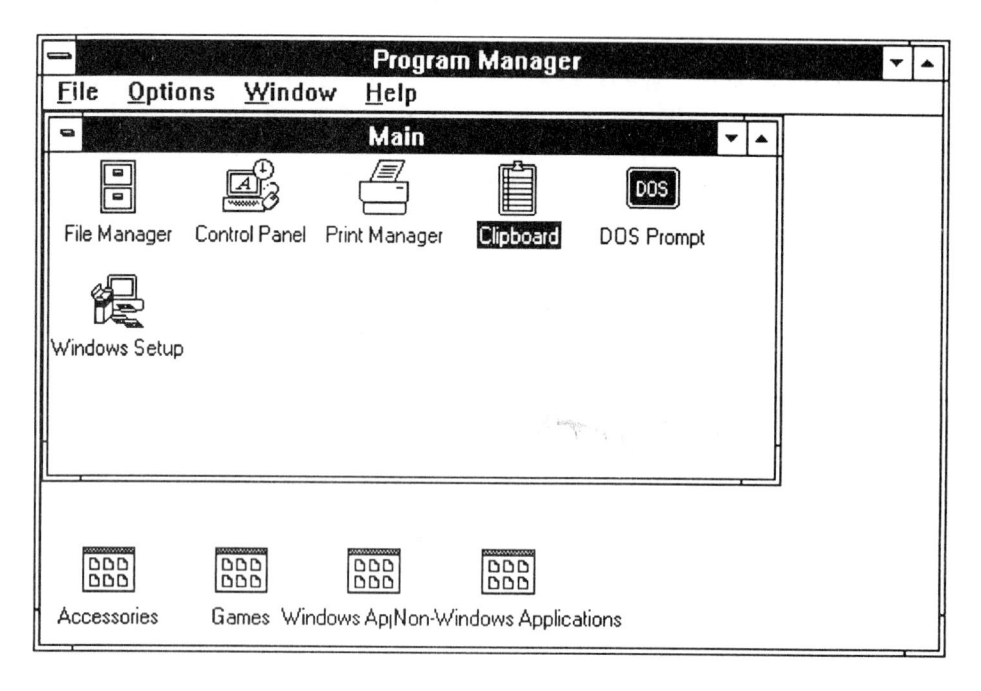

Program Manager created by Setup

Notice that the sub-window shown in the illustration has a Control Box, Title Bar and Minimise and Maximise boxes, but no Menu Bar. This is because sub-windows share the menus of the main window. In other words the menus of the Program Manager are used to control any of the programs and/or files of the group windows.

Exercise 4.1
Windows and Icons

You can influence the way that the windows and the icons appear by using the Control Box. Whenever you click on an icon the commands in its Control Box appear, just as if the icon was a window and you have clicked on the box in that.

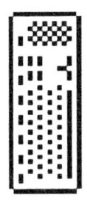

1) Press **Alt-Space** and the menu will pop down. Note that this is the Control Box for the Program Manager, not for the sub-window. (To activate the Control Box on a sub-window you use **Alt-Hyphen**.)

```
Restore
Move
Size
Minimize
Maximize
Close         Alt+F4
Switch To...  Ctrl+Esc
```

Control Box Commands

2) Press **X** and the Program Manager window expands to fill the entire screen.

3) Press **Alt-Space Enter** and the window returns to its previous size. You can press **Enter** because the Restore command is the first one in the menu and thus it is already highlighted.

4) Press **Alt-Space N** and the Program Manager window is reduced to an Icon.

5) Return it to its former size using **Alt-Space Enter** or **Alt-Space R**.

1) Click on the Control Box and then either click on **Maximise** or press **X** and the window expands.

2) Click on the **Maximise** button at the right hand side of the Title Bar to return the window to its former size.

3) Click on the **Minimise** box and the window becomes an icon.

4) Double click on the icon to restore the window to its original size and position.

Program Manager as an Icon

Controlling Windows is much easier with a mouse, but to get the best from the program you should use the mouse and the keyboard in unison. That way you can use two hands at the same time and so increase the speed with which you use the program.

Exercise 4.2
Size is everything

The Program Manager window created by Setup, which appears by default when you first start Windows, is an odd size. It would be much better if it was covering most of the screen with just enough space along the bottom to show any icons that may appear. So let's make it bigger.

1) Press **Alt-Space** to open the Control Box and then press **S**. The pointer turns into a four-headed cross.

2) Press **Left** to move the left border and the framework appears.

3) Press **Up** and the pointer moves to the top left hand corner of the framework and becomes a diagonal arrow.

4) Move the pointer, using the **Left** cursor key, until the top of the framework is as close to the top of the background area as you want it to be.

5) Press **Enter** and the window expands to fill the framework area.

6) Press **Alt-Space S** again.

7) This time press **Right**, followed by **Down**.

8) Move the bottom right hand corner of the framework down, using the **Right** cursor key, until it is at the position you want it to be. Don't forget to leave space for the icons.

9) Finally press **Enter** and the Program Manager window expands to the size you want it to be.

1) Drag the top left hand corner until the framework reaches the position you want. Release the button and the window expands.

2) Now do likewise with the bottom right hand corner. That's it.

Exercise 4.3
A Cascade of windows

Having got the window to the size you want, it's now time to do something with the sub-windows within the main window. By default, Program Manager appears with only the Main sub-window open and the others are shown as icons. Let's open these up and see what we've got.

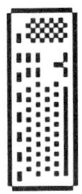

1) Press **Ctrl-Tab** until the name of the icon you want is shown in inverse video.

2) Press **Enter** and the icon becomes a window, overlaying the Main window and offset slightly to the right. By default windows will always be cascaded in this way. Cascade simply means that the group windows lie one in front of the other.

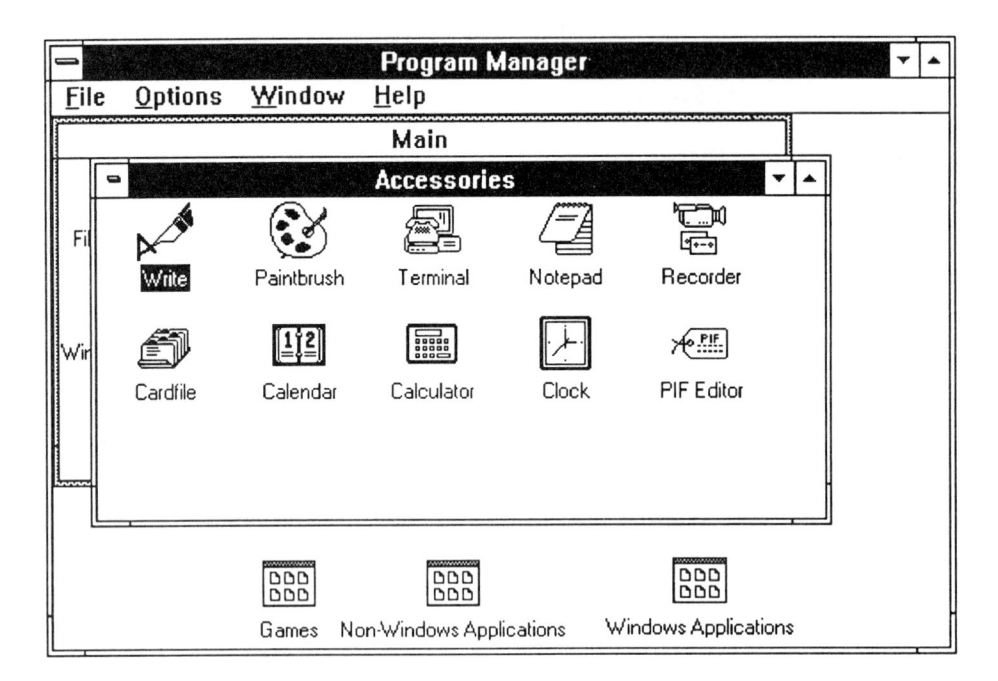

Cascade of Two

3) Press **Ctrl-Tab** again, followed by **Enter** until you have turned all of the icons into sub-windows.

1) Double click on any icon and it will become a sub-window. Do this with all the icons until you have a series of windows one behind the other.

Note that the last icon you restored now overlies all the others. You can change the order of the cascade by clicking on any of the windows and pressing **Shift-F5** again. The active window will always be at the front.

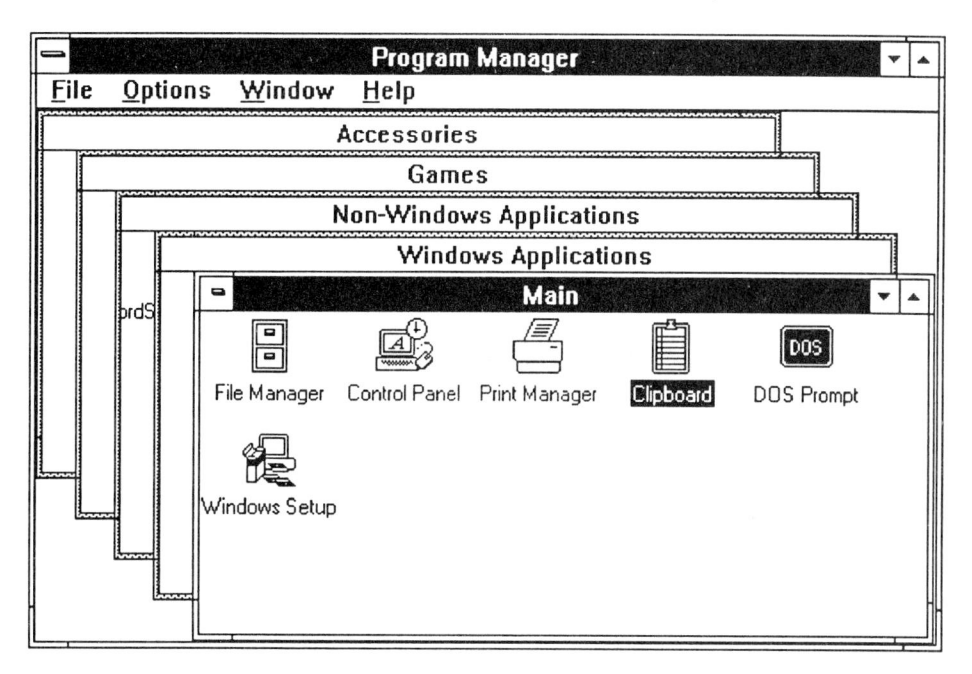

Cascade of Five

Exercise 4.4
On the tiles

The group windows in the cascade is fine if you want to see only one group at a time. But you might just as well have all the other sub-windows as icons and just select the one you want each time. However, you can have the groups displayed in a different way.

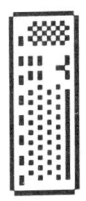

1) Press **Shift-F4** or **Alt-W T** and the sub-windows rearrange themselves so that they lie side by side. You can now see what each group contains at a glance.

1) Click on Window in the Menu bar and then either click on **Tile** or press **T** to tile the group windows.

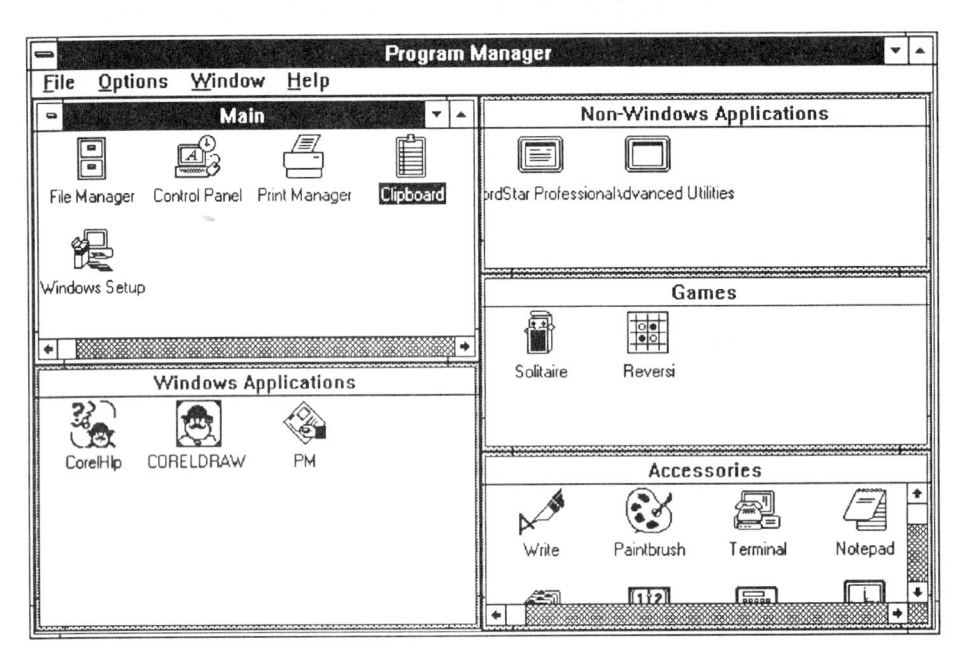

Five tiles

Note that the sub-window that is operational, shown by having its Title Bar illuminated, will always appear at the top left hand corner of the screen when you tile the windows.

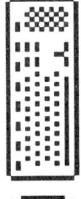

2) Press **Ctrl-Tab** to make one of the other windows the active one and then press **Shift-F4** again. The windows rearrange themselves.

2) Click on any of the windows and then press **Shift-F4**.

As you rearrange the tiled windows, the one that had been in the top left hand corner moves down one place and is replaced by the one you have just activated. Try playing around with this until you get the tiles arranged the way you want them to be. As far as Program Manager is concerned, the order of the tiles is irrelevant.

Groups

A group is a collection of files that have some association with each other. This association can be purely arbitrary, e.g. all the files begin with the letter a, or there can be some specific connection between the files, e.g. MS-DOS programs rather than Windows ones. The way in which the groups are arranged and what each group contains is entirely your own choice, however, as a starting point the Setup program which installed Windows for you will have created a number of groups. These are:

The **Main Group** which contains:

> **File Manager** which is the Windows file and disk organiser.
>
> **Control Panel** it is this program that allows you to make changes in the way that Windows appears.
>
> **Print Manager** which handles the printing from all Windows programs and from MS-DOS programs run from Windows.

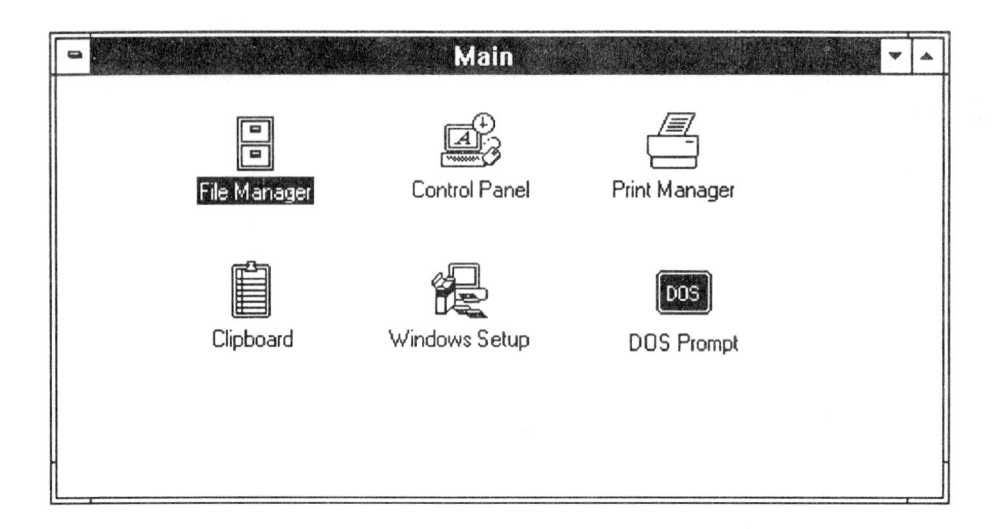

```
┌─────────────────────────────────────────────────────┐
│ ▪                      Main                    ▼ ▲ │
├─────────────────────────────────────────────────────┤
│                                                     │
│       [🗄]          [📅]            [🖨]            │
│   File Manager   Control Panel   Print Manager      │
│                                                     │
│       [📋]          [🖥]          [DOS]             │
│    Clipboard    Windows Setup    DOS Prompt         │
│                                                     │
└─────────────────────────────────────────────────────┘
```

The Original Main Group

Clipboard the facility that allows you to cut and paste from one application to another.

DOS Prompt effectively a window back to the system prompt. If you use this then Windows becomes temporarily memory resident until recalled.

Windows Setup this allows you to change the basic parameters of the Windows environment.

The **Accessories Group** which contains:

Calculator which is simply that.

Calendar a simple day or month organiser with a built-in alarm.

Cardfile which is a (very) simple flat database with limited applications.

Clock provides either an analogue or a digital clock display.

Notepad a pure ASCII text editor.

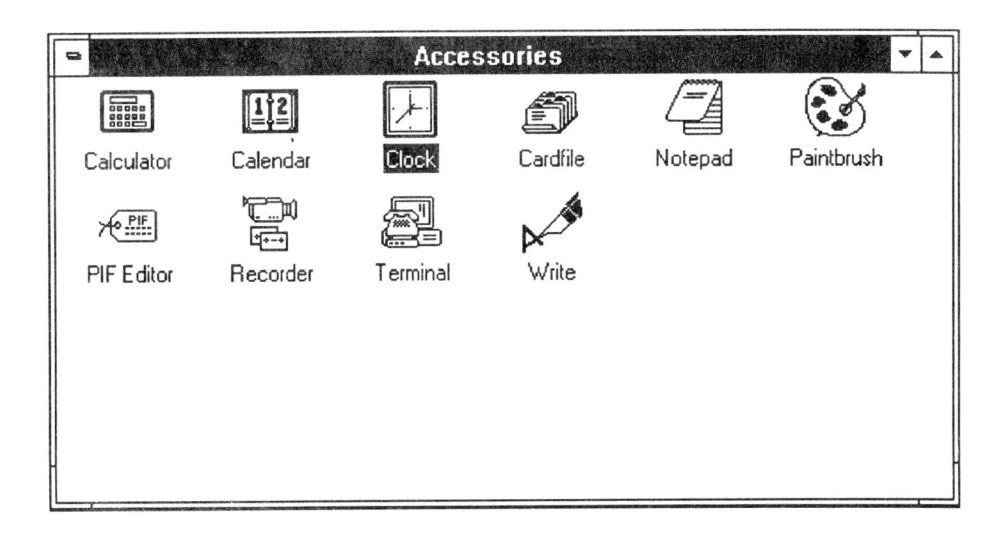

The Original Accessories Group

Paintbrush a full colour, multi-featured paint program.

PIF Editor which is used to create or modify the Program Information Files.

Recorder a macro generator.

Terminal the telecommunications linker.

Write a simple word processor.

The **Games Group** which contains:

Reversi a game of strategy using counters.

Solitaire a card game, known in the UK as Patience.

These foregoing three groups are common to all Windows installations because they are part of the Windows package. The remaining groups and their contents depend on what you had on your hard disk when you installed Windows and which of those programs you decided to include into the Windows environment. The groups as they exist on the machines used for this book are:

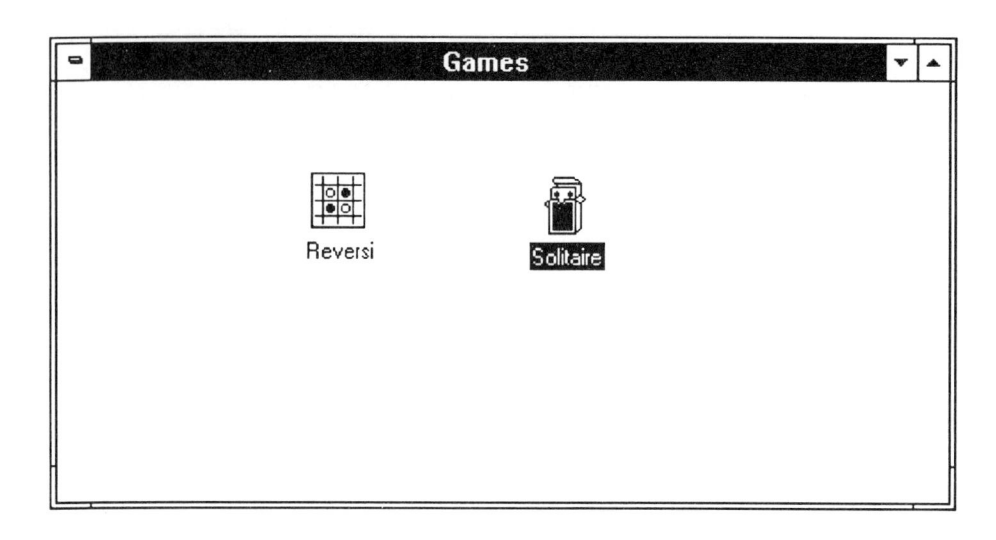

[Screenshot of a "Games" window containing Reversi and Solitaire icons, with Solitaire selected]

The Original Games Group

The **Windows Applications Group** which contains:

> **Corel Draw** probably the best drawing program in the world, especially designed to run in the Windows environment.
>
> **Corel Help** the program associated with Corel Draw.
>
> **PageMaker** the best selling Desk Top Publishing program from Aldus Corporation.

Non-Windows Applications Group which contains:

> **WordStar Professional 6** the character based word processor, which I currently use for writing.
>
> **Norton Utilities** the Advanced edition, my favourite set of utility programs.

Each group exists in its own sub-window and the programs they contain are represented by icons, for example the Print Manager icon looks like a laser printer, Paintbrush is a palette, and so on.

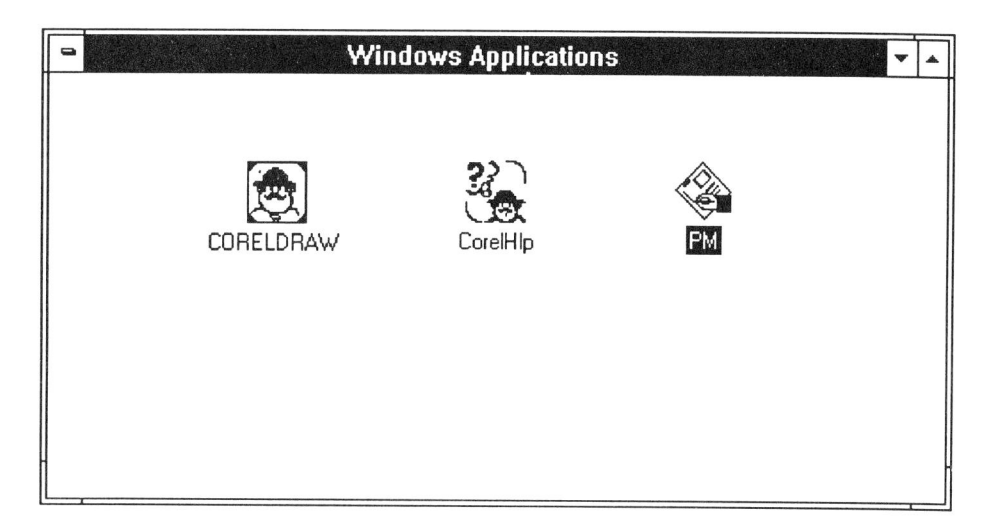

Windows Applications Group

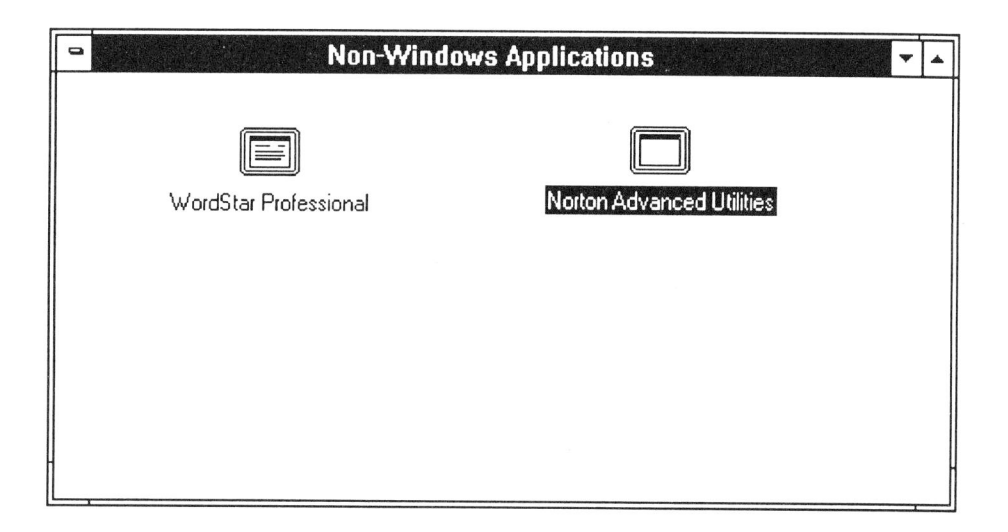

The Non-Windows Applications Group

For each of the groups a special file is created, which has the extension GRP, and this contains the details of the programs that are contained within that group. These are not meant to be looked at, i.e. they are not in ASCII format. If this file becomes damaged, for any reason, then the group ceases to exist and you will have to rebuild it from scratch, something that is easy to do but takes time. I suggest that at the end of each Windows session you make a backup copy of your group files just in case something happens to those on your hard disk. To do so you could create a batch file, called **WINCOPY**, and run this every time you shut down Windows and before you turn off the computer. The batch file looks like this:

```
REM Batch file to copy Group File information.
@ECHO OFF
CLS
REM Ensure you are logged onto the correct drive.
C:
REM Log into the directory containing Windows.
CD\WINDOWS
REM Ask for the backup disk and wait before continuing.
ECHO Please place the backup disk into Drive-A
PAUSE
REM Copy the group files to the target disk.
COPY *.GRP A:
REM Display a message that the files are safe.
ECHO All the Group Files have been copied for safekeeping.
ECHO.
ECHO Please remove the disk and keep it safe. Bye Bye.
ECHO.
PAUSE
REM Return to the root and clear the screen.
CD\
CLS
```

The REM lines are for information only, telling you what happens next, and they do not have to be included. You can create the batch file within Windows by using the Notepad or you can generate it from the system prompt. To do the latter:

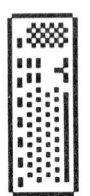

a) At the system prompt, log into a directory that is on the PATH, e.g. WINDOWS.

b) Enter **COPY CON WINCOPY.BAT**, which means copy whatever I type on the keyboard (the CON bit of the command) into a batch file called WINCOPY.

c) Now type the batch file as shown above, pressing **Enter** at the end of each line.

d) When you have finished entering the lines as above, press **F6** and the file will be created.

Once the batch file has been created you can run it from the system prompt by entering **WINCOPY** and it will do the rest. You can also run the batch file from within Windows via the DOS window.

Please note, you should not make any of these group files Read Only because that will defeat the object of the exercise. The whole point of the groups is that they are dynamic, i.e. you can change and modify them to suit your own purposes, whims and ideas, therefore the groups' files have to be capable of change. Making any file Read Only prevents this.

Rearranging group contents

You can move programs from one group to another very easily - after all ease of use is the whole point of Windows, and there are a number of ways that you can do so. The simplest is to pick up an icon and move it from one group window to another. As you do so the group files are updated to remain current. Alternatively you can move the files from one group to another using the keyboard - but it takes longer.

Exercise 4.5
Moving files

For the purposes of this exercise we are going to move the two Games programs from their default group and place them into the Accessories Group. When that is done you can delete the Games group because it is no longer needed.

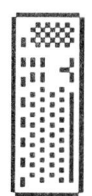

1) Because we are dealing only with two groups, we might as well reduce the others to icons for the duration. Because the Main Group is active we'll reduce that one first. Press **Ctrl-F4** and the window becomes an icon. Do not press **Alt-Space**, because this applies to the Program Manager window and it is not that which we want to shrink.

2) Once the Main window is reduced to an icon the next window in the sequence becomes active. Press **Ctrl-F4** again to reduce this one. If the next window is the Accessories or Games, move on to the one after using **Ctrl-Tab**. Once the unwanted windows are reduced you should be left with just the Accessories and the Games windows on screen.

3) Now press **Shift-F4** to tile the two remaining windows.

4) Make sure the Games window is the one which is active, using **Ctrl-Tab** if necessary. The active window is highlighted. It does not matter whether the active window is the one on the left or on the right.

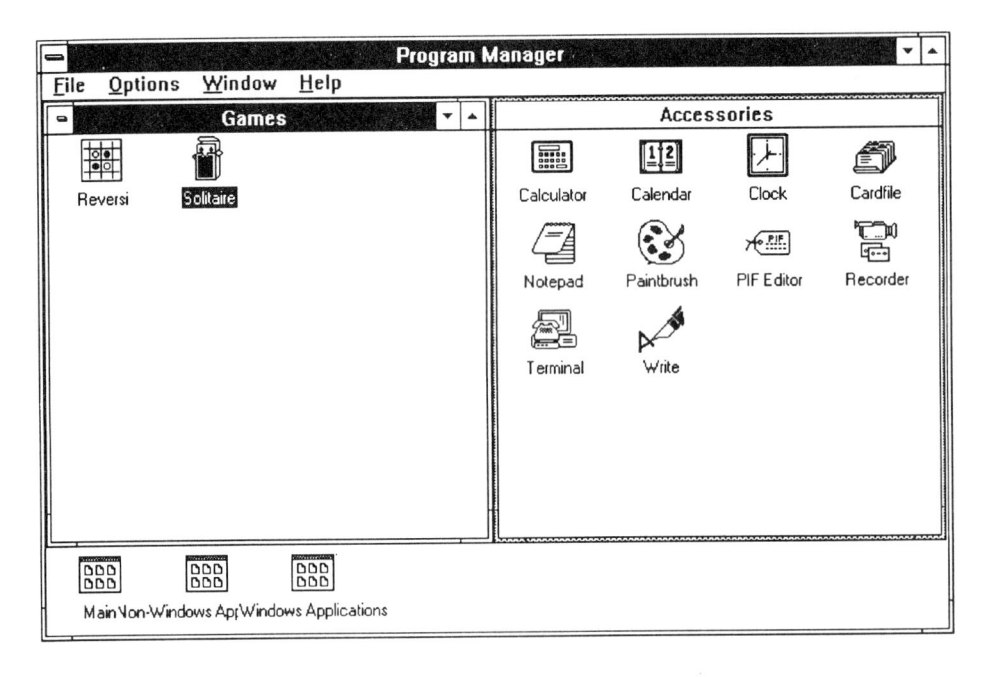

Two windows Tiled

5) Within the Games window the highlighter will be overlying one of the two programs, again it does not matter which. Press **Alt-F M** and a dialogue box appears.

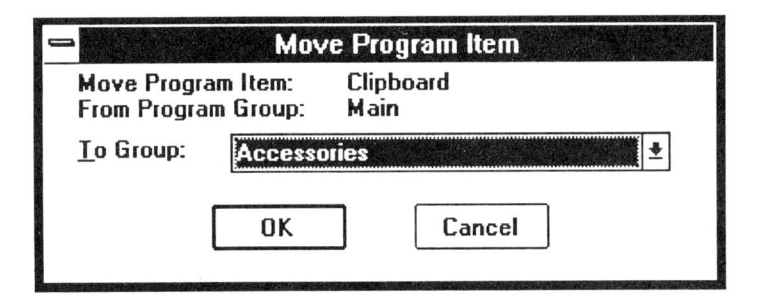

Move Dialogue Box

6) Press **Enter**, to accept the default in the dialogue box, and the program will be moved to the Accessories Window.

7) Because the last action involved the Accessories window, this is the one that is now active. Press **Ctrl-Tab** to return to the Games window. As there is only one program remaining in the window that is the one that will be highlighted. Press **Alt-F M Enter** to move the program across. The Games window is now empty.

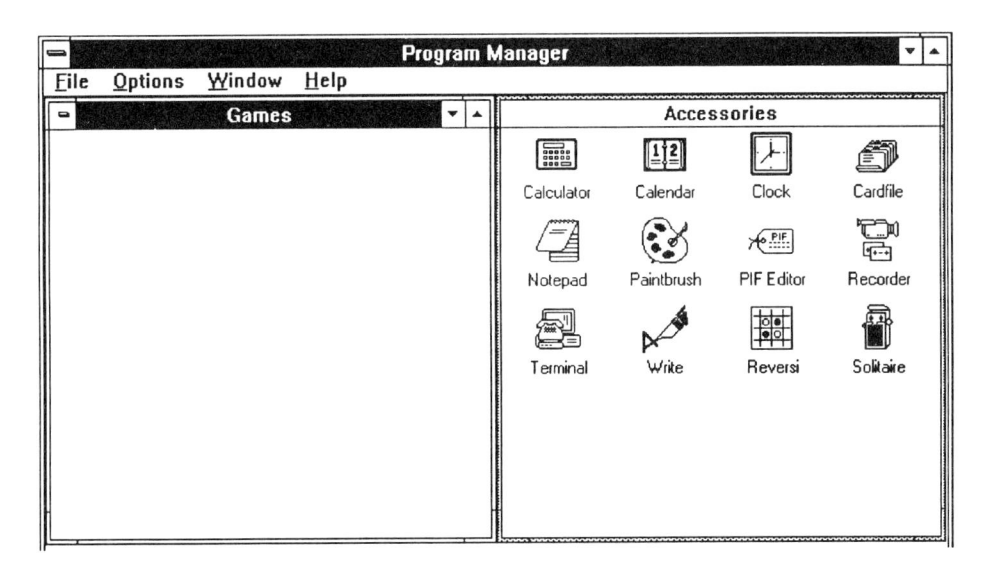

Games Empty

8) Press **Ctrl-Tab** to activate the Games window again, and then press **Del**. A new dialogue box appears:

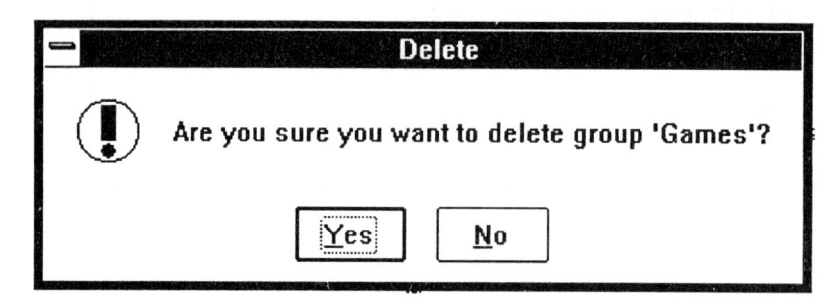

```
┌─────────────────────────────────────────────┐
│ ─                  Delete                   │
├─────────────────────────────────────────────┤
│                                             │
│  (!)   Are you sure you want to delete group 'Games'?  │
│                                             │
│              ┌─────┐    ┌─────┐            │
│              │ Yes │    │ No  │            │
│              └─────┘    └─────┘            │
└─────────────────────────────────────────────┘
```

Delete Group

9) Press **Enter** and the group window vanishes. Press **Ctrl-Tab Enter** and one of the icons at the bottom of the screen will reappear as a window, occupying the same position as it did before you reduced it to an icon. Reselect the other icons in the same way.

10) Finally press **Shift-F4** to tile the remaining windows.

Moving things is very much simpler using the mouse.

1) Click on Reversi in the Games window, hold down the button and drag the icon into the Accessories window.

2) Repeat the action with Solitaire.

3) Click in the Games window to make sure it is active. Press **Del Enter**.

4) Press **Shift-F4** to tile the remaining group windows.

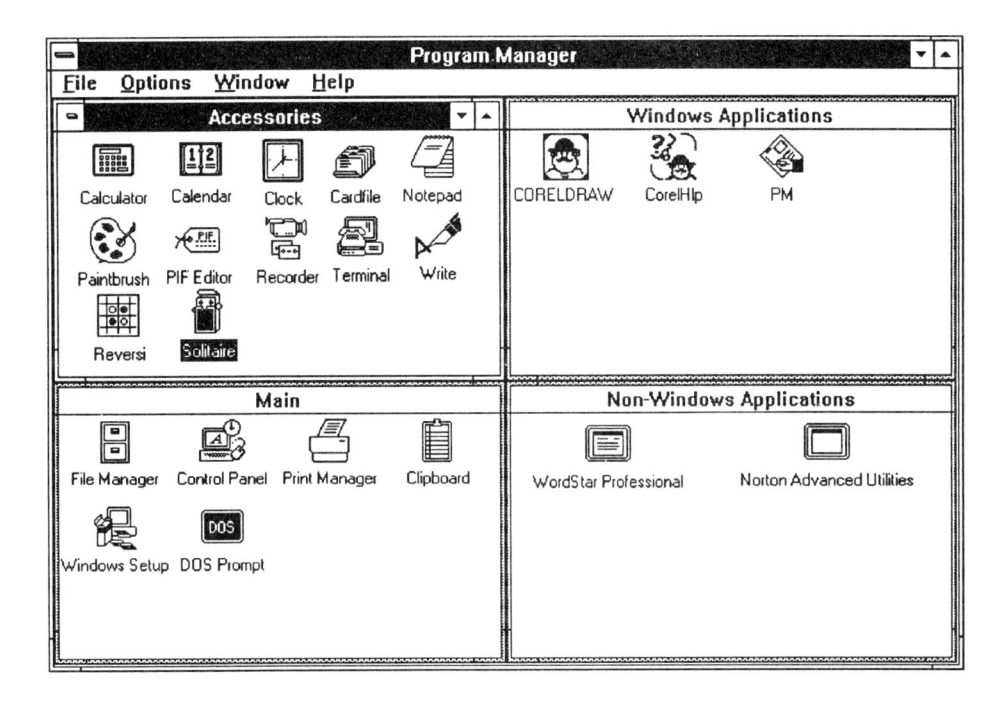

Four groups tiled

Adding things to groups

When Setup installed Windows for you it found a number of programs and gave you the option of adding them into the Windows environment. But it will not have found all the programs on your hard disk. For one thing, it simply cannot. It can only search for certain programs and it will get a few of these wrong. For example, a friend of mine has a program of which is which is called HG.EXE. Setup found this when he installed Windows but insisted it was Harvard Graphics, even though it isn't. This is nobody's fault, there are simply too many programs around for anyone to know what they all are. Windows Setup is intended to find the most common and widely used programs and that's what it looks for.

Another point, Setup only looks for programs which have the extension EXE - it ignores, or rather doesn't bother with, any program with a COM extension. The result is that there could be a great many programs on your hard disk that have not been found by Setup and so they have to be added to the groups manually.

As usual there are a couple of ways that you can do this, one keyboard and the other mouse based. Here's how it's done. By the way, you should not have more than 40 files in any one group for two reasons. Firstly, Microsoft don't recommend it, but more importantly you wouldn't be able to see all the icons in the window - even if it is full sized.

Exercise 4.6
Adding programs using File

Be warned, adding programs into the groups using the keyboard is very long winded - almost to the point of being not worth it. It is much easier using the keyboard and mouse in combination.

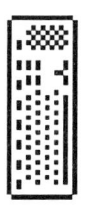

1) Use **Ctrl-Tab** to select the group window into which the program is going to be added.

2) Press **Alt-F,** to open the Files menu, followed by **N** for New. This brings up a dialogue box:

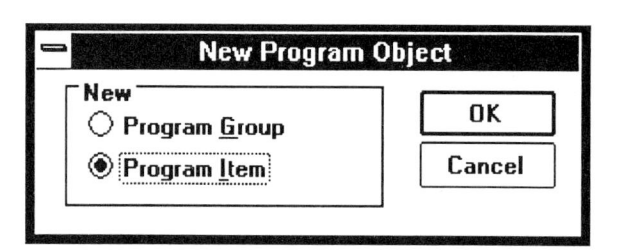

New program dialogue box

3) By default the dialogue box always has New Program Item selected and as this is what we want just press **Enter**. This will bring up a new dialogue box, see top of next page.

4) Press **Tab** three times until Browse is selected, shown by a dotted box surrounding the word, and then press **Enter**. A new dialogue box appears, shown opposite.

Program Item Properties

Description:
Command Line:

[OK] [Cancel] [**B**rowse...] [Change Icon...]

Select a program

5) Because Windows always defaults to its own directory this is what is shown in the Directory box, and the various programs within that directory are shown in the File box. However as these are already installed in Windows we don't need them. Press **Tab** twice until the [..] sign in the Directory box is highlighted by the dotted outline. Now press **Space** to select this option, which represents the parent of the Windows directory - which should be the Root of Drive-C. Press **Enter**.

Browse

File**n**ame: *.exe   [OK]
Directory: c:\winmono   [Cancel]
Files: **D**irectories:

```
calc.exe         [..]
calendar.exe     [system]
cardfile.exe     [-a-]
clipbrd.exe      [-b-]
clock.exe        [-c-]
control.exe      [-d-]
msdos.exe
notepad.exe
pbrush.exe
pifedit.exe
```

Browse the Disk

6) Using the cursor keys select which directory you want to log onto to, i.e. the one which contains the program you want to add to the Windows environment. Once the directory is highlighted press **Enter** to log onto it.

7) Press **Tab** four times, until the selector box moves into the File area of the dialogue box.

8) Use the cursor keys to select the program you want and then press **Enter**.

9) You are now back at the selection box. Press **Tab** twice to move the cursor back to the Description line and then type the description of the program you have just selected. Ideally you want to keep this as short as possible, because what you type here is what appears beneath the program icon.

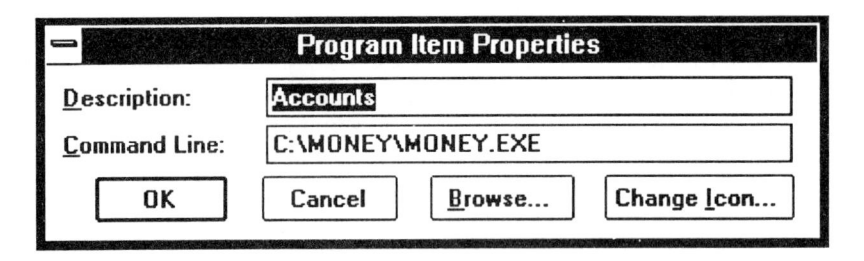

Description of program

10) Now press **Tab** five times, until the Change Icon button is selected, and then press **Enter**. There are a number of different icon styles you can select for the program. Details of these are held in the PROGMAN.EXE which is what is shown as default on the first line of the dialogue box that will appear.

11) Press **Tab**, to move to the box that says Show Next, and then press **Space** or **Enter** to page through the possible icons. Once you find one you want to use press **Tab**, to select **OK**, and then **Enter**.

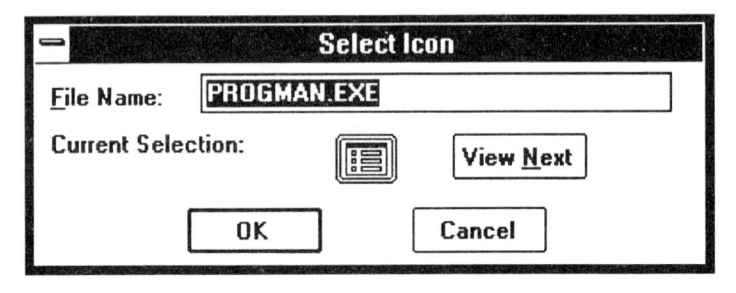

Select an Icon

12) Back at the selection dialogue box, press **Tab** until **OK** is highlighted and then press **Enter**. The program you have chosen, represented by the icon you selected, will now appear in the group window that you activated before you started the selection process.

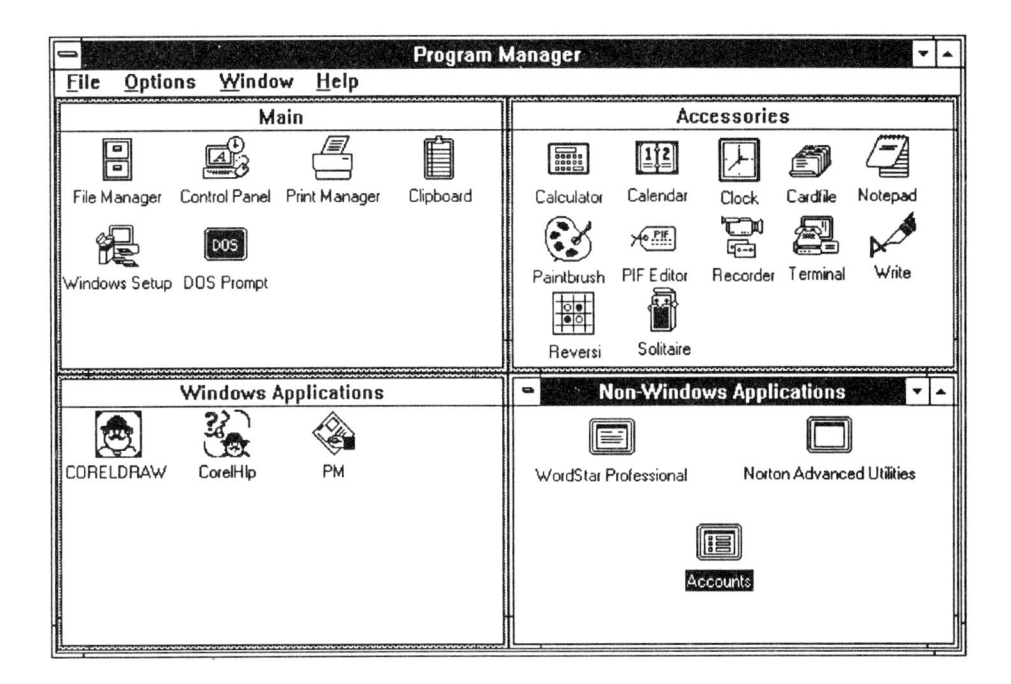

New program added

1) Activate the window you want the program added to by clicking on it.

2) Press **Alt-F N** or click on **File** in the Menu Bar and then on **New**.

3) Click on **OK** in the dialogue box that appears.

4) Double click on **Browse**.

5) Double click on **[..]**.

6) Double click on the directory that contains the file you want to add.

7) Double click on the file name.

8) Type the description and then click on **Change Icon**.

9) Click on **Show Next** until you reach the icon you want. Click on **OK**.

10) Click on **OK** in the main dialogue box and the program, with its icon, is added to the group window.

Exercise 4.7
Adding programs using Setup

When Windows was installed, the Setup program copied part of itself into the Windows directory. At the end of the installation this file was updated to include the details of system parameters under which Windows runs. You can use the resulting Windows Setup program to add programs to the groups within Program Manager.

1) Activate the Main group window.

2) Using the cursor keys select Windows Setup. Note, the **Left** and **Right** keys only allow you to move the highlighter horizontally within a window, **Up** and **Down** move the highlighter vertically only. Once Setup is highlighted press **Enter** to activate it. This brings up a dialogue box which contains details of the system setup:

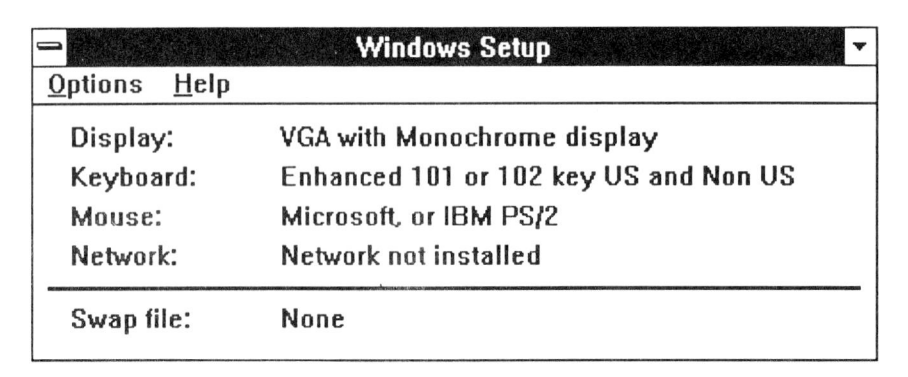

```
┌─────────────────── Windows Setup ───────────────────▼┐
│ Options  Help                                        │
│                                                      │
│   Display:     VGA with Monochrome display           │
│   Keyboard:    Enhanced 101 or 102 key US and Non US │
│   Mouse:       Microsoft, or IBM PS/2                │
│   Network:     Network not installed                 │
│   ─────────────────────────────────────────────────  │
│   Swap file:   None                                  │
│                                                      │
└──────────────────────────────────────────────────────┘
```

System Setup Details

Program Manager 105

3) Press **Alt-O,** to activate the Options menu, followed by **S**. This brings up a new dialogue box:

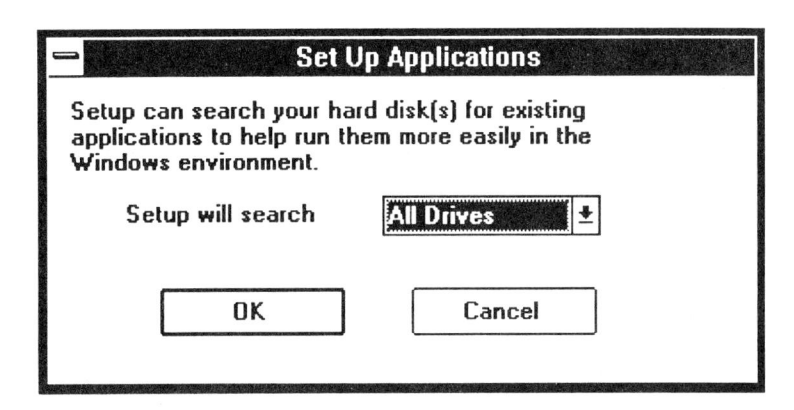

Dialogue box

4) You can use the cursor keys to select which area of your storage you will search to find programs. The options range from All drives to specific disks or the PATH only. Once you have selected one of these press **Enter** to begin the search.

5) The program searches the designated area and then produces a dialogue box containing a list of the programs it has found.

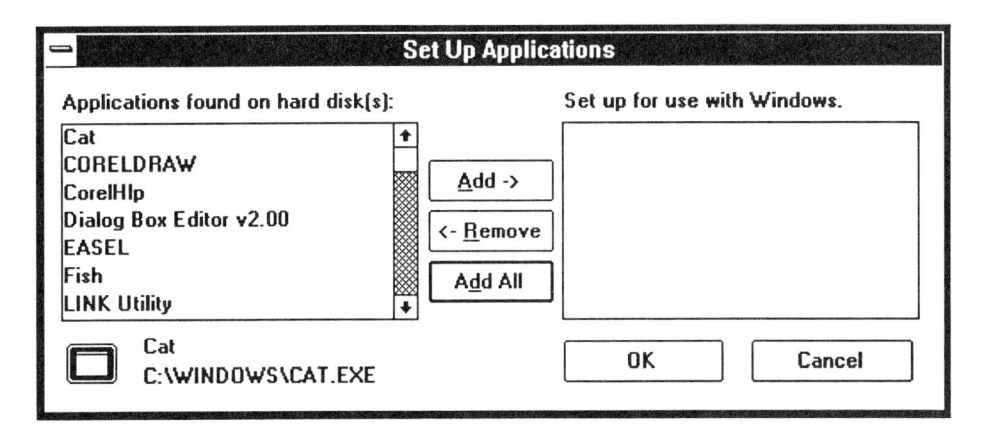

Programs found

6) Use the cursor keys to move the selection box to the program you want to add. Press **Space** to select it. Repeat the action as often as necessary if you want to add a number of files.

7) Press **Tab** to move the highlighter to **Add->** and then press **Enter**. The selected program(s) appear in the right hand box.

8) Use **Tab** to move to **OK** and then press **Enter**.

9) The Program Manager comes to the forefront as the programs you selected are added to the correct groups, e.g. any Windows program is added to the Windows Applications group. As each group is added to it is shrunk to an icon.

10) Once all the programs have been added, the Windows Setup dialogue box reappears. To remove it press **Alt-F4**.

11) Use **Ctrl-Tab Enter** to reinstate any window that has been shrunk to an icon. The icons will reappear as group windows in their former positions.

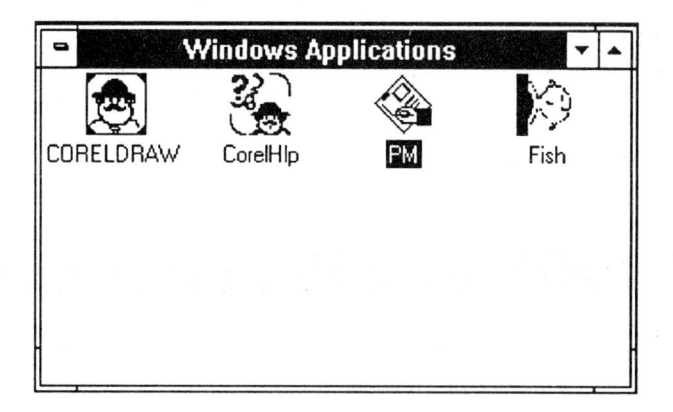

Fish added to Windows Application Group

1) Double click on **Windows Setup** in the Main group window.

2) Click on **Options** and again on **Setup Application**.

3) Click on the drives box to change the selection, if necessary, and then click on **OK**.

4) Click on the programs you want to add, using the scroll bars if necessary. Click on **Add->**.

5) Click on **OK** and the programs are added to the groups.

6) Click on the **Control Box** and then on **Close** to terminate the Setup program.

7) Double click on any icons to restore them to windows.

Deleting files from Groups

If, at any time, you want to delete a file from a group, regardless of the kind of file it is, all you have to do is select the file and then press **Del Enter**. You will be asked if you want to delete the file before it is removed.

Exercise 4.8
Deleting files

The Fish program, which was added in the last exercise, was written to run under Windows/286. It will run in Windows 3 but only if the program is run in Real Mode. As I rarely use this mode, I normally use Standard or 386-Enhanced mode, it would mean that the only time I could run the program would be by purposely deciding to do so. Because the program produces a cartoon of an aquarium, with various sized fish floating back and forth, I have decided that I don't need it and so it can be deleted from the group. Files can only be deleted from the groups one at a time, there is no method of deleting multiple files from a group - unless you delete the entire group.

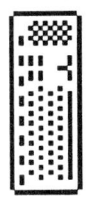

1) Select the appropriate group window, using **Ctrl-Tab** if necessary to change group window.

2) Use the cursor keys to highlight the file to be deleted. Press **Del** and a dialogue box appears.

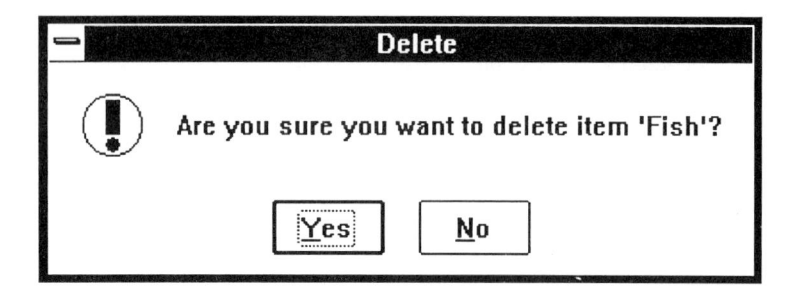

```
        ┌─────────────────────────────────┐
        │ ▬           Delete              │
        ├─────────────────────────────────┤
        │                                 │
        │  (!) Are you sure you want to delete item 'Fish'? │
        │                                 │
        │      ┌─────┐     ┌─────┐        │
        │      │ Yes │     │ No  │        │
        │      └─────┘     └─────┘        │
        └─────────────────────────────────┘
```

Delete File dialogue box

3) Press **Enter** and the file is removed from the group. Note, the program is not deleted from the disk, it is simply no longer part of the group and thus cannot be activated from the Program manager.

1) Click on the file to be deleted. Press **Del**. Click on **OK**.

Creating a new Group

As part of the installation routine, Setup created five groups; Main, which contains the major programs that Windows uses; Accessories, which holds Microsoft produced or licensed Windows applications; Windows-Applications, which contains any Windows-based program that has been found on the hard disk, e.g. PageMaker; and Non-Windows Applications, in other words those MS-DOS programs that you selected to run from within the Windows environment. These will normally be all you need, but there may be occasions when you want additional groups.

A group does not have to be just programs, it can also contain associated files. For example, suppose you were doing a project about Global Warming. You use Write to produce documents; Paintbrush to create graphics; Cardfile to collect basic data and PageMaker to produce the finished report. All these programs and their related files can be put into a single group. This is how you do it.

Exercise 4.9
A new group

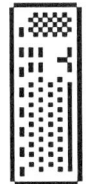

1) Press **Alt-F N** to use the New command. This brings up a dialogue box. Press **Alt-G** to select New Program group and then press **Enter**.

2) In the dialogue box that will then appear enter the name of the new group, e.g. Project.

3) The new group window will appear, as if it was cascaded, over the top of the existing windows. Press **Shift-F4** to tile it into the other windows.

4) Use **Ctrl-Tab** to move into the Accessories group. Then use the cursor keys to select the Cardfile.

5) Press **Alt-F C** to begin the process of copying the Cardfile to the new group. This will bring up a new dialogue box, similar to the Move box.

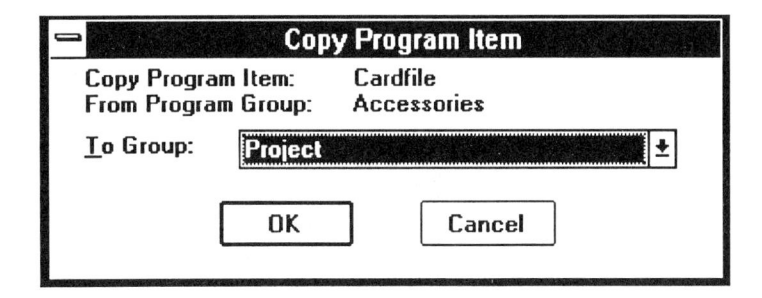

Copy dialogue box

6) Use the cursor keys to change the target group name, by default this will show the group name that is currently active, i.e. Accessories, and you must change it to Project or the program will be copied to the wrong place.

7) Select each of the other main programs, i.e. Write, PageMaker and Paintbrush, and copy them into the Project group.

Project

Cardfile Paintbrush PM Write

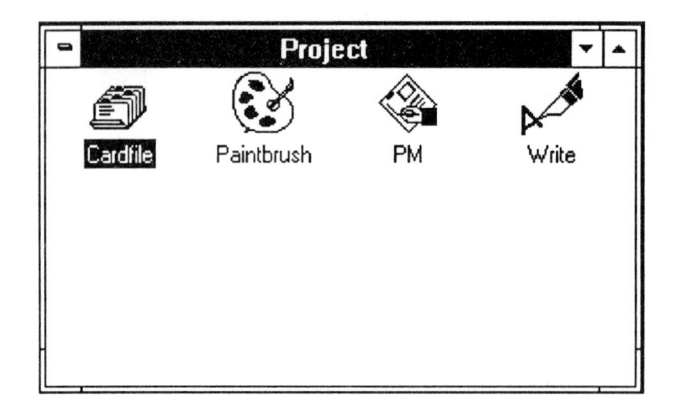

Programs into the group

8) Now for the fun bit. Each program that you place into a group can be primed to load a specific file every time that it is run. You do this by linking the file directly to the program using the Properties command. Suppose you had three Data files, all created by Cardfile. Copy the cardfile icon, within the Project group - so that you have three Cardfile icons. (Any program can appear in a group as many time as you like.)

9) Now, with one of the Cardfile icons selected, press **Alt-F P** and this brings up the program Properties box. Change the description, e.g. to Data 1, on the first line.

10) In the second line you add the name of the data file, plus its extension, to the end of the program name. There must be a space between the program and file name. If the data file is located in another directory, other than the \WINDOWS one, then you must include the full path to it as well; otherwise there is no need to include the path.

11) Once the name of the data file has been added press **Enter** and the icon within the Project group will be renamed.

12) You rename the other Cardfile icons in the same way. Make as many copies of the other programs as you need so that each will load a file automatically. You should end up with something like this:

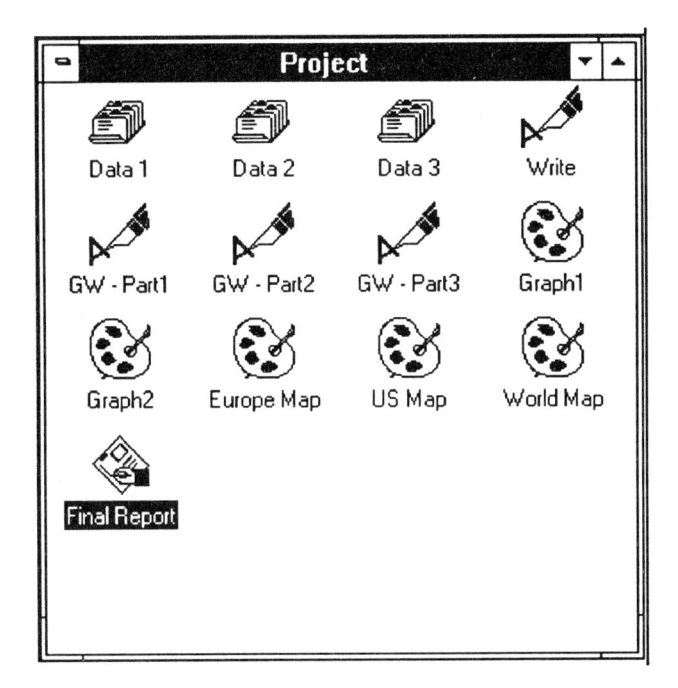

Project group completed

A shortcut to copying the files using the mouse is to press **Ctrl** and then click and drag the required icon while holding down the key. This allows you to copy rather than move the icon. You can only move the icon within the outer boundary of the main Program Manager window.

Now, whenever you activate one of the programs within the Project group, the associated data file will be loaded automatically. The only problem with this is that it means that the application itself is also loaded every time and you may run into memory problems.

By the way, you can also change the icon for each file if you wish. The icon and the description are merely for your reference, they have no bearing on how Program Manager runs the program. As long as the program itself can be found, as shown on the second line, everything will work just fine.

Exercise 4.10
Deleting Groups

If you want to delete a number of files all at the same time then there is an easier way to do other than having to select them all individually. This method makes use of the fact that you can delete an entire group all at once. Note, the files are not deleted from the hard disk, only the group is removed from Program Manager.

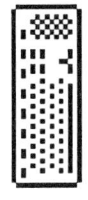

1) Create a new group, e.g. called **Junk**, using **Alt-F N**. Use **Tab** to highlight new Group instead of New program.

2) Move those files that you want deleted into this group as in Exercise 4.5.

3) Reduce the Junk group to an icon using **Ctrl-F4**.

4) With the icon highlighted, press **Del Enter** and the group with its entire contents will be deleted.

1) Click on **File** and then press **Enter,** to create a new group.

2) Cascade the windows and then move the files to be erased into the new group.

3) Click on **Minimise** to reduce the group to an icon.

4) Press **Del** and click on **OK** to delete the group and the files it contains.

Menus

Program Manager is the main program that will be loaded whenever you activate Windows. It is special in a number of ways, not least of which is because it provides services for any and all groups within the main window. Each group window contains its own Control Box, Minimise and Maximise buttons, but no group window contains a menu. Instead each group shares the facilities of Program Manager, where each menu contains its own set of commands and these affect either the groups or the icons that the groups contain.

To activate any of the menus, you either press **Alt** and the initial letter of the menu key word, or use the mouse and click on the menu name. Either action will pop-down the menu from which you then select the command. If you make a mistake and select the wrong menu you can correct the error by simply using the cursor keys to move to an alternative menu. Using the mouse you just click on the menu you actually want. To cancel a menu, without activating any of the commands it contains press **Esc**, using the keyboard, or click anywhere on screen, other than on the menu, using the mouse.

The menus are intended primarily to be used from the keyboard, i.e. without the mouse, although for some actions you must use the mouse and keyboard in combination. To activate any command with the mouse, open the menu and then click on the command you want. The menus and their contents are as follows.

```
┌─────────────────────────┐
│ New...                  │
│ Open            Enter   │
│ Move...                 │
│ Copy...                 │
│ Delete          Del     │
│ Properties...           │
│                         │
│ Run...                  │
│                         │
│ Exit Windows...         │
└─────────────────────────┘
```

File Menu

The **File** menu controls the actions of the files and, within limits, the activities of groups. The commands it contains, and their actions, are:

> **New** This allows you to create a new group or add a new program to an existing group. Once activated it will bring up a dialogue box that allows you to set the options and begin the process of adding programs or creating a group. To activate the command once the menu is open press **N**. Alternatively because this is the first command in the menu, you can simply press **Enter** and the command will be activated.
>
> **Open** This applies specifically to programs and it simply means activate the program. To activate the command once the menu is open press **O**. Alternatively, you can select the program you

want to run, using the cursor keys to select it, and then just press **Enter** without opening the menu in the first place.

Move Allows you to move a program from one group to another. When it has been moved, the program will no longer appear in the original group. To activate the command once the menu is open press **M**.

Copy Similar to Move above, but this command allows you to duplicate the program in another group - or even copy it into the same group as many times as you wish. To activate the command once the menu is open press **C**.

Delete This command allows you to remove a file from a group. Select the program icon you want to remove, press **Alt-F D** or just **Del** and the program is deleted from the group. You can also use this command to delete a group in its entirety but how you do depends on whether or not the group contains any files. If the group is a window then before you delete it you must remove all the files that it contains, one by one, and then delete the group. However, if the group is an icon you can delete the whole thing, files and all, in a single action.

Properties Allows you to change the description, program details and icon of any program. It will also allow you to change the group information, should you so wish. It is this command that you use to make a program automatically load a specific file as the program is activated. If you wish to do this you must include the full information about the file to be loaded, including any extension, after the program name and separate the two with a blank space. To activate the command once the menu is open press **P**.

Run This is identical to Open, above, except that it allows you to run programs that are not included as icons - however, they must be available on the PATH. To activate the command once the menu is open press **R**.

Exit Windows When you have finished with Windows you must close it down before you turn off the computer, if only to remove any temporary files created by the programs you have been using. When you activate this command you will be prompted to make sure that you did intend to leave Windows. You will also be provided with the option of saving the changes you have made. If you choose to use this option, then the next time you run Windows it will appear exactly as you are leaving it now, i.e. the groups will appear as they are now and the icons within the groups will stay the same. If you do not select save changes then the next time you run Windows the groups and icons will appear as they were when you activated the program at the beginning of the day's session. To activate the command once the menu is open press **X**.

The **Options** menu allows you to toggle the appearance of the icons, groups and Windows itself. It contains only two commands:

Auto Arrange With this option toggled on, shown by having a check mark beside the command, every time you return a group icon to a window the icons within that group will be reorganised for you. In other words they will assume new positions within that window subject only to the setting in the Control Panel which determines how close the icons will be. Depending on how many icons you have in a group this can either be of no consequence or a real pain in the butt. For example, consider the contents of the Project window, as shown on Page 135, which contains a large number of icons. Using the mouse it is possible to arrange all the icons that the group contains so that they are all visible, without infringing on each other. If the group is reduced to an icon and then restored to a window with the **Auto Arrange** command On, then all the icons shift around and the scroll bars may appear - thus undoing all the arranging you have done. Whether you have the command on or off is entirely your own preference. Personally I always turn it off for of the reason given above. To toggle the command press **Alt-O A**.

Minimise on Use Again this is a matter of choice. Windows has the facility, provided by this command, to shrink the Program Manager to an icon whenever you activate any program either from a group or using Run. Then when you have finished with the program you restore the Program Manager icon. Essentially, this just means that you have an uncluttered screen. You still have access to the Program Manager, using **Ctrl-Tab**, and it can be restored to a window at any time. This command is, like the one above, a toggle and whether it is on or off will be shown by the presence or not of a tick mark beside the command. To toggle the command once the menu is open press **M** or move the highlighter down to the command and press **Enter**.

```
Cascade                      Shift+F5
Tile                         Shift+F4
Arrange Icons

1 Accessories
√ 2 Windows Applications
3 Main
4 Non-Windows Applications
```

Windows menu

The **Windows** menu controls, believe it or not, the windows and how they appear. The commands it contains are:

Cascade This will change the display of the windows that are open within Program Manager, so that they become rectangular and overlay one another. The active window will always appear at the front of the stack. To select another window you simply click on it and it becomes active. However, it does not change its position within the stack unless you re-cascade the windows. The command has no effect on any group which is being displayed as an icon. You have two methods of running the command; either press **Alt-W C**, which opens the menu and then runs the command, or more simply just press **Shift-F5** which does away with having to open the menu.

Tile Provides the alternative window display method. When the display is tiled, Windows tries to fit the open windows into the main Program Manager window so that they occupy an equal amount of space. The appearance of the tiled windows depends on how many windows there are open. For example, three windows will be displayed side by side as vertical rectangles; five windows will appear as two square-ish ones on the left hand side and three horizontal rectangles on the left hand side; 36 windows appear as six columns of six square-ish windows, and so on. As with Cascade, the command has no effect on any group which is being displayed as an icon. Again there are two methods of activating the Tile command, either press **Alt-W T**, which opens the menus and then runs the command, or just press **Shift-F4** which has the same effect without using the menu.

Arrange Icons This does not, as you might think, apply to any groups which are displayed as icons, unless all the groups are icons. What the command does is exactly what it says - it organises the icons, in the active window, so that they conform with and to the specifications set in Control Panel (See next Chapter for details). If you have any group open as a window, and active as such, then whenever you use this command the icons within that window will be rearranged so that they form neat lines and columns. The order in which they are arranged is based purely on where they lie before you issue the command. For example, the icon that is nearest to the top left hand corner of the window is moved into that position, the icon nearest to that is then moved next to it and so on.

If the groups are being displayed as icons, without any windows active, then the command affects those instead of the icons within a window. The group icons will be arranged in a line along the bottom of the Program Manager window. To use the command, you must go through the menu by pressing **Alt-W A**.

The remainder of the Windows menu contains a numbered list of the groups that are contained with the Program Manager - a check mark appears beside the group that is currently active. You can activate any group window by pressing **Alt-W** and then the number corresponding to that group.

Restore	
Move	
Size	
Mi**n**imize	
Maximize	
Close	Ctrl+F4
Nex**t**	Ctrl+F6

Group Control Box

Each group window also contains its own Control Box which contains a list of commands almost identical to those in the Program Manager Control Box, but these are specific to the group window. You activate the Group Control Box by pressing **Alt-Hyphen**. The commands it contains are:

Restore Returns a group icon to its former position and size within the Program Manager main window.

Move Move the group window, or icon, within Program Manager.

Size Allows you to change the size of the group window using the cursor keys.

Minimise Reduces the group window to an icon.

Maximise Expands the group window so that it fills all the available space within the Program Manager main window.

Close Reduces the group window to an icon.

Next Switches to the next group window. The sequence of windows is given in the Windows menu.

Exercise 4.11
Tidy Icons

This exercise will show you the effect of arranging the icons.

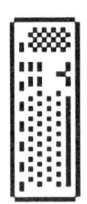

1) Reduce all the open windows, except the Accessories one, to icons. Use **Ctrl-tab** to move to the window to be shrunk and then press **Ctrl-F4**. Repeat the action to shrink the remaining windows.

2) Enlarge the Accessories window to the maximum size by pressing **Alt-Hyphen X**.

3) Use the Arrange Icons command by pressing **Alt-W A**. The icons within the window will rearrange themselves so that they line up one after the other.

4) Toggle the Auto Arrange option by pressing **Alt-O A**.

5) Return the Accessories window to its original size by pressing **Alt-Hyphen R**. The window is restored and the icons automatically reposition themselves.

6) Restore the other group icons. Use **Ctrl-Tab** to select each in turn and then press **Alt-Hyphen R** for each one. As they are returned to their former positions the icons within them will be reorganised.

7) If you want to turn the Auto Arrange facility off, press **Alt-O A** again.

1) Reduce all group windows, except Accessories, to icons by clicking on the **Minimise** button of the windows.

2) Click on the **Maximise** button of the Accessories window.

3) Click on **Window** in the Menu Bar and then again on **Arrange Icons**.

4) Click on **Options** and then press **Enter** to toggle the Auto Arrange facility.

5) Click on **Maximise** in the Accessories window again to restore it to its former position and size. The icons within the window will be rearranged as the window changes size.

6) Restore the other group windows by double clicking on the group icons. Again the program icons will be rearranged.

Help

Windows 3 provides a continuous and on-line help facility for just about everything. The help facility can be activated at any time by pressing **F1**. All the Windows 3 programs that come as part of the package, except Clock, provide a help facility. In each case the help is specific to the program concerned.

Once you have activated help you use the pointer, which changes into a pointing finger, to select the topic you want help with. Along the top of the screen there is a set of buttons that allow you to navigate your way around the help system. Simply click on the one you want and the program does the rest.

It has to be said that the help facility is superb, far superior to that which was available in Windows/286, but it does take some getting used to. Because help now covers every aspect of the program you can very easily get lost as you move through the various screens.

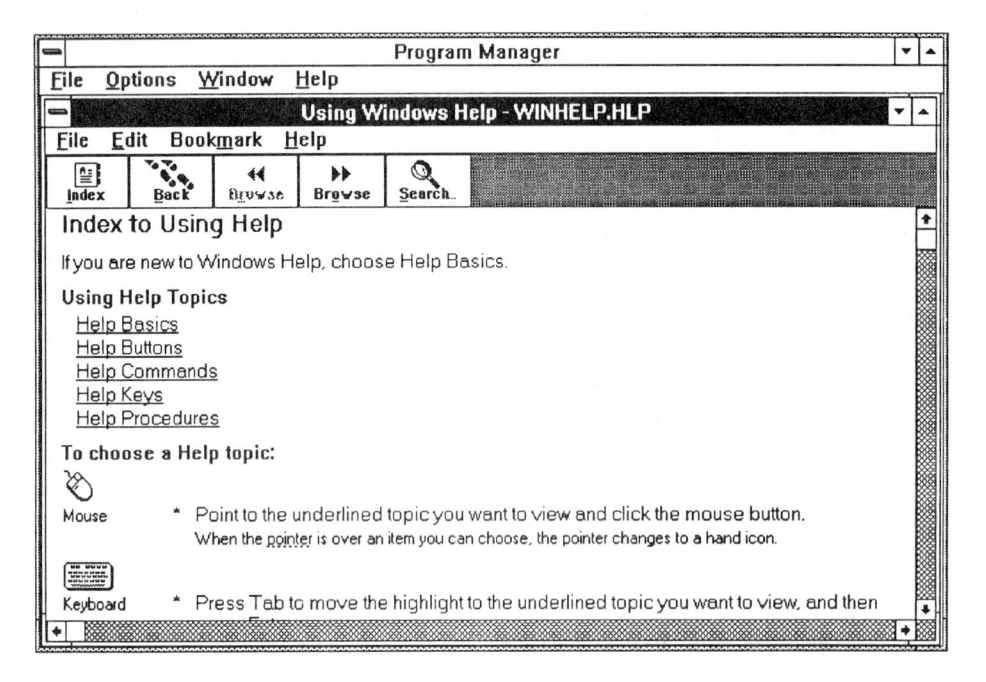

Program Manager Help

When you activate Help by clicking on it, or by press **Alt-H,** a menu pops down showing the following:

> **Index** This takes you directly to the main Help index for the particular program you are running. From here you can access any part of the Help system.
>
> **Keyboard** This section provides help only with those commands and actions that can be accessed from the keyboard.
>
> **Commands** This gives a full list of the commands available under Windows, broken down into convenient sub-sections.
>
> **Procedures** Gives help on exactly what it says. Again you can select specific areas to look at.
>
> **Using Help** How to use the help facility!

About Gives you information about the program you are running, e.g. its copyright details. Within Program Manager this also tells you which mode Windows is running in.

Once you have logged onto help, at any point, you can add comments to a file using **Alt-E A**. This brings up a dialogue box into which you type your comment. Pressing **Enter** then adds you comment to the help screen. The command is shown by a green paper clip overlaying the help screen. Clicking on this returns the dialogue box and its contents so you can view them.

Program Manager Summary

- Program Manager is a program organiser that allows you to sort programs into associated groups to your own preference.

- Program Manager can display groups as sub-windows and/or as icons.

- Groups as sub-windows have no Menu Bar, they share the menus and commands of the Program manager.

- Setup will automatically create up to five groups for you as part of the Windows installation.

- You must return to the Program Manager to terminate Windows.

- Group windows can be arranged as a Cascade, i.e. one in front of the other, or as Tiles, i.e. side by side.

- On-line help is available at all times.

Keyboard Summary

The following is a list of the keystrokes that can be used within Program Manager and what they do.

Alt-F4	Terminate Windows and return to MS-DOS.
Alt-F C	Copy a program from one group to another.
Alt-F D	Delete a selected icon within a group or delete a group if it appears as an icon or an empty window.
Alt-F M	Move a program icon from one group to another.
Alt-F N	Create a new group or add a program to a group.
Alt-F O	Activate a program. Select the program icon and then use this command to run the program.
Alt-F P	Pops-up the Properties dialogue box about either the group or a selected program.
Alt-F R	Run the entered program.
Alt-F X	Terminate the Windows program and return to the system prompt.
Alt-H A	Displays a box containing details of the program copyright and, only within Program Manager, also tells you the mode that Windows is using.
Alt-H C	Pops-up help about Windows commands.
Alt-H I	Activates the Help Index.
Alt-H K	The Keyboard Help system.
Alt-H P	Details help about Windows procedures.
Alt-H U	Provides help about using the help facility!
Alt-Hyphen C	Reduce group window to an icon.
Alt-Hyphen M	Move group window within Program Manager.
Alt-Hyphen N	Minimise group window, i.e. reduce it to an icon.
Alt-Hyphen R	Restore group window to its former size and position.
Alt-Hyphen S	Change the size of a group window.
Alt-Hyphen T	Activate the next group in the list.
Alt-Hyphen X	Maximise window to its fullest possible extent within the Program Manager main window.
Alt-O A	Toggle the icon arrangement facility.
Alt-O M	Toggle the facility that allows the Program Manager to be reduced to an icon whenever any selected program is run.
Alt-Spacebar C	Terminate the Windows program and return to the system prompt.
Alt-Spacebar M	Move the window.
Alt-Spacebar N	Minimise a window, i.e. reduce it to an icon.
Alt-Spacebar R	Restore an icon to a window occupying the same size and position as it had before it was shrunk to an icon.

Alt-Spacebar	S	Change the size of a window.
Alt-Spacebar	W	Switch to another program.
Alt-Spacebar	X	Maximise a window so that it fills the entire available space of the screen.
Alt-W A		Arrange the icons, either within a window, if one is active, or the group icons with the main Program Manager window if no group window is active.
Alt-W C		Cascade the group windows.
Alt-W T		Tile the group windows.
Ctrl-Tab		Move from one window or icon to another.
Ctrl-Esc		Switch to another program.
Ctrl-F6		Move from one window or group to another.
Del		Delete a selected icon, an empty group window or programs within a window.
End		Move directly to the last item in a list box.
Enter		Activate the selected program.
Esc		Cancels an operation.
F10		Activate the first menu on a Menu Bar. You then have to press Enter or a command letter to truly use the menu.
Home		Move directly to the first item in a list box.
PgDn		Scroll items in a list box - downwards.
PgUp		Scroll items in a list box - upwards.
PrScrn		This will copy the entire screen into the Clipboard so that it can be pasted into an application. (The illustrations in this book were created in this way.)
Alt-PrScrn		Copies only the active window to the Clipboard.
Shift-F4		Tile the group windows.
Shift-F5		Cascade the group windows.
Shift-Tab		Move the selector through options in reverse order, i.e. backwards, within Dialogue Boxes.
Spacebar		Toggle items within a Dialogue Box.
Tab		Move the selector through options to the next item within Dialogue Boxes.

Chapter 5
Control Panel

Running the program

The Control Panel, not to be confused with the Control Box on windows, is the program which allows you to adjust the way that the computer system is configured for running Windows 3. It also allows you to set a large number of parameters: from deciding which fonts to use to the complete colour scheme that Windows will use, from network features to the special properties used when running in 386-Enhanced mode.

The program is sub-divided into a number of minor features, the exact number depending on the kind of system you are using, e.g. in Standard Mode there are ten major parameter types that can be changed. The options available are:

Color This will allow you to change the colours of the majority of the screen display. You can use the Microsoft installed colours or you can create your own palette and use these instead.

Fonts Allows you to add or remove the fonts that are installed on your system.

Ports Permits you to assign and configure the communication ports of the computer.

Mouse This will allow you to change and/or modify the way that the mouse behaves under Windows.

Desktop The most comprehensive option, this will allow you to change just about every element of the display and how it appears.

Network Allows you to control the connections to the network. Note, this option is only available if the network is installed and running when you run the Control Panel program.

Printers Use this option to install and configure printers within the Windows environment.

International Allows you to set or modify the various national settings, e.g. the currency display, that will be used by Windows.

Keyboard Allows you to change the way that the keyboard operates under Windows.

Date/Time Changes the system date and time.

Sound Toggle the audible warning used by Windows to notify you of errors.

386-Enhanced Allows you to set the parameters for running programs concurrently. Note, this option only appears on the Control Panel if you are running in 386-Enhanced mode - in any other mode the option does not appear.

Each major parameter is displayed on the Control Panel as an icon, complete with a byline beneath it. To activate any of them you simply double click on the icon and the dialogue box concerned pops up, overlaying the Control Panel itself, ready to allow you to make your changes. Each change you make becomes active immediately, i.e. there is no need to reboot the computer as there was under Windows/286, although in some cases you have to come all the way back to the Control Panel, or even the Program Manager, before you can verify the changes.

The Control Panel can be run, and changes made, using the keyboard, but certain areas of the program really need a mouse. To get or change an effect with the keyboard, particularly the colours or the desktop, may take you several minutes, whereas using the mouse the same changes can be done in seconds. I strongly recommend that you use a mouse if you are going to do anything with the Control Panel.

1) Run Windows as normal by entering **WIN** from the system prompt.

2) Once the Program Manager appears on screen select the Main window, using **Ctrl-Tab** if necessary.

3) If you have not already done so toggle the setting that will shrink Program Manager to an icon by pressing **Alt-O M**.

4) Then, using the cursor keys, select the icon labelled Control Panel (It looks like a computer with the letter **A** displayed on the monitor.) and press **Enter**. The Control Panel program will be activated and the Program Manager is reduced to an icon that sits at the bottom left hand corner of the screen.

Control Panel

Control Panel Icon

1) Run windows as normal from the system prompt.

2) Once the Program Manager appears, click on **Options** in the menu bar to check that the **Minimise on Use** switch, in the Options menu, is **On** - by having a check mark against it. If no tick is present click on the command, otherwise click anywhere on the screen to discard the menu.

3) Double click on the icon in the Main window labelled Control Panel and the program will be activated.

Control Panel

There are only two possible menus available with the Control Panel, Settings and Help. The Settings menu contains a list of those major parameters that appear on the Control Panel as icons, i.e. they are used if you want to use the keyboard. The Help Menu is, like all Windows Help menus, specific to the particular program being run.

128 Windows 3 - A User's Guide

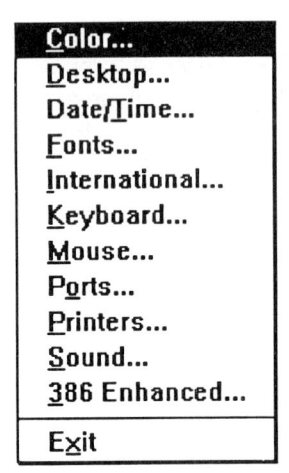

```
Color...
Desktop...
Date/Time...
Fonts...
International...
Keyboard...
Mouse...
Ports...
Printers...
Sound...
386 Enhanced...
Exit
```

```
Index
Keyboard
Commands
Procedures
Using Help
About Control Panel...
```

Settings & Help Menus

To use either menu either click on the key word in the Menu bar or press **Alt** and the initial letter of the menu you want to activate.

When you have finished with the Control Panel, the easiest and quickest way to close it and return to the Program Manager is to press **Alt-Space C** or **Alt-F4**.

Color

The colour option within Control Panel allows you to change, modify, create and save new colour schemes that will be used by Windows. Because Windows is really intended to be used with a colour VGA monitor - nothing else gives the superb colours it can use - the program provides facilities for producing an almost infinite range of colours. (Unfortunately within this book, for production reasons, we can only show the monochrome version of this element of the program, which is a great pity because the colours are superb.)

1) Because the Color option is, by default, pre-selected you can just press **Enter** to activate it.

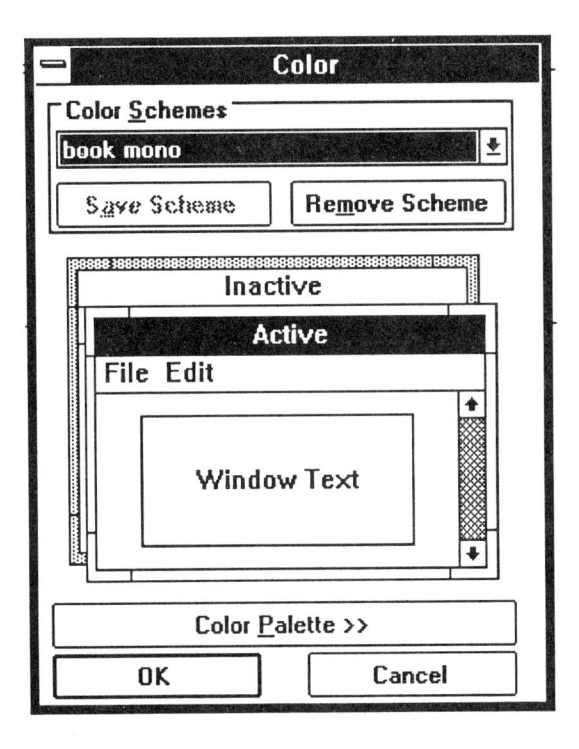

Control Panel Color, Part 1

1) Double click on the **Color** icon and this section of the program is activated.

The illustration above shows the following:

a) The **Color Scheme** currently in use. As you have just installed Windows, the program will be running under the Windows Default. Windows comes complete with a number of alternative, pre-defined colour schemes - some of them awful.

b) A representation of the various areas of the Windows environment to which you can make changes.

c) The **Color Palette** activator. You need to engage this to make individual changes to the colour scheme.

d) A button marked **OK**. Clicking on this will activate any changes you have made and return you to the Control Panel.

130   Windows 3 - A User's Guide

e) **A Cancel** button. This terminates the Color section and returns you to the Control Panel but does not instigate any changes you may have made.

2) Press **Tab** twice until the Color Palette button is selected, a grey dotted box will appear on the button, and then press **Enter**.

2) Click on **Color Palette** and the screen display doubles in size.

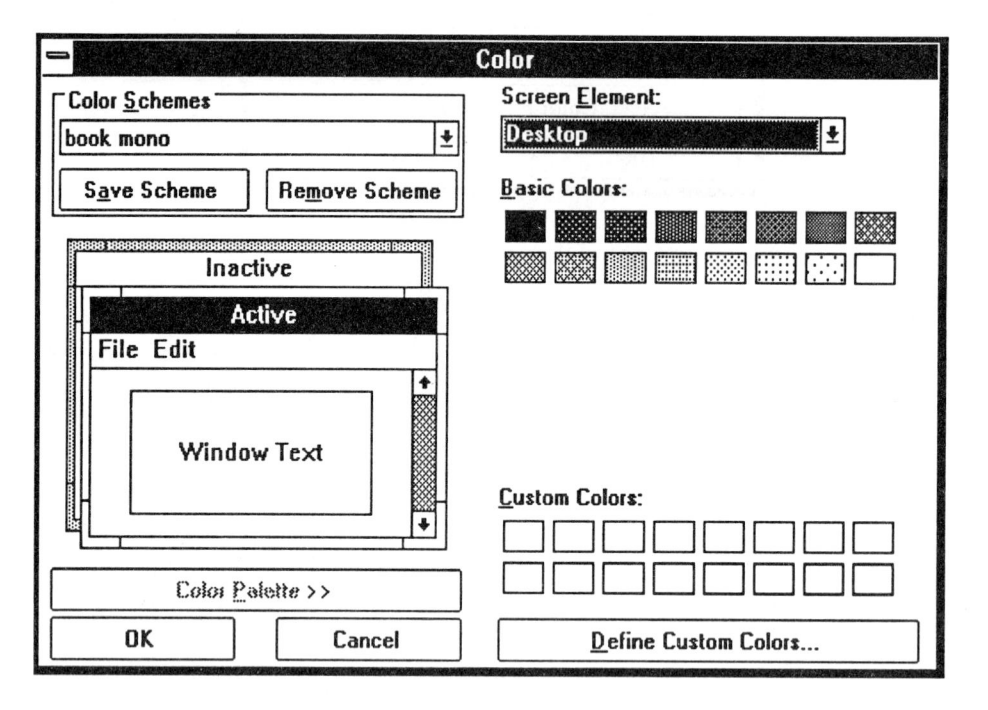

Control Panel Color, Part 2

The screen display now shows all of the original options plus the following:

f) **Screen Element**, with Desktop pre-selected in the box. This section allows you to select individual areas of the Windows environment and identify or change the colours used for them.

g) A series of 48 little boxes, in six rows of eight, each containing a different colour and labelled **Basic Colors**. You can select any one of these colours and apply it to the chosen screen element. (The illustration shows less than this because it is in monochrome.)

h) A series of 16 boxes, in two rows of eight, labelled **Custom Colors**. Windows will allow you to create your own colours, rather than using the pre-defined ones, and when you have done so the created colour will appear in these boxes.

i) A large button labelled **Define Custom Colors**. This activates another dialogue box wherein you can create your own colours.

Exercise 5.1
Colour Schemes

Windows 3 comes with ten colour schemes already pre-defined and you can select any one of these and apply it to the Windows environment. The colour schemes vary from extremely bright to pastel hues. It may well be the case that you don't like any of these and so you will have to create your own colour scheme, see later. For now we're just going to use the schemes supplied by Microsoft.

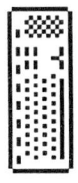

1) At the moment the word **Desktop** in the Screen Element box is shown in inverse video, i.e. this is the section of the program that is selected. Press **Tab** until the phrase Windows Default in the Color Schemes box is selected, i.e. becomes inverse video. Alternatively you can press **Alt-S**.

2) Press **Down** and Windows Default is replaced with Arizona. The area immediately below the box, where the environment itself is shown, will instantly change to reflect the newly selected scheme.

3) You can press **Down** again to move through the list of pre-defined colour schemes one at a time.

1) Click on **Windows Default** and it becomes inverse video.

2) Click on the arrow at the right hand side of the box and a list box will appear. Click on **Arizona**, or any of the other schemes, and the colours will be shown in the area below. You can scroll through the colour schemes using the Scroll Bars at the edge of the list box.

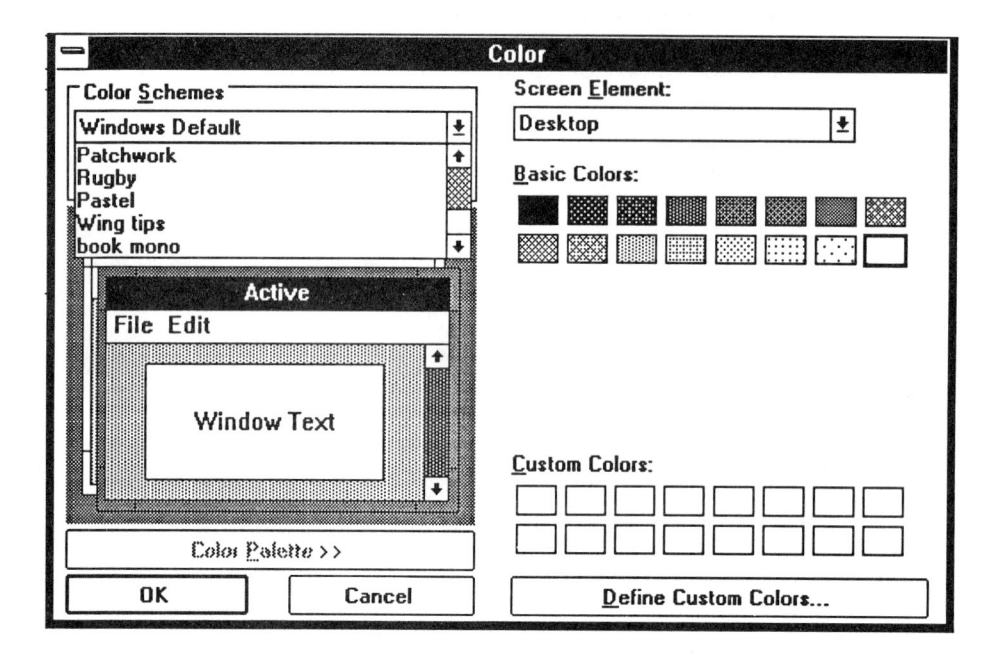

Colour Scheme

I suggest that you have a look at each of the pre-defined schemes, maybe one of them will be to your liking and it will save you the hassle of creating your own. Personally, I don't like any of the pre-defined ones and so I made my own custom scheme.

Exercise 5.2
Design a scheme

To create your own colour scheme you need to allocate a colour to each area of the screen display. The quickest way to do this is to select one of the pre-defined schemes that is closest to what you want and then tweak it by changing selected areas. Alternatively you can select the Windows Default and then re-define every area of the screen.

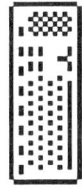

1) Having chosen the base scheme, press **Tab** until Desktop in the Screen Element is selected.

2) Press **Tab** to move down to the Basic Colors. The colour that is already assigned to that screen element will be shown by having a box around it.

3) Use the cursor keys to move to the colour that you want to use. Once there press **Space** to select it and assign it to the screen element. As soon as you press the spacebar the area to the left of the Basic Colors changes to reflect your changes.

4) Press **Alt-E** to move back to the Screen Element box and then press Down to select the next element.

5) Repeat the actions from (2) to (4) until you have changed as many of the colours as you wish.

1) Select a base colour scheme or the Windows Default, as in the previous exercise.

2) Click on the **Screen Element** box so that Desktop is highlighted.

3) Click on the colour, in the Basic Colors areas, that you want to use for the screen element. As soon as you click on the colour the display to the left of the basic colours changes to reflect your choice. You can click on any other colour and it will be assigned in place of your first choice. This is the big advantage of using a mouse, the selected colours can be changed so easily and rapidly.

4) Once you are happy with the colour of the Desktop, click on the arrow at the right hand side of the Screen Element box to select the next area. A list box will appear from which you can choose the area you want to change.

5) Assign the colour to that in exactly the same way. Continue until you have changed as many colours as you wish.

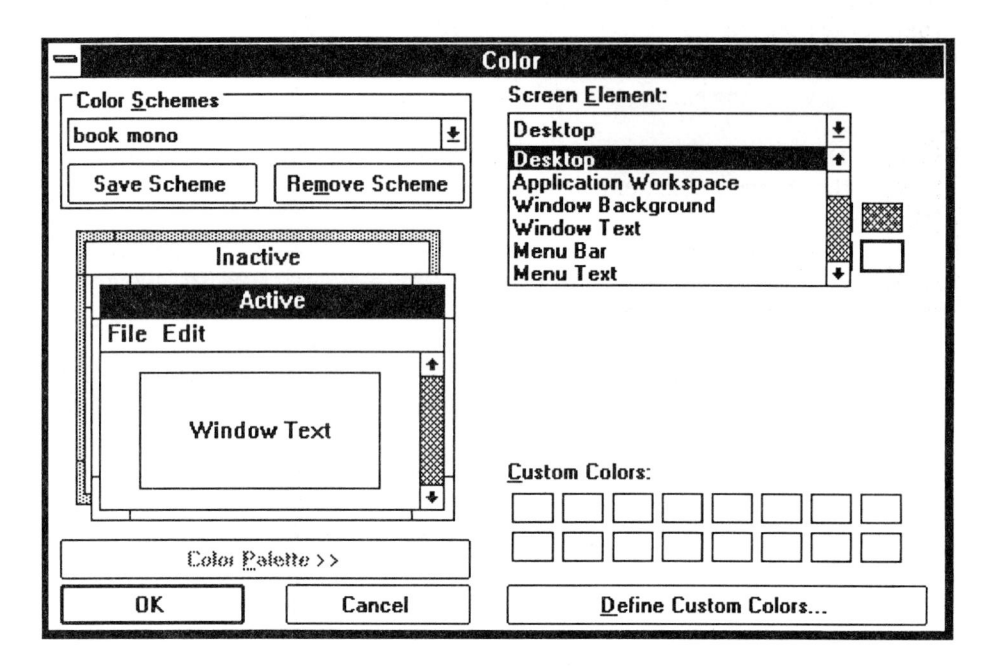

Screen Element selection

Exercise 5.3
Create a colour

The 48 colours that Windows is provided with should be sufficient for most needs but Microsoft have recognised that you may want to use alternative colours by creating your own. So they have provided a facility for doing just that. You can create up to sixteen new colours at a time. This area of the program is far easier to use if you are using a mouse rather than the keyboard. Using the keyboard to make custom colours is so much hassle I would not recommend it - although it is possible.

Control Panel

1) Press **Alt-D,** or use the **Tab** until you select Define Custom Colors and then press **Enter.** A new screen appears.

1) Click on Define Custom Colors and the new screen appears.

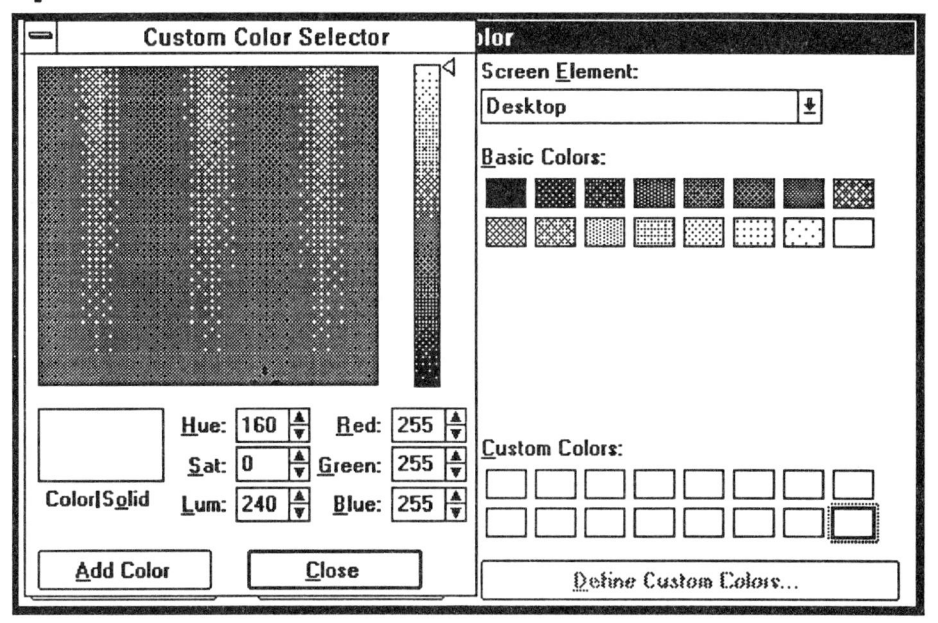

Custom Screen Definition

Notice that the Custom Colour Selector overlays part of the original screen. The new screen is broadly divided into four areas.

a) A square area that shows all the possible colours and hues. This area contains an open cross which is the colour selector cursor.

b) A vertical band to the right of the above. This is used to define the luminosity of any colour, from zero, which is black, to maximum which is white.

c) A series of six boxes in two rows of three. The first set are:

Hue, i.e. the property of the colour, its shade and appearance. This can have any value from 0 to 239.

Sat, short for Saturation, is the density of the colour. This can have a value in the range 0 to 240.

Lum, short for Luminosity, is the brightness of the colour. This can have the same range as Saturation, i.e. 0 to 240.

The second set are used to define the colour. All colours are made up of relative amounts of Red, Green and Blue. (The colours refer to the colour guns within the monitor that control how any colour appears.) Each separate colour can be in the range 0 to 255. A word of caution, if you make each of the colours the same value, regardless of the degree of Hue, Saturation and Luminosity, you get grey. Thus 96 Red, 96 Green and 96 Blue is almost identical to 200 Red, 200 Green and 200 Blue. (In reality the colours are slightly different but the vast majority of monitors are not capable of showing such minor colour differences.)

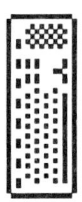

2) Use the **Tab** key to select the Hue box, the value will be shown in inverse video when you have done so.

3) Type the new value. Do not press **Enter** unless you do not want to change the other definition areas.

4) Press **Tab** to move down to Saturation. Type the new value.

5) Tab to Luminosity and type a new value. Note that as you make changes the colour selection cursor moves on the large square and on the vertical bar.

6) **Tab** to Red, type the value you want and then continue using **Tab** until you have changed each colour value. Your custom colour will be shown in the box to the left of the colour definition boxes. If you do not like this then go back to step 2 and make changes.

7) Press **Tab** until you select **Add Colour** and then press **Enter**. Alternatively press **Alt-A**. The customised colour will be placed in the top left hand box in the Custom Colors area of the right hand side of the screen.

8) You can go back to step (2) and define additional colours. Each time you add a colour it will be placed in the next empty Custom Color box; first the top row is filled from left to right and then the bottom row. If you try to define more that 16 colours then the seventeenth will overwrite the first and so on.

9) Once you have created all the colours you want, or are allowed, press **Alt-C** to close the Custom Color definition and return to the main Color area.

2) Using the mouse you can drag the Color Selector Cursor to any part of the square area. The boxes at the bottom of the screen automatically change their values as you do so.

3) Adjust the luminosity of the colour by dragging the arrow head beside the vertical bar. The defined colour appears in the box labelled Color Solid.

4) Click on any of the empty boxes in the Custom Colors area of the main screen to select it. Then click on **Add Color** and the colour you have designed appears in that box.

5) Continue defining colours until you have as many as you want or can have. Then click on **Close** to return to the main screen.

Having designed the custom colours you can now assign them to any part of the screen elements in the same way as you did the Basic Colors.

Exercise 5.4
Save the Scheme

Once you are happy with the new colour scheme you should save it so that Windows can use it. Notice that all the changes you have made so far are only reflected on the main Color screen, they do not appear in the main Windows environment yet. However once the scheme is saved and the Color option terminated the scheme becomes active. If you do not save the scheme then Windows will still use it, even if you terminate the Windows and then restart it, but it will only remain valid until you make any further changes.

1) Press **Alt-A** and a dialogue box appears.

1) Click on **Save Scheme** to get the same thing.

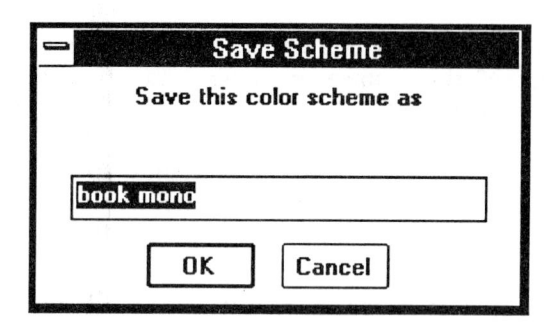

Save Scheme Dialogue Box

2) Type a name for the scheme. You can use a maximum of 32 characters to name the scheme, including blank spaces.

3) Press **Enter** or click on **OK**. The Color option of the Control Panel will disappear and there will be a pause while the changes you have made are implemented. Within a few seconds your new scheme has been applied to the Windows environment and will remain active until you change it.

Fonts

Every Windows application, and some areas of the Windows environment itself, uses text to a greater or lesser degree, how much so depends on the application. Text is a collection of letters, numerals and symbols and it must be a particular typeface. A typeface is a design for the characters, for example Helvetica is a typeface with no serifs (fiddley bits at the top and bottom of the characters) and Times Roman (so called because it was designed for the Times newspaper in London and it was based around a very old typeface called Roman) is one which does have serifs.

There are literally hundreds of different typefaces and generally speaking each one is a copyrighted design. For instance, most people have heard of Zapf Dingbats, that set of characters that produces semi-graphical figures rather than letters and numbers, but most people do not realise that the copyright for the typeface is held by International Typefaces Corporation. If your printer is capable of producing the Dingbats then the printer manufacturer has had to licence the typeface from ITC so that it can be incorporated into the printer. (This is one of the overheads that printer manufacturers have to pass on to their customers as part of the purchase price of the machine.)

A font on the other hand is the characters of a typeface in one particular size or style. Thus Helvetica 15 point, Helvetica 12 Point and Helvetica 99 Point are all different fonts - even though they are the same typeface. Equally Helvetica Bold 15 Point, Helvetica Italic 15 Point and Helvetica Normal 15 Point are all different fonts.

Pitch and Point

The size of the characters you produce will depend on the type of printer that you are using. Dot Matrix printers, without exception, and Daisywheel printers to a lesser extent, base their printed character size on Pitch. This is a measure of the number of characters which can be printed in a 1 inch space across the width of the paper. The Pitch size is actually the number of characters within that space and it is based on the letter O which is taken to be the average size of all the characters, which is why wider letters like W and M will sometimes impinge on the letters to either side of them in the printed text. Thus 10 Pitch means you can print ten characters to the inch, 12 Pitch is twelve per inch and so on. Therefore the higher the pitch value the smaller the characters, because you are printing more characters into the same space.

Laser printers on the other hand base their printed character size on Points. A point is One Seventy Second of an inch and it refers to the height of the character. It also influences the width of the character but to a much lesser extent. Thus 12 Point means that the characters are Twelve Seventy-seconds, or one sixth, of an inch high and so you can print them 6 lines to an inch down the length of the paper - which is the normal default for most printers anyway. On the other hand 36 Point being Thirty Six Seventy-seconds, or one half, of an inch means that you can only print 2 lines to the inch down the paper. Therefore the higher the Point value the larger the characters and so you can print less of them into the same space. (In some application programs, e.g. WordStar or PageMaker, you can define Point sizes, but not Pitch, in decimals, e.g. 12.6, but that gets really confusing - besides which things works better if you stick to whole sizes rather than divisions of them.)

However that is not the end of the matter. Neither the Pitch nor the Point sizes refer to the actual characters, although to all intents and purposes you can treat them as if they do. Both sizes are a hangover from the days when printers set type using little lead character blocks. The sizes actually refer to these rather than the symbols they contain because the blocks contained a built-in separator, i.e. a blank space above and below the characters, to allow the proper spacing of the letters or symbols. (Equally you will notice that the sizes are defined in inches - don't ask me why because I don't know and haven't been able to find out from any source that I tried.) Around each character is a blank area which is the automatic spacing that needs to be allowed so that the characters do not butt up tight to each other when they are printed. The space on either side is allowed for this purpose. The spaces above and below the letter or character are to prevent the character from hitting the symbols on the lines above and below. The spaces, both types, are more or less constant on the lead blocks, regardless of which letter is being used.

However on a computer this is not the case. All characters on any computer occupy the same character area, e.g. 9 pixels by 9 pixels or 14 pixels by 9 pixels - the exact block size depends on the monitor type, and the letters and symbols are distorted to make them fit into that block. (A pixel is the smallest area of the screen that can be illuminated independently.) Thus the spacing around the characters will vary from letter to letter and symbol to symbol as necessary to make them fit the block. In other words, the typeface is distorted to make it fit the character block size. This is why when you look at text on the screen the lines are separated by only a single pixel or two. But when you come to print it out the text will normally be separated properly because the printer uses a different resolution and different character blocks.

Even though a letter is regarded as 10 Point the actual character might only physically occupy 70% of this. Equally while the height of the entire block might be 36 Points the letter only occupies 27 points or 75% of the total height. And then just to confuse matters further different typefaces use different amounts of blank space around their characters. Thus if you are using Courier, then the figures above might be correct but if you change to Times Roman then the actual character size may be 65% and 60% respectively. The size of the characters on their blocks cannot be changed, it is preprogrammed by the font designers. This is why you can suddenly find that changing the typeface of a single line of text makes an enormous difference to your layout. You might expect the characters to stay the same size but they don't and all the rest of the text reflows to accommodate the new size.

Fonts in Windows

Windows uses two different kinds of fonts:

Raster Fonts, which are actually bitmaps of the characters, are used mainly for displaying. Raster Fonts cannot be scaled, they are one size only, and so if you want to use different sized letters on the screen you have to have those sizes installed or you cannot see them. Some dot matrix printers also use Raster fonts but in the normal course of events they are not printed.

Vector Fonts, which are scaleable so that they can be stretched or compressed to make different sizes. The advantage to Vector fonts is that it is only necessary to install one size and this can then be made any size that is necessary. Most laser printers, and all PostScript printers, use vector fonts because it reduces the amount of memory needed.

The sizes of the fonts within Windows are always given in Points, never in Pitch. This is another indicator that Windows 3 is intended to be used with high quality systems, as laser printers are not exactly low cost for all that they have dropped in price and continue to do so.

Windows already has a number of typefaces, and their associated fonts, installed as part of the original Setup. The typefaces should be sufficient to cover all of your needs. Some Windows based programs, e.g. Corel Draw, come complete with their own fonts and so you don't have to worry about them.

Windows will automatically substitute one font for another as necessary. For example, suppose you were using PageMaker with a PostScript printer and you wanted to use the typeface called Palatino. This is not one of the typefaces installed in Windows and so you cannot actually see it. The typeface is still applied to the text concerned, and will appear when the document is printed, but for the purposes of showing the text on screen Windows will use another typeface of similar style and definition. In this case it will probably use Roman because there is not a great deal of difference between the two typefaces. Because the program 'knows' you are using Palatino, all the various characteristics, spacing and kerning will be handled as if the on-screen typeface was Palatino - which is wider than Roman.

Exercise 5.5
Adding and removing fonts

You can add extra typefaces and fonts to the Windows environment if you wish, but each one will require additional disk and memory space with the result that unless there is a very definite reason for wanting the typeface displayed, there is very little point in adding these. Equally you can free memory space, but not disk space, by removing typefaces from the Windows environment. The typefaces remain stored on the hard disk so that they can be restored to Windows at a later date.

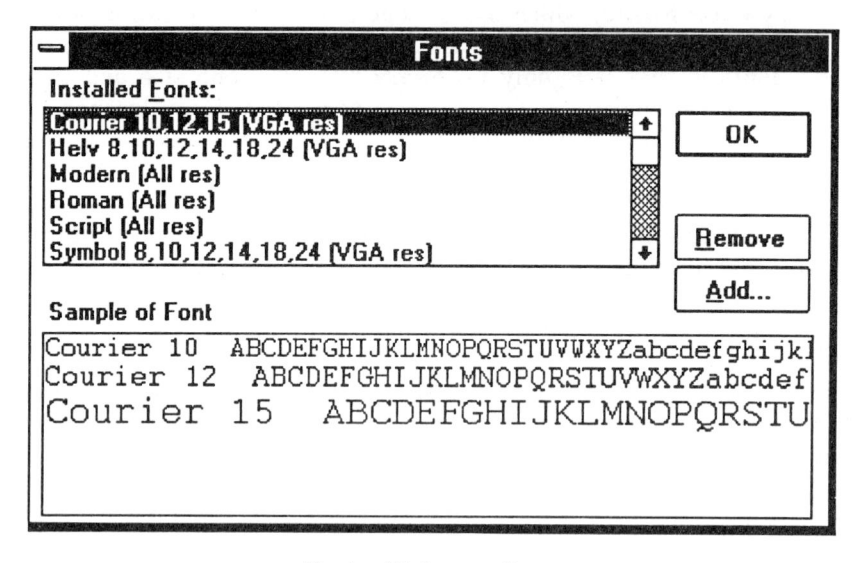

Fonts Dialogue Box

1) Activate the Control Panel and then select Fonts. Press **Enter** to bring up the Fonts dialogue box.

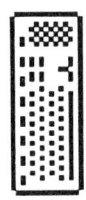

2) You can move through the installed typefaces, and their associated fonts, using the cursor keys. As you do so the bottom box displays the highlighted typeface in a range of sizes proving that the font is a Raster. If the selected typeface is a Vector one then only the base size is shown, it is from this size that the other sizes are created.

3) To add a font use the **Tab** to select Add and then press **Enter**. Alternatively just press **Alt-A**.

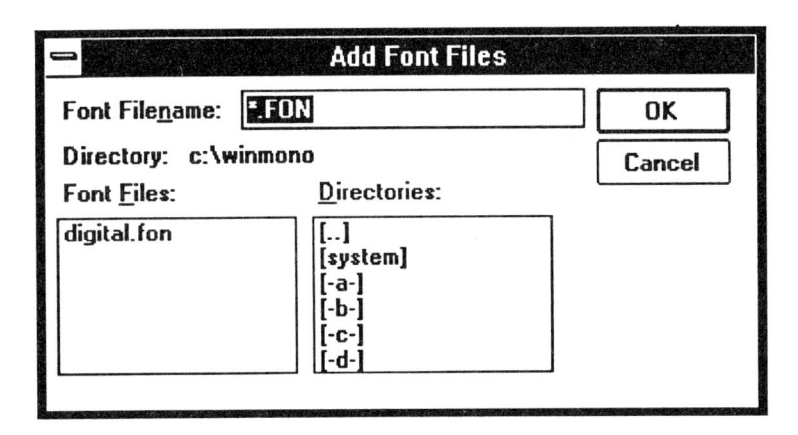

Add Fonts

4) Select the font you want to install, using the cursor keys to select it, and then press **Enter**. As part of the Setup, Windows was installed with the fonts contained in a file called DIGITAL.FON. You cannot reinstall these.

1) Activate the Control Panel as normal and then double click on the icon labelled Fonts. The dialogue box shown on the opposite page appears.

2) You can click on any of the installed fonts to see what they look like, using the scroll bars if necessary to see others.

3) To add a typeface or font click on **Add** and the necessary dialogue box appears. Click on the font or typeface you want to install and then on **OK**.

To remove any typeface or font select it in the Installed Fonts box and then press **Alt-R** which brings up another dialogue box. You use this in exactly the same way as you did the Add Fonts one.

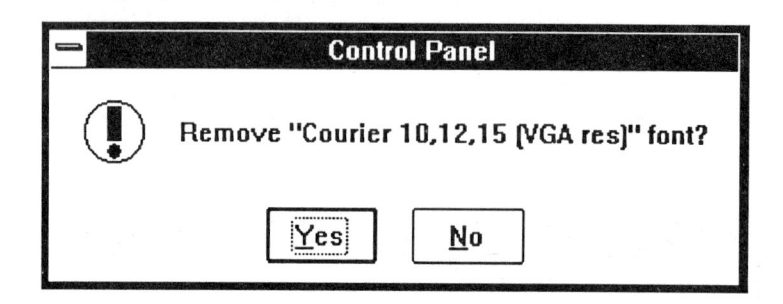

Remove Fonts Dialogue Box

Warning: Do not delete the Helvetica typeface because it is used in all the Windows menus, dialogue boxes, list boxes and what have you. If you remove it then you will not be able to read most of these within the Windows environment.

Exercise 5.6
Port changes

The Control Panel will allow you to make changes to any of the four possible serial ports that are attached to your computer. The settings you make affect how the information from the ports is transferred to the computer or vice versa. The various settings for the ports should conform to those required by the devices attached to the ports. Refer to the product manual for details of what these should be.

1) From the Control Panel use the cursor keys to select **Ports** and then press **Enter**.

2) Again using the cursor keys, highlight the Port you want to change and then press **Alt-S** - this brings up a new dialogue box.

3) Use the **Tab** key to move from area to area and the cursor keys to move within the areas and make changes.

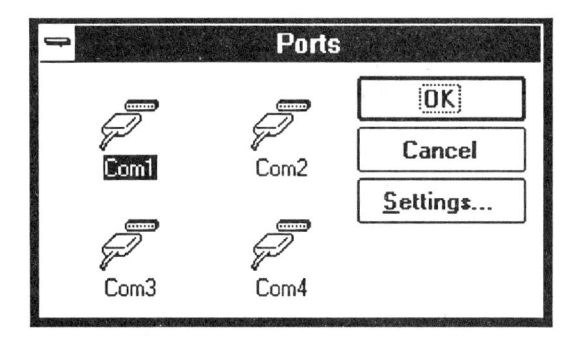

Ports, Part 1

4) Use **Tab** again to select OK and then press **Enter**. The changes will be made and you return to the Ports selection. If you want to make changes to the other ports, repeat steps 2 to 4 again.

5) When the ports have been changed to your satisfaction press **Enter** to return to the Control Panel.

6) Press **Alt-Space C** to return to the Program Manager.

1) Double click on **Ports** in the Control Panel.

2) Click on the icon of the port you want to change and then on Settings.

3) Click on the various settings to change them.

4) Click on **OK** to accept the changes and return to the Ports selection dialogue box.

5) When you have changed the ports as necessary, click on **OK** to return to the Control Panel.

6) Press **Alt-Space C** to return to the Program Manager.

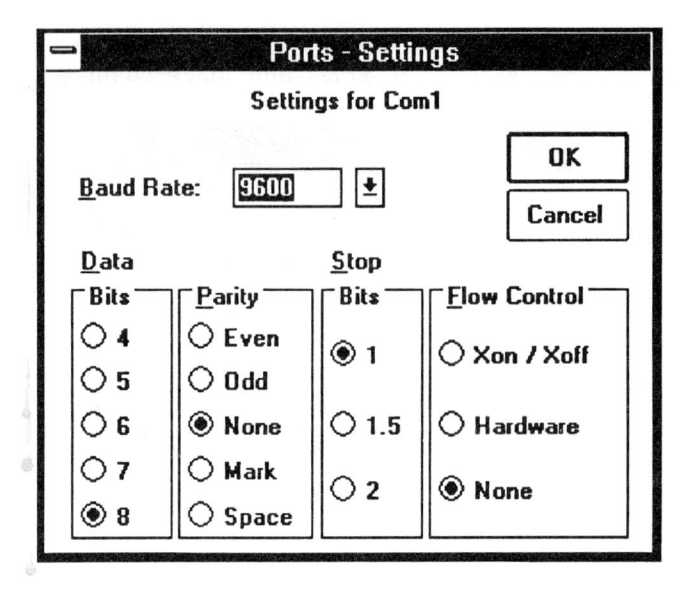

Ports, Part 2

Mouse

Windows 3 is designed to be used with a mouse. While it is possible to use the program with only the keyboard, it is like trying to play football without wide receivers. Possible, but who would want to? As the program is installed, it is configured to handle input from the mouse in a particular way. However, you can use the Control Panel to change this. If you are only using the keyboard then there is no point.

Exercise 5.7
Mouse work

1) Activate the Control Panel in the usual way and then double click on **Mouse** to bring up the dialogue box.

2) The Mouse Tracking Speed controls how fast the mouse moves on screen. Click on the scroll bar arrow at the right hand

side of this box until the indicator is butted up again it. Now try moving the mouse in a random fashion. Notice how fast it moves.

3) Move the indicator all the way to the other end of the scroll bar. Move the mouse again and the difference is obvious. You should set the Tracking Speed to whatever you feel most comfortable with.

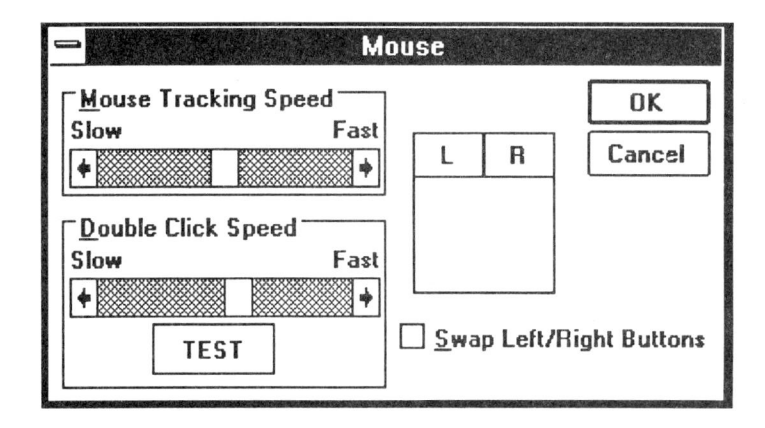

Mouse Dialogue Box

4) The Double Click Speed is slightly different: it controls how fast you have to press the mouse button for a double click to be recognised. Move the indicator all the way to the right and then try double clicking on the box labelled **TEST**. Unless you have got lightening fingers the Test will remain in inverse video after the first click. The second click should return it to normal.

5) Move the indicator all the way to the left and try the **TEST** again. This time you may be clicking too fast for the command to be recognised. Play with different settings, testing each one, until you find one that works best for you.

6) If you are left handed you will probably find it easier to swap the mouse buttons. By default, Windows is installed to be used by someone who is right handed, i.e. that is the hand they use to control the mouse and they use the left hand button to click with. If you are left handed it is easier to press the Right Button rather than the Left Hand one. By clicking on Swap Left/Right Buttons you can switch the clicking to accommodate this.

(Microsoft have always provided this facility in Windows and they are to be congratulated for thinking of it in the first place.)

7) Once you have made the settings you want click on **OK** to save the settings. Warning: do not terminate this option unless the double click test works or you will be unable to activate anything using the mouse and you will have to use the keyboard instead.

Desktop

While the Color option allows you to set and/or change the colour scheme that Windows will use, the on screen display is more complex than that. This option, Desktop, allows you to further customise the screen. It also controls a number of settings to do with where and how things are displayed. One of its major features is that it will allow you to take any graphic that exists in the new BMP (Short for Bitmap.) format, which can be generated from Windows Paintbrush, and use this as a backing display on screen.

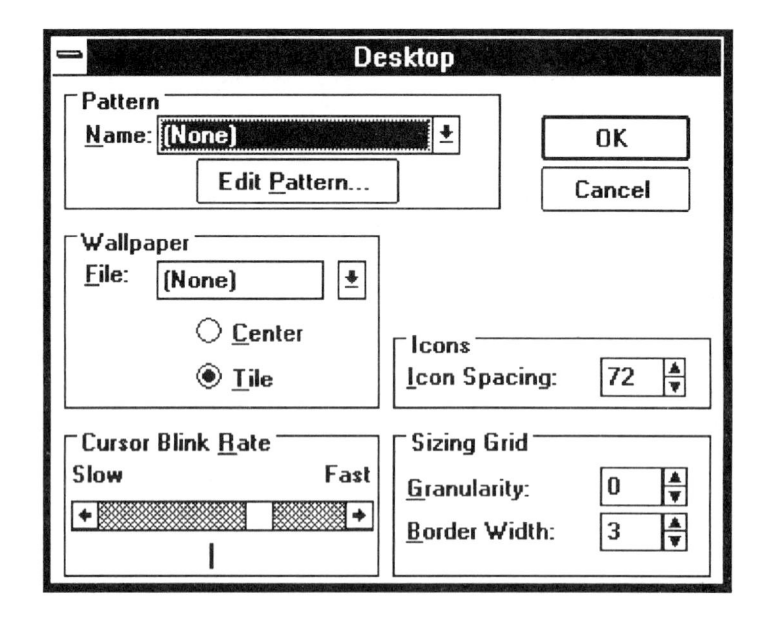

Desktop main screen

The dialogue box that appears is divided into five major areas:

a) **Pattern**, it is this that replaces the blank background.

b) **Wallpaper**, select this option to use a bitmap as a replacement for a pattern, or in conjunction with it.

c) **Cursor Blink Rate**, determines how fast the on screen cursor within applications flashes.

d) **Icons**, use to set how close together icons within windows will be.

e) **Sizing Grid**, allows you to change how close icons will be and how wide window borders are.

Exercise 5.8
Choose a pattern

The Desktop will allow you to use a grid pattern as a Pattern in place of just a blank screen background. The pattern, on a VGA monitor at least, is made up of a series of 64 dots arranged in an 8 by 8 grid. Not very much, you might think, but the way that Windows uses them means that you can create quite complex and visually stunning patterns.

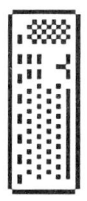

1) Activate the Control Panel and the select Desktop using the cursor keys. Press **Enter** to activate this option.

2) As Windows is installed, there is no pattern used for the background, i.e. you simply get a blank screen, albeit in colour. However, Windows comes complete with a number of pre-designed patterns that you can use instead. These are always in black and white. To change to one of these patterns press **Alt-N** and a list box appears containing the names of the existing patterns.

3) Use the cursor keys to select a pattern.

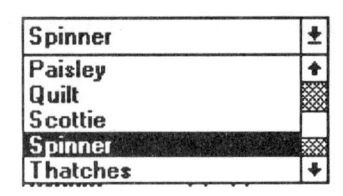

```
Spinner
Paisley
Quilt
Scottie
Spinner
Thatches
```

Pattern List box

1) Instigate the Control Panel as normal and then double click on the **Desktop** icon.

2) Click on the arrow head at the right of the Pattern Name to see the list box.

3) Click on the pattern you want to use.

Exercise 5.9
Design a pattern

Having selected the pattern, using either the keyboard or the mouse, you cannot see it until you go back to the Control Panel. In other words you have to close the Desktop facility before your changes take effect. If you don't like the pattern you then have to go back to the Desktop to change it. (I think this is a major fault, considering how user friendly Windows is in other areas.) However, there is a way to get an idea of what the pattern will look like, even though the facility was not intended for this use.

1) Having selected a pattern, press **Alt-P** for Edit Pattern. This will bring up a new dialogue box that will allow you to change the pattern or create new ones.

1) Once you have selected a pattern click on **Edit Pattern**.

Control Panel 151

The dialogue box that appears is divided into two main parts:

On the left hand side is a box labelled Sample, this shows you what the pattern will look like when it is used as a background pattern.

The main area contains the pattern itself in an 8 by 8 grid. You can only change this if you are using a mouse. There is no way to modify the pattern using the keyboard.

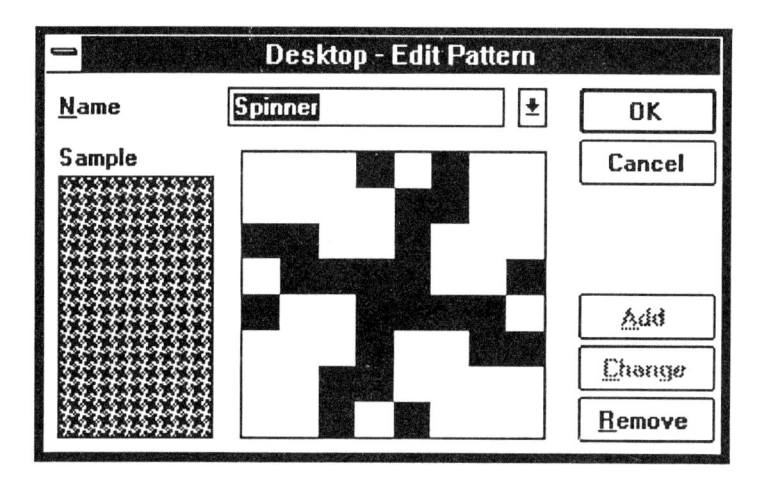

Edit Pattern Dialogue Box

2) You can cycle through the other pre-defined patterns using the cursor keys and so view what each of them will look like. Once you find one that you like, pressing **Enter** will return you to the Desktop main dialogue box.

2) Move the cursor over the pattern grid.

3) If you click on a white square, remember the grid is 8 by 8, it will become black. If you click on a black square it becomes white. This allows you to change the pattern.

Tip: If you want to change a lot of one colour to the other, click and drag the cursor and it will change all the colour squares it moves over.

4) Having designed a new pattern you can save it and add it to the existing ones. Click on **Add Pattern,** provide a name and the pattern is saved. You don't need to press **Enter** at this stage unless you want to terminate this part of the program.

5) At any time you can remove a pattern by selecting it and then clicking on **Remove**. (You can also remove patterns using the keyboard.)

Exercise 5.10
Internal Decoration

Windows 3 will allow you to use any bitmap graphic, even full colour ones, as wallpaper on the background. The wallpaper will take precedence over any pattern or colour that you have used. To be used as wallpaper the graphic must be in the new BMP format that is created by Windows Paintbrush. This is not as much as a problem as it might sound, because Paintbrush will allow you to import a PCX graphic and export it as BMP. Thus if you have a favourite graphic in PCX format you can, with a bit of help from Paintbrush, use this as the wallpaper.

The program comes complete with a number of new graphics which you can use as the wallpaper. The one called Chess is a nice example of perspective, but this can only appear if Windows is running in Standard or 386-Enhanced mode - it cannot appear if you are in Real Mode. My favourite in those supplied, is Paper which is shown opposite. Whoever designed it must have spent literally hours doing so because there is not a single straight line in it, the graphic consists entirely of dots. When you select a wallpaper, the graphic for it must be in the Windows sub-directory - it cannot be anywhere else on the disk.

1) Activate the Desktop as normal.

2) Press **Alt-F** to bring up the Wallpaper list box.

3) Use the cursor keys to select the graphic of your choice and then press **Space**.

4) Back at the Desktop you can select to have the graphic displayed Centrally, i.e. in the middle of the screen, or Tiled,

i.e. as many pictures as possible laid edge to edge so that they fill the background. Use **Tab** to switch between the two.

1) Open the Desktop as normal and then click on the arrowhead at the right hand side of the Wallpaper File line.

2) Click on the graphics you want to use.

3) Click on either Center or Tile to decide the graphic display mechanism.

Wallpaper List Box

Again, you can only see the wallpaper you have chosen once you terminate the Desktop option and return to the Control Panel.

The Paper Graphic as Wallpaper

Cursor Blink Rate

This is exactly what it says it is. The cursor as it appears in the majority of Windows applications flashes to show its position. You can use this option to set the speed at which the flash occurs.

Icon Spacing

When you Arrange Icons on the Program Manager the distance apart that these are set depends on the value set here. The value in the box refers to the number of pixels, the smallest area of the screen that can be illuminated, that Windows will allow for any icons and its caption. Normally icons can occupy as little as 50 pixels but you may find that the captions exceed this and so they overlay one another. You can correct this by increasing the value here. Again you don't see any effect until you return to the Program Manager and activate one of the two icon arranging commands.

Sizing Grid

Windows uses an invisible grid to align icons and windows. You can adjust the grid size using the Granularity option. Normally this is set to 0, in other words the grid is turned off. With the grid off any icon you move to a different position will remain in that position. Once you increase the granularity value the grid becomes operable and the icons align themselves to it when they are moved. Again, the value is in terms of pixels and it must be in the range 0 to 49.

Border width

By default the window Borders are set when you install Windows in the first place. However you can change the width by increasing the value here, the number must be in the range 1 to 49. Increasing the value makes the borders wider.

Network

If you are using Windows on machines that are networked together and that network is active, then the Control Panel will include a Network icon. Activating this will allow you to edit or view the network details. Because each network is different it is impossible to give extensive details of this option here. The contents of the associated dialogue box will always be specific to the type of network you are using.

Printers

Windows 3 can be used with an almost infinite number of printers. The disks as supplied with the program contain enough printer drivers to allow you to use just about any printer that currently exists in the market - and a few more besides. If the program does not have your particular printer, then it will definitely have an emulation that can be used in its place. The printer drivers are very important because they supply Windows with information about the printer; the fonts it contains, the layout, page size, control characters and so on.

You can install any number of printers as part of the Windows Setup or you can add extra ones via the Control Panel. In actuality, it is the Control Panel that Setup uses to install the printer drivers. Even though you have installed the drivers, you still have to configure the printer for it to work correctly. The steps involved in using a printer with Windows are:

   a) Install the printer driver.

   b) Assign a port to the printer.

   c) Configure the printer driver to match the actual printer.

   d) Select an active printer for each port, if necessary.

   e) Nominate one of the printers you have installed as the default printer, i.e. the one you will use most often.

In the following section we are going to cover all of this, using my StarScript printer as an example. The StarScript is a Star LaserPrinter 8II with an added PostScript emulation that allows it to be configured as an Apple LaserWriter Plus - it can also be installed as a number of non-PostScript laser printers. It helps when you are installing the printer if you know what emulations it can perform. By default it uses A4 paper, that is 210 mm by 297 mm, in portrait orientation, i.e. the paper is fed lengthwise.

Exercise 5.11
Adding a printer

Even though you can install printer drivers as part of the Windows Setup, you can install additional printers directly into the Windows environment through the Control panel.

1) Activate the Control Panel in the usual way. Then, using the cursor keys select Printer and press **Enter** which will bring up the main Printer dialogue box.

1) Run the Control Panel as normal and once it appears on screen double click on the **Printer** icon.

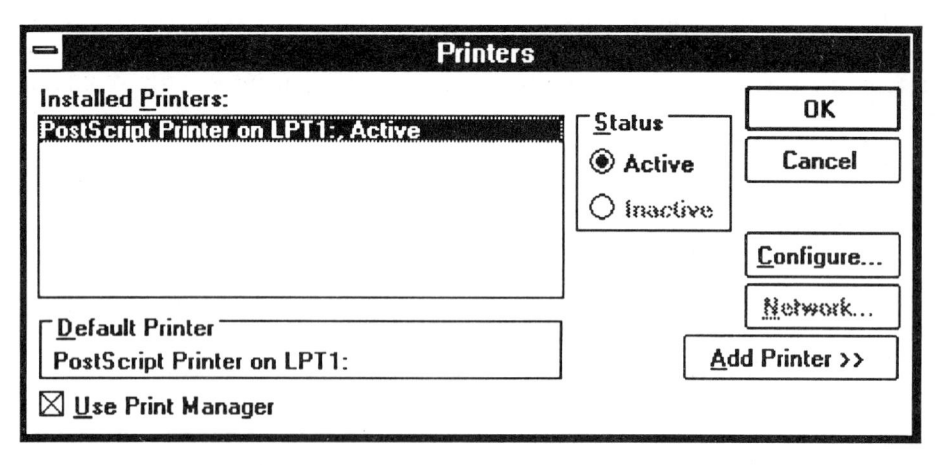

Printer Main Dialogue Box

The dialogue box as it first appears is not all there, there is another section to it that allows you add printers but we'll come to that in a minute. The dialogue box as it first appears on screen in divided into four main areas:

a) Installed Printers, this contains a list of the printers, actually the printer drivers, that you installed as part of the Windows Setup.

b) Default Printer, the printer that you will normally use.

c) Status, this tells you whether the printer highlighted in the Installed Printers list is on line or not.

d) A series of buttons that activate additional dialogue boxes.

2) Use the **Tab** key to select **Add Printer** or simply press **Alt-A**. This will expand the dialogue box and give you a list of installable printers.

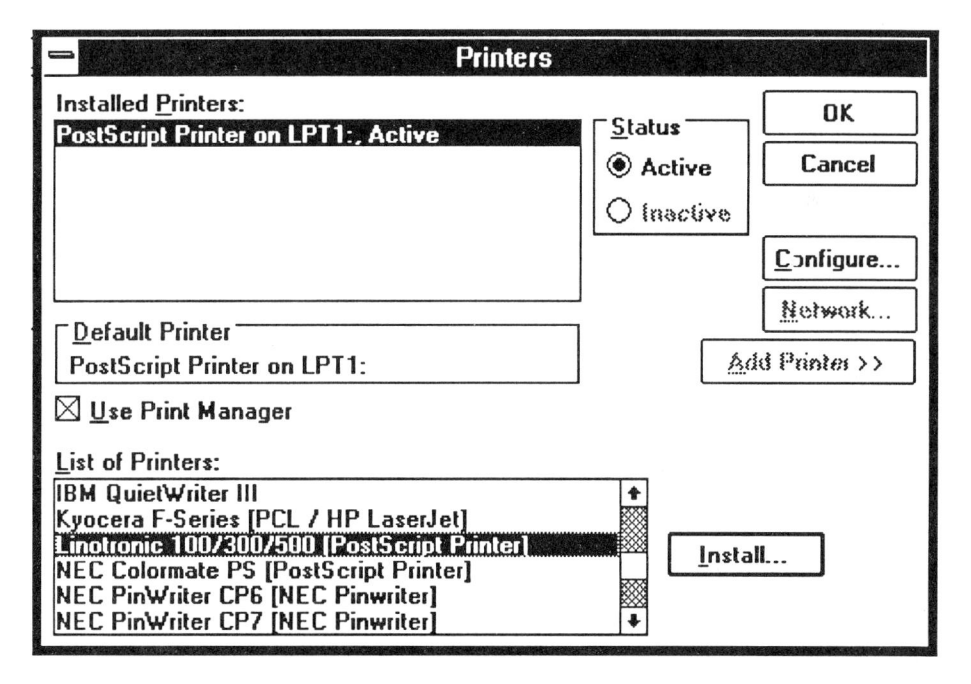

Add Printer Dialogue Box

2) Click on **Add Printer** to expand the dialogue box.

3) Use the cursor keys to move through the list of printers until you find the one you want, either the actual printer or the emulation. Once you find it press **Space** to select it and then press **Alt-I**.

3) Use the scroll bars to move through the list of printers and once you find the one you want, select it by clicking on it and then click on the button labelled **Install**.

If your particular printer is not shown in the list of printers then you will have to use an emulation in its place. What happens next depends on the printers you already have installed. If the selected printer uses the same printer driver as an installed printer a message box will pop up telling you so. This gives you the option of installing the same driver again, using the existing driver or cancelling the installation. Select whichever is appropriate - you can use the same driver as many times as you wish.

If you are installing a printer for which the driver does not already exist on your hard disk, or if you have elected to reinstall the driver, you will be prompted to insert a specific disk into Drive-A so that Windows can copy the necessary driver to your hard disk.

Once the printer driver has been copied, or you have elected to use an existing driver, a new printer name appears in the Installed Printers box. Note, the name is generic not specific. Thus the StarScript is billed as a PostScript printer, along with Linotronic and Apple LaserWriter NTX. Now that the driver has been installed, the next step is to configure the printer for use. You can if you wish, or need, install as many printers as necessary before going on to the next step - just repeat steps 2 and 3 again.

4) Press **Alt-C** to bring up the next dialogue box.

5) Use the cursor keys to select the port to which the printer is attached. The list of possible ports will roll up if you continue

to press **Down,** until you reach the bottom of the list.

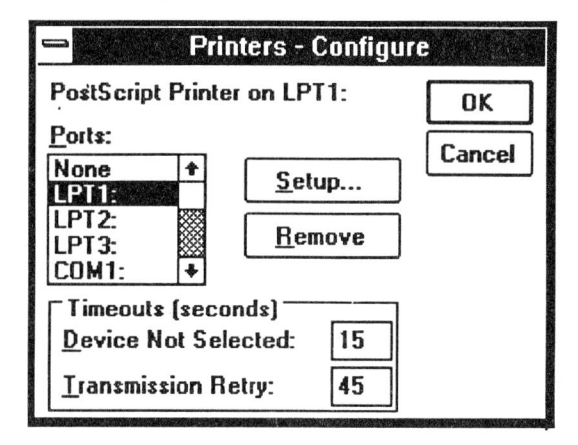

Configure Printer Dialogue Box

4) Click on **Configure** to begin the process.

5) Use the scroll bars, if necessary, to move though the list of ports. When you find the one to which the printer is attached, click on it.

There are four type of port available:

LPT which refers to the Parallel ports, i.e. the ones normally used for printing.

COM refers to the Serial ports, some printers can be run from these but they tend to be slower than using the Parallel ports. If you intend using a serial port you will probably have to change settings using the Ports option of the Control Panel.

EPT is a special port used by some printers. To use this you must have the necessary add-on board installed in your computer.

FILE will allow you to send documents directly to a disk file rather than have then printer on paper.

Thus far you have installed the printer driver, or used an existing one, and assigned the port that will be used. Now you have to tune the driver in fine detail. Before you continue, if you wish to remove a printer from

160   Windows 3 - A User's Guide

your installed printers list, you should select it on the previous dialogue box and then press **Alt-R** here. The printer will be removed but the driver remains on your hard disk to allow you to reinstall the printer at a later date.

The other settings in this dialogue box, under the heading Timeout, set the amount of time that Windows will wait before it presents you with an error message that something has gone wrong, and the time that it will wait before trying the printer again. Both values are given in seconds and the defaults should not need to be changed.

6) Use the **Tab** key to select Setup, or press **Alt-S,** to bring up the next dialogue box.

6) Click on **Setup** to continue the configuration.

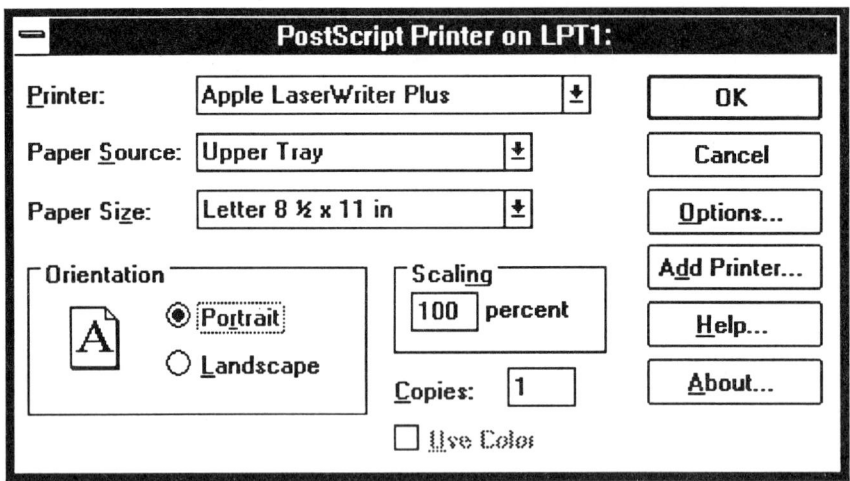

Setup Printer Dialogue Box, Part 1

The details shown in the dialogue box are the default settings used by the particular printer driver you have installed. They may be correct, in which case you need do nothing to them, but it is more likely that they will need to be changed, especially if you are using a printer emulation.

What you have to do next is to select the actual printer, or the emulation, that you want to use.

7) Because the printer name is already highlighted, you can move through the list of printers that use that particular driver by simply using the cursor keys. As you do so the details in the Paper Source and Paper Size boxes will change at the same time.

7) Using the mouse you have to do something slightly different. Click on the arrowhead at the right of the Printer line and a list box of printer names will appear. Scroll through this until you find the printer you want and then click on it.

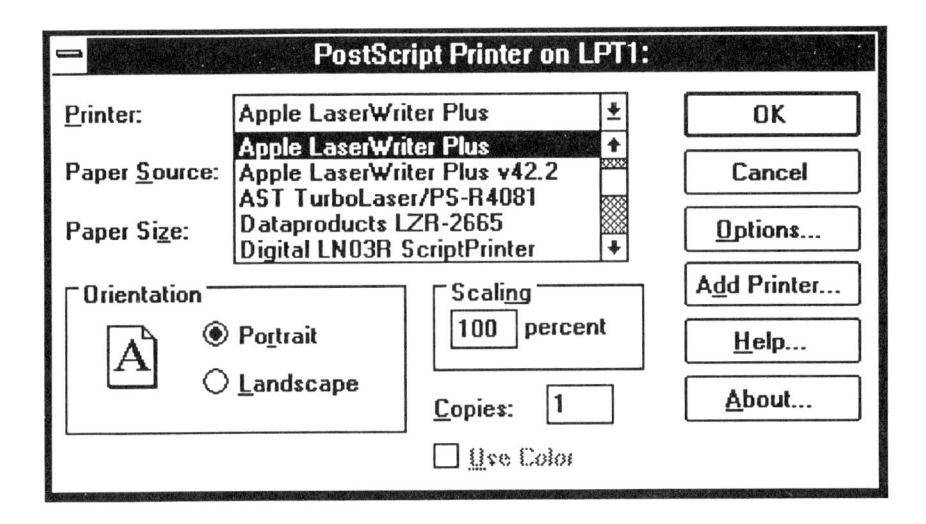

Printer Name List Box

8) If the Paper Source details are correct you need do nothing. The Paper Source refers to the tray that is normally used to contain the paper for the printer - in most cases installing the Upper Tray works fine. On the other hand if the Paper Source is wrong, you need to press **Tab** to move to this line and then use the cursor keys to select the correct tray.

8) Click on the arrowhead at the right of the Paper Source line and a list box appears. Scroll through this and then select the correct tray by clicking on it.

The next step is the default Paper Size that you will be using. The size displayed in the relevant box may be correct, in which case just move on to the next step.

9) The paper sizes default to American sizes, e.g. Letter 8.5" by 11", and these are rarely used in the U.K. Use the cursor keys to move through the list until you find the correct size.

9) Click on the arrowhead at the right of the Paper Size line and this will bring up the size list box. Use the scroll bars, if necessary, to move through the list until you find the correct size.

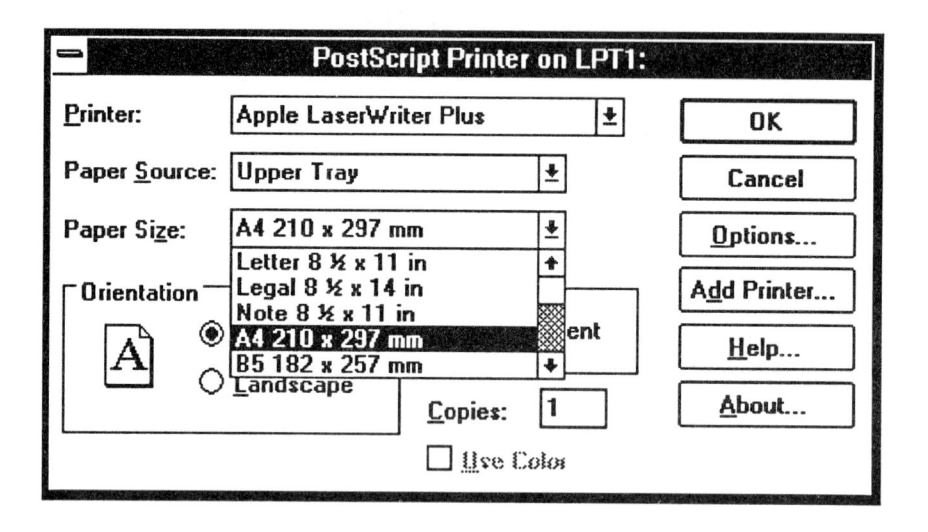

Paper Size List Box

Normally, all printers will use a paper orientation of Portrait, i.e. the paper is fed and used lengthwise, and it is this that is the default. However if you want to change to Landscape you must change the orientation.

10) Use **Tab** to move down to the relevant section of the dialogue box and then press **Alt-L** to change to Landscape. Pressing **Alt-R** switches to Portrait.

10) Simply click on the orientation you want to use.

If you are installing a PCL printer, i.e. a non-PostScript laser, you will also have the option of selecting the Graphics Resolution to use. By default this will be 75 dots per inch, which produces coarse pictures, but you can increase this to a maximum of 300 dpi which produces relatively good images.

11) Tab to the Graphics Resolution box and then use the cursor keys to select the one you want to use. 75 dpi is the faster but produces poor quality images. 150 dpi is medium speed and medium quality. 300 dpi is the slowest but produces the finest quality possible on most laser printers.

11) Click on the resolution you want to use.

If you are installing a PostScript printer you do not have this option because Windows uses the highest resolution it can get. In its place you can select what Scaling to use, i.e. how much an document or graphic will be enlarged or shrunk. By default this will 100% and I suggest that you leave it at that. It is far better to change the scaling from within an application rather than here, both PageMaker and Corel Draw for example will allow you to scale documents.

The next step depends on the type of printer being used. If it is non-PostScript then you can install additional fonts, provided they exist on your hard disk and have not already been installed as part of the font creation. Using a PostScript printer you set the optional parameters that will be used instead.

PostScript Printer Options

The defaults that will be set in this dialogue box work perfectly, at least with my StarScript, and so I have never needed to change them. However, this is what they mean:

Print to allows Windows to send the file to a particular destination. By default this will be Printer but you could send the file to an Encapsulated PostScript File instead. An EPS file can then be incorporated into other programs.

Job Timeout, by default this will be 0, refers to the number of seconds that Windows waits before sending you an error message if something goes wrong. Personally I like to know immediately and so I have left the setting alone.

Margins refers to exactly that, how close to the edge of the printed page you want the document to be. As these are normally set on the printer itself it is best to leave the setting of Default.

Header refers to the PostScript information file that must be sent to the printer before printing can begin. The default setting is Download each job, which means that the data will be sent to the printer every time you print a document. This is the best setting to use because it leaves as much of the printer's RAM as possible free and so speeds up the printing. The alternative option is

Control Panel 165

Already Downloaded which allows you to send the information now so that it will reside in the printer RAM. This reduces the amount of memory the printer has available and also tends to slow down printing.

The button labelled **Header** allows you to send the header information to the printer or to a file. Activating this brings up another dialogue box that will allow you to send the information now or later.

Handshake is concerned with the way the printer and the computer communicate. Again you have the choice of sending the information to a file or to the printer.

Having made the settings you want you can now return to the main Printer dialogue box and determine whether the printer is to be the active, default one or not.

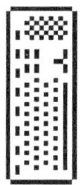

12) Press **Enter** in each dialogue box in turn until you get back to the main dialogue box.

13) You can only have one printer Active. Use the **Tab** to move into the relevant box and then the cursor keys to select.

14) Finally press **Enter** to close the main dialogue box and return to the Control Panel.

12) In each successive dialogue box click on **OK** until you reach the main printer dialogue box again.

13) Click either **Active** or **Inactive** as necessary.

14) Lastly, click on **OK** in the main dialogue box to return to the Control Panel.

International

The International section of the Control Panel allows you to modify how various national characteristics are used, displayed and identified within the Windows environment. If you are using Windows in the

166 *Windows 3 - A User's Guide*

United States of America in English then you should not need to make any changes to this option because that is what Windows automatically defaults to. However, anywhere else in the world you will probably need to adjust certain parts.

The **International** section is very straightforward and it will allow you to make changes very rapidly, for example changing the country setting automatically changes a range of other parameters at the same time. This section makes extensive use of List Boxes and pop-up dialogue boxes, but nowhere near as many as the Printer section does.

1) Activate the Control Panel as normal and then use the cursor keys to select International before pressing **Enter** to run the program.

1) Run Control Panel as usual and then double click on the **International** icon.

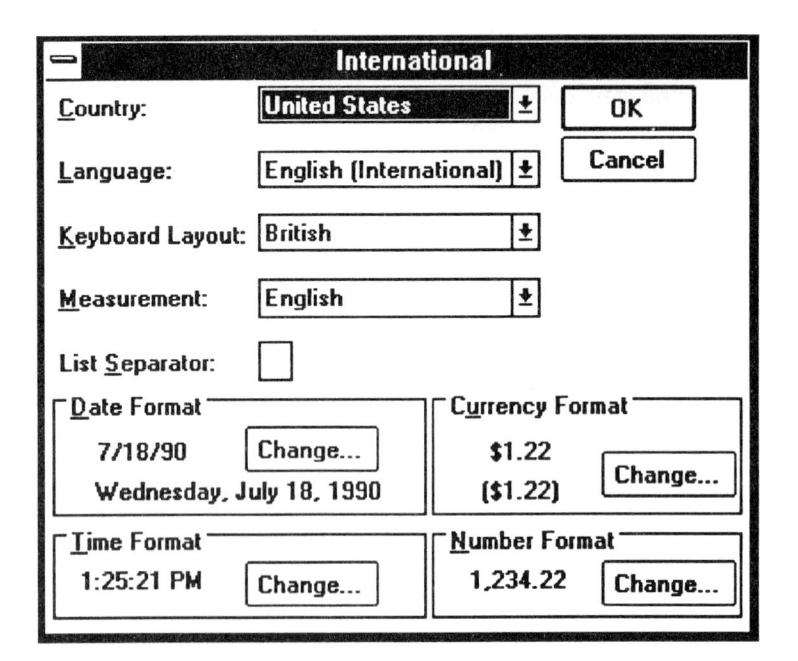

International Main Screen

The dialogue box is divided into two main sections:

a) Four lines at the top of the box, each of which use a separate List Box, which controls the main characteristics.

b) Four boxes, each of which uses a pop-up dialogue box, which allow you to modify specific characteristics.

2) Because the **Country** line is already selected, i.e. it is in inverse video, you can select a specific country just using the cursor keys. As you press the keys so the program will page through the possible countries, one by one, until you get to the one you want.

2) Click on the arrowhead at the right of the **Country** line and a List Box appears. Page through this, using the scroll bars if necessary, until you reach the correct one. Clicking on this will remove the box and return you to main screen.

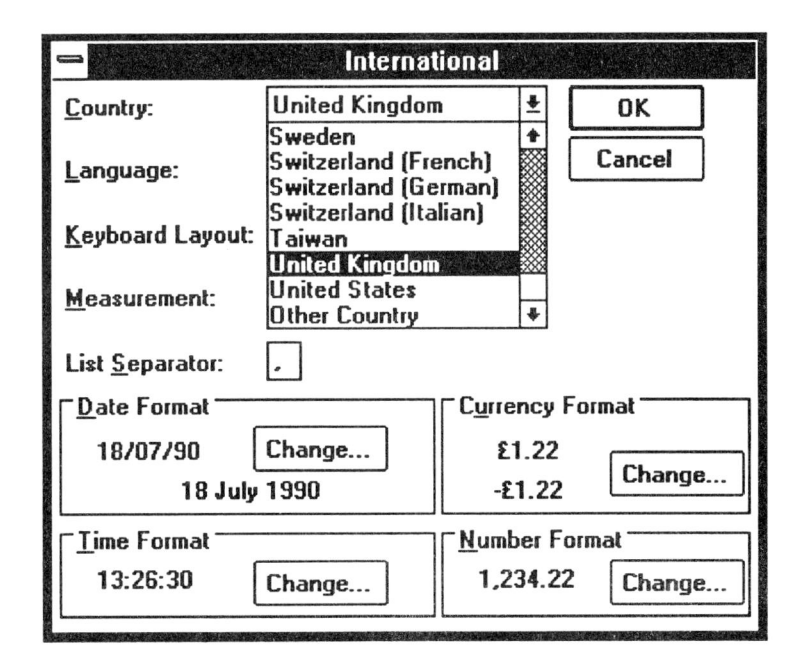

Country List Box

3) Use **Tab**, or press **Alt-L**, to move to the next line. Again using the cursor keys will allow you to select a Language. There are a total of 27 possibles plus an option for a non-listed language.

3) Click on the arrowhead at the right of **Language** and then select the language you will be using.

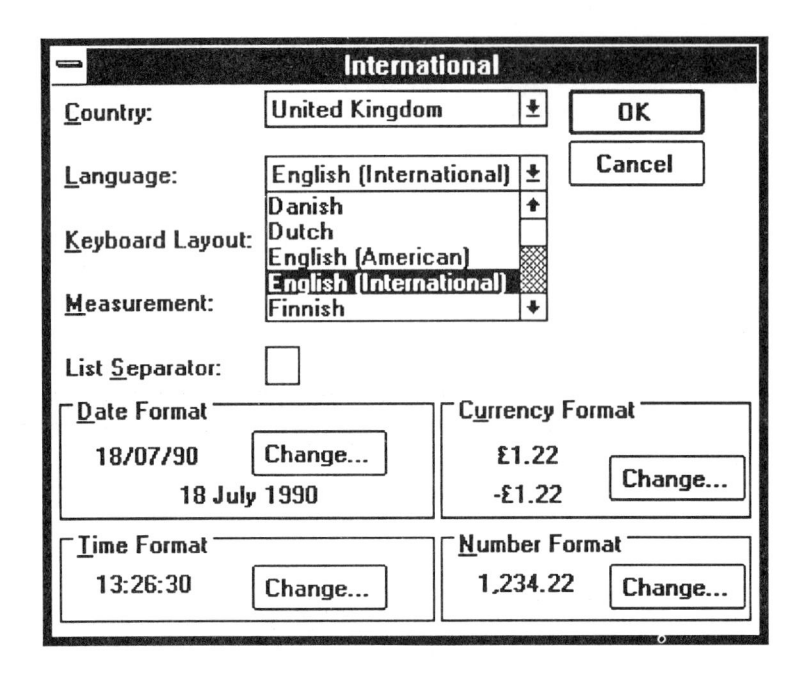

```
┌─────────────────── International ───────────────────┐
 Country:      United Kingdom  ▼      ┌─── OK ───┐
                                      ┌─ Cancel ─┐
 Language:     English (International) ▼
               Danish                ▲
 Keyboard Layout: Dutch
                  English (American)
                  English (International)
 Measurement:  Finnish               ▼

 List Separator:  □

 ┌ Date Format ──────────────┐  ┌ Currency Format ──────────┐
   18/07/90    [ Change... ]      £1.22
                                  -£1.22    [ Change... ]
   18 July 1990
 ┌ Time Format ──────────────┐  ┌ Number Format ────────────┐
   13:26:30    [ Change... ]      1,234.22   [ Change... ]
```

Language List Box

4) The **Keyboard Layout** refers to exactly that. Which national keyboard are you using? Again press **Tab** to move down to here and then the cursor keys to select the correct one.

4) Click on the arrowhead and click on the correct layout for your keyboard.

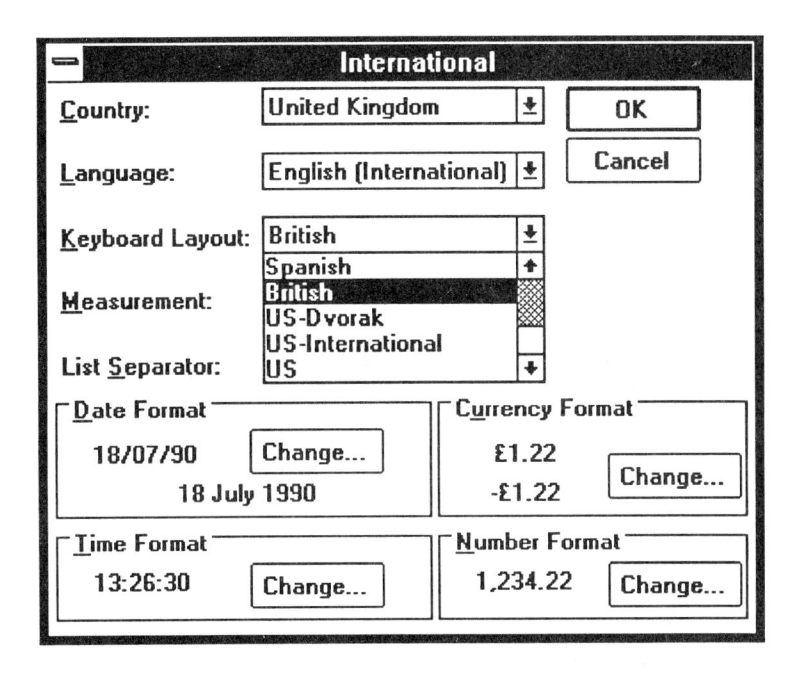

Keyboard Layout List Box

5) You can use one of two measurement systems; **English**, which gives you inches, or **Metric** which is in centimetres. Select the one you want.

5) Click on the arrowhead and then choose your preference.

The **List Separator** is the character that you want to use for subdividing long lists. By default this is a comma but it can be any character you wish.

The short format for the date depends very much on the national characteristics you are used to. For example, in the U.K. we place the day before the month which is before the year. In America the month appears first, followed by the day and then year. As you change the Country so the format displayed here will change but you can also modify it directly.

6) Press **Alt-D** to select the option. A new dialogue box then appears.

6) Click on **Change** in the Date Format box and the dialogue box pops-up.

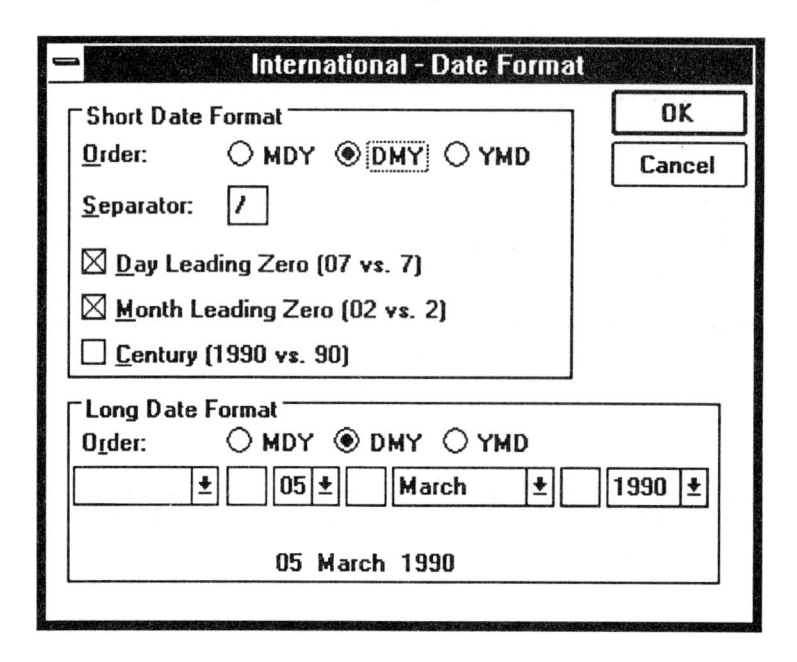

```
┌─ International - Date Format ─────────────────┐
│ ┌─Short Date Format──────────────┐  ┌──────┐  │
│ │ Order:    ○ MDY  ◉ [DMY] ○ YMD │  │  OK  │  │
│ │                                │  └──────┘  │
│ │ Separator:  [ / ]              │  ┌──────┐  │
│ │                                │  │Cancel│  │
│ │ ☒ Day Leading Zero (07 vs. 7)  │  └──────┘  │
│ │ ☒ Month Leading Zero (02 vs. 2)│            │
│ │ ☐ Century (1990 vs. 90)        │            │
│ └────────────────────────────────┘            │
│ ┌─Long Date Format──────────────────────────┐ │
│ │ Order:    ○ MDY  ◉ DMY  ○ YMD             │ │
│ │  [  ▼] [05▼] [March ▼] [1990▼]            │ │
│ │             05 March 1990                 │ │
│ └───────────────────────────────────────────┘ │
└───────────────────────────────────────────────┘
```

Date Format Dialogue Box

7) Use the **Left** and **Right** cursor keys to select the principle format for the date. Month, Day, Year; Day, Month, Year; or Year, Month, Day.

8) Use **Tab** to move to Separator and then type the character you want to use to sub-divide the format.

9) **Tab** to the next element. Pressing the **Spacebar** will toggle the switch on or off. Leading zeros mean that you get a zero appearing before any single digit, thus July 8th. will appear as 07/08 with a leading zero, or as 7/8 without one. Change the other elements to your taste.

Control Panel   171

7) Click on the date layout you want to use.

8) Move the cursor to the **Separator** box. Click once to place a vertical character cursor into the box and then delete the default and replace it with your own choice. If you are happy with using the shown character then go on to the next step.

9) Each of the next three elements are toggles. Clicking on any of them will turn the toggle on or off.

The final section of this dialogue box deals with the long format of the date and how it will appear. You have the option of displaying the Day, the Date, the Month and the Year in a variety of different ways.

10) Press **Tab** to move down to this section. The three letter option will be highlighted. Use the **Left** or **Right** cursor keys to select the main format.

11) Press **Tab** again to move down to the box beneath the word Order. Pressing **Down** or **Up** will page through the possible selections. A blank line for no day to be displayed, a short format, e.g. Sun, or the full day name, e.g. Sunday.

12) Use the **Tab** key to move from one element to another and the cursor keys to select the one you want. Finally press **Tab** until **OK** is selected and then press **Enter** to return to the International main dialogue box.

10) Click on the layout you want to use. The arrangement of the boxes beneath this will change to reflect your choice.

11) Click on an arrowhead to pop-up the list boxes of choices for each sub-element and then click on the one you want.

12) Click on **OK** in the dialogue box to return to the original dialogue box.

The **Currency Format** allows you to define how the currency symbol and related aspects will appear. The dialogue box contains four selections:

Placement determines whether the currency symbol appears before or after the amount of money.

Negative establishes how a negative value is shown, e.g. with a minus sign before it or enclosed in brackets.

Symbol is exactly that. What symbol do you want to use for the currency? The default value here is set by you when you select a Country.

Decimal digits is used to say how many digits you want to appear after a decimal point, by default this will be two.

13) Press **Alt-U** and a new dialogue box appears.

14) You change the various elements in exactly the same way as you did those in the Date Format dialogue box. When you have finished press **Enter** to return to the main screen.

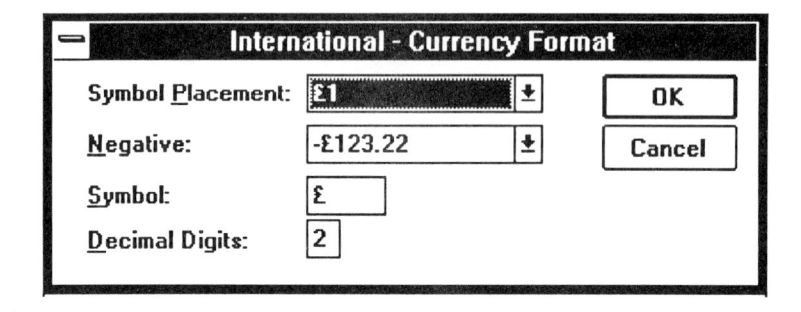

Currency Format Dialogue Box

13) Click on **Change** in the Currency Format box to bring up the new dialogue box.

14) Make your changes as before. When done click on **OK** to return to the main screen.

The **Time Format** controls how the time will be displayed in applications and in the Clock. You can select either 24 Hour display or 12 Hour. If you use the latter then you can select whether you want an AM and PM denominator to appear. You can also toggle the leading zero setting.

Time Format Dialogue Box

Number Format controls the displaying of numbers. The dialogue box will allow you to change the separator used for thousands and for decimals. It also permits you to fix the number of decimal places that will be used and whether or not to use leading zeros.

Number Format Dialogue Box

Once you have finished making changes and have returned to the International dialogue box press **Enter** or click on **OK** to return to the Control Panel. You may find that because you have made changes Windows now requires you to supply one of the original disks so that it can make changes. Just insert the disk in the drive and press **Enter**. The file will be copied to your hard disk which then works like fury as Windows updates its internal files.

Keyboard

This option simply allows you to adjust the speed of the keyboard response. It provides a test strip so you can experiment when you make changes.

Date/Time

Selecting this section will bring up a two line dialogue box that allows you to set the system time and date.

Sound

Allows you to turn the audible warning on or off and that's all.

386-Enhanced

When you are using Windows in 386-Enhanced mode, and only then, the Control Panel will contain an additional icon which is specific to that mode. The options available under this section of the program allow you to set the parameters by which programs will run concurrently. You need to set these because when you have two or more programs running at the same time they might both try to use the same device, e.g. a printer, at the same time. Therefore you have to specify which device will have priority, and thus which program goes first. These settings only need to be changed if one of the applications being used is an MS-DOS program. If you are only using Windows programs then you need do nothing because Windows handles device requests from its own concurrent programs automatically.

The dialogue box is divided into two parts, Device Contention and Scheduling. The first deals with shared devices and how they are allocated as follows:

Always Warm means that the every time a program tries to use the device connected to that port, when the device is already being used, will produce an error message. At that point you then have to manually determine which program gets priority. In other words you are liable to keep getting interrupted with error messages overlaying whatever else you are doing.

Never Warm specifies than any program may use the device at any time without producing an error message. The problem with this is that if you have two or more programs trying to use the same printer, for example, at the same time then all you will get is a load of gibberish.

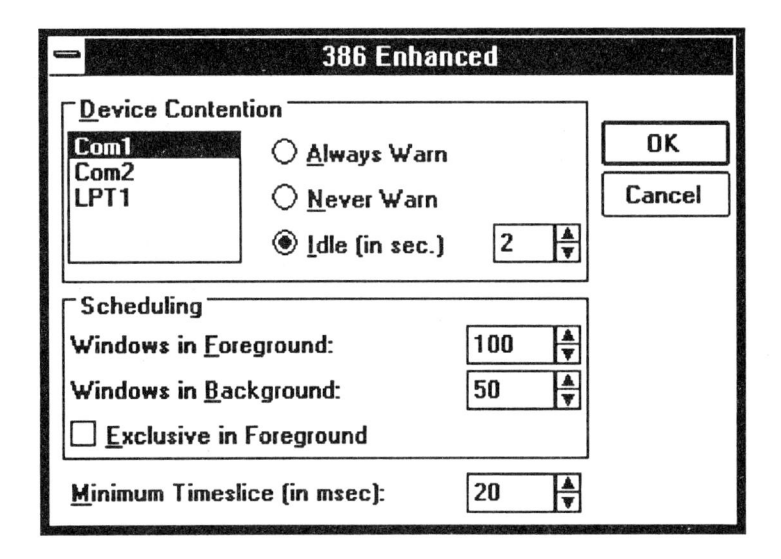

386-Enhanced Dialogue Box

Idle allows you to set a number of seconds that a device must be unused before another program can use it. The delay value must be in the range 1 to 999. If the device is idle for that period of time then the second program can take over use of the device without any problems. By default the value in this box is 2 seconds which is more than enough.

The Scheduling section of the dialogue box is concerned with the actual multitasking of programs and how Windows behaves when doing so.

Windows in Foreground is used to specify the amount of time that the various concurrent applications will share. The value selected is the relative time allowed for the program running in the foreground against the time given to the program running in the background. The value must be in the range 1 to 10,000, the higher the number the more priority is given to the foreground application. However the important factor is not the value but the ratio of this number, with that in the next box.

Windows in Background is the amount of processing time shared by Windows applications when an MS-DOS program is running in the foreground. The range is the same as for the previous setting.

Exclusive in Foreground, which is a toggle switch, means that any Windows application that is active gets 100% of the processing time available. In other words MS-DOS programs will be temporarily suspended while the Windows program is running.

Minimum Timeslice is the number of milliseconds that any program runs for before the processor power is given to another program. All Windows applications share the same timeslice automatically but each MS-DOS program needs its own.

In essence the default values that are given for the 386-Enhanced option should be perfectly adequate for any program running concurrently and you are unlikely to need to change them.

Summary

- Control Panel is the program that allows you to make major changes to the way in which Windows operates.

- The program is sub-divided into a number of elements so that you can customise only those areas of Windows that you wish to.

- Any changes made with the Control Panel will be recorded in the WIN.INI file.

Chapter 6
Setup

What is it?

As part of the Windows 3 installation, a program called Setup was copied to your hard disk. This is not the same thing as the Windows Setup which installed Windows for you, rather it is a source file that contains the information about your system and how it has been configured for Windows. The program, for such it is, can be activated to allow you to make changes to the basic parameters by which Windows operates.

In addition it can be used to configure a range of programs so that they will run in the Windows environment. However, the number of programs you can install in this way is very limited. Windows only looks for program files with an extension of EXE. If you wish to include programs with an extension of COM then you have to use alternative means, the quickest is to use File Manager which is covered in the next chapter.

When you first run Setup within Windows it gives you a list of the basic settings that you have used when you installed Windows in the first place.

```
┌─────────────────────────────────────────────────────┐
│                    Windows Setup                  ▼ │
│ Options   Help                                      │
├─────────────────────────────────────────────────────┤
│   Display:      VGA with Monochrome display         │
│   Keyboard:     Enhanced 101 or 102 key US and Non US│
│   Mouse:        Microsoft, or IBM PS/2              │
│   Network:      Network not installed               │
├─────────────────────────────────────────────────────┤
│   Swap file:    Permanent (8192 K bytes on Drive C:)│
└─────────────────────────────────────────────────────┘
```

Windows Setup Main Screen

1) Start Windows as normal. Once the Program Manager appears on screen move into the Main window, using **Ctrl-Tab** if necessary, and then select Setup using the cursor keys. Press **Enter** to activate the program.

1) Run Windows as normal. In the Main window or Program Manager double click on **Setup**.

Note that along the bottom of the box that appears, Setup tells you what type and size of Swapfile you are using. You cannot change this from here, it is for information only.

Changing the settings

Setup will allow you to change the basic settings for the Windows environment, although unless you have changed elements of the computer system you should not need to do so. There are only four areas that you can change in this way, any other changes to the system will be handled automatically by Windows.

Display allows you to change the type of monitor that you are using.

Keyboard permits you to change the keyboard type, these are mainly manufacturer specific rather than generic.

Mouse allows you to use a different mouse. Again, the types you can use are mainly specific types.

Network lets you install a new network or delete an existing one.

2) Once the Main Setup screen has appeared, press **Alt-O** to open the Options menu and then press **Enter** to activate Change System Settings.

2) Click on **Options** in the Setup menu bar and then again on **Change System Settings** in the menu that will appear.

Change Settings Dialogue Box

The dialogue box is identical to the original display except that it will allow you to actually change things.

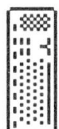

3) To change the monitor type, because this option is already highlighted, you simply use the cursor keys to page through the list of available choices. Alternatively to view the list box press **Alt-Down**.

3) Click on the arrowhead at the right of the line and then select the monitor you want from the list box. Clicking on this selects the monitor type and removes the list box.

Display List Box

180   Windows 3 - A User's Guide

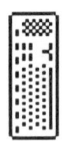

4) To change the keyboard, press **Tab** to move down to the second line and then use the cursor keys to run through the list of available types.

4) Open the Keyboard list box and select the type you are now using.

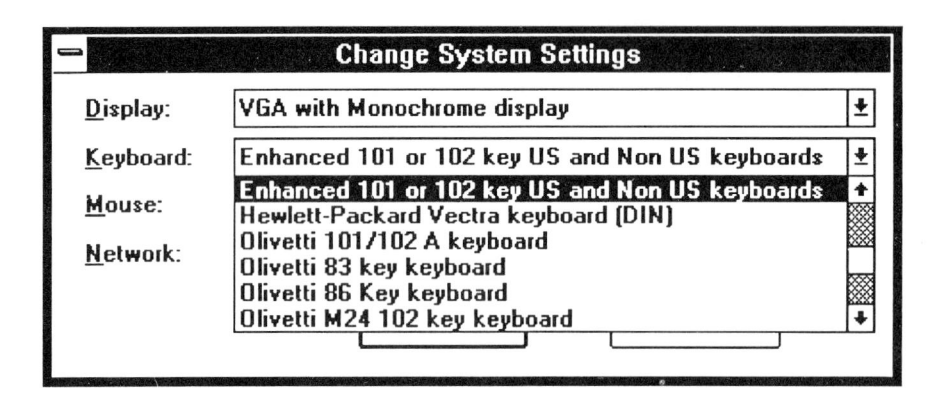

```
┌─────────────────── Change System Settings ───────────────────┐
│                                                              │
│  Display:    │ VGA with Monochrome display              │ ↕ │
│                                                              │
│  Keyboard:   │ Enhanced 101 or 102 key US and Non US keyboards │ ↕ │
│              ┌──────────────────────────────────────────┬───┐│
│  Mouse:      │ Enhanced 101 or 102 key US and Non US keyboards │ ↑ ││
│              │ Hewlett-Packard Vectra keyboard (DIN)    │   ││
│  Network:    │ Olivetti 101/102 A keyboard              │   ││
│              │ Olivetti 83 key keyboard                 │   ││
│              │ Olivetti 86 Key keyboard                 │   ││
│              │ Olivetti M24 102 key keyboard            │ ↓ ││
│              └──────────────────────────────────────────┴───┘│
└──────────────────────────────────────────────────────────────┘
```

Keyboard List Box

5) To change the mouse, press **Alt-M** to select the correct line and then use the cursor to page through the list of mice.

5) Open the Mouse list box and select the one you are using.

If you have installed a network you need to tell Windows that you have done so. The Network must be installed and running before you make any changes here.

6) Press **Alt-N** to select the Network line. Use the cursor keys to page through the supported networks one at a time.

Setup 181

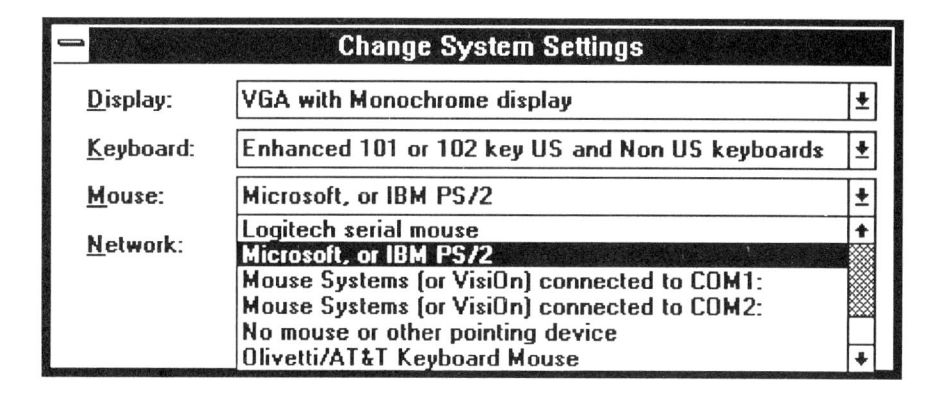

```
┌─────────────────────────────────────────────────┐
│  ─        Change System Settings                │
│                                                 │
│ Display:   │VGA with Monochrome display      │↕││
│ Keyboard:  │Enhanced 101 or 102 key US and Non US keyboards│↕││
│ Mouse:     │Microsoft, or IBM PS/2           │↕││
│            │Logitech serial mouse            │↑││
│ Network:   │Microsoft, or IBM PS/2           │ ││
│            │Mouse Systems (or VisiOn) connected to COM1:│ ││
│            │Mouse Systems (or VisiOn) connected to COM2:│ ││
│            │No mouse or other pointing device│ ││
│            │Olivetti/AT&T Keyboard Mouse     │↓││
└─────────────────────────────────────────────────┘
```

Mouse List Box

7) Having made your changes press **Enter** to close the dialogue box.

6) Open the Network list box, it contains 10 possible choices, and select the one you are using.

7) Finally click on **OK** to instigate the changes.

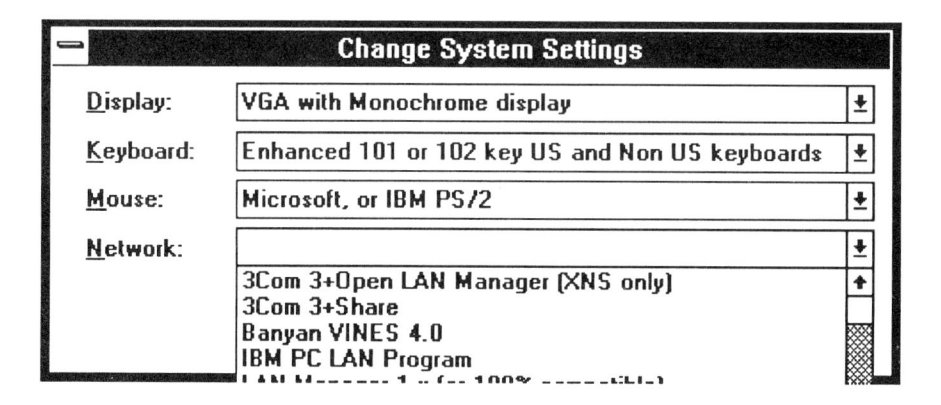

```
┌─────────────────────────────────────────────────┐
│  ─        Change System Settings                │
│                                                 │
│ Display:   │VGA with Monochrome display      │↕││
│ Keyboard:  │Enhanced 101 or 102 key US and Non US keyboards│↕││
│ Mouse:     │Microsoft, or IBM PS/2           │↕││
│ Network:   │                                 │↕││
│            │3Com 3+Open LAN Manager (XNS only)│↑││
│            │3Com 3+Share                     │ ││
│            │Banyan VINES 4.0                 │ ││
│            │IBM PC LAN Program               │ ││
└─────────────────────────────────────────────────┘
```

Network List Box

Once you have made changes Windows has to update itself to use them. Depending on what changes you have made you may be asked to supply one of the original Setup disks. This will certainly be the case if you have just installed a network or a different monitor, so that certain files can be copied. Once the files have been copied you will be given the choice of rebooting Windows or returning to MS-DOS. Personally, I would always choose the latter so that I can perform a number of disk management tasks, including compacting the hard disk, before rebooting the entire machine rather than just Windows - but you don't have to.

Adding programs

As well as allowing you to make changes to the system, Setup can be used for configuring ordinary MS-DOS programs to run in the Windows environment - within limits. What actually happens is that Windows creates a separate Program Information File, PIF, for each such MS-DOS program and then runs each one in a separate MS-DOS window. Windows programs don't need PIF data because Windows handles them automatically.

Setup can also add any Windows programs, including those that were used with an earlier version of Windows, so that they will run under Windows 3. You should remember however, that any program which was designed to run in an earlier version of Windows can only be used in Windows 3 if it is running in Real Mode. Trying to run old programs in anything else may cause the computer to hang up and at the very least you will get some screen corruption.

Setup will only search for EXE files, it ignores any program with an extension of COM for some reason, so this automatically limits the use of the program for adding software to the Windows environment. A much better way to add programs is to use the Program Manager or, providing you have a mouse, the File Manager. The advantage of using Setup is that it allows you to add a number of programs at a time.

1) Run Setup as previously mentioned. Once the main screen appears press **Alt-O S** to activate the Set Up Applications procedure.

Setup **183**

1) Once you have Setup running, click on **Options** in the menu bar and then on **Set Up Applications** in the menu that appears.

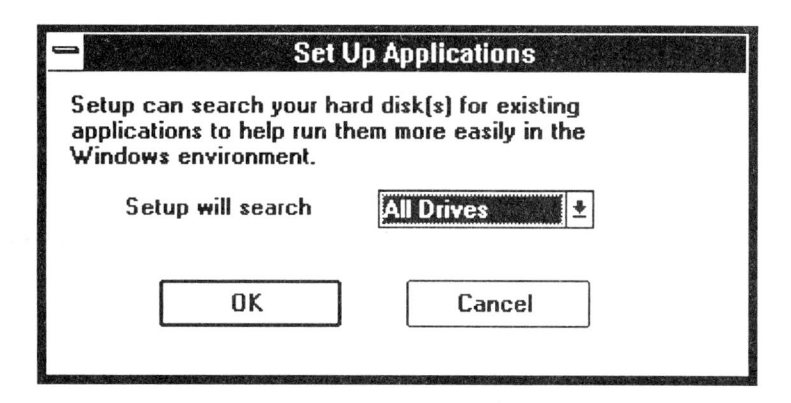

Set Up Applications Main Screen

You have a choice of which drives the program will search trying to find programs, which you choose is up to you. The possible selections are:

> **All Drives** Will search through every hard disk on your computer looking for files. Floppy disks are ignored and so you cannot use Setup to install new software. It can only be used to add programs that already exist on your hard disks.
>
> **Path Only** Windows will only look in those directories and sub-directories that you have mentioned in your PATH statement in the AUTOEXEC.BAT. Using this option presupposes that you have a PATH in existence.
>
> **Specific Drives** The program can be told to look only on a single logical drive you have installed in your system. (A logical drive is one that is a separate entity. Thus a partition is a logical drive and so a large hard disk may contain a number of logical drives.)

The simplest way to select which to use is to page through them using the cursor keys. Once you have made your selection press **Enter** and the program begins its search. Once it has finished it displays the following dialogue box.

184 *Windows 3 - A User's Guide*

```
┌─────────────────── Set Up Applications ───────────────────┐
│                                                            │
│ Applications found on hard disk(s):    Set up for use with Windows. │
│ ┌─────────────────────────┬─┐         ┌──────────────────┐│
│ │CORELDRAW                │▲│         │                  ││
│ │CorelHlp                 │ │ ┌─────┐ │                  ││
│ │LINK Utility             │ │ │Add ->│ │                  ││
│ │Norton Advanced Utilities│ │ ├─────┤ │                  ││
│ │PFS File                 │ │ │<- Remove│                │││
│ │PM                       │ │ ├─────┤ │                  ││
│ │Wfn Font Converter       │▼│ │Add All│ │                 ││
│ └─────────────────────────┴─┘ └─────┘ └──────────────────┘│
│    ┌──┐ CORELDRAW                                          │
│    │  │ C:\WINDOWS\COREL\CORELDRW.EXE   [ OK ]   [Cancel]  │
│    └──┘                                                    │
└────────────────────────────────────────────────────────────┘
```

Set Up Applications - Programs Found

Once the dialogue box has appeared you can select which of the found programs will be added to the Windows environment. The dialogue box is divided into three parts:

On the left is a box labelled **Applications found**. This will contain a list of the programs that Setup has found on the nominated drive(s) which it can add to the Windows environment.

On the right hand side is a blank box labelled **Setup for use**. Once you select programs they will appear here.

Between the two boxes are three buttons; **Add**, which is used to add individual files and copy the filenames from the left to the right; **Remove**, which moves filenames from the right to the left; and **Add All**, which allows you to add all of the found programs in a single action.

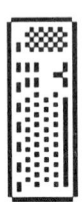

2) Use the **Tab** key to move the selector on to the list of found programs. The selector is a grey, dotted box that may be hard to see when it is on the buttons but it is fairly clear in the list box.

3) You can move through the list of programs using the cursor keys. For each program you want added, move the selector to it and then press **Space**. You can select a number of programs in the list before moving on to the next step.

4) Press **Alt-A** and the filenames will be instantly transferred to the box on the right hand side of the screen. Alternatively you can use Tab to move the selector to the button marked **Add->** and then press **Enter** to get the same effect.

2) Select each program you want to add by clicking on it.

3) Once you have made your selection click on **Add->** and the filenames are transferred to the other box.

If you have added some programs that you don't want then select them in the right hand box and then press **Alt-R** to remove them from the list or click on **Remove**.

4) Having selected the files you want to add press **Enter** and the process begins. The Program Manager will reappear as a full window, even if it has been shrunk to an icon, and Setup adds the found programs to existing group windows. Unfortunately, Setup is very specific about what groups it uses. For example, if you have renamed the Non-Windows Applications group as something else, then Setup creates another group with that name to copy MS-DOS programs into. This can be a real nuisance because you then have to move the files into the group you want them to be in.

Once all the programs have been added to their groups, then Setup Main Screen appears overlaying the Program Manager window. To remove it press **Alt-F4** or **Alt-Space C**.

Problems with Setup

Running Setup under Windows is intended to allow you to make changes to the existing system configuration as outlined above. However, there may be occasions when the changes you want to make are so fundamental that you effectively need to re-install Windows, or large parts of it, e.g. because the devices you want to use are not supplied with Windows and so files have to be copied from a floppy disk.

You can run Setup directly from MS-DOS - one of the few Windows programs that you can do this with - by simply entering **SETUP**. When you do so you get the same screens that appeared at the original Windows installation. A word of warning, if you are going to do this you must be back at the system prompt. Do **not** use the MS-DOS window that is supplied with Windows or you are likely to hang up the machine completely. The reason is that a number of Windows will be recopied and this is liable to corrupt the existing file and thus cause Windows to fail with catastrophic results.

Whenever you run Setup from MS-DOS the program examines your hardware and lists the components that the system is using. To do so, Setup has to perform hardware checks on your system. Very occasionally, and only with unusual systems, this might cause the entire system to hang-up. If it does then don't panic, there is a cure.

Reboot the machine, either by turning it off or by pressing the reset button. Once the computer is back to normal, run Setup again but add the /I switch, i.e. enter **SETUP/I** at the system prompt. This prevents Setup from examining the hardware and so the program will display the normal default settings for the system. You will then have to change these manually as you go along.

Summary

- Setup allows you to change the basic system component elements.

- The program can also be used to add some programs to the Windows environment.

- Setup can be run from MS-DOS to reinstall Windows if necessary.

- The program makes use of hardware examination to check the system components. This may cause problems when run from MS-DOS. To cure the problem use **SETUP/I**.

Keyboard Summary

Alt-F4	Terminate Setup and return to Program Manager.
Alt-H	Activate help.
Alt-O A	Add programs to the Program Manager.
Alt-O C	Change the system setup.
Alt-O X	Terminate Setup.
Alt-Space C	Terminate Setup
Alt-Space M	Move Setup window.
Alt-Space N	Reduce Setup window to an icon.
Alt-Space R	Restore Setup icon to previous size and position.
Alt-Space W	Activate Task Switching.
Ctrl-Esc	Activate Task Switching.

The Setup window cannot be maximised or resized.

Chapter 7
File Manager

What is it?

File Manager is just that, a program that will allow you to manage your files. However it is not a disk utility and should not be thought of as one. Essentially the File Manager is the replacement for the old MS-DOS Executive that was found in earlier versions of Windows and it can function in much the same way. File Manager is a tool that will allow you to organise your files and directories but it can also be used to run programs from, instead of using the Program Manager.

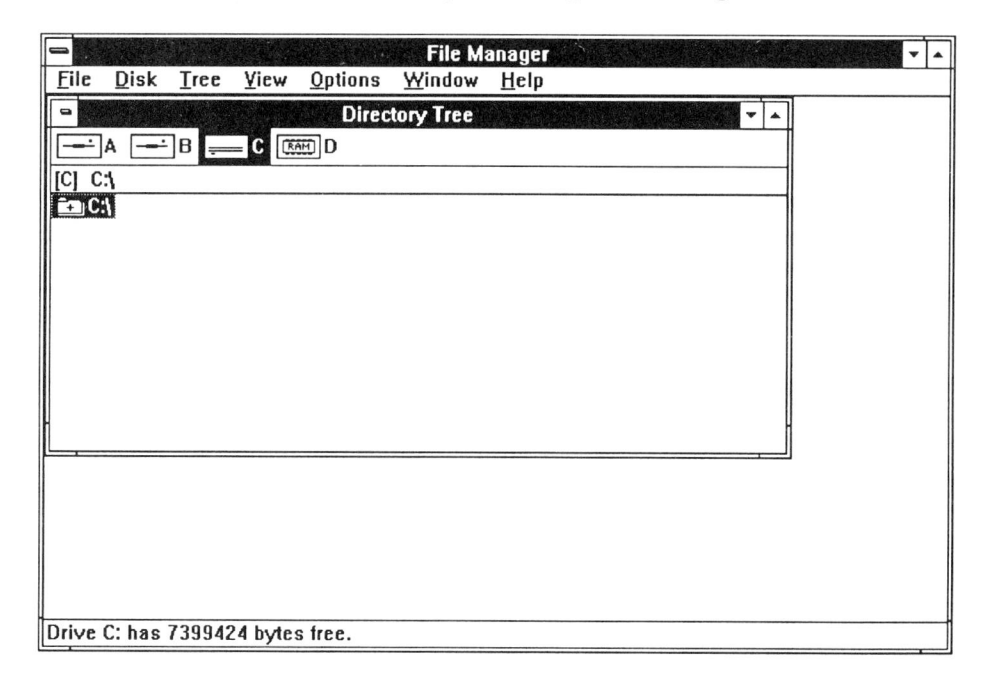

File Manager

File Manager normally contains only one window, the Directory Tree window, which gives you a graphical representation of the directories on your hard disk. Each directory is represented by a folder, with the directory name beside it. If the directory contains sub-directories then the folder will have a plus sign on it. Selecting this, by moving the highlighter to it using the cursor keys, and then pressing + will display the sub-directories it contains. To close the display up again, select the directory and then press -, either the one on the numeric keypad or the hyphen - they both have the same effect. The Directory Display window does not show any files - only directories and it is used to navigate your way around your hard disk, rapidly and smoothly. (It is very much faster and easier to use than the MS-DOS Executive used to be!) This program, more than any other except Paintbrush, almost demands that you use a mouse. The whole point of File Manager is that you can do things quickly and accurately - using the keyboard by itself negates this.

To run File Manager simply select the icon as normal and then press **Enter** or double click on it.

Before getting into using the program, let's examine the basic window layout. This is essentially the same as any other Windows program.

The top line contains the Control Box, the Title of the program, and the Minimise and Maximise buttons. Beneath this is the menu bar containing the menu keywords.

Along the bottom of the window is the Status Bar. This tells you which drive you are currently logged onto and how much free space remains on that drive.

Between the Menu Bar and the Status Bar is the area wherein sub-windows appear.

When you first start File Manager it automatically includes the Directory Tree window of the drive you are logged onto. This contains the following:

> A line of disk icons, the first one is always Drive-A, a floppy drive. If you have a second floppy installed then this appears as Drive-B. Then there is the first hard disk, labelled C. Every computer has to have Drive-C for MS-DOS to boot from.
>
> The drive icon represents the first logical drive, not the physical one. A logical drive is a single drive that MS-DOS recognises as a single entity, i.e. a partition. Thus if you are running MS-DOS 3.3 or earlier, Drive-C will always be a maximum of 32 Mb - because 3.3 cannot use drives of larger sizes, except in special circumstances where the hardware has been tweaked by third

party software. If you are using MS-DOS 4 then the logical drive can be, and probably will be, the size of the whole hard disk. A physical drive is the whole thing, i.e. the bit of hardware that is fitted into the slot. A physical drive may contain one or more logical drives.

Following on from the first hard disk icon there will be others, if they exist. Next come any Ramdrives that are installed, these will bear the label RAM on the icon and have the drive designator letter beside them. Finally come any network drives. These contain the word NET.

Immediately below the drive icons is another line of information. This contains the Volume Label of the selected drive and the current directory path.

Next comes the bulk of the sub-window containing a single folder, overprinted with a plus sign, and labelled C:\. This tells you that you are logged onto the Root Directory of Drive-C. If you press + the display will open up and give you a list of the first level directories on that drive.

When you display the directories a scroll bar may appear at the right hand side of the window. This allows you to page up and down through the directory listing.

Basic actions

a) To enlarge the File Manager window.

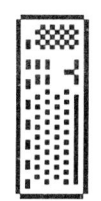

1) Press **Alt-Space S** to select Size. The cursor becomes a cruciform shape.

2) Press the cursor key that corresponds with the side of the window you want to expand, e.g. **Left** to move the left hand border. The cursor moves to that border and becomes two headed. Using the cursor keys you can now move the border to where you want it.

3) Repeat the steps 1 and 2 for the other borders.

4) Alternatively, if you want to maximise the window so that it fills the entire screen, press **Alt-Space X**.

5) If you want to Tile the window so that it fills all the screen except for a narrow border along the bottom where the Program Manager icon and any other icons lie, press **Alt-Space W,** to open the Switch To dialogue box, and then **Alt-T**.

1) Drag whichever border you want to enlarge to the position you want it to be in. You can drag two adjacent sides at the same time by dragging the corresponding corner, i.e. dragging the lower left hand corner will move the left and the bottom border at the same time.

2) To maximise the window click on the upwards pointing arrow at the extreme right hand top corner of the window.

3) To Tile the entire window, click on the Control Box, in the upper left hand corner, and then on **Switch To**. In the dialogue box that appears click on **Tile**.

b) To switch from one drive to another.

Either press **Ctrl-[drive letter]** or click on the drive you want. As you do so the Status Line at the bottom of the main window changes accordingly.

c) To expand the Directory Tree window.

To fill the entire available space, press **Shift-F4**. This will tile the window within the main window but because there is only one sub-window open it expands to fill the entire area. To return it to normal press **Shift-F5**. (By default all sub-windows are always cascaded.)

d) To page through the directory listing:

1) Use **Tab**, if necessary, to move into the Directory tree window and then use the cursor keys to move the highlighter within the window. Pressing **PgUp** or **PgDn** will always move the highlighter to the last totally visible directory name in the window.

1) Use the scroll bars to page the display. Clicking on an arrowhead will move the display up or down one line at a time. Clicking on the scroll bar itself will move the display up or down one screen at a time, depending on whether you click above or below the button on the scroll bar. If you want to page rapidly through the listing drag the scroll bar button up and down, the display scrolls accordingly.

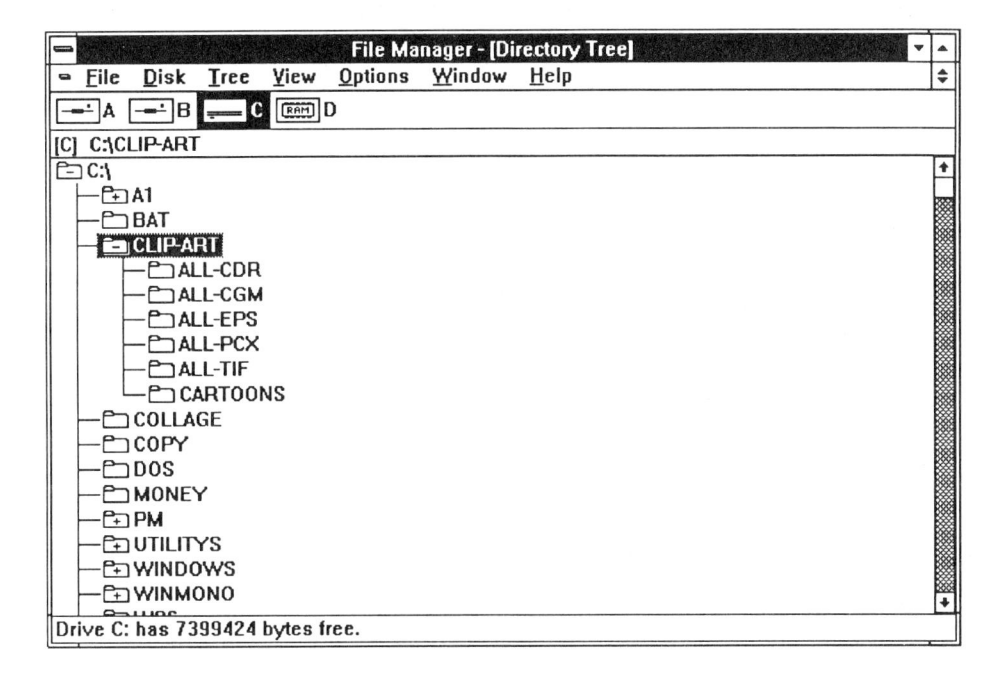

Sub-directory detail

e) To display the sub-directories.

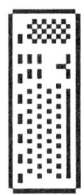

1) Use the cursor keys to select the directory you want to open. Any directory that contains sub-directories will have a plus sign on the corresponding folder.

2) Press + and the sub-directories are revealed. The plus sign changes to a minus sign. To close the directory press minus.

3) To display the entire branch of the directory tree, i.e. show the sub-directories and sub-sub-directories of a directory, press * instead of +.

4) To show every branch of the directory and all sub-directories at whatever level press **Ctrl-***. Unfortunately there is no quick way to collapse the full display again and so you have to close each level individually by highlighting it and then pressing minus.

1) Click on the folder of the directory you want to open. Don't click on the directory name itself or you will bring up another window containing the files and sub-directories of that directory. To close a directory click on the directory folder again.

f) To display the contents of a directory.

1) Highlight the directory you want to log onto using the cursor keys.

2) Press **Enter** and another window appears, in cascade format, bearing the contents of that directory.

1) Double click on the directory name, not the folder, and another window appears containing the contents of that directory.

g) To close a window:

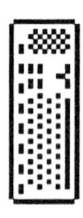

1) Select the window you want to close using **Ctrl-Tab**, and then press **Ctrl-F4**.

1) Click on the Control Box of the window you want to close and then click on **Close** within the menu that will appear.

Note: You cannot close the Directory Tree window if it is the only window on screen. It can be reduced to an icon at any time but it cannot be closed.

h) To reduce a window to an icon:

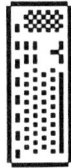

1) Select the window you want to minimise using **Ctrl-Tab**.

2) Press **Alt-Hyphen N** and the window becomes an icon.

1) Click on the **Minimise** button at the right hand corner of the window you want iconised.

Be warned: There is a limit on the number of windows and icons you have on screen at any one time. The more windows you have open, or the more icons you have, the slower File Manager works - so much so that at times it appears to have hung up on the machine if it is running in Real Mode. (In fact if I have more than about a dozen windows open at the same time on the Samsung 80286 in Real Mode and I try to open another one, I can go away and have a cup of coffee while I'm waiting for it to appear! Again, it's a system resource problem.)

i) Moving from one window to another.

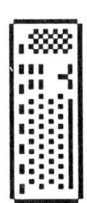

1) Pressing **Alt-W** pops down the Window menu and you can select the window you want to log onto by pressing the corresponding number.

2) Use **Ctrl-Tab** to switch from window to window in turn.

3) Press **Alt-Hyphen T** to switch to the next window in the sequence.

4) **Ctrl-F6** has the same effect as **Alt-Hyphen T**.

1) Just click anywhere on the window you want to move to.

2) If the window is not visible you can use the Window menu by

clicking on **Window** and then on the window you want in the list that will be presented.

j) To select multiple files.

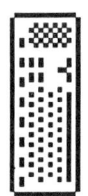

1) Use the cursor keys to move to the first file you want selected and then press **Space** to highlight the file. Then press **Shift-F8**. The selector box flashes and can be moved while still leaving the previous file selected.

2) Using the cursor keys again, move the selector to the next file, press **Space** again. Continue doing this until all the files you want have been selected.

1) Click on the first file and it is highlighted.

2) If the remaining files you want are in sequence, i.e. one after the other, you can press **Shift** and then click on the last file in the sequence and all the intervening files are highlighted.

3) If you want to select separated files, press **Ctrl** and click on the next wanted file. You can select as many files as you wish in this way.

File Manager Menus

File Manager has seven menus plus the Control Box, and each sub-window also has its own Control Box. Certain menus and/or some commands are only operable when you are using certain types of window. Any command that cannot be used will be shown in grey rather than as solid black.

The Control Box is accessed by clicking on the button at the top left hand corner of the screen or by pressing **Alt-Space**. The commands the menus contains are:

Restore which will return an icon to a window such that the window occupies the same size and position as it did prior to it being reduced to an icon.

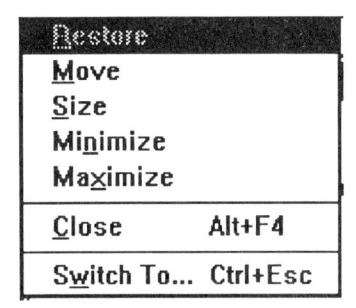

File Manager Control Box

Move which allows you to pick up the window or the icon and move it to another position on the screen.

Size allows you to change the size and shape of a window.

Minimise will shrink any window down to an icon.

Maximise expands any window so that it fills the total available space. If the window is a main one, e.g. File Manager itself, then the window expands to fill the entire background area. A sub-window on the other hand expands to fill the available space within the main window.

Close, not available on the Directory Tree sub-window, terminates a window.

Switch to, only available on main windows, allows you to activate the Task Switching facility of windows so that you can activate another program.

Next, only available on sub-windows, allows you to deactivate the current window and move to another one.

File Menu

All of the commands within this menu are only available if the window you have open contains files. If you are using the Directory Tree window then about half of the commands are not available to you because they are specific to files. Certain commands within the menu will instigate dialogue boxes once they are activated, these are shown by having three dots after the command.

Open	Enter
Run...	
Print...	
Associate...	
Search...	
Move...	F7
Copy...	F8
Delete...	Del
Rename...	
Change Attributes...	
Create Directory...	
Select All	Ctrl+/
Deselect All	Ctrl+\
Exit	

File Manager File Menu

Open allows you to run a selected program, i.e. the one that is currently highlighted. As an alternative you can simply highlight the program and press **Enter** or double click on the program name.

Run is used to activate a named program. This is similar to Open but instead of highlighting the program first you simply enter the name, and, if necessary, the full path to the program in the dialogue box that appears. Pressing **Enter** then runs the program. You can use this command to run any program that has not been installed as an icon in Windows.

Print allows you to print a document file, via the Print Manager. This is rather useful because it allows you to print a pure ASCII file to a PostScript printer - something that is not possible from MS-DOS. However, if you don't want a load of gibberish and sheets of almost blank paper, don't use this command to try and print a graphic.

Associate is used to tell Windows that certain files are linked with specific programs. Once a file has been associated you can run the program by running the file. For example, you have a file called ALPHA.DOC and you associate it with Windows

Write. You can then run the file, either by selecting it and pressing **Enter** or by double clicking on it, as if it were a program. What actually happens is that the association causes the program to run and automatically load the document file. In a sense it is like combining a program and filename in the Program Manager.

Search is extremely useful - it is almost worth having Windows just for this command, especially if you have a large hard disk and a complex directory structure. Quite simply the command allows you to search for a specified file. You can use the wildcard characters in the search, e.g. ***.TXT** to find every file with an extension of TXT. Normally Search is used only to look for the files in the directory you currently have open, but you can also ask it to search the entire hard disk.

Move allows you to move a file, or group of files, to another location. The shortcut is to press **F7** once the files have been selected.

Copy is similar to the above but it only copies the files rather than moving them. Use **F8** as the shortcut.

Delete allows you to delete selected files and sub-directories. One advantage, or disadvantage depending on how you look at it, of the command is that it can be used to delete directories that are not empty. (Within MS-DOS you can only delete an empty directory.)

Rename is used to rename files or directories. Select the file or directory and then activate this command. In the dialogue box that appears simply enter the new name. A tip: When you enter the new name do not include a path, even though the first line of the dialogue box that appears does so. If you do so you get an error message.

Change Attributes allows you to modify the attributes of any file. Again this is better than the MS-DOS command because it allows you to change the System and Hidden attributes - something that is not possible with pure MS-DOS.

Create Directory does just that. It is the equivalent of the MS-DOS **MKDIR** command. You can create the directory at any point in the directory structure by including the full path.

Select All provides a shortcut for selecting every file in a directory, e.g. to move or copy them. To use the command directly from the keyboard press **Ctrl-/**.

Deselect All is the opposite of the above. The keyboard shortcut is **Ctrl-**.

Exit terminates the File Manager and brings up a dialogue box that will allow you to save any changes you have made so that they become the default characteristics for the program.

Disk Menu

```
Copy Diskette...
Label Disk...

Format Diskette...
Make System Diskette...

Connect Net Drive...
Disconnect Net Drive...
```

File Manager Disk Menu

The Disk Manager is concerned with a number of disk activities. The first four commands are available at all times, whereas the final two will only be active if you are using a network. Each of the commands brings up its own dialogue box.

Copy Diskette is the equivalent of MS-DOS **DISKCOPY**. Before you can use the command you must be logged onto a floppy disk drive, otherwise you get an error message. The dialogue box asks you to select a floppy drive that you wish to copy and then tells you to swap source and target disks as the process is carried out. One peccadillo with this command is that it does not tell you it has finished - all that happens it that the disk stops spinning and the dialogue box vanishes - and so you do not get the opportunity to copy another disk.

Label Disk is similar to the MS-DOS **LABEL** command. The command allows you to add a volume label to any floppy disk. Again you have to be logged onto the drive that contains the disk you want to label. The standard MS-DOS rules about disk labels applies, i.e. you cannot use the reserved characters.

Format Diskette can only be used with floppy disks - you cannot use this command to format a hard disk. The command operates in the same way as the MS-DOS **FORMAT**, even to the extent of asking if you want to format another diskette when you have finished. The command uses two dialogue boxes, the first to select the drive you want formatted and the second to select the type of disk, e.g. High Capacity or not, and whether or not you want to create a system diskette.

Make System Diskette allows you to copy the system files to a floppy, just like the MS-DOS **SYS** command.

Connect Net Drive is only available on networked systems, otherwise the command is greyed, i.e. inoperable. The command pops up a dialogue box which allows you to log onto a network drive, including a password if one is in operation.

Disconnect Net Drive does the opposite of the above and allows you to leave a networked drive. Again the command is only available if you are using a network, otherwise the command is greyed.

Tree Menu

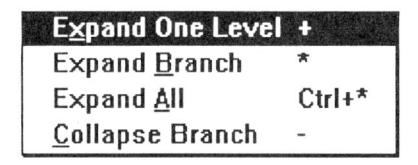

Expand One Level	**+**
Expand Branch	*
Expand All	Ctrl+*
Collapse Branch	-

File Manager Tree Menu

The Tree menu is concerned with directories and sub-directories only and as such it is not available if you have a window open which only contains files.

Expand One Level allows you to view the sub-directories contained within any individual directory. A directory which contains sub-directories is shown by having a plus sign (+) on the directory folder. You can open this without using the menu by selecting the directory and then pressing +.

Expand Branch does much the same thing but it will open the directory to display sub-directories and any sub-directories that these, in turn, contain. Select the directory you want to open and then use this command or press *.

Expand All is similar to the above but it will show you the complete directory structure for the whole disk. You can activate the command from anywhere, it doesn't matter what directory or sub-directory you are logged onto. The direct shortcut is to use **Ctrl-***.

Collapse Branch is the opposite of Expand Branch. It returns the display to showing only the first level of the selected directory. The keyboard shortcut is to press minus once the directory is selected.

View Menu

```
√ Name
  File Details
  Other...
√ By Name
  By Type
  Sort by...
  Include...
  Replace on Open
```

File Manager View Menu

The View Menu applies to files only - not to directories. However, the menu commands are all active when you are using the Directory Tree window, even though they apparently do nothing. Basically, the menu and its commands are concerned with the way in which the files are displayed. The menu is divided into four parts, each concerned with a different aspect of the display. The first part is concerned with the information that is given about the files, the second part changes the way in which the files are presented, the third allows you to change what is included in the display, and the final part is about the display itself. Most of the commands include dialogue boxes.

Name, the default option, is the first of the display options. With this option selected all you can see are the names of the various files contained within that directory.

File Details is an adjunct to the above. It allows you to display not only the filename but also the details of the file's size, date and time stamping, and the file attributes.

Other affects the previous command. It allows you to nominate which of the file details, other than the name, will be displayed. For example, you could turn off the date and time stamping but leave the other details.

By Name is the first of the sorting routines and is the default option. With this option selected the files will be shown sorted on the basis of the filenames, in normal alphabetical order. In other words A comes before B which comes before C and so on. You cannot have reverse order unfortunately. Symbols come before Numbers which are followed by Letters. Sub-directory names appear before everything else regardless of their names but listing in the same order as the files.

By Type changes the display so that the files and sub-directories are sorted on the basis of the file types, i.e. they are sorted according to the file extensions. With this option selected the files are shown in ascending alphabetical order based on the filenames but within groupings of ascending alphabetic order of extensions.

Sort By allows you to sort the display by a number of alternatives, e.g. by file size. This option will override any other selection.

Include allows you to preselect or modify which files are included in the display. You can toggle the setting so that all hidden and system files are displayed or not.

Replace on Open applies to directory windows. Instead of opening a different window for every directory and thus having a number of different windows on screen, you can use this option. What it does is use two windows, one for the main directory tree and then one other for everything else. When you open any other directory its contents will replace those of this second window instead of being in a window of their own. Thus you can reduce the number of windows on screen at any time.

Options Menu

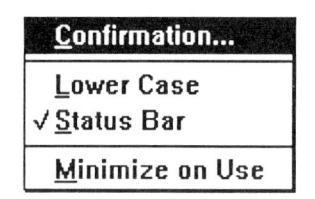

```
┌─────────────────────┐
│ Confirmation...     │
├─────────────────────┤
│ Lower Case          │
│ √ Status Bar        │
├─────────────────────┤
│ Minimize on Use     │
└─────────────────────┘
```

File Manager Options Menu

This menu has to do with the way that the main File Manager window appears and also with what happens with certain commands.

Confirmation brings up a dialogue box that will allow you to preset the validation of certain actions, e.g. if you have the Confirm on Delete option set then you will be doubly prompted before any file or directory is deleted. By default all four options within the dialogue box are turned on.

Lower Case changes the way that filenames appear. By default Windows will use upper case letters, i.e. capitals, for everything within a sub-window. You can change this so that all filenames and directory names are shown in lower case. Unfortunately you cannot mix the two, e.g. to have directories in upper case and filenames in lower.

Status Bar is a toggle switch that determines whether or not the line along the bottom of the File Manager window gives you details about which drive and directory you are currently logged on to.

Minimize on Use is also a toggle that will reduce File Manager to an icon when you run any program from within it.

Window Menu

The Window menu applies to the sub-windows contained within the main File Manager window in the same way that the menu on Program Manager works.

Cascade	**Shift+F5**
Tile	Shift+F4
Refresh	F5
Close All Directories	
√ 1 Directory Tree	

File Manager Window Menu

Cascade, the default, allows all sub-windows to overlay one another.

Tile shapes the sub-windows so that they are all visible within the main window.

Refresh is unnecessary in the vast majority of cases, the command has been included primarily for networked drives. Whenever you open a window the display should change to reflect this. However on some networks this is not always the case. By using this command the window is properly displayed.

Close all directories will terminate, i.e. close, every sub-window you have open except the main Directory Tree one.

Exercise 7.1
Copying files

Because your disk and its directories are different from mine in most respects we are going to have to use a single directory for all of the following exercises because there is only one directory that I know your hard disk contains - the Windows one. However, the principles of the exercise apply to all files, directories and sub-directories. If you want to use another directory then by all means do so, just substitute the appropriate directory name for every occurrence of WINDOWS that appears hereafter in this chapter.

The first thing we'll do is create a new sub-directory within the main Windows directory.

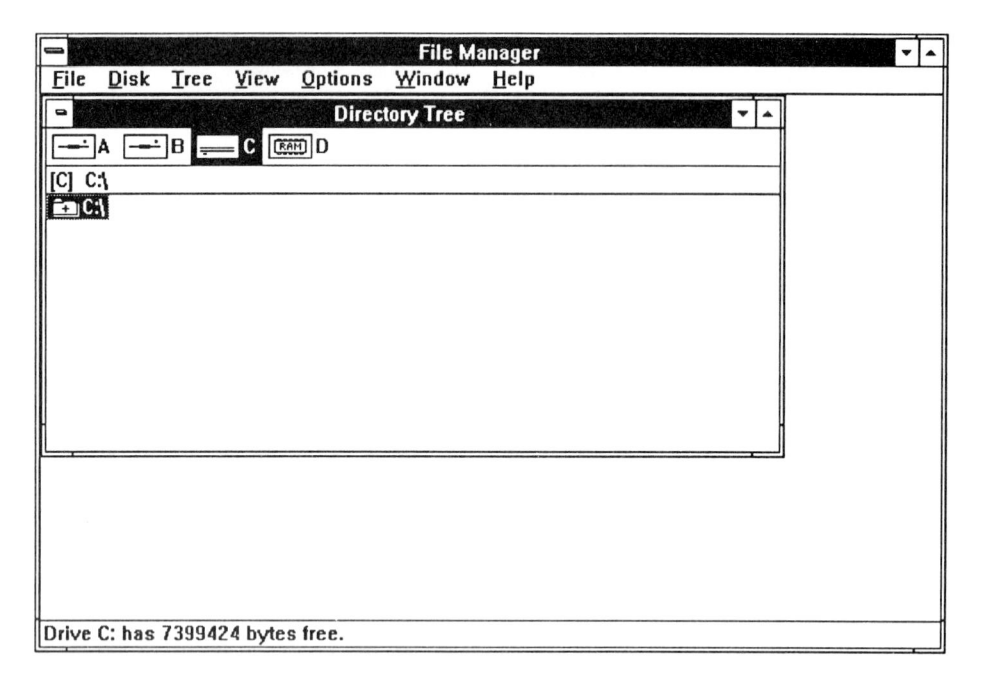

File Manager

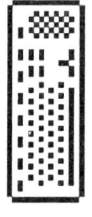

1) Run the File Manager from the Program Manager by selecting the icon and then pressing **Enter**. You should have set the **Minimize on Use** toggle of the Program Manager to on so that only the File Manager is on screen as a window.

2) If the only thing that appears in the Directory Tree window is **C:** then you are logged onto the Root Directory of the drive. The folder beside the label will have a plus sign on it. **Press +** to open the folder and display the first level directory tree of your disk.

3) Press **Down** until you have selected the WINDOWS sub-directory and then press **Enter**. A second window appears.

4) Press **Alt-F R** and a dialogue box appears. Type **ALPHA-1** and then press **Enter**. Almost instantly the new sub-directory will appear at the top of the Windows window, just below the line saying [..].

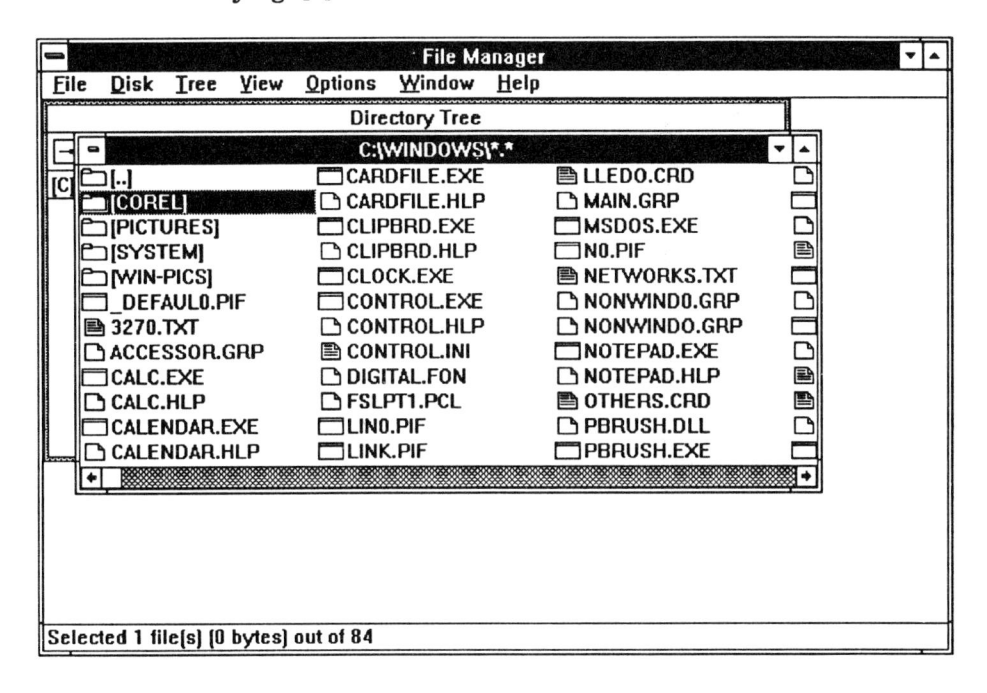

```
┌─────────────────────── File Manager ───────────────────────┐
│ File  Disk  Tree  View  Options  Window  Help              │
├────────────────────── Directory Tree ──────────────────────┤
│                      C:\WINDOWS\*.*                        │
│ [..]           □ CARDFILE.EXE      ≡ LLEDO.CRD             │
│ [COREL]        □ CARDFILE.HLP      □ MAIN.GRP              │
│ [PICTURES]     □ CLIPBRD.EXE       □ MSDOS.EXE             │
│ [SYSTEM]       □ CLIPBRD.HLP       □ N0.PIF                │
│ [WIN-PICS]     □ CLOCK.EXE         ≡ NETWORKS.TXT          │
│ _DEFAUL0.PIF   □ CONTROL.EXE       □ NONWIND0.GRP          │
│ ≡ 3270.TXT     □ CONTROL.HLP       □ NONWIND0.GRP          │
│ □ ACCESSOR.GRP ≡ CONTROL.INI       □ NOTEPAD.EXE           │
│ □ CALC.EXE     □ DIGITAL.FON       □ NOTEPAD.HLP           │
│ □ CALC.HLP     □ FSLPT1.PCL        ≡ OTHERS.CRD            │
│ □ CALENDAR.EXE □ LIN0.PIF          □ PBRUSH.DLL            │
│ □ CALENDAR.HLP □ LINK.PIF          □ PBRUSH.EXE            │
├────────────────────────────────────────────────────────────┤
│ Selected 1 file(s) (0 bytes) out of 84                     │
└────────────────────────────────────────────────────────────┘
```

Windows sub-directory

1) In the Program Manager Main window double click on the File Manager icon.

2) When you use File Manager for the first time it automatically logs onto the Root Directory of Drive-C and does not show the sub-directories that this contains. Click on the folder beside the C:\ label and the directory names appear.

3) Double click on the word WINDOWS and a new sub-window appears bearing the names of the sub-directories and files contained within the Windows directory.

4) Press **Alt-F R** and a dialogue box appears. Type **ALPHA-1** and then press **Enter**. Almost instantly the new sub-directory will appear at the top of the Windows window, just below the line saying [..].

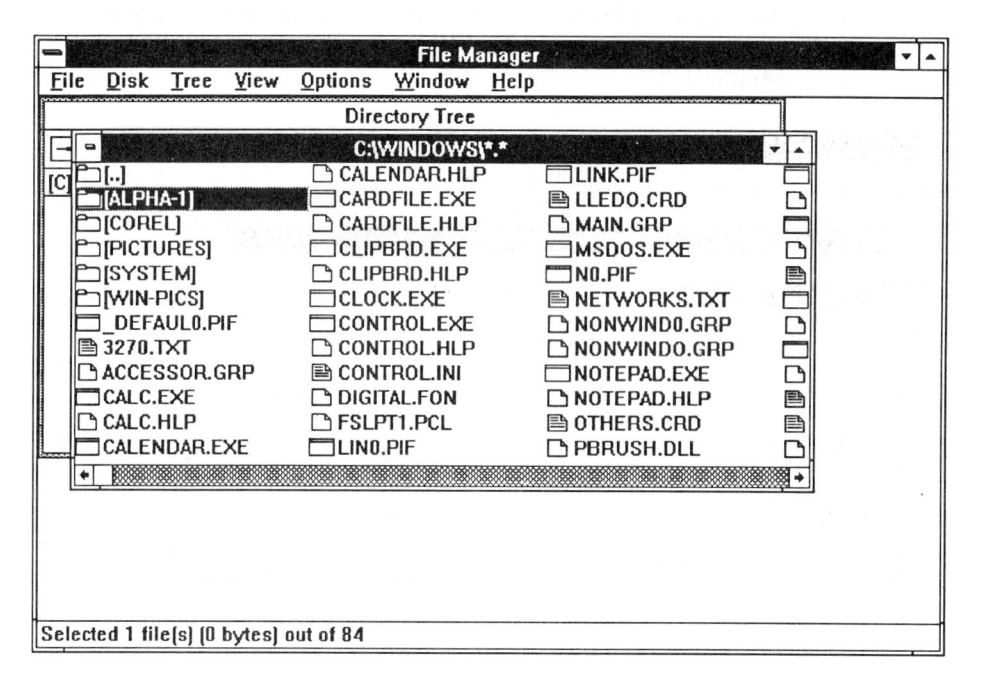

New directory created

Exercise 7.2
Copying Files in one window

Copying files within Windows is very easy, you simply select the files you want and then tell Windows where to put them. In this exercise we're going to copy all the files with an extension of BMP into the sub-directory we previously created.

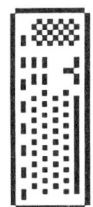

1) Because there are so many files in the Windows directory it would be handy if we expanded it to fill the entire available area. Press **Alt-Hyphen X** and the window will fill the entire area, overlaying the Directory Tree window in the process.

2) Press **Alt-V T** and the files will be shown sorted on their extensions, the directories at the top left followed by the files.

3) Use the cursor keys until you reach the first file with a BMP extension. Press **Shift-F8** and the selector box, which may be difficult to see, flashes. While still holding down **Shift**, continue using **Down** until you have selected all the files with a BMP extension.

4) Press **F8**, or **Alt-F C** if you want to go through the menu, and a dialogue box appears. Enter ALPHA-1 and the files will be copied into the directory. If you wish you can include the full path to the destination directory, i.e. C:\WINDOWS\ALPHA-1, but it is not necessary in this case because the target directory is a sub-directory of the directory you are logged on to.

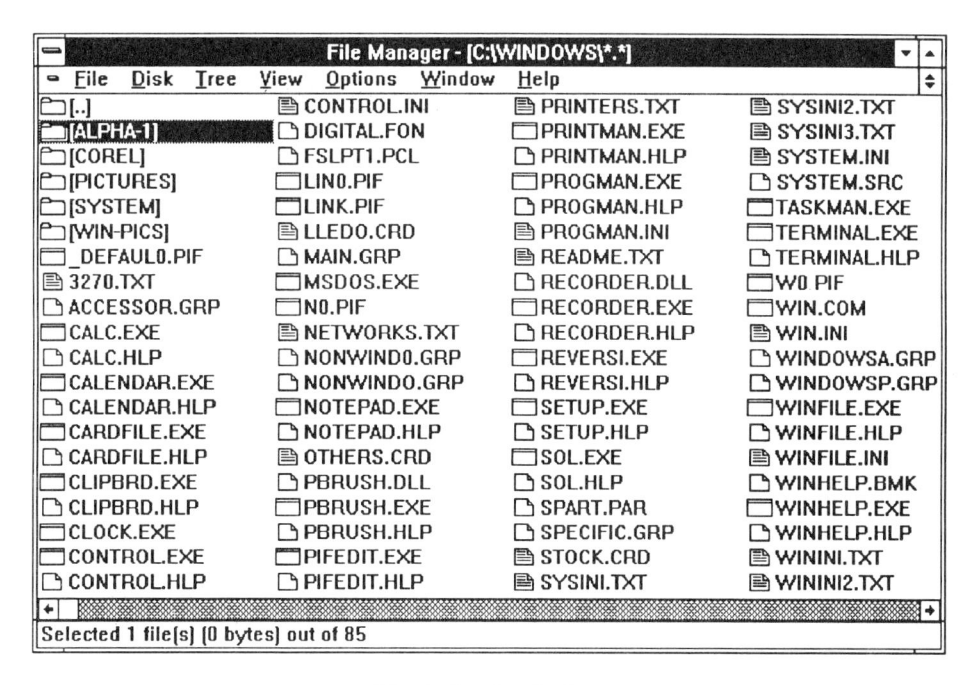

Maximised window

1) Click on the **Maximise** button at the extreme right hand top corner of the Windows window.

2) Click on **View** in the menu bar and then on **By Type** in the menu and the display is changed.

3) Click on the first file with a BMP extension. Then hold **Shift** and click on the last file with that extension, release the **Shift** key. All the intervening files will be selected automatically.

4) Hold down **Ctrl** and then click the mouse button. The cursor will change into a graphic that looks like a stack of cards. Drag this, while still holding **Ctrl**, until it overlies the directory name ALPHA-1. Release the mouse button and **Ctrl**. A dialogue box appears asking if you want to copy the files into the directory. Click on **OK** and they will be copied.

Warning: Make sure you press **Ctrl** and not **Shift** otherwise the files will be moved and not copied.

Exercise 7.3
Copying files using Search

Rather than having to rearrange the display you can use the search facility to select a number of files and then copy them en masse. Search will produce a new window containing the results of what it finds.

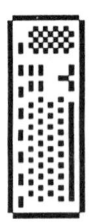

1) Press **Alt-F H** and a dialogue box appears.

2) By default this is set to show *.* as the search criteria. Type *.BMP instead. **Tab** down to the next line and press **Space** to deselect the Search Entire Disk facility. **Tab** down again and then press **Enter**.

3) Tile the windows using **Shift-F4** and then, in the Search window, select the files you want to copy as in the previous exercise. The press F8, type **ALPHA-1** in the dialogue box and press **Enter**.

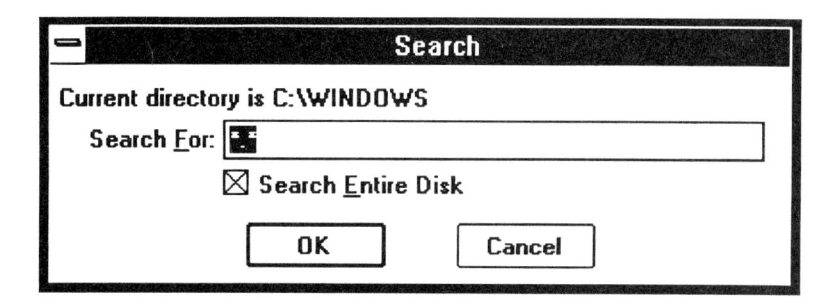

Search dialogue box

4) Because the files already exist in the target directory you will get a message each time Windows tries to copy a file, saying the File already exists and asking if you want to overwrite it. Just press **Enter** to do so or **Esc** not to. Finally close the Search window by pressing **Ctrl-F4** and cascade the remaining windows by pressing **Shift-F5**.

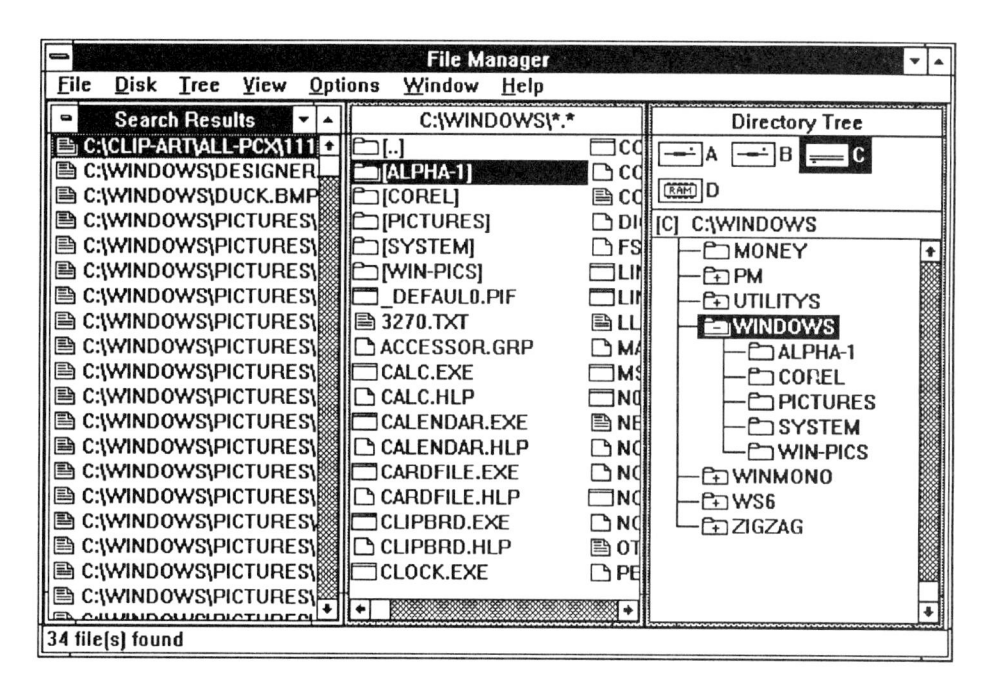

Three windows tiled

1) Click on **File** in the menu bar and then on **Search** to bring up the dialogue box.

2) Type ***.BMP** and then click on **Search Entire Disk** to turn off the toggle. Finally click on **OK**.

A new window then appears bearing the title Search Results. Notice that this not only contains a list of those files within the Windows directory that we want, it also has a list of the files in the \ALPHA-1 sub-directory. The reason is that the Search command considers any sub-directory to be part of the directory you want to look through, which is fair enough but can be a bit of a nuisance.

3) Select the files as in the previous exercise. You can now copy them directly into the Windows window by pressing **Ctrl** and then holding the mouse button. Drag the cursor across into the Windows window and position it over the directory ALPHA-1. Release the button and the **Ctrl** key.

4) Because the files already exist in the target directory you will get a message each time Windows tries to copy a file, saying the File already exists and asking if you want to overwrite it. Just press **Enter** to do so or **Esc** not to. Finally close the Search window by pressing **Ctrl-F4** and cascade the remaining windows by pressing **Shift-F5**.

Exercise 7.4
Deleting files

Windows will allow you to delete a single file or a large group of files in a single action. So we'll use this to delete all the files that are in the ALPHA-1 directory.

1) With the Windows window active select the ALPHA-1 sub-directory using the cursor keys and then press **Enter**. The contents of the sub-directory will appear in a new active window.

2) Press **Ctrl-/** and all the files are selected.

3) Press **Del** to delete the selected files.

1) Double click on the name ALPHA-1 and a new window appears showing the contents of the sub-directory.

2) Click on the first filename in this window, press **Shift** and click on the last filename. All the files will then be selected. Press **Del** to delete the files.

You will now discover one of the quirks of Windows 3. As each file is deleted the screen display is correspondingly refreshed. This slows down the deletion process but that's the way it works and there is nothing you can do about it. However, you can circumvent it. Instead of deleting the files in a window, reduce the ALPHA-1 window to an icon. Then with the icon selected, i.e. highlighted, press **Del**. The files will be deleted rapidly without any refreshing. Finally you get a message asking if the sub-directory should be deleted. If you answer negatively then the directory remains in place but all the files are gone. If you answer yes then the directory will also be deleted. (You will need ALPHA-1 later.)

Exercise 7.5
Renaming files

Windows will allow you to rename files in the same way as the MS-DOS **REN** command does, but it will also allow you to rename directories, which is something you cannot do in pure MS-DOS.

Warning: Do not change the names of any of the files that are supplied with Windows 3 or if you do make sure you make backups of them first.

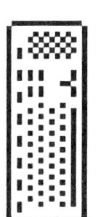

1) Select the ALPHA-1 directory in the Windows window using the cursor keys.

2) Press **Alt-F N** and a dialogue box appears bearing the name of the selected directory on the first line.

3) Type a new name, e.g. **ALPHA-2**, on the second line but do not include any path details - if you do you will get an error message. Press **Enter**. The dialogue box vanishes and the directory has been renamed.

```
┌─────────────────────── Rename ───────────────────────┐
 Current directory is C:\WINDOWS\PICTURES
       From:  [BILLY.BMP BOXES.BMP BRUISER.BMP CAMEL.BMP]
       To:    [                                        ]

              [ Rename ]          [ Cancel ]
```

Rename Dialogue Box

4) You can also rename a number of files at once. Select all the files with a BMP extension as in Exercise 7.1. Press **Alt-F N** to bring up the dialogue box. Notice that this will not, apparently, contain the names of all the selected files. In fact it does, but you cannot see them all.

5) On the second line type ***.ABA** and then press **Enter**. The file extensions of the selected files will all be changed - the names remain the same. Now change them all back to ***.BMP** in the same way - or you cannot use them.

1) Click on **ALPHA-1** to select it.

2) Click on **File** in the menu bar and then on **Rename**.

3) Type the new name on the second line and then click on **OK**.

4) You can also use this command to rename multiple files. Select the BMP files you want renamed as in the first exercise and then open the Rename dialogue box as above.

5) Type ***.ABA** on the second line of the dialogue box and click on **OK**. As each File is renamed the display in the window will

be refreshed and updated. Make sure you change the extensions back to BMP when you are done.

Exercise 7.6
Associating files

This command is used to tell Windows that certain files are related to specific programs. Why? Because once an association exists you can start the program by clicking on the filename instead of the program name. Windows will then load the program and automatically load the selected file into the program for you, i.e. it is a shortcut. You can associate as many files as you like with any program, theoretically you could associate every program on your disk with one or more programs, but you can only associate one extension at a time.

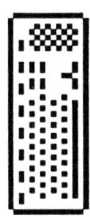

1) Select a filename that bears the extension you want to associate. The association is based on File extensions - not filenames.

2) Press **Alt-F A** and a dialogue box appears.

3) Type the name of the program, including its extension, in the dialogue box and then press **Enter**. That's it.

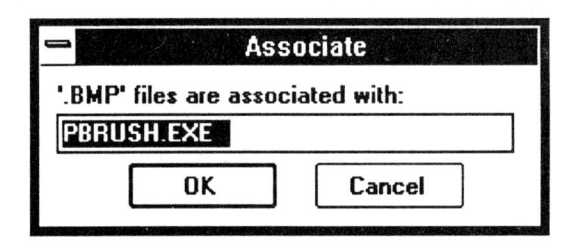

Associate Dialogue Box

1) Click on the file that bears the extension you want to link to a program.

2) Click on **File** in the menu bar and then on **Associate**.

3) Enter the program name the extension is to be associated with.

Exercise 7.7
File Attributes

Every file, regardless of what it is, has a number of attributes about it. There are four possible attributes:

Archive means that the file can be backed up either by MS-DOS itself or by third party software. As a file is created this attribute is automatically set to on.

Read Only means a file is just that - it can be read, i.e. loaded into an application program, but it cannot be changed or modified.

Hidden is used to suppress the visibility of a file. Normally, under MS-DOS, you cannot see any file which has this attribute turned on, i.e. it will not show up when you enter **DIR**. Windows, however, has the ability, which you can turn on or off, to see all files on your disk regardless of what the file attributes are.

```
C:\WINMONO\*.*
WEAVE.BMP        190   1/05/90   03:00:00   ——A
FIG-098.CLP    33787  23/07/90   17:36:40   ——A
FIG-099.CLP    33787  23/07/90   17:38:00   ——A
FIG-100.CLP    33787  23/07/90   17:38:18   ——A
FIG-101.CLP     7107  23/07/90   17:38:46   ——A
FIG-102.CLP    33787  23/07/90   17:38:20   ——A
FIG-103.CLP     8693  23/07/90   17:40:58   ——A
FIG-104.CLP     8693  23/07/90   17:40:44   ——A
WIN.COM        19358   6/07/90   18:28:40   ——A
DATA1.CRD         72  12/07/90   16:28:58   ——A
PBRUSH.DLL      7724   1/05/90   03:00:00   ——A
RECORDER.DLL   11774   1/05/90   03:00:00   ——A
```

Files and their Attributes

System are special files which are used by the operating system. They should never be changed or your computer is liable to hang up in glorious fashion.

Under MS-DOS you have only ever been able to change the first two attributes. There are a number of both commercial and shareware programs that will allow you to change any attribute but MS-DOS itself provides no facility for altering Hidden or System attributes. However Windows now does. It will allow you to change the attributes of any file and/or directory so you can now have hidden directories.

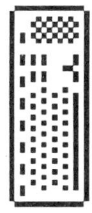

1) Still in the Windows window, press **Alt-V F** and the display will change to show you the Name, Size, Date, Time and Attributes of the files. Note that each file has only one attribute turned on, the Archive one shown by the letter A.

2) Select all the BMP files as before.

3) Press **Alt-F G** and a dialogue box appears. Use **Tab** and **Space** to select **Archive, Read Only** and **Hidden**. Press **Enter**. The display changes so that the selected files now say RH-A. In other words that are now Read Only, Hidden and have their Archive attributes turned on.

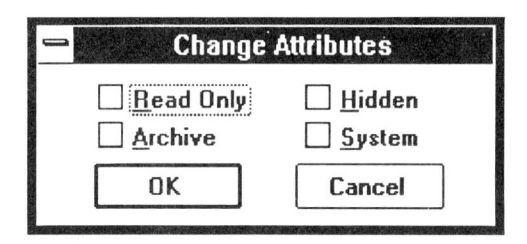

Change Attributes Dialogue Box

1) With the Windows window active, press **Alt-V F** and the display will change to show you the file details and attributes. Note that each file has only one attribute turned on, the Archive one shown by the letter A.

2) Select all the BMP files as before.

3) Click on **File** in the menu bar and then on **Change Attributes**. In the dialogue box that appears, click on **Read Only, Archive** and **Hidden**. Then click on **OK**. The display will then be updated to show the changed attributes.

To see the effect of the changes you have just made, press **Alt-V C**. Click on the box that says **Show Hidden/System Files**. The files will then either appear or disappear according to what the previous setting was. With the command turned on, shown by a diagonal cross in the box, the files are visible. If the command is turned off then the display behaves like it would under the MS-DOS **DIR** command and the files cannot be seen because they are hidden. I suggest that you change the attributes on the files again so that only the Archive attribute is active.

You can also use this command to change the attributes of directories - something that is impossible under MS-DOS. Thus you can create a directory, store files in it, and by making it hidden have it disappear from view.

Exercise 7.8
Formatting floppy disks

Windows 3 is designed to be used in place of pure MS-DOS if you should want to. In essence it is an extension to MS-DOS, but one that is more colourful, more intuitive and easier to use than the system prompt. The File Manager provides most of the major functions you would expect to use from MS-DOS including the ability to handle floppy disks.

Before any disk can be used it must first be formatted: you can purchase pre-formatted floppies but why buy them when it is so easy to format your own?

1) Place a floppy disk into the disk drive. If the disk already contains data then it will be lost as a result of this exercise. Ideally you want to use either a brand new disk or one that does not contain any data that you are liable to want.

2) Press **Alt-D F**. Select the drive which contains the disk you are wanting to format, it has to be either A or B because Windows will not allow you to format the hard disk.

3) A message box then appears informing you of the consequences:

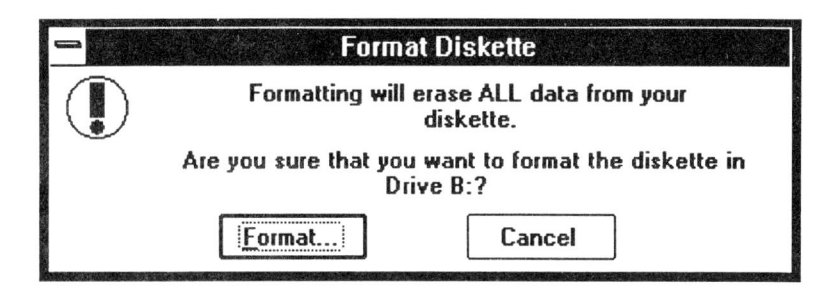

```
┌─────────────────── Format Diskette ───────────────────┐
│                                                        │
│  (!)   Formatting will erase ALL data from your        │
│                         diskette.                      │
│                                                        │
│        Are you sure that you want to format the diskette in │
│                         Drive B:?                      │
│                                                        │
│           [ Format... ]        [ Cancel ]              │
└────────────────────────────────────────────────────────┘
```

Format Warning Message Box

4) Pressing **Enter** then brings up a dialogue box that allows you to choose the kind of disk you want to create. You can select High Capacity, if that is the type of disk you have inserted. (Don't format a standard disk to high capacity, you run the risk of damaging the disk drive and the formatted disk will have a awful lot of bad sectors.) You also have the choice of making a system disk, i.e. one that contains the system files and which can be booted from. Select whichever option you want, using **Tab** and **Space**, and then press **Enter**.

1) Place the disk to be formatted in the drive you want to use.

2) Click on **Disk** in the Menu bar and then on **Format diskette**. Select the drive you are using and then click on **OK**.

3) In the dialogue box that appears make your selection of the type of disk being formatted and then click on **OK**.

As the disk is being formatted you get a running commentary of how far the process has run as a percentage. Once the process is complete you will be asked if you want to format another disk or not.

I had a lot of trouble with this command the first time I tried to use it. Every time I wanted to format a disk in Drive-B, which is 3.5" 1.44 Mb, I got an error message saying that the disk could not be formatted. The odd thing was that the disk would format perfectly using either MS-DOS **FORMAT** or Norton Safe Format. The resulting disk could then be read by Windows and even used to copy files to but I couldn't reformat it. I spent ages trying to solve it and got nowhere. In the end I solved the problem more by luck than by good judgment. I formatted a disk in Drive-A, which is 5.25" 1.22 Mb, and then I found I could also format in Drive-B. Since then it has worked perfectly but I still don't know why it wouldn't work in the first place. I'm not the only who's encountered the problem either. To ensure that it wasn't just the machines at fault, the problem occurred on each of the four machines used for writing this book, I asked a couple of friends to try the command on their machines with exactly the same results. They couldn't format Drive-B until they had formatted at least one disk on Drive-A!

Exercise 7.9
Adding to the Program Manager

You can run programs directly from the File Manager instead of using the Program Manager if you wish. Simply move through the directory structure until you find the program you want, select it and then either press Enter or double click on it. The program will then run.

You can also use the File Manager to add programs to Program Manager - but only if you have a mouse - you cannot do this with the keyboard. This is the only time that you can move a file outside the main Program Manager or File Manager window.

1) Run Windows as normal so that the Program Manager is on screen.

2) Resize the main window by dragging the right hand border into the middle of the screen. The easiest way to do this is to click on the **Control Box**, in the upper left hand corner, of either window and click on **Switch To**. In the dialogue box that appears click on **Tile** and the two windows will be tiled for you. Then press **Shift-F4** to tile all the open windows within the Program Manager.

3) In the main window double click on **File Manager**. Resize this so that it occupies the space beside the Program Manager, as opposite.

4) Open a directory window in File Manager that contains the program or programs you want to add.

5) Select the programs as if you were going to copy them - which is what you're going to do.

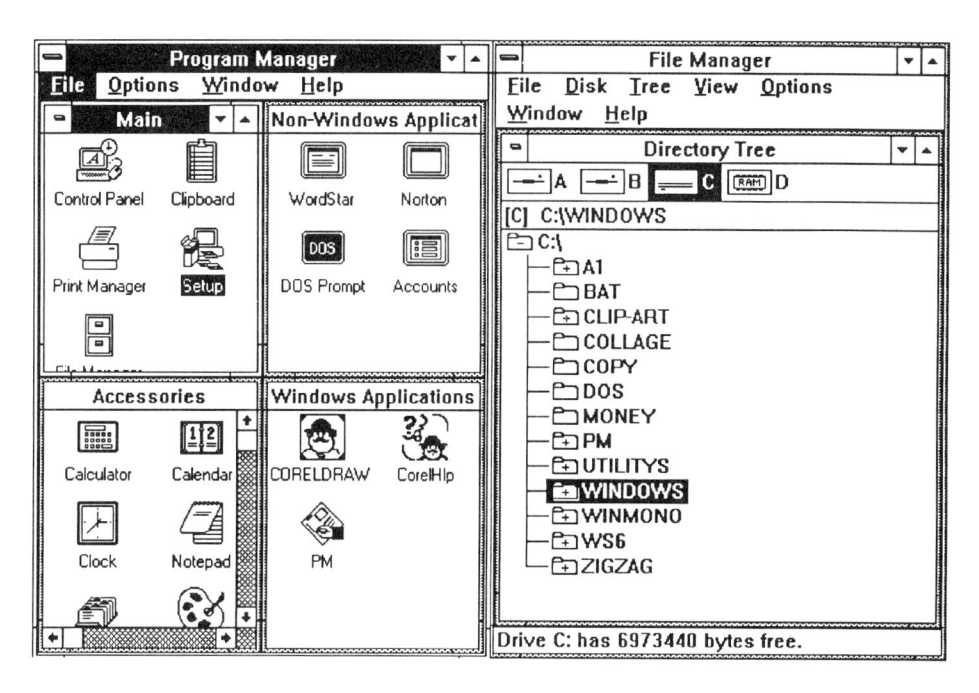

Program Manager and File Manager together

6) Drag the selected file across to the appropriate window in Program Manager. A new icon will appear bearing a label that matches the program name. Carry on doing this until you've got all the programs you want copied across.

7) Reduce the File Manager to an icon by clicking on the **Minimise** button or close it by pressing **Alt-Space C**. Resize and retile the Program Manager window and arrange the contents of the sub-window to your satisfaction. Finally reduce Program Manager down to an icon.

Exercise 7.10
Pruning and Grafting

Windows 3 will allow you to do something that just wasn't possible under any previous versions of the program, Prune and Graft directories. In fact if you wanted to do this you had to have a special utility like PC Tools because there was no simple way to do it under MS-DOS either. Again to do this you really need to use a mouse rather than the keyboard.

1) Close the Windows window using **Ctrl-F4** and you're back to the Directory Tree window.

2) Close all the branches of the directory structure except the Windows directory. (You might find this easier if you maximise the Directory Tree window first.)

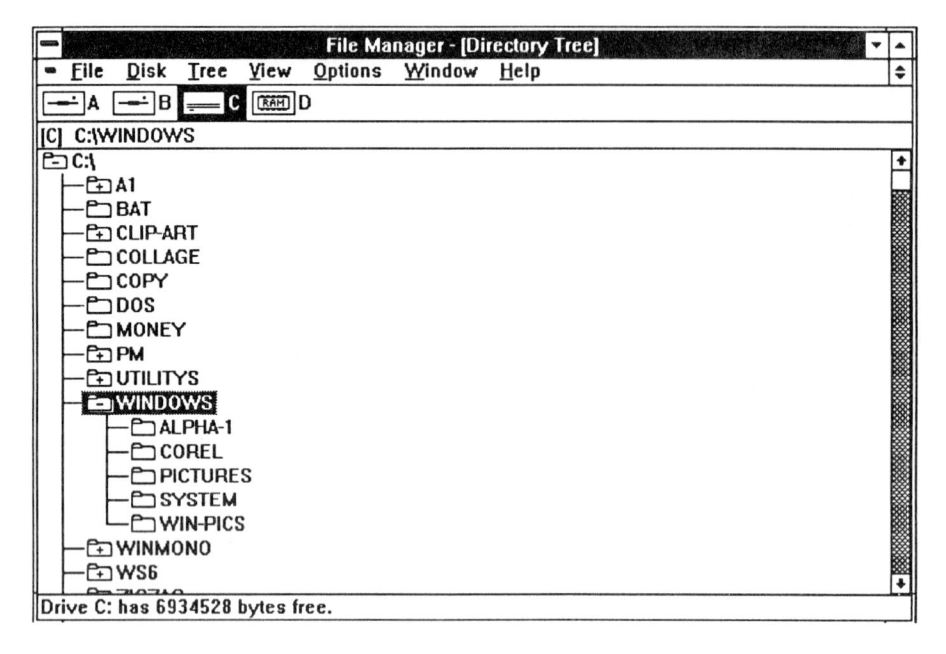

```
┌─                    File Manager - [Directory Tree]              ▼ ▲
│ File  Disk  Tree  View  Options  Window  Help                      ◆
│ [─]A [─]B [═]C [RAM]D
│ [C] C:\WINDOWS
│ ┌─┐C:\                                                              ▲
│    ├─┌+┐A1
│    ├─┌┐BAT
│    ├─┌+┐CLIP-ART
│    ├─┌┐COLLAGE
│    ├─┌┐COPY
│    ├─┌┐DOS
│    ├─┌┐MONEY
│    ├─┌+┐PM
│    ├─┌+┐UTILITYS
│    ├─┌─┐WINDOWS
│    │    ├─┌┐ALPHA-1
│    │    ├─┌┐COREL
│    │    ├─┌┐PICTURES
│    │    ├─┌┐SYSTEM
│    │    └─┌┐WIN-PICS
│    ├─┌+┐WINMONO
│    ├─┌+┐WS6                                                        ▼
│ Drive C: has 6934528 bytes free.
```

Windows branch open

3) Click on **ALPHA-1** to select it, assuming you haven't deleted it yet, and then drag it up until you have highlighted C:\ at the top of the window. Release the mouse button and you get a

message asking if you want to move all the files to this point. Click on **OK**. The sub-directory and all the files it contains will be grafted on to the Root Directory of Drive-C.

4) You will then be asked if you want to remove the sub-tree C:\WINDOWS\ALPHA-1. Click on **OK**. The original sub-directory will be removed. If you answer negatively then the original sub-directory remains in place and you have simply copied it, and its contents, into the Root.

Exercise 7.11
Closing File Manager

To close the File Manager and return to Program Manager, press **Alt-F4**. A dialogue box appears asking you to confirm this. If you click on Save Changes then the Directory Tree window display will appear exactly as you leave the next time you run File Manager. Otherwise it will default to the prior setting.

Summary

- File Manager is a utility program that will allow you to manage the files and directories on your disks quickly and easily.

- The program can be used with the keyboard but it is much easier to use if you combine both keyboard and mouse actions.

- File Manager is such a huge improvement on the old MS-DOS Executive in Windows/286 that it is hard to believe that both programs came from the same company.

Keyboard Summary

Alt-D C	Copy the contents of one floppy disk to another.
Alt-D D	Disconnect from a network drive.
Alt-D F	Format a floppy disk.
Alt-D L	Apply or change a volume label to a disk.
Alt-D M	Copy system files to a preformatted floppy disk.
Alt-D N	Connect to a network drive.
Alt-F A	Associate file extension with particular programs.
Alt-F C	Copy selected files to another directory or disk.
Alt-F D	Delete selected files, sub-directories or icons.
Alt-F E	Create a directory.
Alt-F G	Change file and directory attributes.
Alt-F H	Search the disk to find specific files or groups of files.
Alt-F L	Deselect all the files in a directory.
Alt-F M	Move selected file to another directory or disk.
Alt-F N	Rename selected files or directories.
Alt-F O	Run the selected program.
Alt-F P	Print any file directly.
Alt-F R	Run any program that is available on the PATH.
Alt-F S	Select all the files in a directory.
Alt-F X	Terminate File Manager.
Alt-F4	Terminate File Manager.
Alt-Hyphen C	Close sub-window. Not available on Directory Tree window.
Alt-Hyphen M	Move sub-window within File Manager.
Alt-Hyphen N	Minimise sub-window, i.e. reduce to an icon.
Alt-Hyphen R	Restore icon to sub-window.
Alt-Hyphen S	Resize sub-window.
Alt-Hyphen T	Change to next sub-window in sequence.
Alt-Hyphen X	Maximise sub-window.
Alt-O C	Select what confirmations will be used.
Alt-O L	Change display to lower case only.
Alt-O M	Minimise File Manager when running other programs.
Alt-O S	Toggle Status Bar display.
Alt-Space C	Terminate File Manager.
Alt-Space M	Move File Manager main window.
Alt-Space N	Reduce File Manager main window to an icon.
Alt-Space R	Restore File Manager main window.
Alt-Space S	Reshape main File Manager window.
Alt-Space W	Activate Task Switching.
Alt-Space X	Enlarge File Manager window to fill entire screen area.
Alt-T A	Show entire directory structure of the disk.
Alt-T B	Show all sub-directories and sub-sub-directories of a

	directory.
Alt-T C	Collapse branch display.
Alt-T E	Show sub-directories of a directory.
Alt-V B	Sort file display alphabetically by name.
Alt-V C	Select what type of files and directories will be shown.
Alt-V F	Show full or partial file details.
Alt-V N	Show names of files.
Alt-V O	Show selected file details.
Alt-V R	Limit the number of windows that are displayed.
Alt-V S	Sort file display by selected criteria.
Alt-V T	Sort file display by extension.
Alt-W A	Close all windows except Directory Tree.
Alt-W C	Cascade open windows within File Manager.
Alt-W R	Refresh window display.
Alt-W T	Tile open windows within File Manager.
Ctrl-Esc	Activate Task Switching.
Ctrl-F4	Close sub-window.
Ctrl-F6	Switch to next sub-window in sequence.
Ctrl-*	Show entire directory structure of the disk.
Del	Delete specific selected files, directories and icons.
F5	Refresh window display.
F7	Move selected files to another directory or disk.
F8	Copy selected files to another disk or directory.
Shift-F4	Tile open windows within File Manager.
Shift-F5	Cascade open windows within File Manager.
*	Show all sub-directories and sub-sub-directories of a directory.
+	Expand Directory to show sub-directories.

Chapter 8
Print Manager

What is it?

In the normal course of events, when you want something printed you simply activate the appropriate command within whatever program you are using and that's it. Depending on the program concerned, you may find that your machine is effectively locked up, to a greater or lesser degree, for the duration of the print run. That brings up the first point about printing - it's memory hungry. Whenever you send a document to the printer from an application it does not go straight down the printer cable and into the printer as you might expect. The program concerned has to add the printer commands to the document first. For example, suppose you are printing a document from WordStar to a PCL Printer. (A PCL printer is one that uses Printer Control Language, which was developed by Hewlett-Packard, to describe the fonts, layout and so on. The majority of non-PostScript laser printers use PCL.) The document uses three different fonts, all of the same typeface, in three different sizes. When the document is being prepared for the printer, the application has to find the fonts on your hard disk, download them to the printer so they are ready for use, and then send the details of the pages themselves. All this takes time but more importantly it requires using the processor. This is why you find that you are unable to do certain things as the printing operation is being carried out.

Even if you are using a PostScript printer, there is still a delay while the application generates the appropriate coding regarding the page. (PostScript is actually a computer language, albeit a specialised one, that is used to describe the contents of the page.) If the application makes a mistake in the PostScript code then the printer will, in all likelihood, hangup and generate an error message. A PostScript printer does not normally need to have the different fonts sent to it because there are a number of vector fonts already installed in the printer and it uses those. In fact, if you stick to using the fonts and typefaces supplied with the printer you will find that printing is faster. Even so, the process still takes time and processor power. For instance, when you are printing from WordStar 6 you find that you cannot open a second document or save an existing one until the printing is finished.

All this would limit the primary ability of Windows, the purpose of which is to allow you to have a number of applications running concurrently and to relegate additional functions, such as printing, to the background. So how does Windows get around the problem? It cheats and uses another program to handle the printing - Print Manager. When you send something to the printer from any Windows application it is not sent directly to the printer, instead the application generates a print file which is sent to the Print Manager which then handles the actual printing from that point on. Because the printing is now being controlled by another program, which has been designed to work in the concurrent Windows environment, you can continue to use other applications as if you were not printing anything.

Actually, that's not quite true. Depending on the system resources you have available and the type of machine you are using, you may well find that even using the Print Manager slows down everything else. The file to be printed has to be stored somewhere and it will normally be stored on a Ramdrive, if you have one, or on the hard disk. Whether or not you use a Ramdrive will depend on how much free RAM you have available. By trial and error I found that with a Ramdrive of less than about 1 Mb, the printing process was so cumbersome that it wasn't worth doing, however it has to be said that I tend to generate very large print files. Instead I now use the hard disk as temporary storage and that slows down everything else. Because most applications must access the disk from time to time and because the Print Manager is also doing so, the whole Windows environment slows down considerably when I use the Laser 80386. I cannot measure it accurately but printing from this machine slows Windows down by at least 50%. Everything still works, it's just slower. Mind you, it has to be said that the speed of the hard disk on this machine leaves a lot to be desired and this is the major limiting factor on the speed with which Windows, and thus Print Manager, works. Windows can only work with the resources it has available and if these are in any way below par, then the whole thing is hampered and restrained.

As far as the Samsung 80286 is concerned, I have never bothered trying to print from that after the first time - there just isn't enough in the way of system resources available on that machine to make printing as I'm going along a viable proposition. Instead I found that the best thing to do was leave the printing until I wasn't doing anything else, not even playing Solitaire, and do all the printing necessary at that time. I suspect, but haven't had time or money to verify, that if I increased the amount of RAM on the 80286 to at least 4 Mb then I could get that machine to print just as effectively.

Printing from the 80386SX is no problem whatsoever, but then it has the best system resources. The Ramdrive is used for temporary storage and printing fairly flies along without any particularly noticeable deterioration or slowing of the other Windows programs.

The moral of the story is - when it comes to printing, in particular, the system resources rule, okay.

The Print Manager handles the printing from all Windows based applications, but what about printing from MS-DOS programs from within the Windows environment? Again this depends on the system resources. Theoretically, when you use an MS-DOS program from within Windows, the way that I am using WordStar to write this book for instance, then any printing from that program will be done with the program's own printer drivers as if you were running under MS-DOS and not Windows. However that doesn't quite happen, though it does depend on the program involved.

On the Samsung 80286 and the Laser 80386 printing from WordStar under Windows is impossible. (This is a result of the system resources shortfall and it certainly doesn't apply to all 286 and 386 machines.) There is insufficient memory on both machines to allow printing to occur. Because the Windows environment is still in the background, using memory, there just isn't enough left for the program to print. In WordStar 6 you can find out how much memory you have available. On the Laser 386, which is my base machine, the resulting information from WordStar running within Windows is:

WordStar	173k
Text and data	100k
Messages	25k
Printing	0k
Spelling	71k
Thesaurus	71k
Hyphenation	29k
Total	469k
Unused memory	24k

The same thing running under MS-DOS rather than Windows gives:

WordStar	173k
Text and data	100k
Messages	25k
Printing	0k

Spelling	71k
Thesaurus	71k
Hyphenation	29k
Total	469k
Unused memory	75k

From this you can see that Windows isn't using that much memory, 51 Kb is virtually nothing, but it is sufficient to prevent WordStar from printing when running under Windows. I could play around with the various settings and free enough memory so that I could print but as I also use WordStar from MS-DOS I don't want to. The result is that I'm stuck - if I want to print from WordStar I have to run the program from MS-DOS! Alternatively I could increase the amount of RAM on the machine itself - after all WordStar is a memory hog itself. So why am I using WordStar in the first place? Habit: I've been using the program for so long I don't have to think about it anymore and that makes it very easy to use. Still it has to be said that it is time I changed to something else, WordStar is purely text based and as such it is showing its age. I have just got Ami Professional from Samna and I'll be using that from now on. At least with that I'll be able to print without any hassle - but then the program is designed to run under Windows.

Printing from Windows

When you select Print from any Windows application the program generates a print file and sends this to the Print Manager, providing you have this turned on. If you are not using Print Manager, i.e. you have not turned it on in the Control Panel, then the document to be printed is sent directly to the printer. In that case you will find that the printing takes priority over everything else - you will be unable to use any Windows program, or any MS-DOS program for that matter, until the printing is finished. The reason for using the Print Manager is then apparent - it allows you to carry on using an application while the printing is relegated to the background. As soon as you send a document to be printed the Print Manager icon appears at the bottom of the screen.

You can send a number of files to be printed, even while the first one is still being processed, and these form the Print Queue. This is simply a list of files waiting to be printed. You can check which files are being printed and their order in the queue by selecting Print Manager from the Program Manager and having it appear in a window.

![Print Manager window screenshot showing Options, View, Help menu; Pause, Resume, Delete buttons; message "The PostScript Printer on LPT1 (Local) is Paused"; queue listing PostScript Printer on LPT1 [Paused] with (untitled) 0% of 9K 16:46 24/7/1990, 2 Cardfile - DATA1.CRD 9K 16:47 24/7/1990, 3 PageMaker - MAH-JONG.PM3 16K 16:48 24/7/1990]

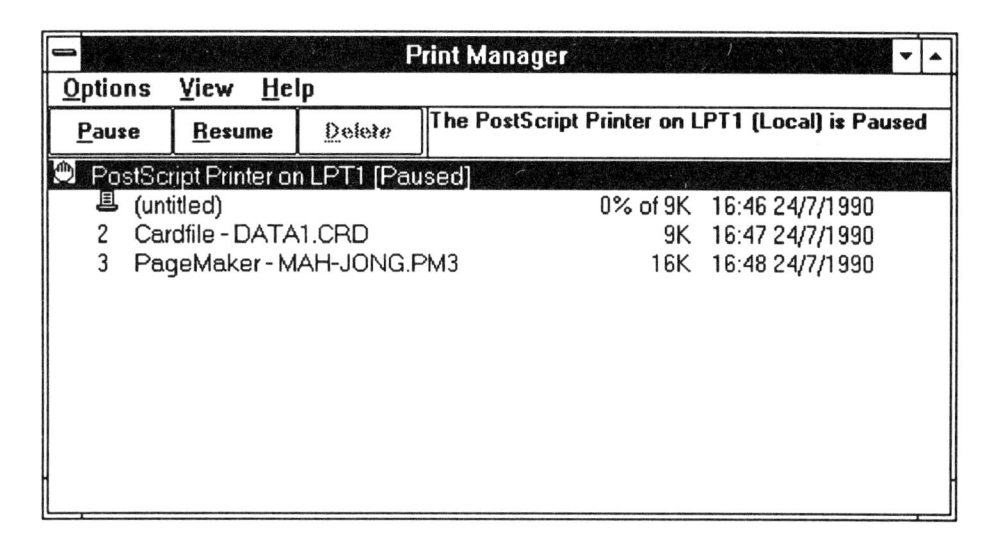

Print Manager

The Print Manager window is much the same as other windows. The top line contains the Control Box, Title Bar, Minimise and Maximise buttons, beneath that is the Menu Bar with three keywords. The difference is on the next line. This contains three buttons and the Message Box:

> **Pause** which is a button that will allow you to temporarily suspend the printing of the highlighted file.
>
> **Resume** is the opposite of the previous button. This will also need to be used if the printer itself has gone off line for some reason, e.g. it runs out of paper.
>
> **Delete** allows you to eliminate a file from the print queue.

The Message Box tells you what printer is currently being used and what its status is.

Immediately below this is the main area of the Print Manager window. This will contain a list of those files that are waiting to be printed. For each file you are also told the associated information as follows:

The position of the file within the print queue. The first file has a little icon of the printer beside it, this tells you that this particular file is in the process of being printed, the others have numbers beside them. You can change the position of any of these numbered files by dragging them around so that they assume a new position within the queue. You cannot however move the file that is being printed.

The originating program, e.g. Cardfile, Write, Notepad, followed by the name of the actual file.

The size of the file is next, expressed in kilobytes, followed by the time and date that the file was sent. The first file, i.e. the one being printed, will also give details of how much of the file has been sent to the printer in percentage terms.

These last details are optional, you can turn them on or off using the View menu.

Print Manager Menus

Print Manager comes with three menus; Options, View and Help. Help provides the customary help facilities that we have now come to expect from Windows 3, it is detailed and extensive if somewhat over anxious to please.

Options Menu

```
Low Priority
√ Medium Priority
  High Priority

  Alert Always
√ Flash if Inactive
  Ignore if Inactive

  Network...

  Exit
```

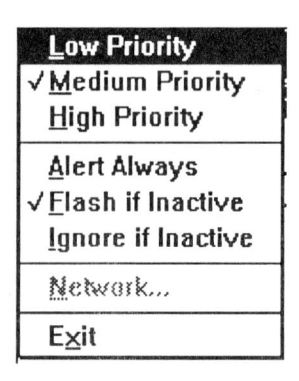

Print Manager Options Menu

The **Options** menu controls the printing speed and how messages appear. The menu is divided into four parts:

The first three lines are concerned with the speed at which the printer is used. The selected speed is shown by having a check mark beside it.

By default, i.e. as it is set when you install Windows 3 in the first place, the Print Manager speed is always set to **Medium Priority**. This means that the Print Manager and any application you also have running share the processor time equally, it produces hard copy output fairly quickly but not as fast as it would if you were printing directly from an MS-DOS application.

Low Priority slows down the Print Manager because it allocates more of the processor's time and resources to applications. This will very effectively slow down the printing, on my StarScript, which can print 8 pages per minute, printer it roughly halves the printing speed.

High Priority does the opposite, it gives precedence to the printing and less processor time to the applications. Using this means that the printer functions at roughly normal printing speed, though it does depend on which application you have running at the time.

The next three lines have to do with the way that Print Manager provides you with fault information, e.g. the printer has gone off line for some reason, that you are required to respond to. These commands do not interfere with system messages, such as Printer Off-line, they are only concerned with direct Print Manager messages.

Always Alert will cause Print Manager messages to pop up on screen, overlaying any other application that might be running, whenever a fault occurs.

Flash if Inactive, the default setting, causes the Print Manager icon to flash and also produces a beep to draw your attention to it. The flashing continues until you enlarge the icon into a window, when the error message will be displayed.

Ignore if Inactive does nothing if the Print Manager is an icon or an inactive window. Only when you engage the Print Manager will you be told of any problems.

The next element concerns network printing and it provides a number of dialogue boxes that affect how the printer runs under the network.

The final element, **Exit,** allows you to terminate the Print Manager window. If you try this when there are documents being printed or waiting to be printed then you will be prompted with a message telling you that all print jobs will be terminated as a result. The message provides you with the option of cancelling the closure or continuing with it.

View Menu

The **View** menu allows you to change the way that information about the files is presented.

```
√ Time/Date Sent
√ Print File Size

  Update Net Queues

  Selected Net Queue...
  Other Net Queue...
```

Print Manager View Menu

Those items which have a check mark beside them are the ones which are active. By default the first two are operable so that you can see the time and date that the file was sent and the size of the file being printed. This latter is always worth having on view because it gives the real file size and as the file is being printed you can see how much more of it there is to be done.

Problems with printing

Print Manager is very effective at what it does but it is not omnipotent and so you may encounter the occasional problem. One of the major difficulties may be nothing to do with Print Manager at all, but may instead be caused by the type of printer you have installed - or rather the emulation you are using.

When I first installed Windows 3 I also installed my StarScript printer as an Apple LaserWriter NTX. After all this is what the printer had run as from Windows/286 and it had worked with no problems. But the first time I tried to print from Windows 3 under this emulation I got an error message on the printer itself. Not being one to go screaming for technical support every time something goes wrong, I played around with the thing and tried the different emulations. Eventually I found that the StarScript would work if it was installed as an Apple LaserWriter Plus and everything has been fine since. The odd thing about this is that I couldn't use this emulation in Windows/286. So the moral is - if you get printer problems and the printer hangs up, try changing the emulation before you do anything else.

While I think of it - before you try to do any printing make sure the printer is turned on. I know it sounds silly but it does happen. A friend of mine, who's a consultant, once earned a rather nice fee fixing someone's system. He had installed the system and checked it thoroughly and everything was fine. The next day the company who had bought it tried to print a document and found that they couldn't. So they rang my friend but he wasn't available, so they went elsewhere. Another consultant then came in, he turned everything off and then rebooted the system. Without any problems he managed to produce a print out and so everything was okay. He got his fee and the company was happy. Come the next morning the system wouldn't print anything again. The guy in charge had a minor fit and then called my friend again. This time he was available and he went right round. He turned everything off and then told the operator to boot up the system. The operator carefully switched everything on except the printer! That's called how to earn a nice fat bonus in one easy lesson.

The point behind both of these stories is that you shouldn't expect all problems to be the fault of Print Manager. Whenever anything goes wrong with a computer system and its peripherals check the bits and pieces first.

>   a) Is the printer turned on?
>   b) Are the cables connected to the right ports?
>   c) Have you installed the printer in the software?
>   d) Is there paper in the printer?
>   e) Is there toner in the printer?

Check all these first and then worry about the software, not before.

If everything with the hardware is okay, check that you have the printer properly configured in the Control Panel. When you install a printer all you are doing is copying the device driver for a particular printer, which has then got to be configured for the actual printer. (See Chapter 5 for details.) Make sure that you have the correct options set and the correct port assigned. If you are using the serial port make sure the settings are right. Having checked all that, if the printer still doesn't print, exit from Windows and try printing from an MS-DOS application. If that works then I suggest that the emulation needs to be changed. If it doesn't work then the fault lies with the printer itself.

Printing from Windows is dependent on a number of factors:

>   a) The printer must be configured correctly in the Control Panel. If it isn't then it just will not work.
>
>   b) You must have selected the correct printer as the default. If you have one printer set as the default and you have used another one for a document then you need to log on to the correct printer or you may get gibberish. This is especially true is you are using a PCL printer by default and a PostScript one for the document you currently want printed.
>
>   c) The fonts you are using must be available to the printer. With a PostScript printer you shouldn't have any problems in this area but with a PCL printer you may have. Have you created the fonts you are trying to use and are they in the correct directory? If not then the printer cannot use them and the resulting printout, if any, will be wrong.

The Windows manual gives a range of possible problems and possible remedies for them. If you are encountering problems and you have tried all of the above then dig out the manual and have a look at that. The printing problems section is on pages 211 to 216.

Summary

- Print Manager controls the printing of Windows applications.

- You can use the Print Manager to allocate how the processor time is allocated to printing and running programs.

- Within the Print Manager you can change the position of files in the queue, delete files and rearrange the print queue.

- Printing is resource hungry, trying to use other programs at the same time may cause problems.

Keyboard Summary

Alt-D	Delete file from print queue.
Alt-F4	Terminate Print Manager.
Alt-O A	Set error message to override applications.
Alt-O F	Set default error message status.
Alt-O H	Set High Priority printing.
Alt-O I	Override Print Manager error messages.
Alt-O L	Set Low Priority printing.
Alt-O M	Set Medium Priority printing.
Alt-O N	Activate network dialogue boxes.
Alt-O X	Terminate Print Manager and all printing.
Alt-P	Pause printing.
Alt-R	Resume printing.
Alt-Space C	Terminate Print Manager and all printing.
Alt-Space M	Move Print Manager window.
Alt-Space N	Reduce Print Manager window to an icon.
Alt-Space R	Restore Print Manager icon to window.
Alt-Space S	Change size and shape of Print Manager window.
Alt-Space X	Enlarge Print Manager to cover entire screen area.
Alt-V O	Alternative network print queue.
Alt-V P	Toggle print file size.
Alt-V S	Selected network print queue.
Alt-V T	Toggle Date and Time stamping of print files.
Alt-V U	Update network print queues.
Ctrl-Esc	Initiate Task Switching.
Del	Delete selected file from print queue.

Chapter 9
Odds and Ends

Clipboard

The Clipboard is a fundamental part of the Windows environment. It is this program that allows you to cut and paste text and graphics from one program to another. Without the Clipboard, Windows would not be half as much use as it is.

Normally you would use the Clipboard without even thinking about it. Whenever you use Copy or Cut on any Windows application program, the selected text or graphic will be copied into the Clipboard ready to be pasted in elsewhere. Up to this point the Clipboard is the same as it was under all earlier versions of Windows. But Clipboard has one huge improvement in Windows 3 - you can save the Clipboard files to the hard disk and then reload them later. Normally any information that is copied into the Clipboard remains there until you copy something else, and then the original contents are lost, but you can now copy things to the Clipboard and write the resulting file to your hard disk where it can be stored ready for use later.

Clipboard has been improved even further though. It is now possible to capture the entire screen or an open window and copy this to the Clipboard. All the illustrations in this book were captured and then stored using this facility. You can even grab shots of the Clipboard containing shots of the Clipboard containing shots of the Clipboard! Clipboard works in full colour, if that is what you are using, and so you can produce very dynamic presentations.

All in all the improvements that Microsoft have made in Clipboard are praiseworthy: I just wish they had gone a little bit further and allowed it to import files directly rather than having to go through an application. For instance it would be nice if the Clipboard could load PCX or BMP files without having to run Paintbrush first and copy the images from there. Still, one cannot have everything - unfortunately.

Within the majority of Windows applications, other than the ones we have already covered and the games, you will find a menu entitled Edit.

This contains a list of commands that will always include the following:

> **Cut** which allows you to copy selected data from the application into the Clipboard and then delete it from the application itself. The data is then held in the Clipboard ready to be pasted back elsewhere.
>
> **Copy** is similar to the above but the data also remains in the application. But because it is also in the Clipboard you can duplicate it as many times as desired or necessary.
>
> **Paste** takes the data from the Clipboard and places it into the application. The data also remains in the Clipboard, until other data is copied or cut to it, so that it can be included as often as necessary.

You can also grab a screen shot and copy this into the Clipboard by pressing **Print Screen**. If you press **Alt-Print Screen** then only the active window or dialogue box will be copied.

The Clipboard can also be run in its own window, rather than just in the background to assist with cutting and pasting.

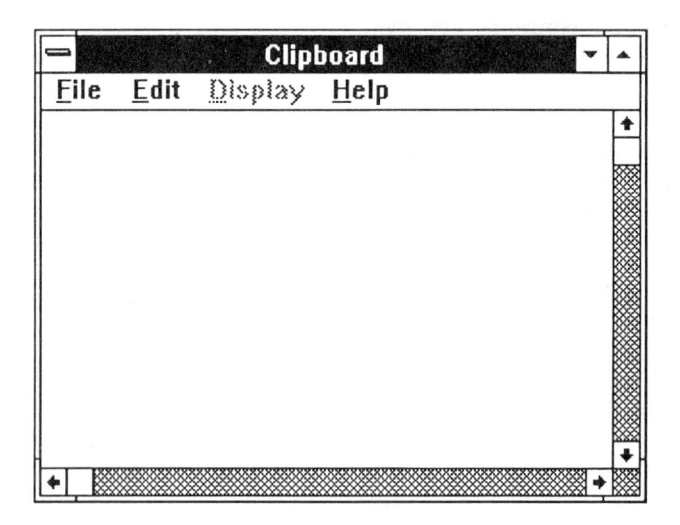

Clipboard

Exercise 9.1
Grab an image

The Clipboard allows you to grab either the entire screen or just the active element, either a window or a dialogue box.

1) From the Program Manager, select Clipboard and then press **Enter**. The Clipboard window will appear on screen. Using the mouse, double click on the Clipboard icon and it will appear. As it first appears the Clipboard window is very small. For the purposes of this exercise you want to enlarge it so that it fills about half of the screen - which half does not matter.

2) Press **Print Screen** and the image of the Windows background, complete with the open Clipboard window will appear in the Clipboard window.

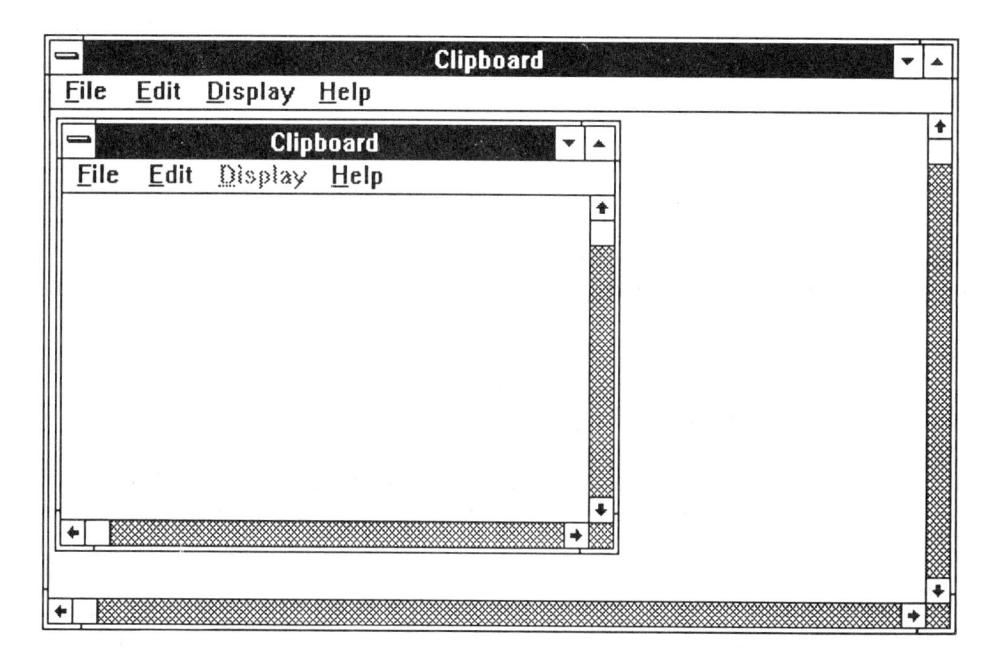

Clipboard in the Clipboard

3) Use the scroll bars to move around the image area. Press **Alt-F A** and a dialogue box appears. This will bear the words DEFAULT.CLP on the first line. Change this to **TEST1**, without any extension and then press **Enter**. The image you have captured will be written to the disk - Clipboard automatically appends the CLP extension - and the dialogue box vanishes.

4) Now press **Alt-E D** and this will clear the Clipboard.

5) Press **Alt-Print Screen** and a new image appears in the Clipboard window. This time it consists only of the Clipboard itself because that is the only active window. Save this as **TEST2**.

6) Reload the original file by pressing **Alt-F O** and then double clicking on, or by entering, TEST1 in the dialogue box that appears. You don't need to add the extension because the Clipboard assumes that you want a CLP file. A message box appears asking if you want to delete the Clipboard contents. Press **Enter** because you do and the first image reappears. You can now paste this into any Windows program that can handle graphic files.

Exercise 9.2
Pasting to MS-DOS

You can also use the Clipboard to paste data into an MS-DOS program that is running in the Windows environment - but it is not so easy as using a Windows program.

1) Get the information you want to paste into the Clipboard using whatever method you wish. Ideally you should save this to the hard disk just to be on the safe side.

2) Run the MS-DOS program, load the file you want to paste the data into and place the cursor where you want the data to be pasted. You should be aware that some MS-DOS programs will not accept graphic files from Windows, for instance you cannot paste a graphic into WordStar.

3) Switch back to Windows by pressing **Alt-Esc**. This will take you directly back to Windows and reduce the MS-DOS program you are using to an icon.

4) Click once on the MS-DOS program icon and the Control Box menu will appear. Within this is the word **Paste**. Click on this and the program resumes its former position and size.

5) The data will be pasted in where the cursor lies. (When I do this in WordStar, on the 386 machine, I have to press a key, which one doesn't matter, before the data appears.)

Clipboard Summary

- Clipboard is a fundamental part of Windows, it is this program that allows you to copy data between others.

- Normally Clipboard is used in the background but you can display it as a window or an icon if you wish.

Clipboard Keyboard Summary

Alt-D A	Toggle Automatic mode.
Alt-D B	Switch to Bitmap mode.
Alt-E D	Clear Clipboard contents
Alt-F A	Save current contetns to a file.
Alt-F O	Load a previously saved Clipboard file.
Alt-F X	Close Clipboard window.
Alt-F4	Terminate Clipboard window.
Alt-H	Activate Help.
Alt-Space C	Close Clipboard.
Alt-Space M	Move window or icon.
Alt-Space N	Reduce window to an icon.
Alt-Space R	Restore icon to a window of former size and shape.
Alt-Space S	Resize window.
Alt-Space W	Activate Task Switching.
Alt-Space X	Maximise window or icon.
Ctrl-Esc	Activate Task Switching.
Del	Clear Clipboard contents.
F1	Activate Help.

Task Switching

In the Control Box of every Windows application the final command is **Switch To...**. This allows you to activate any other already running program, whether it is an icon or a window and whether it is a Windows application or an MS-DOS one. This is one of the major advances of Windows 3 - you can switch from one application to another just by pressing a couple of keys.

When you press **Ctrl-Esc**, which is the shortcut to activating the Task Switching, what happens depends on the type of application you are using. If you are running an MS-DOS program then you find yourself back in Windows proper and the former program is reduced to an icon. If you are running a Windows program then the current window is deactivated. Either way the Task Switching box appears.

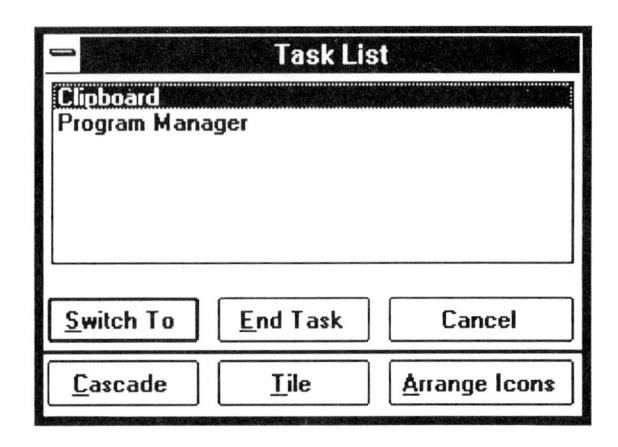

Task Switching Dialogue Box

Within the box you can select any of the programs listed and run this without having to switch to it manually, e.g. by clicking on the window or icon, by clicking on **Switch To**. The selected program will be run for you. If the selected program exists as an icon it will be restored to its former size and shape in the process.

But Task Switching can do more than that. It also allows you to terminate programs directly. By selecting a program and then clicking on **End Task** the program is terminated, and you will be prompted about saving any modified file beforehand.

Clicking on **Cancel** leaves you in the Windows environment but the Task Switching dialogue box vanishes and you can select whatever program you want in the normal way.

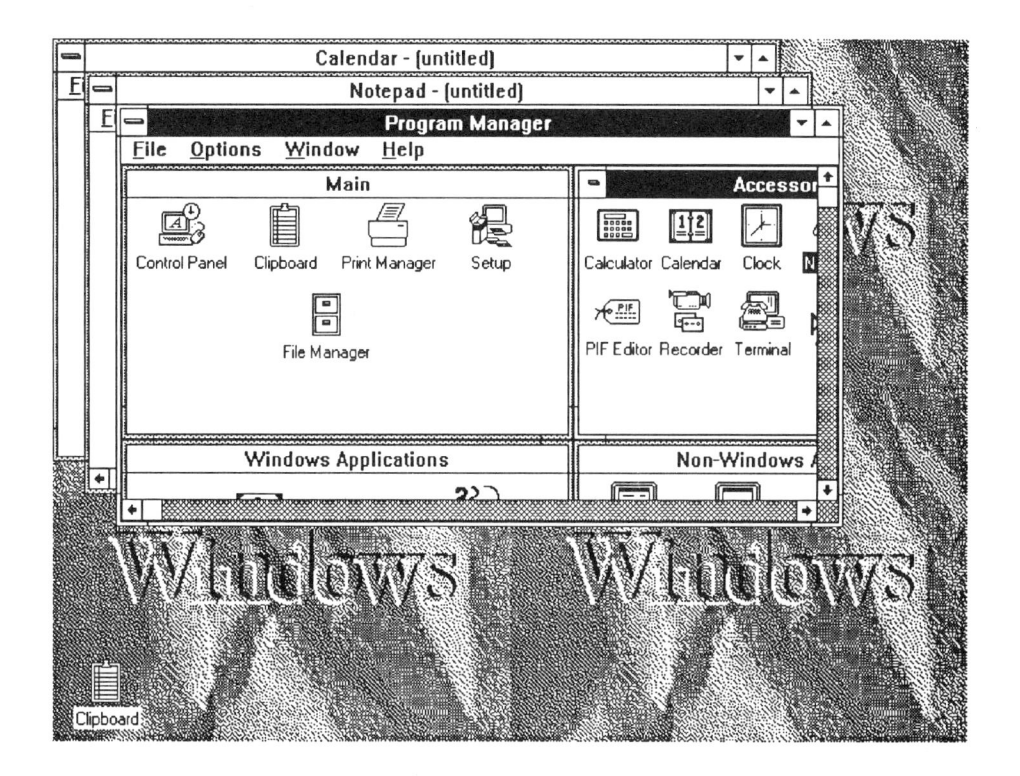

Three Windows Cascaded

The three buttons along the bottom of the dialogue box allow you to arrange open windows and/or icons on the screen. Clicking on **Cascade** will produce a display identical to cascading sub-windows within Program Manager or File Manager except that it is entire windows that are involved. Tile arranges the windows so that they fit into the background. The final option, **Arrange icons**, sorts the program icons into neat lines along the bottom of the screen.

You can also switch directly from one application to another using **Alt-Esc**. When you do this the Task Switching dialogue box does not appear but you move directly to whatever program is next in line. Thus if you had three programs open; Program Manager, Notebook and Calendar in that order, and you were using Notebook and pressed **Alt-Esc** you would find yourself in Calendar - even if this had been an icon. If you press **Alt-Esc** again you will go directly to the Program Manager.

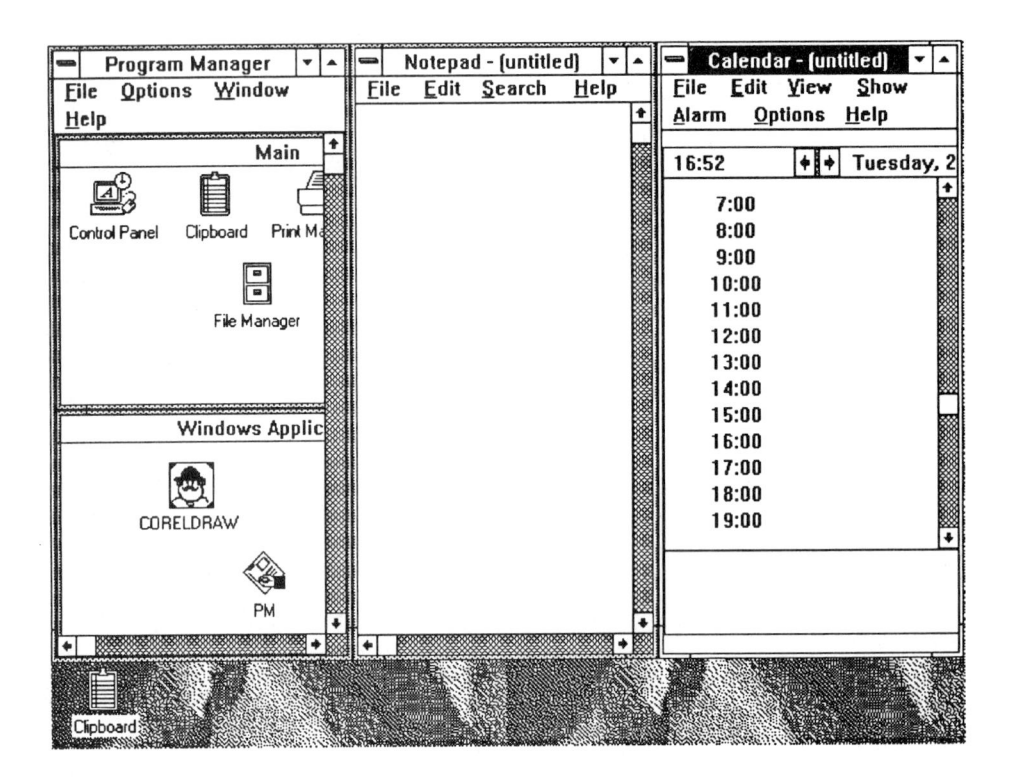

Windows Tiled

DOS Window

As part of the installation routine, Setup automatically creates an icon labelled DOS Window. This is exactly what it says it is, a window back to MS-DOS and the system prompt. This is something entirely new - it has not been available on previous versions of Windows.

When you activate this program what you are doing is running COMMAND.COM - apparently the only application program on the disk with an extension of COM that Windows bothers to look for. The DOS window forces Windows itself to become temporarily memory resident while you return to the system prompt. Once there you can run any standard MS-DOS program as normal, subject only to memory limitations because Windows will be using a chunk of the RAM. Once you have finished you can reinstate Windows by entering **EXIT** at the system prompt.

When you are using MS-DOS in this way you should avoid running any program that changes the File Allocation Tables of the disk, e.g. a compression program or **CHKDSK.**

Chapter 10

Paintbrush

What is it?

Windows Paintbrush is a vast improvement to the Paint program that was available in Windows/286, and it is based on the Zsoft Paintbrush program. The program will allow you to create full colour graphics, or monochrome ones if you prefer, that can then be saved in either PCX or the new Windows BMP format. So what exactly is it? Windows Paintbrush is a painting program, i.e. one that produces bit mapped images. It will allow you to create a graphic and then flood any part of it with a colour or a monochrome pattern. It is not a drawing program - for that you need something like Corel Draw.

Essentially there are two types of graphic programs, Paint programs and Drawing programs. The former produces bit mapped graphic images that tend to be fairly large when stored as files because the file has to contain details of every aspect of the graphic. Drawing programs, on the other hand, tend to be object orientated. This means that instead of keeping a log of what each individual pixel does, the program keeps track of objects by saying 'there is a square measuring x by y positioned at a,b and its colour is black'. Object orientated disk files can be much smaller than bitmap files, but because they tend to be used for much more complex graphics they are generally much larger.

Windows Paintbrush is a wonderful introduction to computer graphics, but don't expect to become a Da Vinci overnight. Curiously enough, many artists who normally work with pen and ink or paint and brush have a lot of difficulty when it comes to computer art, while computer users tend to be the opposite. This is not a hard and fast rule, rather it is a general guideline, but it is valid. My step-father is an artist, and a very good one, but he has no end of problems trying to use a computer based graphic program. The reason he has so much trouble stems from the fact that on the computer the drawing area is very limited and by definition it is flat and thus it is difficult to generate true perspective. Because a line is of one thickness, rather than graduated, you cannot create pictures in proper perspective and if you want to try you have to work with a zoomed in image and create the image almost dot by dot. In other words, if you want to produce a good picture you have to spend a long time doing so, whereas with pen and paper you can do a passable picture in minutes.

The biggest failing of all computer graphic programs, not just Windows Paintbrush, is the inability to produce your colourful graphic as a printed copy, because the majority of people have monochrome printers. Granted you can get inkjet printers which will produce high quality colour images, but they are not common, they tend to be expensive and the printed image rarely matches the screen image. You can print any graphic generated in Windows Paintbrush on a standard printer but, of course, only in black and white. This therefore limits the use of the program. However, you can create wonderfully bright and dynamic pictures and then use them as Wallpaper for the Windows itself, and there is a vast range of Clip-Art available, most of it not copyright, that you can purchase and modify. Any Clip-Art that you want to use with Windows Paintbrush must be in PCX or BMP format, the latter is rather new and so there is not much of it around, but there are literally tens of thousands of PCX images available in a vast range of subjects, styles and content.

Windows Paintbrush is fun. Whatever you do with it, it is fun to produce images and it can be used as the basic program on which to learn to use Windows. It produces tangible results, quickly and easily, but it can also be terribly frustrating. You know what you want to do but actually getting it on screen can be extremely difficult - but don't give up, persevere and your troubles will be rewarded. To run the program select the icon, the most colourful one in the Windows environment, shaped like a painter's palette and double click on it. Paintbrush, more than any other Windows program, must be used with a mouse. Trying to use the program with only the keyboard is an utter nonsense. Throughout this chapter there are no exercises that are keyboard based. If you don't have a mouse and you want to use Paintbrush then I suggest you go and buy one!

Paintbrush Layout

When you run the program for the first time, the window that is activated is rather small and so you should resize it or maximise it to get the full benefit.

The top line of the window contains the usual Control Box, Title Bar, Minimise and Maximise buttons, and beneath this is the Menu Bar.

Down the left hand side of the screen is the Toolbox, which contains icons of the various drawing implements you can use. To select any tool you just click on it.

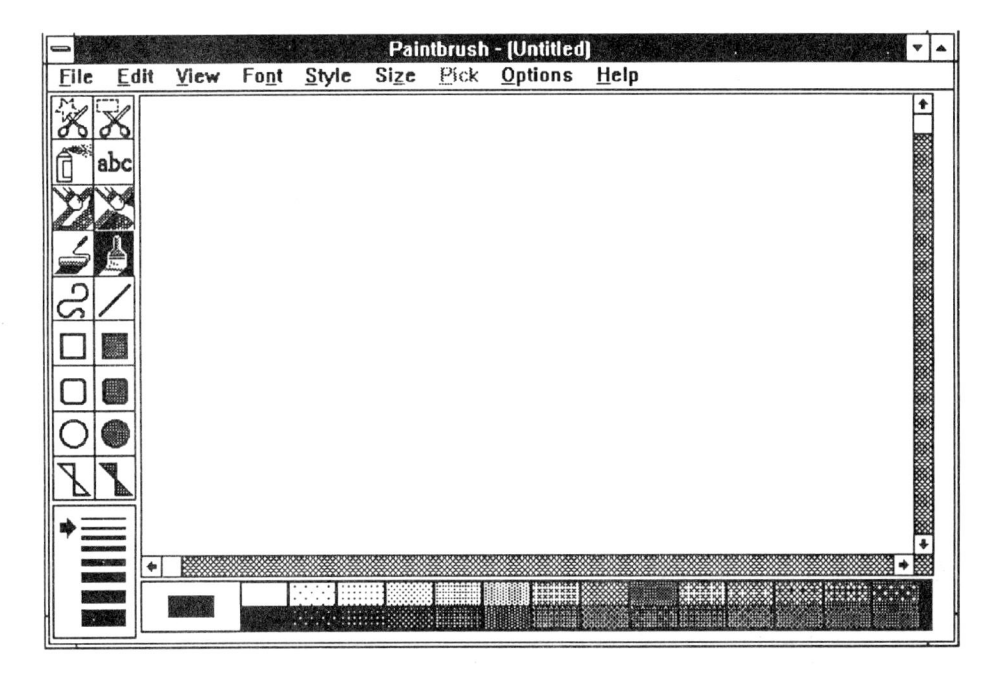

Windows Paintbrush

In a separate box at the lower left hand corner of the window there are a series of lines in different thicknesses - this is the Linesize box. By clicking on any individual line you select the thickness of the line that will be used for drawing.

Across the bottom of the window is the Palette. This contains a series of boxes, each of which contains a separate colour. Only a few of these colours are pure, the majority of them are made up of two or three different colours. To the left of the palette is a rectangular box, coloured white, containing another box, coloured black. These show the current foreground and background colours, the larger area is the background or paper colour, and the small box is the foreground or ink colour. To select a new foreground colour click on one of the boxes in the palette using the left hand button - the colour will appear in the smaller of the two boxes. To change the background colour, click in the palette using the right hand button - the larger box now contains the chosen colour.

The main area of the window is the Drawing Area, i.e. it is here that you produce you picture. The size of the drawing area depends on how much memory you have available: Paintbrush more than most Windows programs is very memory intensive. Normally the drawing area covers the entire available space and more besides, hence the scroll bars within the open window, but if you have only a limited amount of memory then it will be reduced, leaving an unusable border around the drawing area. Whenever you start a new drawing, the foreground and background colours you have set affect how the screen clears. For instance, if you selected Red as the background colour and then start a new drawing, the entire drawing area is coloured red.

Overlying the drawing area is the cursor. The shape of this depends on what tool you have selected, and to a lesser extent the line thickness you have chosen to use. For instance, using the brush tool produces a small square cursor - the size of this is dependent on the line thickness; using the scissors tool produces a cross; using abc, the Text tool, produces a vertical bar.

Exercise 10.1
Changing Colours

Windows Paintbrush makes it very easy to change the ink and paper colours, all you have to do is click on the one you want.

1) Change the background colour to Red by clicking the right hand button on the third box of the top row of the palette. The large area to the left of the palette becomes red.

2) Change the foreground colour to Yellow by clicking the left hand button on the fourth box in the top row of the palette. The small box in to the left of the palette becomes yellow.

3) Now start a new drawing. There are three ways to do this:

a) Click on **File** in the menu bar and then on **New**.

b) Double click on the **Eraser** tool, the one below abc.

c) Press **Ctrl-N**.

A message box appears asking if you want to save the current image, click on **No**. The new drawing area then appears and it is bright red. If you used method (b) the cursor has become an outlined box.

4) Change back to the default colour scheme, click on White with the right hand button and on black with the left hand one. Notice that you do not have to change tool to do this. Just by moving the cursor on to the palette it changes into an arrow. The tool cursor only appears when you are on the drawing area. Double click on the **Eraser** again and you're back to the original layout.

Exercise 10.2
Draw a line

Because the first thing you will want to do is draw something that's what we'll do.

1) Click on the **Brush** tool to select it and then move the cursor onto the drawing area. The cursor becomes a small solid square.

2) Move down to the Line thickness box and click on the top line. The arrowhead within the box moves up to lie beside the line you have just clicked on.

3) Move the cursor back onto the drawing area. The solid square is now smaller than before.

4) Let's do a squiggle. While holding down the left hand button, move the mouse in a figure of eight. The cursor follows your movement and leaves a trail behind it.

5) Release the button and move the mouse again. This time the cursor moves but there is no trail. Any of the Paintbrush tools only becomes active when you press the button, otherwise they are dormant.

6) Click on the fattest line in the Line thickness box and draw another figure of eight. Try each of the line thicknesses in turn.

7) Double click on the **Eraser** again and click on No in the message box that appears. Once the screen has cleared, click on the **Line** tool, the one below the Brush, and select the thinnest line.

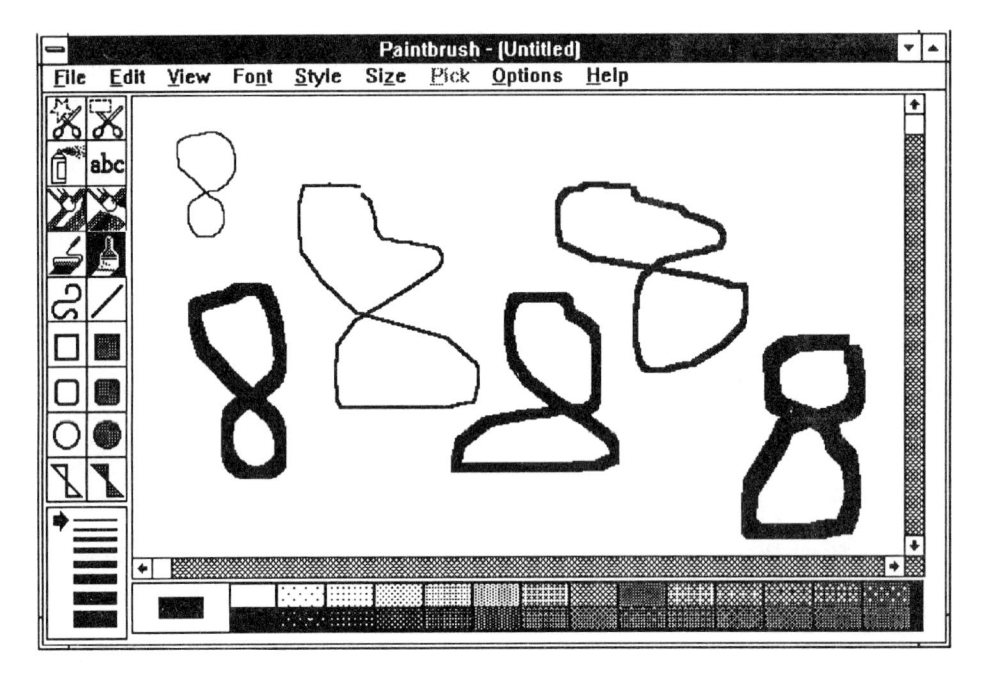

Figures of Eight

8) Move the cursor onto the drawing area, this time it is a thin cross shape, somewhere near the top left hand corner. Click and hold the left hand button and then drag the cursor to the right. You leave a trail behind you, but this time it is not fixed. If you move the mouse up or down the line follows you but remains pivoted on the position you first clicked at. Get the line straight and then release the button. The line now appears on the drawing area.

9) Select the next line thickness and repeat the previous step. Notice as you do so that the line is apparently the same thickness as the previous one. It is not until you release the button that the line assumes the thickness you have selected.

10) Draw a series of lines, one above the other, using all the different thicknesses.

11) Click on the Roller tool and select another foreground colour. Move the cursor onto the drawing area and it becomes a roller with a triangular area beneath it. The Roller allows you to flood an enclosed area with the foreground colour and the paint comes from the tip of the triangular area. Place this over the thickest line and then click the left hand button once. The line is flooded with the ink colour. If you missed the line then the drawing area is flooded.

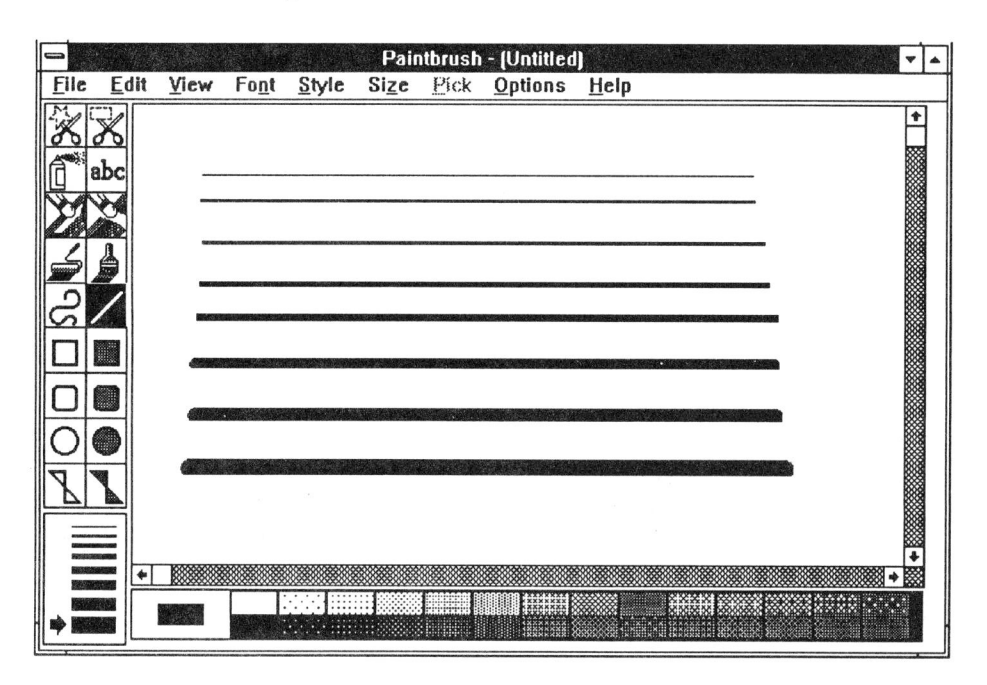

A Stack of Lines

12) Without changing tool, select another foreground colour and flood another line and then do all the other in different colours - but don't change tool.

13) Click on **Edit** in the menu bar and then on **Undo,** or use the shortcut **Alt-Backspace**. All the colours you have just flooded vanish and you are back to black lines on a white background. The Undo facility will undo whatever you have done since you last changed tool.

14) Try flooding the lines again and at some point change to another tool and then back to the Roller. Then press **Alt-**

Backspace again. Only those lines that have been flooded since you changed tool are returned to black.

Exercise 10.3
Boxes and Circles

Windows Paintbrush will allow you to draw simple shapes besides just straight lines and the program provides a total of eight different tools for doing so.

1) Start with a clean drawing area, in black and white, by double clicking on the **Eraser** again.

2) Click on the tool that is shaped like an open square, i.e. the one below the backward S-shape. This produces unfilled quadrilaterals. When you move the cursor onto the drawing area it is again shaped like a thin cross.

3) Select the thinnest line thickness. Place the cursor where you want one corner of the square to be. Click and drag to the diagonally opposite corner until you get a size and shape you are happy with. As you drag the cursor a set of four lines, linked to form a square or rectangle, follows it. Once you release the mouse button the shape is set in place.

4) Draw some more boxes, using the same tool, but with different line thicknesses until you get something like the figure opposite. Notice that each shape overlays previous ones but you can still see the outline of the first ones.

5) Click on the shaded square tool, the one beside the one you have been using. Draw some more shapes. This time you get filled in squares but each one has a white border.

6) Change the background colour to red and the foreground colour to blue. Draw some more. The shapes now have a red border and are filled with blue.

Tip: If you want to draw only pure squares, hold down **Shift** and then click and drag. The Shift key limits the tool so that it can only draw true squares.

Try using the other shaped tools to see how they work. Using Shift with the circle tools will draw pure circles instead of ellipses. The Polygon tools, which look like two triangles touching each other, allow you to draw many sided shapes. To finish the shape and set in place, including any colour or pattern you have set, double click the button at your final position.

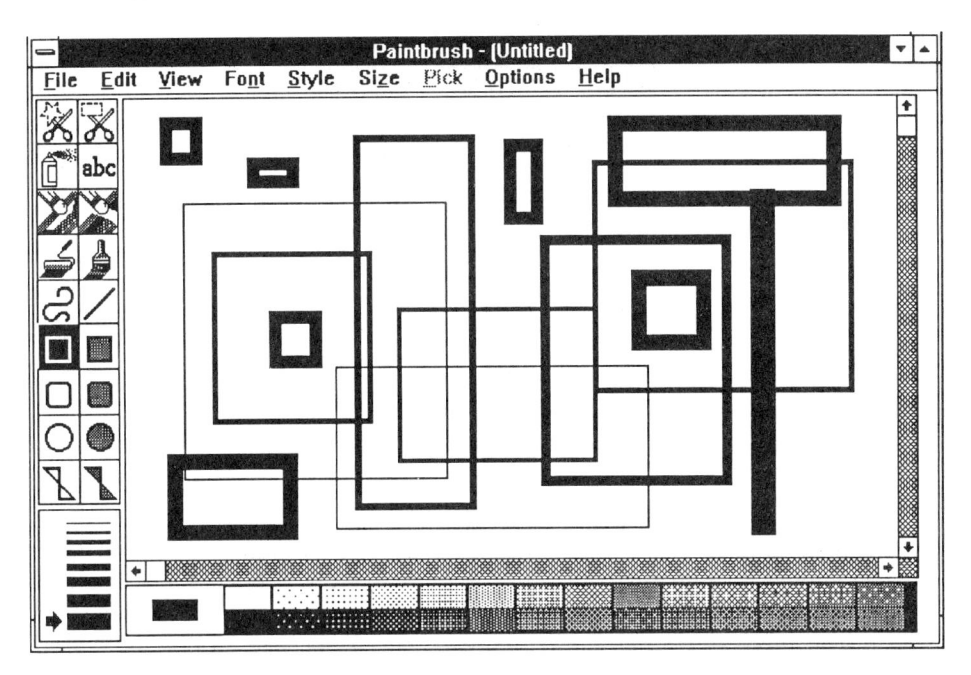

Squares and Rectangles

File Menu

Windows Paintbrush provides eight menus, plus the standard Help one, although three of them are specific to text. The Pick Menu is only active if you have the Pick tool selected, i.e. either of those that looks like a pair of scissors. The first menu is File which is concerned with the loading and saving of files, plus the printer usage. You can open the menu either by clicking on it or by pressing **Alt-F**. The commands it contains are:

New clears the drawing area and presents you with a clean area in which to create your graphics. The colour of the paper will be that which you have selected as the background colour when you activate the command. There are two shortcuts to using this command; either press **Ctrl-N** or double click on the **Eraser** tool. If you have a graphic on screen that has been changed in any way then you will be prompted about saving the file before the screen is cleared. If you want to save the file, click on Yes. You will have to supply a filename if this is a new drawing. If you want to discard the graphic then click on No.

```
New             Ctrl+N
Open...
Save            Ctrl+S
Save As...

Page Setup...
Print...
Printer Setup...

Exit
```

File Menu

Open allows you to load a graphic that already exists on disk. The command brings up a dialogue box, as below, from which you can select the type of graphic and where on your disk it is located. To move though your hard disk directory structure double click on

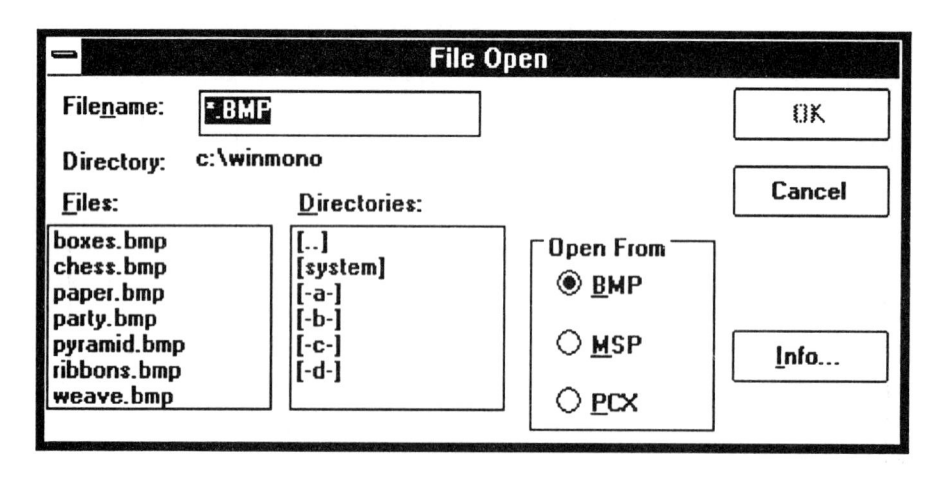

```
                        File Open
Filename:  *.BMP                                      OK
Directory: c:\winmono
Files:          Directories:                          Cancel
boxes.bmp       [..]           ┌Open From─┐
chess.bmp       [system]       │ ● BMP    │
paper.bmp       [-a-]          │          │
party.bmp       [-b-]          │          │
pyramid.bmp     [-c-]          │ ○ MSP    │          Info...
ribbons.bmp     [-d-]          │          │
weave.bmp                      │ ○ PCX    │
                               └──────────┘
```

Open Dialogue Box

the appropriate entry. For example, to move up to the parent of the Windows directory, double click on [..]. If you want to load a file from a floppy disk double click on the appropriate drive letter and the dialogue box contents will change to show what files are available. By default the dialogue box will always show the file type you have selected, e.g. PCX or BMP, and only those files with that extension will be shown in the list box.

Save will write the existing graphic file to your hard disk. The command brings up another dialogue box that allows you to specify which directory or disk you want to save the file to. The command provides a shortcut, **Ctrl-S**. This command should be used for saving any file that has been loaded previously, rather than newly created. You should get into the habit of saving your work often. This applies to any type of document but it is especially true with graphics.

Save As Dialogue Box

Save As is used to write a newly created file to disk. The command pops-up a dialogue box that allows you to specify where on the directory structure the file will be saved to. The dialogue box also contains two buttons which instigate additional dialogue boxes.

Info gives you details of the pictures attributes.

Options allows you to change the format for the graphic, i.e. specify what type of graphic it will be stored as. Before you save

Options Dialogue Box

the file you should select which format you want the graphic to be stored in. Which you chose will affect how large the file is. A rule of thumb is never save a file to a format that contains more colours than the picture does. For example, if you are using a monochrome image then don't save it as a 256-colour bitmap. If you click on **Info** it will tell you how many colours the graphic is using and you should save the file to that format by clicking on the appropriate one. Type a filename in the appropriate line and then press **Enter**. You need not specify an extension because Paintbrush will apply the appropriate one for you.

Page Setup is only necessary if you are using text or if you want to print your graphic. The dialogue box allows you to set the page margins and also provides options for including headers and footers. If you want to use these latter you have to include a code, in upper or lower case, preceded by an ampersand (&) in the appropriate box. The codes are:

```
C ...... Centre text between the margins. This is the default.
D ...... Include the current date set on the computer.
F ...... The current filename of the image.
L ...... Justify text that follows the left margin.
P ...... Include page numbers.
R ...... Justify text that follows the right margin.
T ...... Include the current system time.
```

Paintbrush 261

You can include any of these codes, either singly or in combination, as either headers or footers or both.

Print sends your graphic to the printer, via the Print Manager. The command brings up a dialogue box that allows you to determine which part of the image will be printed and what quality of printing will be used.

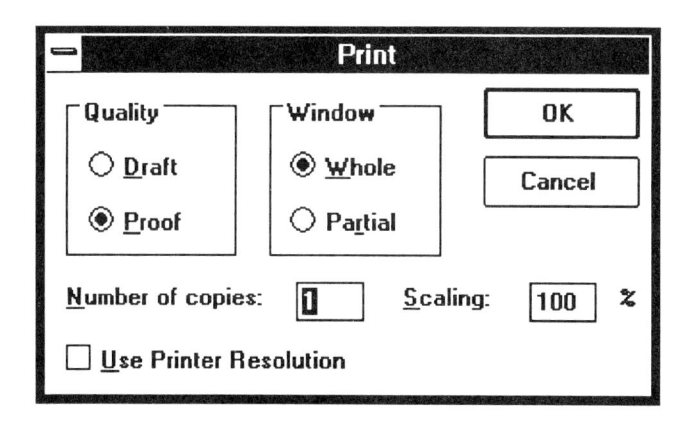

Print Dialogue Box

Printer Setup allows you to select a printer from those you have installed and configured, that the image will be sent to.

Exit terminates Windows Paintbrush. You will be prompted about saving a changed image before the program finally closes and returns you to the Program manager.

Exercise 10.4
Changing format

You can use Paintbrush to turn PCX files into BMP files that can then be used as Wallpaper for your general Windows background.

1) Run Windows Paintbrush and then click on **File** and **Open** in the menu that appears.

2) Change the setting in the dialogue box by clicking on **PCX**. Switch to the correct drive or directory using the list box.

3) Double click on the filename you want and the image is loaded into Paintbrush.

4) Click on **File** and then on **Save As**. Don't press Ctrl-S or that will just save the file back as a PCX file.

5) Click on **Options** in the dialogue box and then select whichever BMP format you want to use.

6) Finally click on **OK** and the image will be saved in the new format. You can then use it as Wallpaper in the Control Panel.

Edit Menu

The Edit menu is used primarily to cut and paste images or parts of images to and from the Clipboard. However Windows Paintbrush also allows you to copy graphics, or parts of them, directly to another file and it will allow you to paste in an image from another graphic directly into the current one. To open the Edit menu, either click on the word or press **Alt-E**.

Undo	Alt+BackSpace
Cut	Shift+Del
Copy	Ctrl+Ins
Paste	Shift+Ins
Copy To...	
Paste From...	

Edit Menu

Undo, which can be activated by pressing **Alt-Backspace,** will revoke whatever you have done with a specific tool since you last changed that tool. Essentially, it provides a failsafe against accidental changes to your graphic. To negate the undo facility change tool whenever you do something that is correct, even if you only click on the current tool in the toolbox.

Cut is only active if you have the Pick tool selected and have used it to outline something. The command, which can be operated using **Shift-Del**, takes the selected image area and removes it to the Clipboard. Once it is there you can then paste the image back in elsewhere. You can use the Undo command to revoke the deletion but the cut element remains in the Clipboard.

Copy is similar to Cut except that the chosen element is copied to the Clipboard but not deleted from the current painting. The command can be activated without using the menu by pressing **Ctrl-Ins**.

Paste is the opposite to Cut and Copy. It allows you to insert the contents of the Clipboard into a graphic. If the Clipboard is empty then the Paste command on the menu will be greyed - telling you it is inoperable. The keyboard shortcut is **Shift-Ins**. The Clipboard retains its contents and so you can paste in the same data a number of times. Whenever you paste something it will always appear at the top left hand corner of the main drawing area window.

Copy To is similar to Save As except that it copies only the selected part of the image to a designated file. You have exactly the same options as you have under Save As.

Paste From is similar to Open but it allows you to incorporate a number of files into one. You cannot select part of another image, it must be the whole file.

View Menu

The View Menu, as you would expect, is concerned with the image of Paintbrush on the screen. **Alt-V** will open the menu or just click on it for it to appear.

Zoom In, the keyboard shortcut is **Ctrl-Z**, is the magnification component of Windows Paintbrush. Unfortunately there is only one magnification available. When you activate the command a selector box, a grey rectangle, appears on screen. Move this to the area you want to enlarge, click the left hand button and the area will be enlarged for you.

264 Windows 3 - A User's Guide

Zoom In	Ctrl+Z
Zoom Out	Ctrl+O
View Picture	Ctrl+C
√ Tools and Linesize	
√ Palette	
Cursor Position	

Ziew Menu

When you have enlarged an area there are only two tools that you can use - the Roller and the Paintbrush. The Roller works just as normal, but the Paintbrush is slightly different. Clicking the left hand button uses the foreground colour, the right hand button uses the background one. The areas that are affected when you are using Zoom can only be one colour.

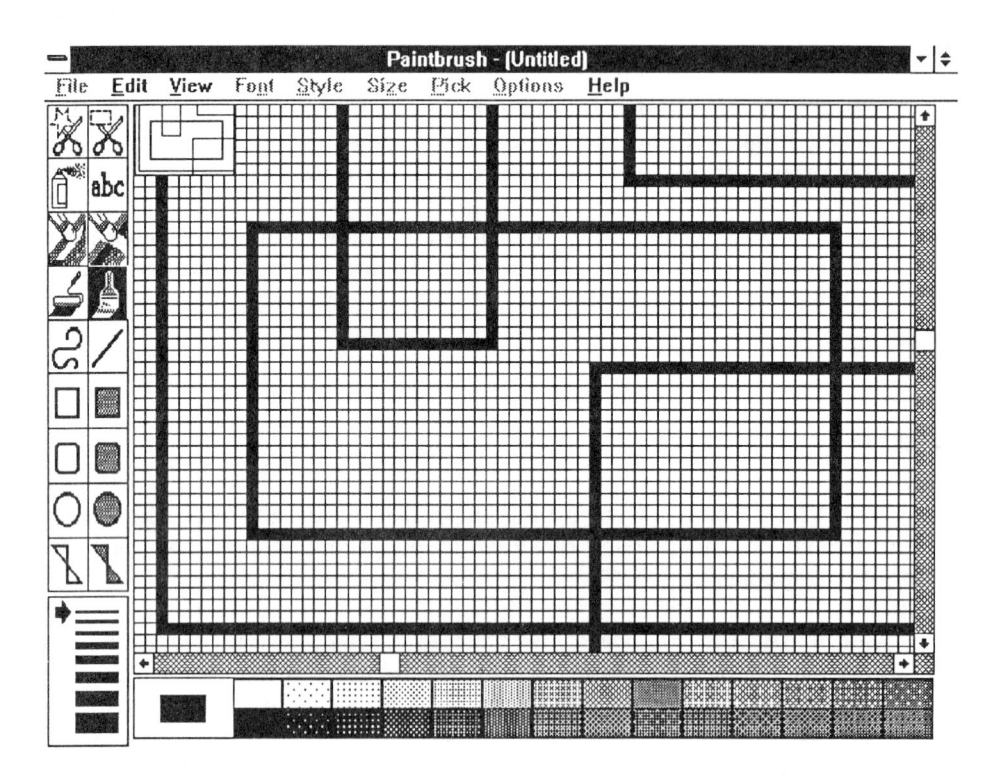

Area Enlarged

Zoom Out is the opposite of the previous command. It will take you from the magnified image back to the original drawing area size. The keyboard shortcut is **Ctrl-O**. However you can also use the command to zoom out from the drawing area - the result is that you get most of the page visible on screen. If you do this then you have to use **Ctrl-Z** to get back to the normal view.

View Picture, the shortcut is **Ctrl-C**, shows the page without having the Paintbrush window in the way. The entire screen fills with a white area against which your picture is shown. To get back to the Paintbrush window press any key.

Tools and Linesize is a toggle and it controls whether or not these are shown. By default they are always On, i.e. they have a check mark beside them. If you turn them off then you have to turn them on again before you can change either option.

Palette is also a toggle that controls whether or not the Palette is visible.

Cursor Position, which is also a toggle, produces a mini-window that gives the coordinates for the cursor at all time. It is very useful if you want to produce images that contain precisely aligned elements. By default it is Off. You can move or reposition the mini-window around anywhere outside the main drawing area: simply drag it to where you want it to be. To remove the cursor position window, either click on its own Control Box and then on **Exit** or toggle it again in the View menu. Alternatively make it the active window and then press **Alt-F4**.

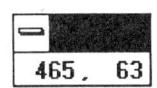

Cursor Position

Text menus

The next three menus are all related to each other and their actions apply only to text with the abc tool active.

Font allows you to select any of the installed typefaces. The current one is shown by having a check mark beside it. By default this is always System.

The **Style** menu allows you to apply different effects. By default the selection is Normal but you can change this in a number of ways:

Bold, the shortcut is **Ctrl-B**, produces thicker, denser characters.

Italic, for which the shortcut is **Ctrl-I**, makes the top of characters slope to the right.

Underline, the keyboard shortcut is **Ctrl-U**, places a solid line under all characters, including spaces.

These previous three characteristics can be applied individually or in any combination. To remove all effects click on **Normal**.

Outline produces characters in outline form only. These might be hard to see unless you have increased their size.

Shadow places a thin shadow, in the background colour, around the characters. Therefore if you are using a white background the shadow doesn't show up!

Outline and Shadow are mutually exclusive - you can use one but not both.

The **Size** menu allows you to change the point size of the characters according to the typeface you are using. Some typefaces can be used only in specific sizes.

When you select the Text tool, click on the Drawing area where you want the text to start. Then just type it on the keyboard and it will appear in whatever typeface, effect and size is currently active. Provided you don't do anything else, including clicking on the scroll bars, you can apply any typefaces, style, size and colours to the text you have just written. The text will not be fixed in place until you change tool or click on the scroll bars.

It has to be said that Windows Paintbrush does not handle text very well - certainly nowhere near as well as Corel Draw does. When you enter some text it may not all appear in the Drawing Area, especially if you enlarge the point size. However, is it still all there. But once you fix it in place, e.g. by changing to another tool, any text that is not visible in the Drawing Area is lost irretrievably. In addition, once the text has been fixed in position it cannot be altered - it becomes part of the painting and has to be treated as such. Thus you can rub it out or flood it with different colours but you cannot change the size, style or typeface.

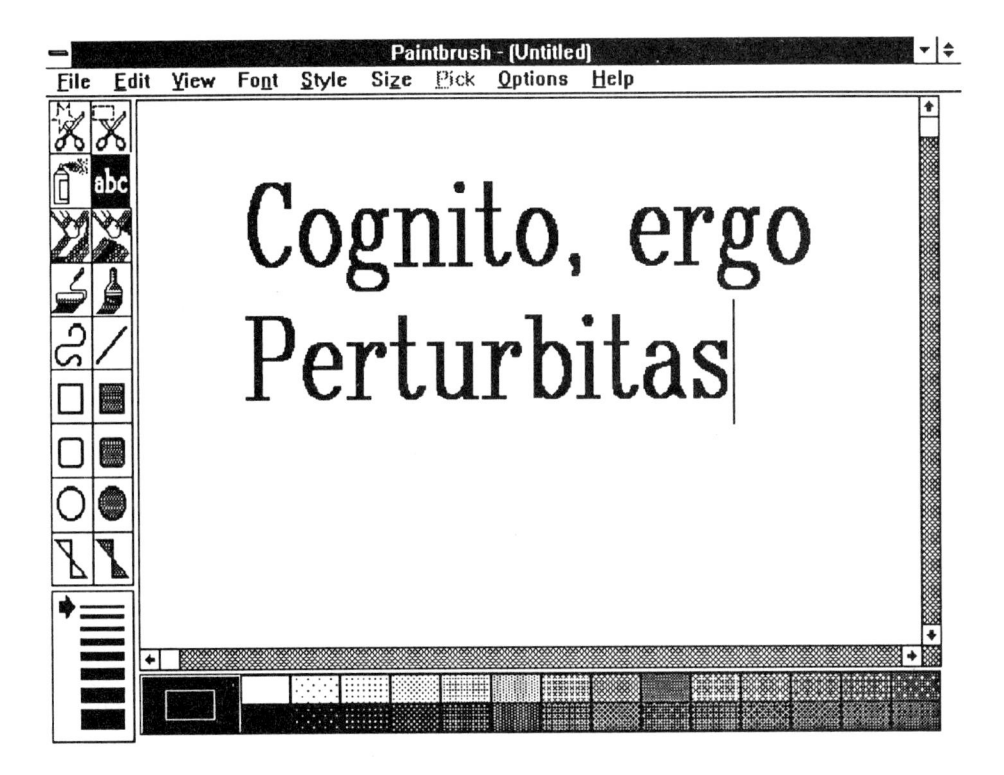

Text (I think, therefore I am confused!)

Pick Menu

This menu is only active if you have already selected and used one of the Pick tools, the ones represented by a pair of scissors. When you select a Pick tool you use it to contain an area of the image, in the same way that you draw a box, and once you have released the button this menu becomes active. The command it contains control the Pick effects.

Flip Horizontally turns your selected area around a vertical axis so that the left hand side becomes the right and vice versa.

Flip Vertically rotates the selected area around a horizontal axis so that the top becomes the bottom and the bottom becomes the top.

Inverse changes the colours of the selected area. This should turn colours into their complements, i.e. blue into yellow, red into green and vice versa, but it doesn't quite work as you would expect. Blue becomes Ochre, Red becomes a dirty Cyan, Yellow becomes dull purple and Green becomes a dark Magenta. What seems to be happening is that the colours are being inverted but so is their brightness, thus dark colours become bright and vice versa.

Shrink and Grow is a toggle, which remains active until you deselect it. What it allows you to do is change the size and shape of the selected item - as many times as you wish until you deselect the command. Thus you can pick a square, for example, and produce as many distorted quadrilaterals you want. The original item you selected remains in place.

Tilt allows you to angle the selected object any way you wish. When you use this command, either the top of bottom of the object stays in place and the remainder is other object it tilted according to how you move the mouse - producing a parallelogram shape. Again the command is a toggle and so remains active until it is deselected.

Clear applies to the original selected area. If you select this command the original picked area comes back to the forefront, anything you have done with the other commands remains in place, and you can then do what you want with it.

Options Menu

The Options menu provides a range of control devices for use within Paintbrush.

Image Attributes allows you to change the size of the default drawing area. By default, the first time you run the program, the dialogue box that appears will contain a size that is based on the amount of memory and the type of monitor you have. You can adjust this up or down, within limits. The three units of measurement are Inches, Centimetres or Pixels. As you change from one to another so the values in the Width and Height box adjust themselves. The settings you make here become the new defaults. Until you start a new graphic or restart Paintbrush the settings do not come into effect. Thereafter, every time you use Paintbrush these settings will be used.

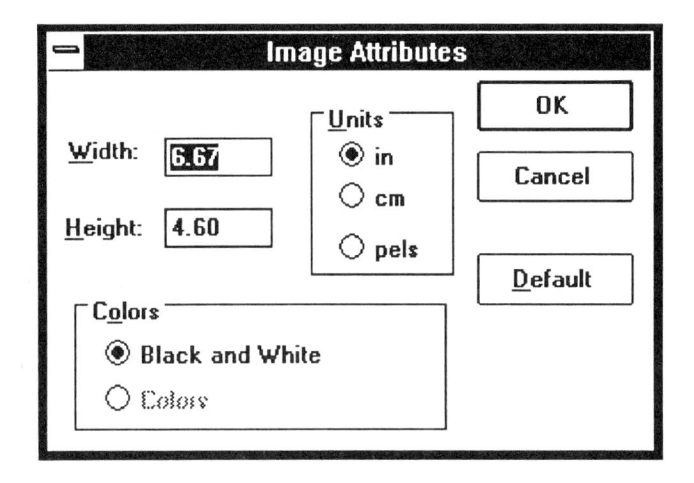

Image Attributes Dialogue Box

Brush Shapes brings up a dialogue box from which you can select the shape of the brush you will use. The brush shape has an effect on most of the tools you will use for drawing.

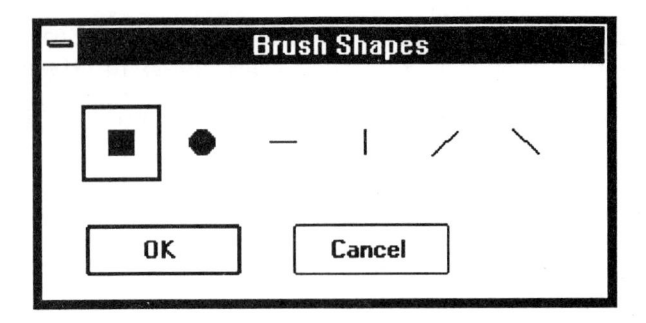

Brush Shapes Dialogue Box

Edit Colours allows you to create your own custom colours - although the colours that appear are very dependent on the type of monitor you are using. You can change the three basic colours, Red, Green and Blue, in single steps from 0 to 255. Theoretically therefore you could have 16,581,375 different colours but there isn't a monitor available that is capable of showing these. Come to that, the human eye couldn't distinguish them anyway. The colour you change is the one that is currently selected as the foreground colour. Paintbrush remembers what the default colour scheme is and so you can reset any custom colour back to the original at any time.

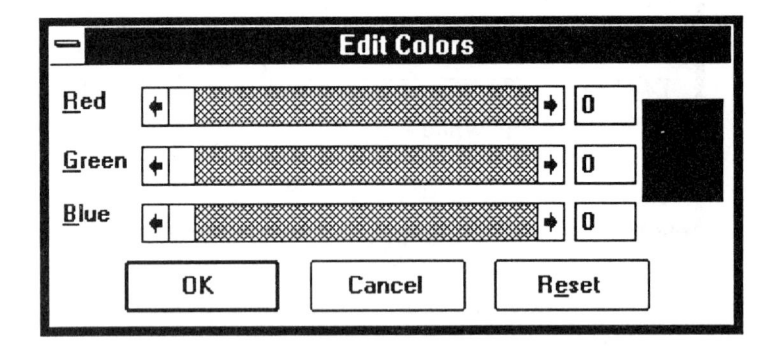

Edit Colours Dialogue Box

Get Colours allows you to reload a palette of previously saved colours. Until you create such a thing there isn't one!

Save Colours will allow you to save a palette of colours onto the disk so that they can be loaded back later. It is worth spending some time designing a number of custom palettes and saving them because you can use any number of different palettes in any one graphic.

Paintbrush Tools

Paintbrush provides a total of twelve tools: there are eighteen shown on the Toolbox but some of these are merely filled and unfilled aspects of the same thing. Reading from left to right and top to bottom of the Toolbox, the tools available are:

Scissors or polygon Pick, the tool that looks like a pair of scissors with a star above it. This allows you to mark out irregular shapes for use with the Clipboard or with the Pick menu. To use the tool select it and then click at the point you want to begin shaping the cutout. Drag the cursor around the shape you want until you eventually arrive back at your starting point. Release the mouse button and the area you have just delineated will be shown by a dashed line.

Square Pick, the one that looks like a pair of scissors with a rectangle above them. This tool is similar to the above but it only allows you to select rectangular areas. Select the tool by clicking on it and then click where you want one corner, normally the upper right hand one, of the selected area to be. Drag the cursor to the diagonally opposite corner. Release the button and the area is selected. You can now use the Clipboard and/or the Pick menu.

Airbrush, the one that looks like a spray can. (Hopefully it is CFC free!) This tool produces a random scattering of dots in the foreground colour. The size of the area that these dots cover depends on what thickness of line you are using. The sprayed area is always round. To use the tool, select it and the colour you want to spray with. Position the cursor and then click and hold the left hand button. A series of dots appears but nothing else happens until you move the cursor. Actually, the tool is not very good - the one in PC Paintbrush is much better.

Text, shown as abc, allows you to place text into the graphic as we've already mentioned. How the text appears depends on the settings you have made in the three text menus. You can make changes to the text only until you click on the scroll bars or on the drawing area. Once you perform either of these actions the text is frozen in place as a graphic and cannot be changed using the text tool.

Colour Eraser, the one below the spray can, allows you to change one colour into another. The colour shown in the foreground box will be changed into the colour shown in the background box. Thus if you wanted to change red into blue, you select red as the foreground and blue as the background. When you select this tool the cursor appears as an open box, and you can change the size of this by varying the line thickness. To use the tool, select the colours and then drag the cursor over the area that contains the colour you want to change. Be warned: some of the colours in the palette consist of multiple colours, for instance the colour shown in the last box, the right hand one, on the top row is made up of Red, White and Yellow. As a result using the colour eraser can produce some odd changes that you were not expecting.

Tip: If you change every occurrence of a colour in a graphic to another colour then do this. Select the colour you want to change as the foreground colour and the colour you want it to become as the background colour. Now, double click on the Colour Eraser and every occurrence of the foreground colour will be changed automatically, without you having to drag the tool across the graphic.

Eraser, the one below abc, rubs out things in the background colour. It size is adjusted by using the line thickness box.

Roller, shaped appropriately, allows you to flood an enclosed area with the current foreground colour. The area to be flooded must be enclosed, or bounded, in some way otherwise the colour leaks out all over the place. A bounded area can consist of a single line. When you flood an area, only those parts of the area that are the same colour and touching each other will be flooded. The flooding will only fill the area that is in the colour of the point at which you position the apex of the triangle. For example, if you have a yellow filled rectangle with a blue border and you then change the foreground colour to red, when you position the roller tool so that the tip of the triangle is touching the yellow area, then all the yellow will become red. If you are touching the blue area then that becomes red. If you missed the rectangle completely, then the entire background area, that is not blocked off by other lines or shapes, will be flooded.

Brush allows you to draw freehand lines, of the thickness that is set in the linesize box, in the foreground colour. To use the tool drag the cursor across the drawing area and the line follows you.

Curve, it looks like a backwards S, allows you to draw a straight line and then bend it in two different directions. The line will be the current thickness and colour. To use the tool, click at the starting point of the line and then drag the cursor to the ending point. Release the button and the beginning and end of the line are anchored in place. The line contains two points, which are invisible unfortunately and which lie somewhere on the line, that allow you to distort the line. Move the cursor onto the line and then click and drag, as you do so the line will move to follow your actions. When you are satisfied with the curve release the mouse button. Now move the other point in the same way. It is not until you have moved both points that the line actually becomes fixed in its colour and thickness. This description sounds complex, but using the tool is not as difficult as it sounds.

Line, shown as a diagonal line, allows you to draw straight lines of the current foreground colour and thickness. To use the tool click at the point where you want the line to begin and then drag the cursor to where you want the line to end. Releasing the button fixes the line in place.

Rectangle, shown as an unfilled box, will draw a quadrilateral using the current colour and thickness as the border of the box. To use the tool, click at the point where you want one corner to be and then drag the cursor to the diagonally opposite corner. Releasing the button fixes the rectangle in place. You can force the tool to draw squares by holding down **Shift** while you are dragging.

Filled Rectangle is similar to the above but it produces rectangles that are filled with the current foreground colour and bordered with the current background colour. You can limit this tool to drawing squares by holding down **Shift** while dragging the cursor.

Rounded Cornered Box, immediately below the Rectangle tool, draws boxes which have rounded corners. (What a surprise!) The border of the box will be coloured with the foreground colour. You use the tool in exactly the same way as the Rectangular one. Unfortunately there is no way to change the aspect of the rounded corners - you will have to make do with what the tool provides.

Again you can limit the action of the tool by holding **Shift** while dragging.

Filled Rounded Cornered Box, identical to filled rectangle but with rounded corners.

Ellipse, shown as an unfilled circle, produces ellipses or circles in the current foreground colour, the border of which is in the currently selected line thickness. To use the tool click at the point that is the imaginary rectangle containing the ellipse. Then drag the cursor to the diagonally opposite corner of this imaginary box. You can force the tool to produce circles only by holding down **Shift** while you drag the cursor.

Filled Ellipse is identical to the above except that the circles are drawn with a border of the current background colour and then filled with the current foreground colour.

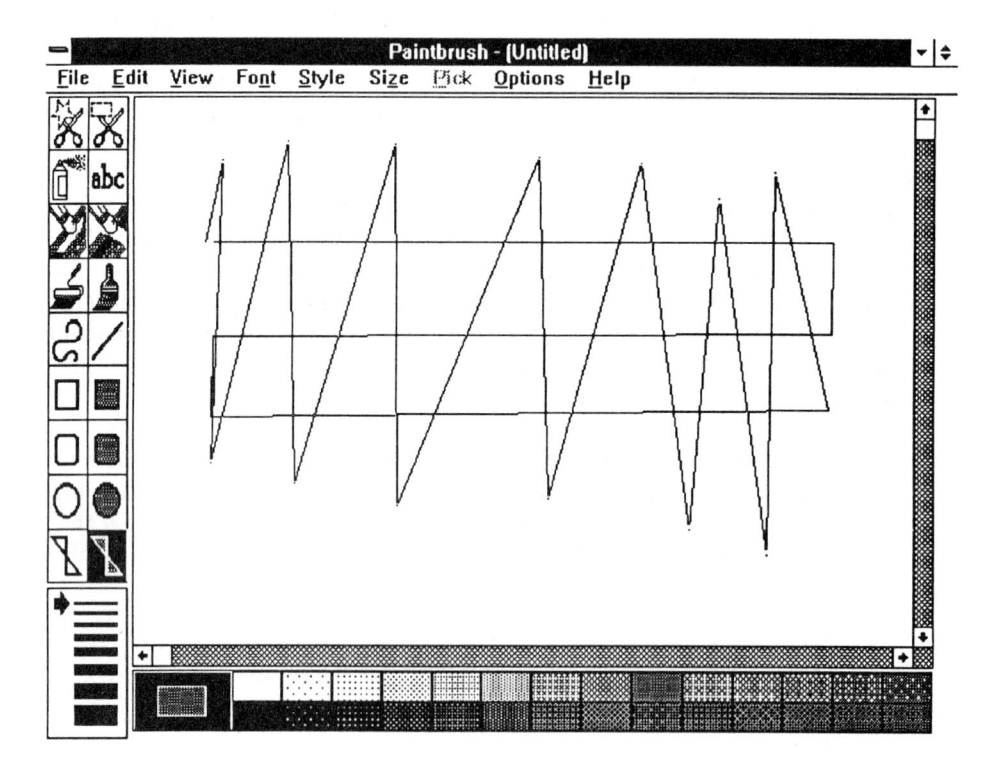

Polygon

Paintbrush

Polygon, shown as two triangles joined at their apexes, allows you to draw multi-sided shapes. To use the tool, click at the point where you want the shape to start, drag the cursor to the end of the first line - just as if you were using the Line tool - and release the button. Now move the cursor to the end point of the next line, click once and a line from the last point to your current position appears. Move the cursor and click at the next position and so on. When you want to finish the polygon double click and a line appears from your last position back to the starting point. You can force the tool to produce only straight lines, i.e. horizontal, vertical or diagonal at 45 degrees, by holding down **Shift**.

Filled Polygon works in exactly the same way as above except that the line will be drawn in the background colour and the resulting shape will be filled with the foreground one. When you finally double click the areas that are filled in are those that are totally contained:

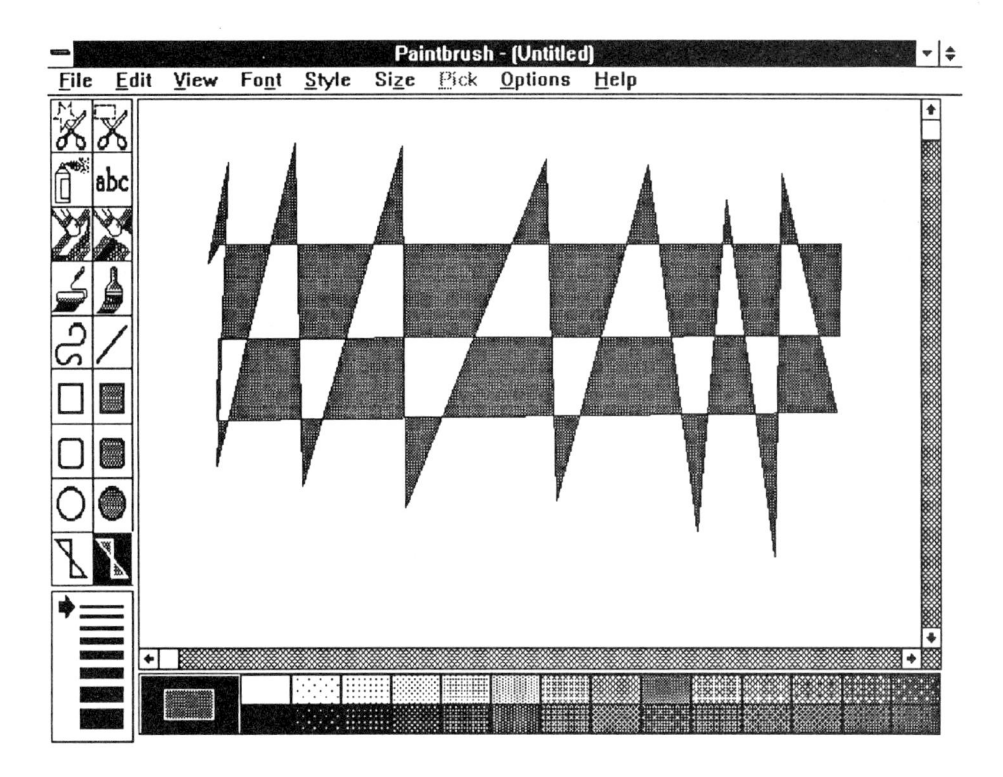

Polygon - Filled

Exercise 10.5
Pick a Piece

When you use the Pick tool you can do much more than just cut and paste or flip the selected part of your drawing. You can use the tool to create special effects that can produce very interesting images. The figures in this exercise are all pieces of Shareware Clip-Art, just to give an example of what is available in this area. And because I can't draw!

1) Create a drawing of something, it doesn't matter what. Then select the **Square Pick** tool and mark out an area. I've used a picture of a Elephant because it's a decent size and shape to begin with. The entire animal is enclosed in the Pick box.

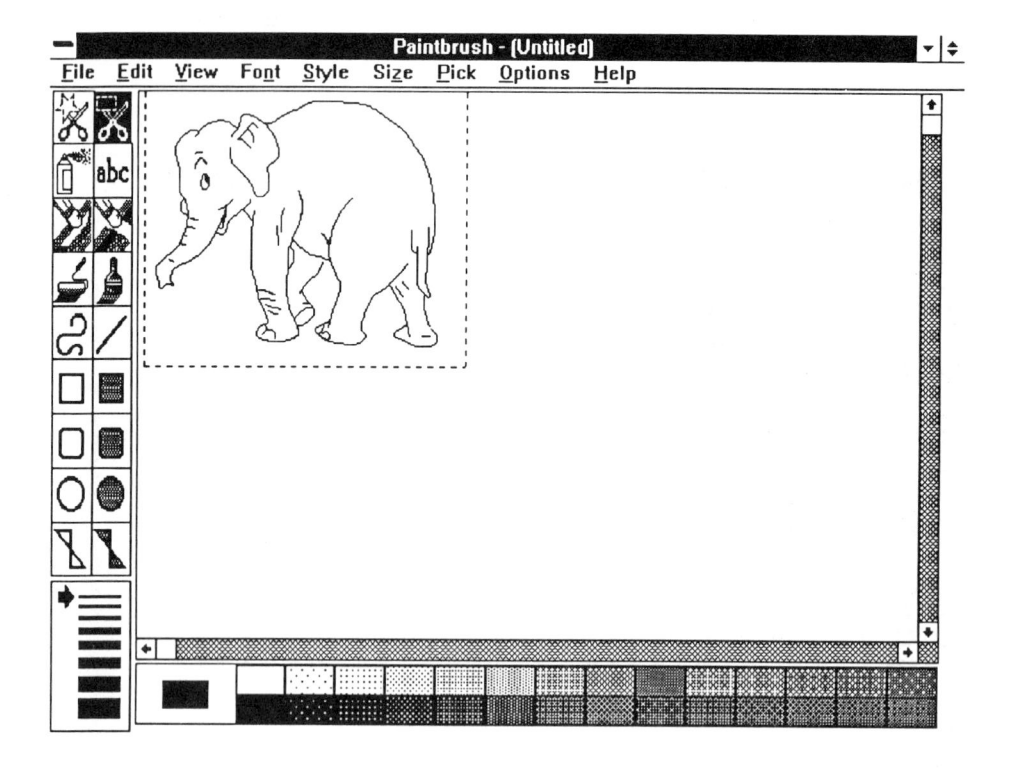

The Original Elephant

2) Copy the selected area into the Clipboard by pressing **Ctrl-Ins**.

3) Click on the **Pick** menu and then on **Shrink and Grow**. The Pick box around your selected area vanishes but the cursor remains the same.

4) Click and drag a rectangular box elsewhere on the drawing area. When you release the button your selected part of the image is placed into the box you have just outlined. The image is distorted to make it fit the box you drew. The Shrink and Grow command remains active until you deselect it and so you can reproduce as many different sized copies of your original area as you want.

Three Elephants

5) You can do other things with the Pick though - like drag the selected object to make sweeps of it. Outline an object with the Pick tool or import one via the **Paste From** command in the Edit menu.

278 *Windows 3 - A User's Guide*

6) Move the cursor inside the boxed area, hold down **Ctrl** and then drag the cursor around the screen. The selected image area now acts as a giant brush that uses the colours and shape of the area you have selected.

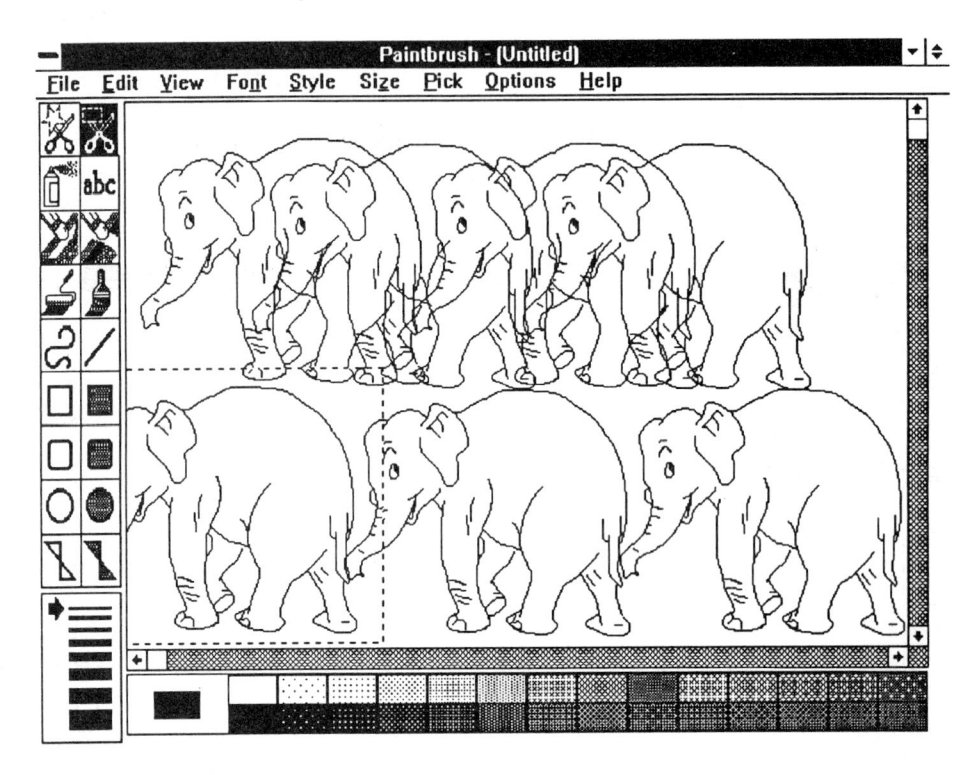

Sweep of Elephants

Exercise 10.6
Print a Picture

Windows Paintbrush will allow you to print your artistic creations although the quality of the hard copy will depend very much on the type of printer you are using.

1) Create your image.

2) Save the graphic you have just created by pressing **Alt-F A**

or by clicking on **File** in the Menu bar and then on **Save As**. It does not matter what format you save the graphic in, just so long as you save it before going any further. Especially with graphics you should get into the habit of saving your work often.

3) Press **Alt-F P** and this brings up the Print dialogue box.

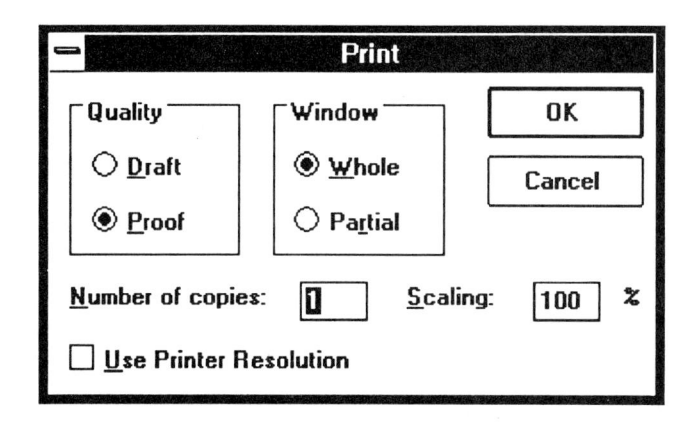

Print Dialogue Box

On here you make your selection about the quality, view and scaling of the image. You have the choice of two qualities, Draft or Proof, with the latter being the default. **Draft** quality produces blocky pictures very quickly, **Proof** will be slower but will produce much higher quality images.

The Window box allows you to print either the Whole image, i.e. including those parts of the image that are not visible in the Drawing Area window, or only that part of the image that is visible on screen. The default setting is to print all of an image.

How many copies do you want? By default this is set to 1 but you can have as many as you wish. Equally, what size do you want your image to be? By default the scaling is set to 100%, which means it doesn't use any scaling, this produces an image roughly the same size as it is on the screen - give or take a bit. However you can reduce or enlarge your pictures by decreasing or increasing the value.

Once you have set these parameters pressing **Enter** or clicking on **OK** will send the picture to the printer. If you have made the picture too big to fit the page size, e.g. by increasing its size, then you will be prompted with an error message telling you so.

Summary

- Windows Paintbrush is a painting program, which produces bitmapped images.

- The program is a good introduction to computer graphics. It will not make you a Rembrandt but it can produce pictures on a par with Lowry stick figures.

- Paintbrush can be used to produce or modify images that are then usable as Windows Wallpaper.

- Only by playing with the program will you discover what it is capable of and you might be surprised at your own artistic ability too. Examine the BMP files that come as part of Windows to see just what the program is capable of.

Keyboard Summary

Alt-Backspace	Undo last action.
Alt-E C	Copy picked area to Clipboard.
Alt-E F	Paste existing file into current painting.
Alt-E O	Copy picked area to a disk file.
Alt-E P	Paste Clipboard contents into painting.
Alt-E T	Cut picked area into Clipboard.
Alt-E U	Undo last action.
Alt-Esc	Switch to next program without using Task Switching.
Alt-F A	Save image to new filename.
Alt-F N	Start a new painting.
Alt-F O	Load a disk file image.
Alt-F P	Activate print dialogue box.
Alt-F S	Save current image to existing filename.
Alt-F T	Change page setup.
Alt-F X	Terminate Paintbrush and return to Program Manager.
Alt-F4	Terminate Paintbrush and return to Program Manager.
Alt-H	Open Help menu.

Paintbrush

Alt-O	B	Select new brush shape.
Alt-O	E	Customise colours.
Alt-O	G	Load previously saved colour palette from disk.
Alt-O	I	Open Image Attributes dialogue box.
Alt-O	S	Save existing colour palette to disk.
Alt-P	C	Select original picked area.
Alt-P	H	Flip picked area around vertical axis, i.e. horizontally.
Alt-P	I	Inverse colours in picked area.
Alt-P	R	Select a printer.
Alt-P	S	Toggle Shrink and Grow.
Alt-P	T	Toggle Tilt command.
Alt-P	V	Flip picked area around horizontal axis, i.e. vertically.
Alt-S	B	Toggle text into Bold.
Alt-S	I	Toggle Italic text effect.
Alt-S	N	Toggle normal type effects.
Alt-S	O	Toggle Outline text effect.
Alt-S	S	Toggle Shadow text effect.
Alt-S	U	Toggle Underline effect.
Alt-Space	C	Terminate Windows Paintbrush.
Alt-Space	M	Move window against the background.
Alt-Space	N	Reduce window to an icon.
Alt-Space	R	Restore icon to window of former size and shape.
Alt-Space	S	Resize and/or reshape window.
Alt-Space	W	Switch to alternative program using Task Switching.
Alt-Space	X	Maximise window so it covers entire screen area.
Alt-V	C	Toggle appearance of cursor position mini-window.
Alt-V	I	Zoom in to selected area.
Alt-V	O	Zoom out back to main screen or view whole page.
Alt-V	P	Toggle appearance of Palette.
Alt-V	T	Toggle appearance of Toolbox and Line thickness box.
Alt-V	V	Remove main window elements to view whole picture.
Alt-V	Z	Open Size menu,
Ctrl-B		Toggle Bold print effect.
Ctrl-C		View entire picture area.
Ctrl-Esc		Switch to alternative program via Task Switching.
Ctrl-I		Toggle Italic text effect.
Ctrl-Ins		Copy picked area to Clipboard.
Ctrl-N		Clear current image and start a new one.
Ctrl-O		Zoom out to view whole page or to cancel zoom in.
Ctrl-S		Save image to existing filename.
Ctrl-U		Toggle text underlining.
Ctrl-Z		Zoom in to selected area.
F1		Activate Paintbrush Help.
Shift-Del		Cut picked area into Clipboard.
Shift-Ins		Paste Clipboard contents into painting.

Chapter 11
Write

What is it?

Windows Write is a high powered text editor, albeit one that uses its own quirky format for saving files. It is not quite a word processor, for instance it does not have a spell checker or a thesaurus - both of which are essential in today's word processing programs; you cannot use macros nor can you import or export other files, except through the Clipboard which is not always convenient because it means you have to open additional programs first. However, its biggest drawback is that it will not allow you to produce an output file in anything but Write or Word formats. Having said that though, the program is perfectly suitable for producing short documents, say less than a dozen pages, for your own personal use. I certainly would not recommend that it be used in a business capacity, it has too many drawbacks for that, but it is an ideal introduction to using text editors under the Windows environment. The program is simple to use and, apart from some minor hassles, quick to learn. Windows Write exemplifies the principle that once you learn to use the Windows environment, using any Windows-based software then becomes a piece of cake. Within Write you can paste graphics and/or text from other programs via the Clipboard.

The program that is supplied with Windows 3 is identical to that which had been supplied with Windows/286 except for the addition of the Switch To command and the new Help system. It is a pity, I think, that Microsoft did not take, or did not have, the time to improve the program. If you want a proper word processor to run under Windows then you actually have very little choice, there is Word for Windows, from Microsoft themselves, and there is Ami Professional from Samna. But it is early days yet and you can guarantee that before very long there will be a number of Windows-based word processors available.

When you install Windows the SETUP program creates a group called Accessories and it is here that Windows Write is placed. To run the program just select the icon, it looks like a Pen drawing the letter A, and double click on it or press **Enter**. Once the window appears you may find that it is an odd size but that can be easily fixed, either resize the window as with previous programs, or press **Ctrl-Esc** and then click on

Tile. Providing you have shrunk the Program Manager to an icon, the Windows Write window will expand to fill all of the screen area.

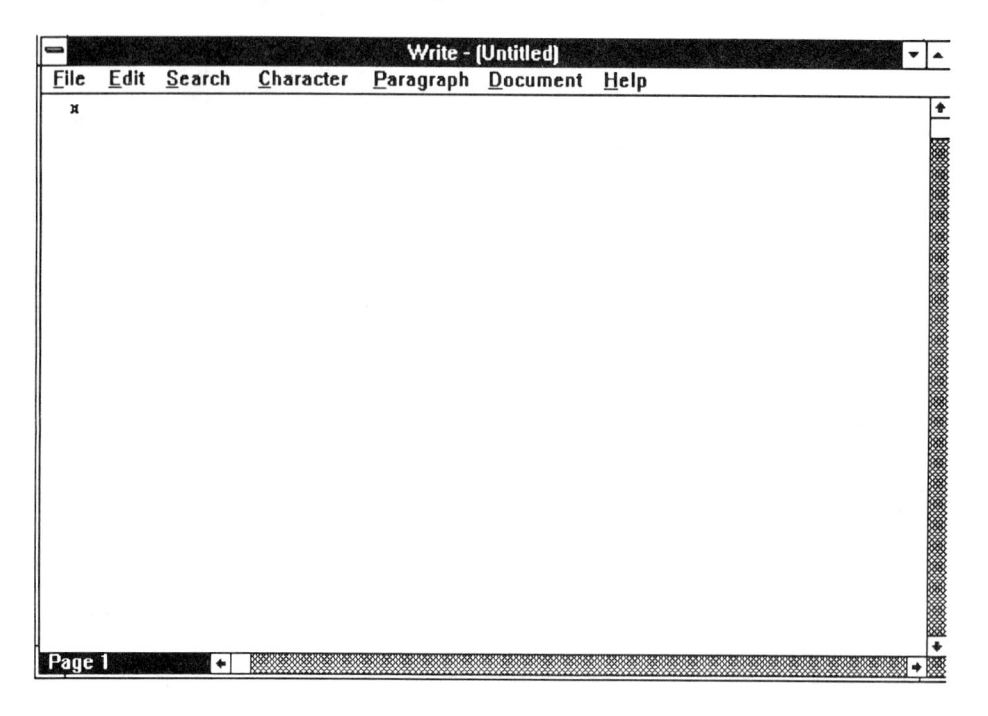

Windows Write

The layout of the window is the same as the majority of other windows programs. Along the top are the Control Box, Title Bar, Minimise and Maximise buttons, and the Menu Bar. Around the window are the scroll bars, but the main bulk of the window is a blank space containing a flashing cursor and the star-shaped end of file marker.

Exercise 11.1
Setting the Format

When you first run Windows Write it uses its own default format but this will probably not be to your taste and so you will need to change it. Doing so is easy, if long-winded, and here's how. The Write Page Format defaults are:

Top and Bottom margins   1 inch
Left and Right margins   1.25 inches
System of measurement   inches.

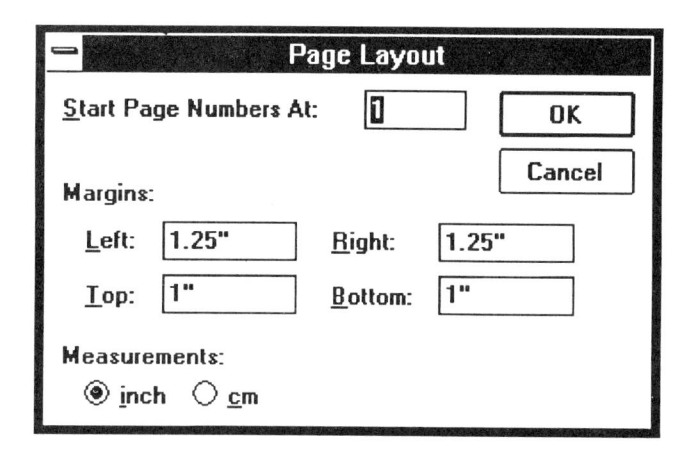

Page Layout Dialogue Box

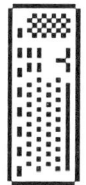

1) Press **Alt-D P** which will bring up a dialogue box in which you can specify the margins and the system of measurement you wish to use. By default the program is set to work in inches.

2) The first box, the one dealing with page numbers, will be highlighted. As you are unlikely, at this stage, to want to change the numbering just press **Tab** to move to the next box. If you want to change the first page number, just type the value you want to use and then press **Tab**. Don't press **Enter** or you will close the dialogue box.

3) The box that is now highlighted, **Left Margin**, contains a value in inches. You can change this to whatever you wish but you should specify a value format, " for inches or **cm** for centimetres. Having typed a value press **Tab** to move on to the next box until you get to the measurements line.

4) To change from inches to centimetres press **C**. If you have entered values for the margins in inches these will be translated into centimetres. You can toggle between the two systems by pressing **I** or **C**, each time you do so the margins change to reflect this. Once you are happy with this press **Enter**. The dialogue box vanishes and you are back to the main window.

1) Click on **Document** in the Menu Bar and then on **Page Layout** to bring up the dialogue box.

2) To change any of the values for the margins, double click on the number. It will then be highlighted and anything you type will overprint it. This double click action is very useful as you will see later, it allows you to highlight a specific word including its trailing space and so change it easily. A number in this case counts as a word. Change each of the margins in this way - don't forget to include the measurement system.

3) To change the default measurement system, click on **cm** at the bottom of the screen. If you have entered margin values in inches these will be adjusted to the new measurement system automatically.

The page size you have just set becomes the format for the current document only. It will not change the default values - Windows Write has no provision for resetting the default page size, which is another reason why it is not a true word processor. Every time you create a document you will have to create a separate format for it unless you always want to use the original default.

Exercise 11.2
Ruler and Tabs

The Write window as it stands is very barren: you can enter text but you have no idea of where it is going to go, no text formatting abilities and only the standard font. Ideally, you want to be able to use tabs and other fonts. This is how to do so.

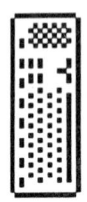

1) Let's bring up the ruler line so you can see the page layout. Press **Alt-D R** and the ruler line appears along the top of the white space area.

This actually consists of three lines, though it may not look like it. Along the top are some little boxes, the first two contain arrows - these can be used to set Tabs if you are using a mouse; the next three control the line spacing; and the third set control the text alignment: you have a choice of unjustified, the default, centred, right aligned or fully justified.

Write Ruler Line

The next line contains a series of markers. These are shown in the measurement system you are using, numbered at every whole point, i.e. every inch or centimetre.

At the extreme left hand side of the third line is a triangular shape, which denotes the left hand margin of the page. There is a similar marker showing the right hand edge although it may not be visible. Overlying the left hand marker is a very small square, shown in white (you cannot see it on the illustration above because it is so small.). This is the first line paragraph indent marker.

2) Let's set some Tabs. Press **Alt-D T** and this will bring up a new dialogue box which has a flashing cursor in the first box but nothing else.

Tabulations Dialogue Box

3) The dialogue box will allow you to set a maximum of twelve tabs and they can be either standard or decimal tabs. Type the position of the first tab, press **Tab** twice to move on to the next

box, type the next value and so on until you have inserted as many tabs as you want. Pressing **Enter** removes the dialogue box and takes you back to the Write window. Notice that the tab positions you have just entered in the dialogue box now appear on the third line of the ruler.

1) To bring up the ruler click on **Document** in the Menu Bar and then on **Ruler On**. The ruler appears across the top of the page.

2) To set a tab, just click at the position you want the tab to be on the third line of the ruler. If you make a mistake just drag the tab marker up or down off the ruler and it will be deleted.

As with the Page Format, these settings you have just made apply only to the current document. By default Windows Write does not include any tabulations and the ruler is always turned off. Having set the page format and tabulations you can now begin to create a document.

Exercise 11.3
Entering, saving and formatting text

Windows Write handles the justification of the text automatically for you. All you need do is type away and the program does the rest, your text will fill as many lines as necessary based on the page format and font size you are currently using. This exercise is intended to be used with both the keyboard and the mouse and so it does not make distinctions between the two as normal. Where you can use key combinations instead of mouse actions these are given in brackets.

1) Type your text as you would normally, don't worry about spelling and justification for now - just type away until you have enough text to fill more than a single screen, i.e. you have to use **PgUp** and **PgDn** or the scroll bars to page through the text.

2) Once all your text is entered press **Ctrl-Home** to return to the first line of the document. If you click on the scroll bars the

text will move in the direction you want but the cursor remains in whatever column position you left it.

3) Click on **File** in the Menu Bar and then on **Save As**. This brings up a dialogue box that allows you to determine how the file will be saved.

Save As Dialogue Box

The main line of this box allows you to enter a filename for your document, and this is the one in which the cursor is flashing. Type a filename, the standard MS-DOS rules about filenames apply, but don't include any extension.

By default, the Write Save option always logs on to the Windows directory of Drive-C. You can change this target directory by clicking on the directory name you want the file to be saved in. For example, if you wanted the file to be saved to the Root Directory of Drive-C you would double click on [..] and the list in the Directories box changes to show this.

The three toggle switches to the right of the Directories box allow you to determine what format the file will be saved in. You can select any of these toggles directly from the keyboard using **Alt-[underlined letter]**, e.g. **Alt-T** for Text only, but it is easier to click on them with the mouse.

The first switch, **Make Backup**, takes any previously saved version of the file and renames the extension to BKP, if the previous file was in Write format, or BAK if the previous version of the file was in Word format so that you have a backup copy of the file. By default this option is always selected for you.

The second switch, **Text Only**, saves the document in Windows ANSI format. This is different to ASCII and so the file will not be pure text. The ANSI format can be used with Windows Terminal but very little else.

The final switch allows you to save the file in **Word** format, this is the Microsoft word processing program that runs under MS-DOS. If you are using graphics in your file then you should not use Word format or the pictures vanish because this file format cannot handle graphics.

Once you have typed the file name and set the format pressing **Enter** will write the file to disk. As the file is being saved the program tells you how many characters the file contains in the lower left hand corner of the window to the left of the bottom scroll bar.

4) Having saved the file you can now make changes to it with impunity. Let's change the typeface and font of the first paragraph. Move the mouse cursor to the left hand side of the text, but still within the main window, and it becomes an arrowhead. Double click and the entire paragraph is highlighted, shown in inverse video, to show it has been selected. If you click just once then only the line beside the cursor is selected.

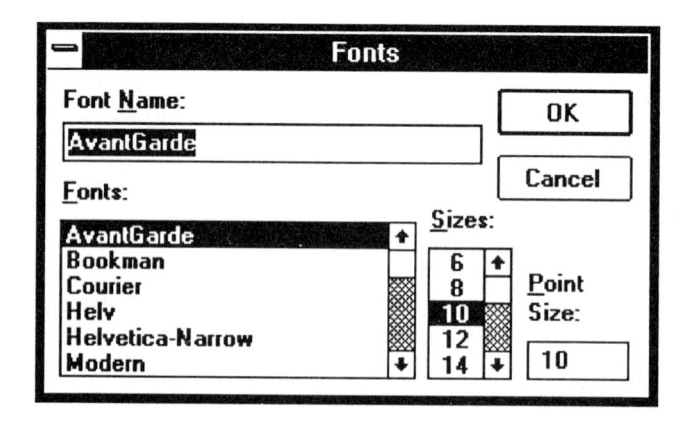

Fonts Dialogue Box

```
    Normal           F5
    Bold             Ctrl+B
    Italic           Ctrl+I
    Underline        Ctrl+U
    Superscript
    Subscript
  √ 1. AvantGarde
    2. Helv
    3. Helvetica-Narrow
    Reduce Font
    Enlarge Font
    Fonts...
```

Character Menu

5) Press **Alt-C F** and up pops the Fonts dialogue box. The typeface that this contains will depend on what type of printer you are using and what fonts you have installed. Click on any typeface name to select it and then double click on a point size. The dialogue box vanishes and the highlighted text is now shown in the typeface and size you have just selected.

6) To get printing effects you use the **Character** menu directly. While the paragraph is still selected, press **Alt-C** again and this pops down the menu. This contains a list of printing effects - click on any one of these and the selected effect is applied to the paragraph. This is one of the advantages of Windows Write, it is truly WYSIWYG. The acronym means What You See Is What You Get, in other words the way the text appears on screen is the way that it will appear on the printed page.

The menu also contains a list of up to three typefaces and clicking on any of these applies that typeface to the selected text. You can also change the size of the font by selecting **Enlarge** or **Reduce**. The text will be adjusted to the next available size, e.g. if it was originally in 12-Point and you select Reduce it now becomes 10-Point, while selecting Enlarge makes it 14-Point.

7) Let's change the justification. With the paragraph still selected, click on the last icon shown on the ruler line, the one that contains four equal lines. The selected paragraph is instantly fully justified, i.e. the words are spread out so that the left and right margins are in straight lines. Click on the penultimate icon and the text is aligned to the right hand margin, leaving the left hand one ragged. Try clicking on each of the justification icons, and the line spacing icons, and see what you get.

8) Now for some indentation. Move the mouse cursor up to the third line of the ruler to the little white square over the left margin marker. Drag this to the right and then release the button. The first line of the highlighted paragraph will now be indented so that the first character lies beneath this marker.

Indent Dialogue Box

9) Let's indent the entire paragraph, rather than just the first line. With the paragraph still selected, press **Alt-P I** to bring up the indent dialogue box. This allows you to set indentations from the left or right margins. The middle line of the box allows you to indent the first line only, as you did in the last step. Change the highlighted setting on the first line to **3** and then press **Enter**. The selected paragraph will be shoved three units, either inches or centimetres, to the right. You can set the First Line indent to be less than the Left indent so that the first line doesn't align with the rest of the paragraph. To remove an indentation either use the dialogue box again or drag the triangular marker on the ruler line back to its original position using the mouse.

Cursor Keys

To move around through your text you can either use the mouse or the keyboard, and which you use depends on what you want to do. Unlike Paintbrush, this time the keyboard is better. Any action that you try which is not allowed will cause the computer to beep at you - providing you have the Warning Beep turned on in the Control Panel.

To move the cursor to the beginning of the next word you press **Ctrl-Right**.

To move to the beginning of the previous word use **Ctrl-Left**.

To move to the beginning of the next sentence use **Goto-Right**. (The **Goto** key is number 5 on the numeric keypad.)

To move to the beginning of the previous sentence you should press **Goto-Left**.

To move to the start of the current line use **Home**.

To move to the end of the current line press **End**.

To move to the beginning of the current paragraph you should press **Goto-Up**.

To move to the beginning of the next paragraph use **Goto-Down**.

To move to the first line within the window, the cursor staying in the same column press **Ctrl-PgUp**.

To move to the last line in the window, the cursor staying in the same column press **Ctrl-PgDn**.

To scroll the page down one line at a time use **Ctrl-Up**. (You can move between pages only after a document has been printed or it has been paginated using **Alt-F E**.)

To scroll the page up one line at a time press **Ctrl-Dn**.

To move to the beginning of the file use **Ctrl-Home**.

To move directly to the end of the file press **Ctrl-End**.

To move to the beginning of the next page use **Goto-PgDn**.

To move to the previous page press **Goto-PgUp**.

Holding down a key combination will force the command to repeat until either you release the keys or the program reaches a point where it cannot continue. For example, if you press **Ctrl-End**, to move to the bottom of the document you have created, and then hold down **Goto-Up**, the page will scroll downwards and once the cursor reaches the top of the document the computer will beep. It will then continue beeping until you release the keys.

Changing Text

Windows Write provides a facility for finding and/or changing specific words and phrases. The program can find whole words, i.e. it searches for exactly what you have requested, and it can be forced to find only those words that match the case you want.

```
┌─────────────────────────────────────────────┐
│                     Find                    │
│  Find What: [                             ] │
│  ☐ Whole Word        ☐ Match Upper/Lowercase│
│              [   Find Next   ]              │
└─────────────────────────────────────────────┘
```

Find Dialogue Box

To activate the Find facility press **Alt-S F** or click on **Search** in the Menu Bar and then press **Enter** because **Find** is the first command in the menu. When the dialogue box appears type the word or phrase you want to find, set the options by clicking on them and then click on **Find Next** or press **Alt-N**. The program will search through your document looking for a match to your specified word or phrase.

Once it has found it, the word or phrase will be highlighted. You can then click on **Find Next** or press **Alt-N** to continue search to the end of the file. The only way to remove the dialogue box is to press **Alt-F4** when it is active.

Write also provides a facility for finding and replacing words. Pressing **Alt-S** brings up a dialogue box similar to the find box, except that you can include what you want the target word or phrase to be changed to.

Change Dialogue Box

The dialogue box provides four basic options, once it has found your target word or phrase:

> **Find Next** does nothing to the found words, i.e. it skips them, and goes on to search for the next occurrence.
>
> **Change, then Find** changes the highlighted words and then searches for the next occurrence.
>
> **Change** changes the currently highlighted words only. You then have to tell it to find the next occurrence if you want to continue finding and changing.
>
> **Change All** allows you to specify that all occurrences of the target words are changed automatically.

As with the Find dialogue box, the only way to close the Change box is to press **Alt-F4** when the box is active.

Exercise 11.4
Moving blocks

Because Write runs under Windows you can very easily move blocks of text around within a document, thanks to the Clipboard. However, you must have a mouse to highlight the block you want to move or copy.

1) Highlight the block of text using the mouse. If you want to use an entire paragraph, or even a number of sequential paragraphs, then move the mouse cursor to the left of this and then click and drag the cursor down until the text is highlighted. If you want to work with only part of a paragraph, move the cursor to where the block begins, click and then drag the cursor until you reach the end of the block. Releasing the button selects the highlighted text.

2) To copy the block to the Clipboard press **Ctrl-Ins, Alt-E C** or click on **Copy** in the **Edit** menu. Even though the block has been copied it remains highlighted.

3) If you want to copy the block and delete it from its current position, press **Shift-Del, Alt-E T** or click on **Cut** in the **Edit** menu. This time the block is removed from the main text and any following text will be reflowed to make up for the block removal.

4) Move the cursor to the position within the document where you want the text to be placed and click to fix the cursor in place. Press **Shift-Ins, Alt-E P** or click on **Paste** in the **Edit** menu. The entire contents of the Clipboard will be inserted at the current cursor position. Existing text will be shunted along to make room. The contents of the Clipboard will remain the same until you use Cut or Copy again and so you can paste the same block into the document a number of times.

Exercise 11.5
Adding Graphics to Write

Windows Write will allow you to incorporate a graphic, or a number of graphics, into a document via the Clipboard. To do so the graphic must be in a format that the Clipboard can handle, usually through being copied from another application, although the new Clipboard will allow you to load previously saved Clipboard files. Either way, before the graphic can be incorporated you must have it in the Clipboard.

>1) Load the graphic you want to use into the Clipboard. You can reduce Write to an icon while you do this or run the other application over the top of the Write window.
>
>2) Move the cursor to the position that you want the graphic placed, usually a blank line. Click to fix the cursor and then press **Shift-Ins**. The graphic is pasted in but it will probably be the wrong size - fortunately Write allows you to resize graphics.
>
>3) Click on the graphic and it will be highlighted. Press **Alt-E S** or click on **Size Picture** in the **Edit** menu. The cursor changes into a dual box shape. By moving this you can change the border positions of the graphic. The borders are shown as grey outlines. Once you are happy with the size and shape click and the graphic assumes the size and shape of the outlines.
>
>4) You can also move the graphic to another position within the page. Click on the graphic to select it again and press **Alt-E M** or click on **Move Picture** in the **Edit** menu. The cursor changes to the same shape as in the previous step and the grey borders appear. As you move the cursor around, so the border moves with it. Place this wherever you want the graphic to be, click and it will be fixed into place. Unfortunately you can only move the graphic laterally, i.e. from side to side, you cannot move it up or down the page.

Exercise 11.6
Printing your document

Write uses the Print Manager, if it is turned on, to handle all printing. This means that all you have to do is send the document to this and then you can get on with using the Write program while the printing is handled in the background.

1) Before you print the document you should paginate it so that you know how many pages there are.

2) Press **Alt-F E** or click on **Repagination** in the **File** menu. This will bring up a dialogue box asking if you want to confirm page breaks. You should accept this one, so that a cross appears beside the command, by clicking on it and then click on **OK**.

3) The pagination process then begins and before a page break is placed, Write will prompt you about the position of the page break. Select whichever option you wish by clicking on it. Clicking on **Confirm** sets the page break and then the program moves on to the next until all the page breaks are in position.

Tip: Never move page breaks down, always move them up or you may encounter problems with lines running off the page.

4) Once the pagination is finished press **Ctrl-Home** to go back to the beginning of the document. Press **Alt-F P** or click on **Print** in the **File** menu and the Print dialogue box appears.

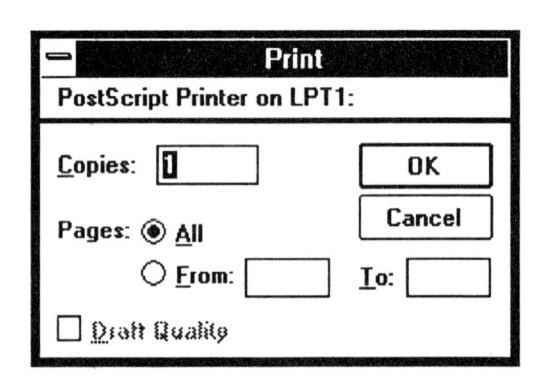

Print Dialogue Box

5) Within the dialogue box you can select the number of copies you want produced, which pages you want printed if you don't want them all and, depending on your printer, whether or not you will use draft or proof quality printing.

6) To change the number of copies, just type a numeral because the relevant box is already highlighted.

7) If you want to print only specific pages, click on **From** and then type the relevant page numbers in the appropriate boxes. The numbers are inclusive, i.e. if you enter **3** and **6** then pages 3, 4, 5 and 6 will be printed. If you want to print all the pages in the document you need do nothing because the **Print All** command is the default.

8) If you wish to produce a draft quality print out, and assuming your printer is capable of doing so, then click on **Draft**. You cannot produce a draft print out on any laser printer - at least none that I have tried. Clicking on **OK** then sends the document to the printer.

Summary

- Windows Write is a super-text editor, it is not a full blown word processor, although it does have a number of word processing features.

- The program is WYSIWYG, What You See Is What You Get, and so the screen image should be identical to the printed output.

- Write will allow you to incorporate graphics, pasted from the Clipboard, into your documents.

Keyboard Summary

Alt-Backspace	Undo last action.
Alt-C B	Apply bold printing effect to selected text and/or any text entered hereafter.
Alt-C C	Activate subscript printing effect.
Alt-C E	Enlarge point size of selected text and/or any text entered hereafter.
Alt-C F	Activate Font selection dialogue box.
Alt-C I	Apply italic printing effect to selected text and/or any text entered hereafter.
Alt-C N	Select normal printing effects, it can also be used to reverse other printing effects.
Alt-C P	Activate superscript printing effect.
Alt-C R	Reduce point size of selected text and/or any text entered hereafter.
Alt-C U	Apply underlining to selected text and/or text entered hereafter.
Alt-C [number]	Select one of three typefaces.
Alt-D F	Activate Footer dialogue box.
Alt-D H	Activate Header dialogue box.
Alt-D P	Activate Page Layout dialogue box.
Alt-D R	Toggle appearance of ruler.
Alt-D T	Activate Tab setting dialogue box.
Alt-E C	Copy selected block to Clipboard.
Alt-E M	Move selected graphic laterally.
Alt-E P	Paste Clipboard contents into document at cursor position.
Alt-E S	Resize graphic.
Alt-E T	Cut selected block to Clipboard.
Alt-E U	Undo last action.
Alt-Esc	Switch directly to another program.
Alt-F A	Save the document to a new filename.
Alt-F E	Paginate the document.
Alt-F N	Begin a new document, any unsaved or modified document will cause a prompt to appear allowing you to save the document before you start another one.
Alt-F O	Load a previously saved document from the disk.
Alt-F P	Print the document.
Alt-F R	Change or modify the printer setup or select an alternative printer.
Alt-F X	Terminate Windows Write.
Alt-F4	Terminate Windows Write.
Alt-H	Activate Help menu.

Alt-O S		Save the current document to the filename shown on the Title Bar.
Alt-P 1		Set line and a half line spacing.
Alt-P C		Set Centre justification.
Alt-P D		Set double line spacing.
Alt-P I		Activate indent setting dialogue box.
Alt-P J		Set full justification.
Alt-P L		Set left justification.
Alt-P N		Toggle normal paragraph style.
Alt-P R		Set Right justification.
Alt-P S		Set single line spacing.
Alt-S C		Activate Find and Replace dialogue box.
Alt-S F		Activate Find dialogue box.
Alt-S G		Jump directly to specific page, only available after the document has been paginated and/or printed.
Alt-S R		Repeat last Find operation.
Alt-Space C		Terminate Write and return to Program Manager.
Alt-Space M		Move Write window against background.
Alt-Space N		Minimise window, i.e. reduce to an icon.
Alt-Space R		Restore icon to window of previous size and shape.
Alt-Space S		Resize Write window.
Alt-Space W		Activate Task Switching.
Alt-Space X		Maximise window to cover entire screen area.
Ctrl-B		Apply bold printing effect to selected text and/or any text entered hereafter.
Ctrl-Esc		Activate Task Switching.
Ctrl-I		Apply italic printing effect to selected text and/or any text entered hereafter.
Ctrl-Ins		Copy selected block to Clipboard.
Ctrl-U		Apply underlining to selected text and/or any text entered.
F1		Activate Help directly.
F3		Repeat last Find operation.
F4		Jump directly to specific page, only available after pagination or printing.
Shift-Del		Cut selected block to Clipboard.
Shift-Ins		Paste Clipboard contents into document at current cursor position.

Chapter 12
All the C's

Rather than deal with each of the remaining Accessories individually, which would produce some very small chapters, they are going to be grouped together. The first such group deals with Calculator, Calendar and Cardfile.

Calculator

Windows Calculator is just that, a calculator that can be popped up over any other Windows application. Unfortunately it cannot be used in conjunction with any MS-DOS program, even if the program is being run from the Windows environment, if you are using Real or Standard mode. It can however appear if you are using 386-Enhanced mode and running the MS-DOS program in a window. The first time that the calculator is invoked it will appear as a standard, short function pocket calculator.

The Calculator can be run using any of the following.

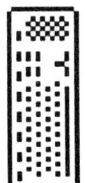

1) To run the Calculator, select the icon, using **Alt-Tab** to change sub-window if necessary, and then press **Enter**.

2) Select the calculator icon in the Accessories window and then press **Alt-F O**.

3) From any sub-window of the Program Manager press **Alt-F R**, then enter **CALC** in the dialogue box that appears.

1) Double click on the calculator icon in the Accessories sub-window.

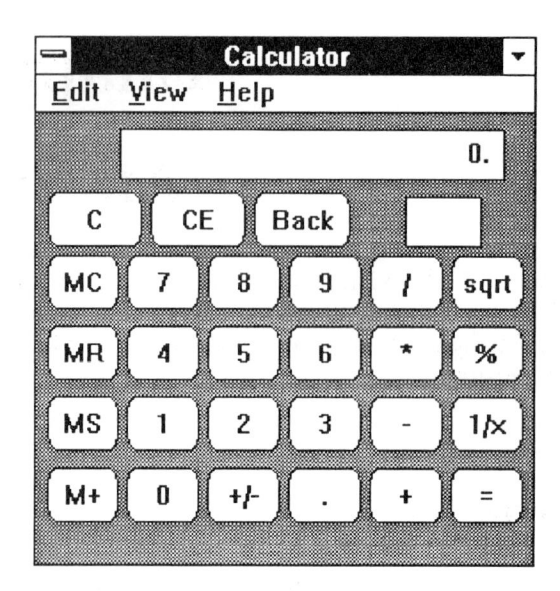

Standard Calculator

The calculator can be used either with the keyboard, specifically the numeric keypad if the **Num Lock** is turned on, or with the mouse. The cursor, when it appears above the calculator remains a white arrowhead.

The calculator includes a number of other functions besides the basic arithmetic operands, i.e. the ones shown on the numeric keypad. The operands and their corresponding keystrokes are:

sqrt	@	Calculates the Square Root of the displayed number.
%	%	Calculates percentages.
1/x	R	Calculates the reciprocal of the displayed number.
+/-	F9	Changes the sign or the displayed number, i.e. negative to positive and vice versa.
CE	Del	Clears the displayed number.
C	Esc	Clears the current calculation.
MC	Ctrl-C	Clears the contents of the memory.
MR	Ctrl-R	Memory recall, i.e. display value in memory.
MS	Ctrl-M	Place displayed number into memory, overwriting any existing value.
M+	Ctrl-P	Add the displayed number to the contents of the memory.

Exercise 12.1
Simple Sums

The best way to learn to the Calculator is to use it. The following exercise incorporates all of the basic operands. Because the calculator is easier to use with the mouse, rather than the keyboard, the exercise is based around the mouse. Keyboard equivalents are included in brackets.

1) Run the calculator from the Program Manager.

2) Enter the value 1024 and store this in the memory. (**Num Lock, 1024, Ctrl-M**)

3) Divide the displayed number by 64. (**64, /, Enter**) The displayed number should be 16. (If you press = again, the result from the previous calculation will be divided by 64 again. The previous calculation remains active until you change it to something else.)

4) Multiply the previous result by 2. (`, **2, Enter**) The displayed number should be 32.

5) Add -32. Click on + 32 then on +/- before pressing equals. (**+, 32, F9, Enter**) The displayed number should now be 0.

6) Clear the calculation by clicking on CE (**Del**) and then retrieve the original number from the memory by clicking on MR. (**Ctrl-R**).

7) Find 50% of the original number. The fastest way to do this is simply multiply the 1024 by .5. (***, .5, Enter**) Or you can use the percentage key. (***, 50, %**) Don't press Enter or click on = or the original number will be multiplied by your result.

8) Click on C and CE (**Esc Del**) and then recall the original number from memory again. (**Ctrl-R**) Click on 1/x (**R**) The resulting answer is 0.0009765625.

9) Finally clear the display again, click on CE and C (**Esc Del**) and retrieve the original number again. (**Ctrl-R**) Click on sqrt (@) and you get the answer 32. Multiply this by itself by clicking on * = (*** Enter**) and you should get 1024 again. Add this to the memory by clicking on M+ (**Ctrl-P**). Click on MR (**Ctrl-R**) and

you should have 2048. Finally click on MC (**Ctrl-C**) to clear the memory and then on C and CE (**Esc Del**) to return the calculator to a pristine state.

The calculator can also be used with the Clipboard, to export values into and to Paste values from. When you paste into the calculator you can include operands as part of the clipboard contents and these then effect how the calculator performs. The letters that have a determining effect are:

C	Clears the memory, the equivalent of **Ctrl-C**.
M	Stores the current displayed value in memory, equivalent to **Ctrl-M**.
P	Add the displayed value to the memory, equivalent to **Ctrl-P**.
Q	Clears current calculation, equivalent to **C** and **Esc**.
R	Displays the value stored in the memory, equivalent to **Ctrl-R**.
:	When a colon is placed before a letter, the calculator interprets the letter as being part of a control sequence, e.g. :C is the equivalent of **Ctrl-C** - clear the memory contents.

The calculator can also be used as a Scientific one which can be used to perform scientific and statistical calculations. To switch from the standard display to the Scientific one click on **View** in the Menu Bar and then on **Scientific** or simply press **Alt-V S**.

Unfortunately I have a mental blind spot about mathematics, so much so that I have trouble with algebra and I cannot understand a word about geometry or trigonometry, and so I am not able to design a valid exercise for this. (Yes, I know I should do something about it and I've just spent an entire year going to classes to try and learn maths again. The result is that I still can't do it!) So you'll just have to play with it all by yourself. The functions, their meanings and keystrokes are given on pages 367 to 369 of the Windows manual. When you terminate the Calculator, whatever mode it is in at the time becomes the default mode for the next activation. Thus if you close the program in Scientific mode, the next time you run the program it appears in this mode.

All the C's 307

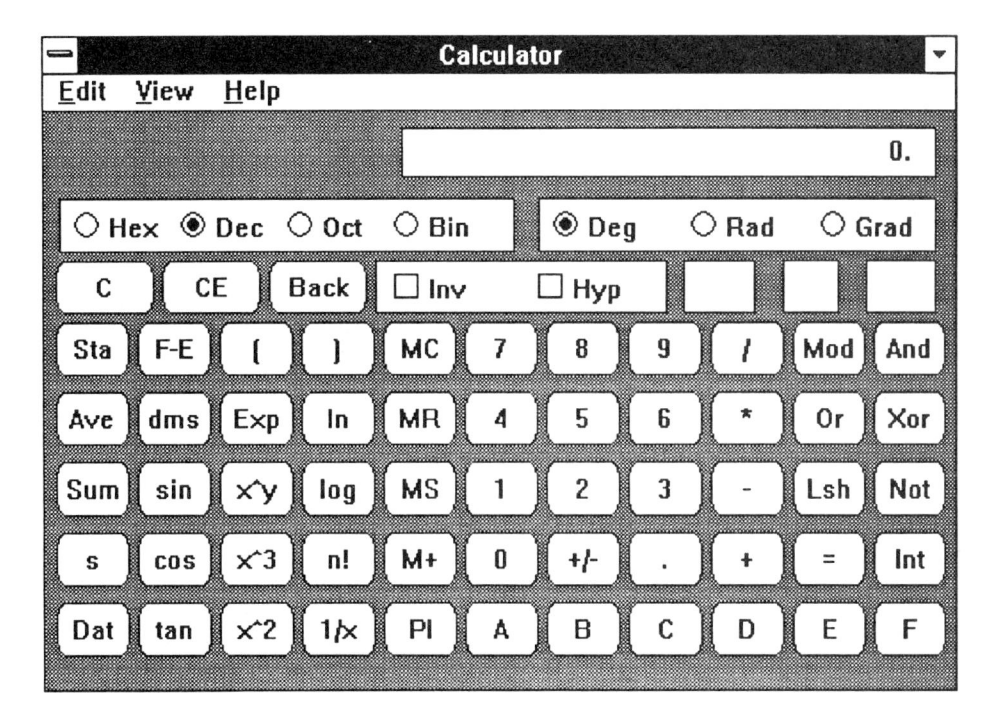

Scientific Calculator

Calculator Summary

- Windows Calculator is a pop-up, single sized window.

- The program runs in two modes, Standard or Scientific.

Calculator Keyboard Summary

Alt-E C	Copy displayed value to the Clipboard.
Alt-E P	Paste Clipboard contents into program.
Alt-Esc	Activate the next program.
Alt-F4	Terminate program and return to Program Manager.
Alt-Space C	Terminate program and return to Program Manager.
Alt-Space M	Move current icon or window against the background.
Alt-Space N	Minimise window, i.e. reduce it to an icon.

Alt-Space R	Restore icon to a window or former size and shape.
Alt-Space W	Activate Task Switching dialogue box.
Alt-V S	Toggle Scientific Calculator display.
Alt-V T	Toggle Standard Calculator display.
Backspace	Delete last digit of displayed value.
Ctrl-C	Clear memory
Ctrl-Esc	Activate Task Switching dialogue box.
Ctrl-Ins	Copy displayed value to Clipboard.
Ctrl-M	Store displayed value in memory, overwriting existing contents.
Ctrl-P	Add displayed value to memory contents.
Ctrl-R	Recall value stored in memory.
Del	Clear displayed number.
Enter	Equals, i.e. perform calculation.
Esc	Clear current calculation.
F1	Activate Help Main Index.
F9	Change sign of displayed number.
Left	Delete last digit of displayed number.
R	Calculate reciprocal of displayed number.
Shift-Ins	Paste Clipboard contents into program.
. or ,	Decimal point.
%	Calculate percentage.
*	Multiply.
+	Add.
-	Minus.
/	Divide.
=	Equals, i.e. perform calculation.
@	Perform square root calculation on displayed number.

Calendar

Windows Calendar is a simple diary program that includes a facility to provide you with an alarm for user defined appointments. You can use the program either as a monthly display or on a daily basis. The program is totally interactive and thus the information you enter affects how the program works. You can use Calendar just as you would any other diary but you can only get 32 characters onto any line. The program is not really meant to be used in place of a paper based appointments book or diary but rather as an adjunct to these. The program can show you any date from January the first 1980 to any date you care to name in the future - all the way to the year 2099. (I cannot really see the point of this - it's totally impossible that we'll still be using MS-DOS or Windows in a hundred years time!)

The calendar uses two different formats for its display: either monthly, which gives you a display showing the entire month; or as a daily appointments book where you can determine the time slots to be used: the default is for hourly slots but you can change this to 15 or 30 minutes. In addition the program allows you to use intervening times if that is not enough.

The program will allow you to set multiple alarms, months in advance if you wish, and set these to provide you with an audible or visual warning of their imminence. Because you can save the data in a diary to disk, as a distinct file, you can set up any number of diaries and reload them as necessary. Within the limitations imposed by character fields the program is actually very versatile.

To run the program select the Calendar icon in the Accessories group window and then either press Enter or double click on it. By default Windows Calendar appears in the Daily Mode. The window contains the usual Control Box, Title Bar, Minimise and Maximise buttons and Menu Bar. Below the Menu Bar is the Status line, this tells you the current system time and the date. The main bulk of the window is given over to the daily display against the window background. This daily display cannot be enlarged, and even if you maximise the display the daily diary just sits in the middle of the background - remember you can only have 32 characters on a line and this limits the overall size of the diary. If you shrink the window so that it is smaller than the daily display then the scroll bar appears on the right hand side of the window.

Calendar Menus

The Menu Bar contents remain the same, regardless of which view of the Calendar you are using. The **File** menu controls the way that files are loaded, saved and printed. The menu contains the following commands:

New starts a new diary. If you have made changes to the current one then you will be prompted about saving the changes before the new one is created.

Open allows you to load a previously saved diary. The dialogue box allows you to select any diary file from anywhere on your hard disks. Within the dialogue box is an option to Read Only. This means that you will copy the selected file contents but not the file itself. Any changes you make will mean that the resulting file will have to be saved as a new file.

Save is used to quickly write the current file to an existing filename. If you use this command with a new file you will be prompted to supply a filename first.

Save As allows you to save the current file to a new filename. By default the program will always place your saved files into the Windows sub-directory.

Print allows you to produce a hard copy of your file including any details that have been set by the next command.

Page Setup is used to include specific information on a print out and to set the page margins.

Printer Setup is used to select which printer you wish to use for printing.

Exit terminates the program and returns you to the Program Manager.

The **Edit** menu allows you to use the Clipboard and contains the following commands:

Cut will copy the selected text to the Clipboard and then remove it from the Calendar.

Copy Similar to the above but the selected text remains in the Calendar.

Paste copies the Clipboard contents to the current cursor position.

Remove allows you to delete all the details for selected dates from the current Calendar.

The **View** menu controls the Calendar display. It contains only two commands, **Day** or **Month,** each of which refers to a specific display mode. Using a mouse you can switch between the two modes by double clicking on the date shown on the status line. Alternatively you can use **F8** or **F9** respectively to toggle the display.

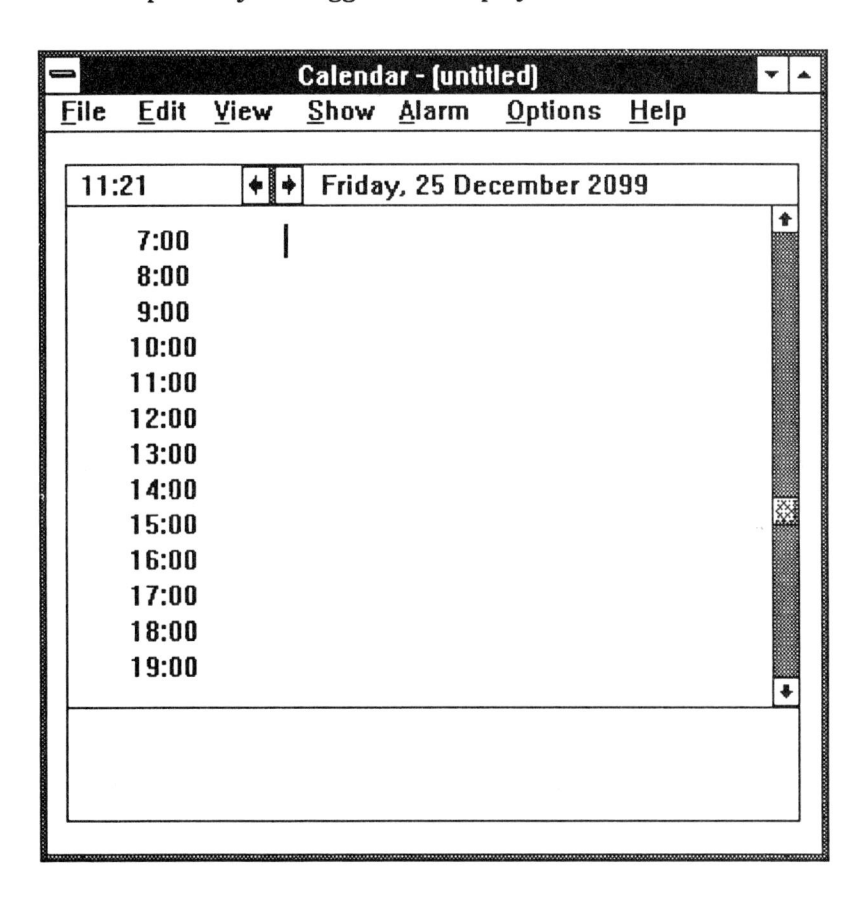

Calendar Default Display

The **Show** menu allows you to move between specific dates on the Calendar.

> **Today** will always bring you back to the current system date. The system date is the date that the computer is set to. If it is set correctly then it will be today and thus Calendar will show this, but if it is set wrongly then it could be anything after January the first 1980.
>
> **Previous** will take you back one day, using the Daily display, or back to last month using the Monthly display.
>
> **Next** takes you on one day, e.g. from Saturday to Sunday, on the Daily display or forward one month, e.g. from June to July, in the Monthly display.
>
> **Date** brings up a dialogue box into which you can enter any valid date and the program then switches directly to the date. A valid date is any one from January 1st. 1980 to December 31st. 2099. Dates must be entered as digits, e.g. 14-11-1990.

The **Alarm** menu is used to set the alarm. The menu contains only two commands, **Set**, which applies the alarm to the time against which the cursor is flashing, and **Controls** which brings up a dialogue box that allows you to adjust the alarm settings.

Options provides a number of adjustments for the way in which the displays are shown. Each command brings up a dialogue box.

> **Mark** allows you to apply any combination of five different characters to a date - only on the Monthly display. Thus you could use squares to mark birthdays, brackets for something else, bullets for important appointments, and so on. You can use all five marks on any date.
>
> **Special Time** is used to add a non-standard time to the Daily display. For example, Calendar will allow you to show the day broken down in 15, 30 or 60 minute time slots, but if you wanted to display 14:50 you would have to use this facility to add it into the display.
>
> **Day Settings** allows you to change the time slots, the starting time and the time format.

Monthly Display

Exercise 12.2
Pick a date

Let's have a quick look at the different ways you can display dates and times. Run the Calendar program by selecting the icon and then pressing **Enter**, or by double clicking on the Calendar icon in the Accessories menu. You can also run the program, from the Program Manager, by pressing **Alt-F R** and then entering **CAL**. By default the Calendar shows today's date in Daily format and it starts at 7 AM.

1) To see tomorrow press **Ctrl-PgDn** or use the menu by pressing **Alt-S N**. Pressing the key combination again takes you to the following day and then the day after and so on. To move back to today either use **Ctrl-PgUp** to move back one day at a time or press **Alt-S T** to move directly to today.

2) Press **Alt-V M** to switch to the Monthly display and find out. If you press **Ctrl-PgDn** now the display moves on one month at a time.

3) Check what day your birthday will be in 1995. Press **Alt-S D** and a dialogue box appears. Enter your birthdate and the year **1995** and the program instantly jumps there.

4) The date can be marked by pressing **Alt-O M** or just **F6** to bring up the dialogue box. Use the **Tab** key and then the **Spacebar** to select a mark. Pressing **Enter** removes the dialogue box and the selected mark is applied to the date. There are five marks to choose from:

    [] which draws a box around the date.
    () brackets the date.
    O places a bullet in the lower left hand corner of the date.
    X places a cross in the upper left hand corner of the date.
    _ underlines the date.

5) Since we're looking so far ahead, we want to make a note of what is special about the date you've just marked. Press **Tab** and the cursor jumps down to the three-line scratch pad at the bottom of the window. The cursor provides its usual effects here and can be moved around using the cursor keys. Press **Tab** to return to the main display.

All the C's 315

6) Back to today, press **Alt-S T**.

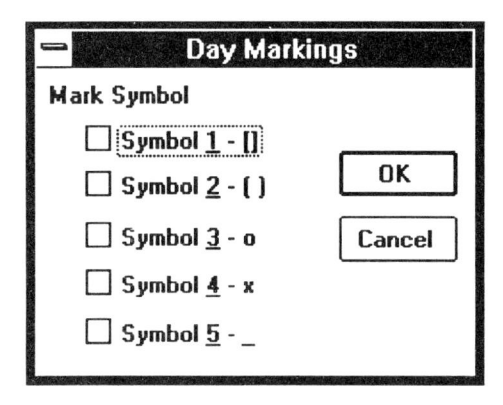

Mark Dialogue Box

1) Click on the arrowhead that points to the right on the **Status Bar** and the display moves on one day. Click again to move to the day after tomorrow. Go back to today either by clicking on the left arrowhead or by pressing **Alt-S T**.

2) Double click on the **date** part of the **Status Bar** and the display changes to the Monthly format. Clicking on the right arrowhead will now move the display on one month at a time.

3) To view a specific date press **F4** and then enter the date into the dialogue box that appears.

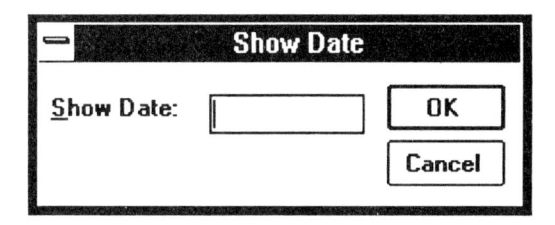

Date Select Dialogue Box

4) Press **F6** to bring up the Mark dialogue box and then click on one of the five marks before clicking on **OK**. The selected mark is applied to the selected date.

5) To make a note about the marked date click in the scratch pad and then type the details. To move back to the monthly display click on any date shown. The notes are specific to whatever date you had highlighted and so if you marked the 14th. and then clicked on the 13th. the notes disappear. Clicking on the 14th. brings them back.

6) Finally back to today by clicking on **Show** and **Today**.

The information you have just entered, including the marking and the notes, are now part of the current file. When you save the file all these details will be stored. If you do not save the file but terminate Calendar, and answer No to the prompt about saving the file, then the details will be lost. A single Calendar file can include any dates from January 1st. 1980 to December 31st. 2099.

Exercise 12.3
Alarm calls

The Windows Calendar will allow you to set any number of alarms for any time of any date that the program can handle. Theoretically this will allow you to set 1440 alarms per day, i.e. one a minute. But who needs that many? The problem is that the alarm will only be active if you are in Windows, and the Calendar is active, either as a window or an icon, and you are not using an MS-DOS -based program. If you are using MS-DOS programs in 386-enhanced mode and the program is windowed then this does not apply.

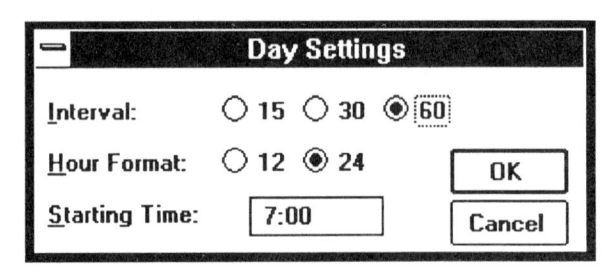

Day Settings Dialogue Box

You have the option of having an audible alarm or not, the choice is yours. If you choose to have it on then the alarm sounds until you turn it off. With the alarm sound off the Calendar window or icon will flash until you negate it. This exercise uses the mouse and keyboard in combination.

1) Before setting the alarm, change the display to show different time slots. Press **Alt-O D** and a dialogue box appears. Click on **30** and press **Enter** or click on **OK**. This accepts the new settings and returns you to the Calendar which now shows 30 minute time slots.

2) Set the alarm for 10:30 AM. Using the cursor keys move the cursor up to **10:30 AM**, alternatively just click to the right of this time, and then press **F5**. A little bell appears to the left of the time to show the alarm has been set. This alarm will use the default settings, i.e. an audible alarm.

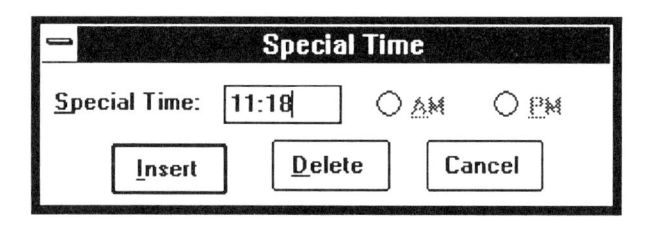

Special Time Dialogue Box

3) But suppose you wanted to set the alarm for 3 minutes from now, what then? You need to insert a special time. Press **Alt-O S** or **F7** and a new dialogue box appears. Type a new time, one that does not appear in the time slots, in the box separating the hours and minutes using a colon, e.g. **15:53**, and then press **Enter**. (The time display depends on what settings you have set as defaults in the Control Panel program.) Once back at the Daily display, the cursor will be lying in the time slot you have just created, press **F5** to set the alarm for this time and then type '**This is a test**' beside the time slot.

4) Reduce the Calendar to an icon by clicking on the **Minimise** button on the Title Bar. At the set time the computer will beep twice and then the icon flashes until you restore the Calendar icon by double clicking on it. When you do so a message box appears like this:

Alarm Message Box

I don't know why the message box is so large because it only ever displays the alarm time that is currently active, along with the text for that time.

5) You can also set an alarm that will go off early. Set another alarm as in step 3 above. Back at the Daily display press **Alt-A C** and a dialogue box appears that allows you to change the alarm settings.

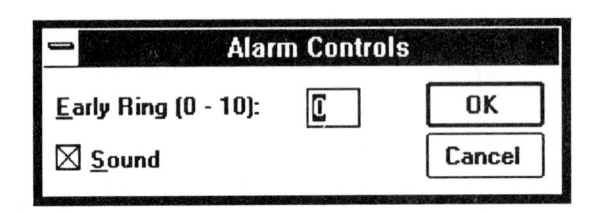

Alarm Settings Dialogue Box

6) In the early ring box type 1, you can use anything from 0 to 10 minutes, and click in the box beside sound. Press **Enter** to remove the box. Once back at the main window restore the Program Manager and then double click on **Clock**. Reduce the Program Manager back to an icon, if you have not already set the Minimise on Use command. The clock should be the active window, overlying but not obscuring the Calendar.

7) Because the Calendar is the inactive window, when it reaches the alarm time the Title Bar will flash and will continue to do until you make the Calendar window the active one. When you do so the message box appears.

You can set alarms for any time and date that the program is capable of displaying, e.g. up 23:59 on December 31st. 2099. When you save the file the alarm settings are included along with the file so that when it is reloaded they can become active.

Exercise 13.4
Printing and saving the Diary

You can produce a hard copy of your diary on any printer that is connected to your computer and which has been configured to work with Windows. There is also a range of information you can include on the printout if you wish.

1) Before you send the file to the printer press **Alt-F T** to bring up the Page Settings dialogue box. This allows you to set the margins for the printed page and also determines what information will be included on the pages. In either the Header or Footer box you can include any of the following, each one must be preceded by an ampersand (&) character, either singly or in combination:

C centre the text within the margins.
D prints the current system date.
F the filename of the printed file - this is the default header.
L left justify the text.
P page numbers - this is the default footer.
R right justify the text.
T include the current system time.

Any of these parameters can be preceded, or replaced, by ordinary text, e.g. **This file is &F** produces the words 'This file is' followed by the filename. To exclude any header or footer leave the boxes blank.

2) Having set the Page Settings you can now print the file by pressing **Alt-F P**. This brings up another dialogue box that

allows you to say what dates you want to be printed. By leaving the bottom box blank only the date mentioned in the top box will be printed.

Page Settings Dialogue Box

When you produce a printed copy it will include any special times, i.e. non-standard time slots, that you have created even if they do not contain any detail; those times for which you have entered text - with the alarms being shown by an asterisk and any notes on the scratch pads for the days within the specified dates - even if there are no appointments that day.

Print Dialogue Box

3) To save the file you have just created press **Alt-F A** and then enter a filename in the appropriate box. You do not have to include an extension because Calendar will supply its own specific one, i.e. CAL. Clicking on **OK** then writes the file to disk. Close the Calendar by pressing **Alt-F4**.

Calendar Summary

- Windows Calendar is a simple, page-a-day diary which can be customised to produce your own preferred time slots.

- The program allows you to set alarms for any time and date it is capable of using, i.e. from January 1st. 1980 to December 31st. 2099.

- You may use either the Daily or the Monthly Display and switch between the two with ease.

- While not as dynamic as some diary programs, Calendar is extremely useful and versatile.

Calendar Keyboard Summary

Alt-A C	Open Alarm Settings dialogue box.
Alt-A S	Set alarm at currently selected time.
Alt-E C	Copy selected text to Clipboard and delete it from the Calendar.
Alt-E C	Copy selected text to Clipboard.
Alt-E P	Insert Clipboard contents at current cursor position.
Alt-E R	Remove details of specific dates from current Calendar file.
Alt-Esc	Activate next program without using Task Switching.
Alt-F A	Save the current file to a new filename.
Alt-F N	Start a new file.
Alt-F O	Load a previously saved calendar file.
Alt-F P	Initiate printing dialogue box and set dates to be printed.
Alt-F R	Select alternative printer.
Alt-F S	Save the current file to the existing filename.
Alt-F T	Set parameters for printed pages.
Alt-F X	Terminate Calendar and return to Program Manager.
Alt-F4	Terminate program and return to Program Manager.
Alt-H	Open Help menu.
Alt-O D	Change day settings.
Alt-O M	Apply mark to a date in Monthly mode display.
Alt-O S	Insert non-standard time into Daily display.
Alt-S D	Move to a specific date.

Alt-S N	Move to the following day's display.
Alt-S P	Move back one day.
Alt-S T	Jump to today's date.
Alt-Space C	Terminate program and return to Program Manager.
Alt-Space M	Move current icon or window against the background.
Alt-Space N	Minimise window, i.e. reduce it to an icon.
Alt-Space R	Restore icon to a window or former size and shape.
Alt-Space S	Resize or reshape the current window.
Alt-Space W	Activate Task Switching dialogue box.
Alt-Space X	Maximise window, i.e. make it fill the entire screen.
Alt-V D	Switch to Daily display mode.
Alt-V M	Switch to Monthly display mode.
Ctrl-Esc	Activate Task Switching dialogue box.
Ctrl-Ins	Copy selected text to Clipboard.
Ctrl-PgDn	Move to the next day, e.g. tomorrow.
Ctrl-PgUp	Move back one day, e.g. yesterday.
F1	Activate Help Main Index.
F4	Move to a specific date.
F5	Set alarm for currently selected time.
F6	Apply mark to specific date in Monthly mode.
F7	Insert non-standard time slot into Daily display.
F8	Switch to daily display mode.
F9	Switch to Monthly display mode.
Shift-Del	Copy selected text to Clipboard and delete it from the Calendar.
Shift-Ins	Insert Clipboard contents at current cursor position.
&C	Centre the text within the margins of printout.
&D	Print the current system date with file contents.
&F	Include the filename of the printed file - this is the default header.
&L	Left justify the text.
&P	Include page numbers - this is the default footer.
&R	Right justify the text.
&T	Include the current system time.

Cardfile

Windows Cardfile is a simple flat database which uses individual index cards to record and sort data. The program presents its data as a stack of index cards. The program can also be used to dial into the telephone network directly, if it is connected and configured to do this. The amount of information you can get onto the cards is very limited and as there is no provision for resizing the individual cards this tends to limit the number of uses that the program can be applied to. Still, for keeping track of small amounts of information the program is ideal and there is no limit to the number of cards you can have in any one file, excluding the memory and disk limits of course. I use the program to store the details of my collection of model vehicles as each card is just large enough to contain the information I want. For more specific and specialised information I have to use something else, but for broad outlines Cardfile is ideal.

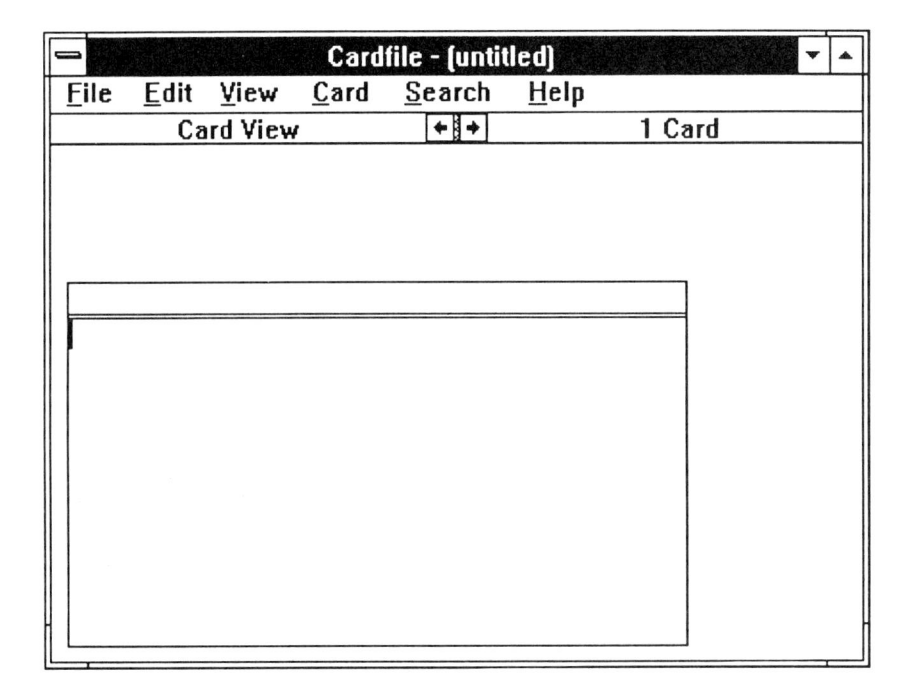

Cardfile

The cards are sorted automatically, based on the contents of the Index line of each card - there is no provision to sort them on the main card contents. Numbers are placed first, don't forget that 10 comes after 1 and before 2 because the sorting is done on one digit at a time, followed by letters, from A to Z, in normal alphabetical, followed by symbols. While you cannot sort the cards on the contents of other than the Index line, you can search through the card text, but not the Index line, using the Search routine.

You can even incorporate graphics, from the Paintbrush program for example, onto any card via the Clipboard, by simply pasting it in. All in all Cardfile is one of the most useful programs that is bundled with Windows 3, although it has its limitations, and it is a shame that you cannot vary the card size.

To run the program select the Cardfile icon, it looks like a stack of index cards, and either press **Enter** or double click on it.

The window layout is standard, the Control Box, Title bar, Minimise and Maximise button and Menu bar along the top. Immediately below the Menu Bar is the Status line, this tells you what view you are using, Card or List, and the number of cards in the current file. It also contains a pair of arrows that allow you to page through the cards, one at a time, by clicking the arrowheads. Below the Status line is the main window area containing a single card - we'll come back to that in a minute or three.

Cardfile menus

Cardfile has a total of five specific menus plus the usual Help one. The **File** menu is, as usual concerned with inputting and outputting files, and contains the following commands:

New which starts a file. If you have modified the existing file and not saved it, you will be prompted to do so before the new file is created.

Open allows you to load a specific, previously saved file. In the process this will over-write any file that is already on screen and so you should save this first - unless it's to be discarded.

Save is used to write the current file to the disk under an existing name, shown in the Title Bar.

```
New
Open...
Save
Save As...
Print
Print All
Page Setup...
Printer Setup...
Merge...
Exit
```

File Menu

Save As allows you to save the current file to a new filename, e.g. to make a duplicate of the current file.

Print will produce a hard copy of an individual file, this option is not available if you are using the List view, see below.

Print All sends all of the cards in the current Cardfile to the printer where they will be printed out as boxed cards, i.e. each card appears in its own box.

Page Setup is identical to that in Calendar, it allows you to set the margins and specify what information will be included on the printout.

Printer Setup allows you to select a printer, other than the default printer to which the file will be sent.

Merge allows you to import an existing file, e.g. to combine two or more files together into one large one. The files have to be selected from disk as if they were being loaded. As the files are merged, the Program will sort them automatically.

Exit terminates Cardfile and returns you to the Program Manager.

The **Edit** menu is a bit of a mix, it contains the usual Clipboard commands plus some extra ones.

Undo cancels the last action, e.g. if you have deleted some text accidentally press **Alt-Backspace** and it reappears.

Cut copies selected text to the Clipboard and then deletes it from the card.

Copy simply copies the selected text to the Clipboard but leaves it in place on the card.

Paste inserts the Clipboard contents at the current cursor position.

Index allows you to modify the Index line of the current card, i.e. the one shown at the front of the stack.

Restore is very handy. It allows you to cancel any changes that you have made to the current card and return it to its original content. However, you must not move the card or change your view before doing so. Equally the command will not restore a deleted card - because it is no longer at the front of the stack!

Text, the default option, allows you to paste text into the card.

Picture is used only when you want to paste a graphic from the Clipboard into the current card. If you don't select Picture then the graphic cannot be pasted.

The **View** menu contains only two commands, **Card** and **List**. By default Cardfile always displays the file contents as cards as shown in the illustration on Page 330. However, you can change the display so that it shows only the index lines of the cards in the file, shown opposite, in which case you get no extra detail. While you are using List, a number of the commands in the menu will be grey, i.e. inoperable.

The **Card** menu is mainly used to insert or remove cards from the current stack, it will also allows you to dial number directly. There are four commands in the menu:

Add which allows you to add a card to the current stack. When you use this command a dialogue box appears asking for the

contents of the Index line of the card being added. Once you have
entered this the card is added to the stack and placed at the front.
The remainder of the stack will be shifted around so that they
remain in the correct order.

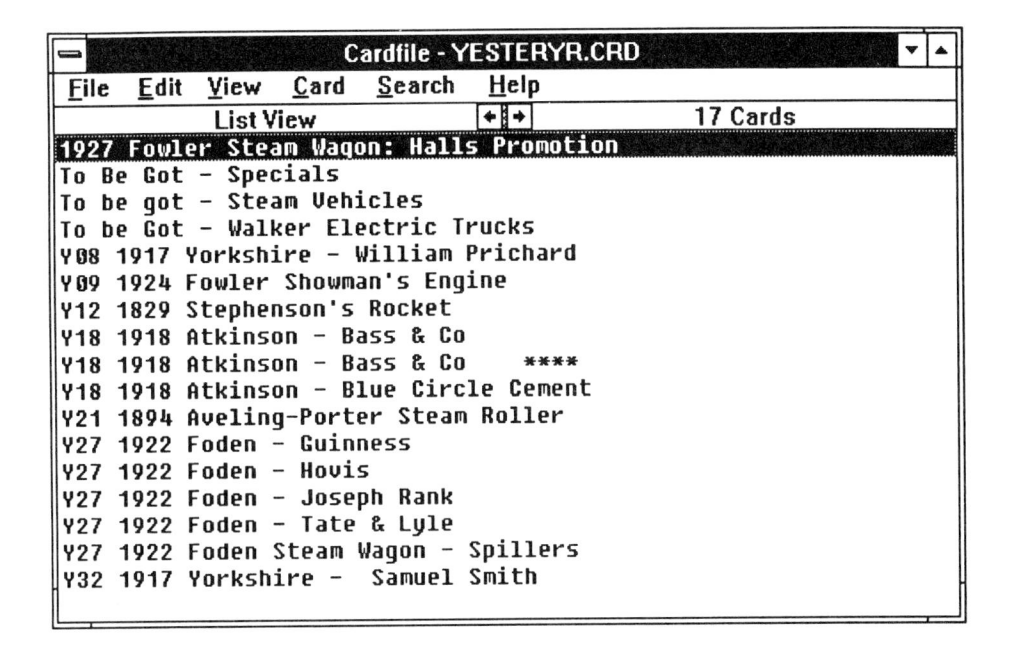

```
┌─────────────────────────────────────────────────────────────┐
│ ─          Cardfile - YESTERYR.CRD                    ▼ ▲  │
│ File  Edit  View  Card  Search  Help                        │
│          List View         ← ▌ →              17 Cards      │
│ ▌1927 Fowler Steam Wagon: Halls Promotion                   │
│ To Be Got - Specials                                        │
│ To be got - Steam Vehicles                                  │
│ To be Got - Walker Electric Trucks                          │
│ Y08 1917 Yorkshire - William Prichard                       │
│ Y09 1924 Fowler Showman's Engine                            │
│ Y12 1829 Stephenson's Rocket                                │
│ Y18 1918 Atkinson - Bass & Co                               │
│ Y18 1918 Atkinson - Bass & Co       ****                    │
│ Y18 1918 Atkinson - Blue Circle Cement                      │
│ Y21 1894 Aveling-Porter Steam Roller                        │
│ Y27 1922 Foden - Guinness                                   │
│ Y27 1922 Foden - Hovis                                      │
│ Y27 1922 Foden - Joseph Rank                                │
│ Y27 1922 Foden - Tate & Lyle                                │
│ Y27 1922 Foden Steam Wagon - Spillers                       │
│ Y32 1917 Yorkshire -  Samuel Smith                          │
└─────────────────────────────────────────────────────────────┘
```

List Display

Delete will remove the current card, i.e. the one at the front of the
stack, from the file. Once deleted a card cannot be recovered - it
is lost irretrievably.

Duplicate does just that, it creates an exact copy of the current
card and then places it at the front of the stack.

Autodial allows you to dial the number given on the Index line of
the current card. Before you use this option you must have the
phone and modem connected and configured.

The final menu is **Search** and this is used to find specific cards, based
on their Index lines, or a string of text within the cards themselves. The
menu contains three commands:

Goto brings up a dialogue box that asks for a key word to search for. You can enter a whole word or part of one. Once you press Enter the program then searches through the index lines of the cards to find a match. Note: the search routine is not case sensitive, i.e. Alpha is identical to ALPHA as it is to alpha.

Find is similar to Goto but it searches through the contents of the cards and ignores the Index lines. Again the routine is not case sensitive.

Find Next allows you to find the next occurrence of the string you have entered in the Find command without having to activate the dialogue box again.

Using the program

1) Whenever you run Cardfile it will always present you with a single blank card by default. To change the Index line, i.e. the top line above the double line, on this card press **F6** to bring the dialogue box. Enter the details for the Index line, you can use up to 40 characters in all, and they will be applied to the blank card. For the sake of this exercise use your name, forename then surname, for this card.

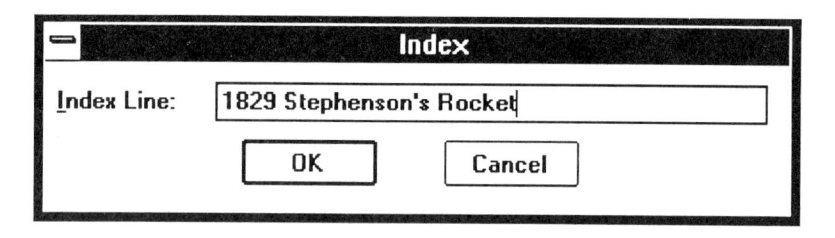

```
┌─────────────────── Index ───────────────────┐
│                                             │
│ Index Line:  │1829 Stephenson's Rocket│     │
│                                             │
│           ┌────OK────┐   ┌──Cancel──┐       │
└─────────────────────────────────────────────┘
```

Index Line Dialogue Box

2) To add another card to the existing one you can click on **Card** in the Menu Bar and then on **Add** or simply press **F7**. (In many ways, Cardfile is actually easier to use with the keyboard than with the mouse. The mouse provides the occasional shortcut but because the program is heavily text based, the keyboard is usually just as fast, if not faster.) This brings up a dialogue box similar to the first one but the details you enter

here will be applied to the new card. When you press **Enter** the new card is placed in front of the old one.

You can move through the stack of cards, regardless of how many it contains, by clicking on the arrowheads in the Status Line or you can move to a specific card by clicking on the edge of it. For example, if you wanted the card about halfway through the stack you can either click on its Index line or on any part of the card that is visible. This will bring the card to the front and reflow the remaining cards so that they remain in alphabetical order.

3) But suppose you wanted to store the same details of each person, what then? Go back to the original card, the one with your name on it. The cursor will be flashing on the first line of the card below the Index line. Enter the following so that you have six lines of text on the card, press **Enter** after each colon and you move down one line:

Birthdate:
Current Age:
Favourite Colour:
Favourite Flower:
Favourite Food:
Pet name:

4) We're going to copy all of this to the second card. Click just before the **B** on the first line and then drag the mouse downwards, while still holding the mouse button down. As you do so the text in each line will be highlighted. Providing you press **Enter** after the last colon you should be able to highlight the last line by dragging past it. If you didn't press Enter then you will have to drag left to the colon. Release the button.

5) Press **Ctrl-Ins** to copy the text into the Clipboard. Now click on the second card and it comes to the front, again the cursor is on the first line. Press **Shift-Ins** and the text from the Clipboard is pasted in. The Clipboard still retains its contents so you can could create more cards in the same way.

6) Duplicating cards this way is okay if you are only doing a couple at a time but if you want a number of almost identical cards there is an easier way. Press **F7** and press **Enter**. A new card appears with nothing on its Index line. Paste in the Clipboard contents again using **Shift-Ins**. Now click on **Card** in the Menu Bar and then on **Duplicate** in the menu that

appears. A new card will be created that is identical to the current one, i.e. it contains the same details and has nothing on the Index line. Press **F6** and put another family member's name on the Index line. Click on the blank card again and duplicate it, in the same way, until you have about ten cards - changing the Index line on each so that it bears the name of a family member. You should then have something like the illustration below. (The figure shows some of my steam vehicle models.)

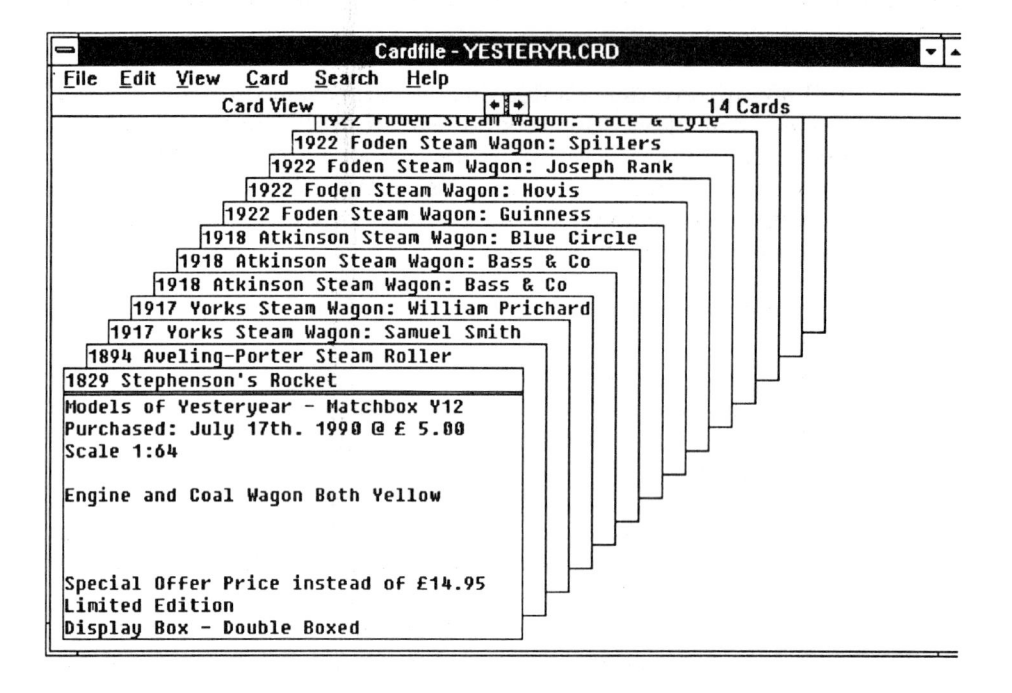

```
┌─────────────────────── Cardfile - YESTERYR.CRD ───────────────── ▼▲
 File  Edit  View  Card  Search  Help
                  Card View         ←▯→                    14 Cards
                             ┌1922 Foden Steam Wagon: Tate & Lyle
                            ┌1922 Foden Steam Wagon: Spillers
                           ┌1922 Foden Steam Wagon: Joseph Rank
                          ┌1922 Foden Steam Wagon: Hovis
                         ┌1922 Foden Steam Wagon: Guinness
                        ┌1918 Atkinson Steam Wagon: Blue Circle
                       ┌1918 Atkinson Steam Wagon: Bass & Co
                      ┌1918 Atkinson Steam Wagon: Bass & Co
                     ┌1917 Yorks Steam Wagon: William Prichard
                    ┌1917 Yorks Steam Wagon: Samuel Smith
                   ┌1894 Aveling-Porter Steam Roller
                  │1829 Stephenson's Rocket
                  │Models of Yesteryear - Matchbox Y12
                  │Purchased: July 17th. 1990 @ £ 5.00
                  │Scale 1:64
                  │
                  │Engine and Coal Wagon Both Yellow
                  │
                  │
                  │
                  │Special Offer Price instead of £14.95
                  │Limited Edition
                  │Display Box - Double Boxed
                  └─────────────────────────────────────
```

A Card Stack

7) Delete the blank card by bringing it to the front of the stack and then clicking on **Card** in the Menu Bar, then on **Delete**. Click on **Yes** in the dialogue box that appears. Save the remaining cards by pressing **Alt-F A** to bring up the Save As dialogue box. Enter a filename and the file is written to disk. You need not apply any extension because Cardfile automatically adds its own CRD extension. Once the file has been saved the name you gave it will appear on the Title Bar, e.g. **Cardfile - [filename].CRD**.

8) Fill in the relevant details on each of the cards you have just created. You'll have to enter the details on one and then page to the next and so on. To move from one line to another on a card use the **Up** and **Down** keys. If you press **Enter** then you add a blank line after the line you are currently on. Because you are only allowed eleven lines on each card the computer will soon beep if you do this too often. When you have entered all the details on each card save the file again by pressing **Alt-F S**. This time no dialogue box appears because you are saving the file to the same name as before.

Save As Dialogue Box

9) Print the file and see what it looks like. You can print the details in two ways, either as just a list of Index line contents or as individual cards which gives the card contents as well as the Index line. Try doing both. Click on **View** in the Menu Bar and then on **List**. You get a listing of cards like the figure shown over the page.

10) Open the **File** menu and click on **Page Setup**. By default you should have **&f** as the Header and **Page &p** as the Footer. If you have just click on **OK**, if not then enter these details into the relevant boxes before doing so.

11) Open the **File** menu again and click on **Printer Setup**. Double click on whichever printer you want to use for printing the file. If you have only one printer installed and configured then you can skip this step.

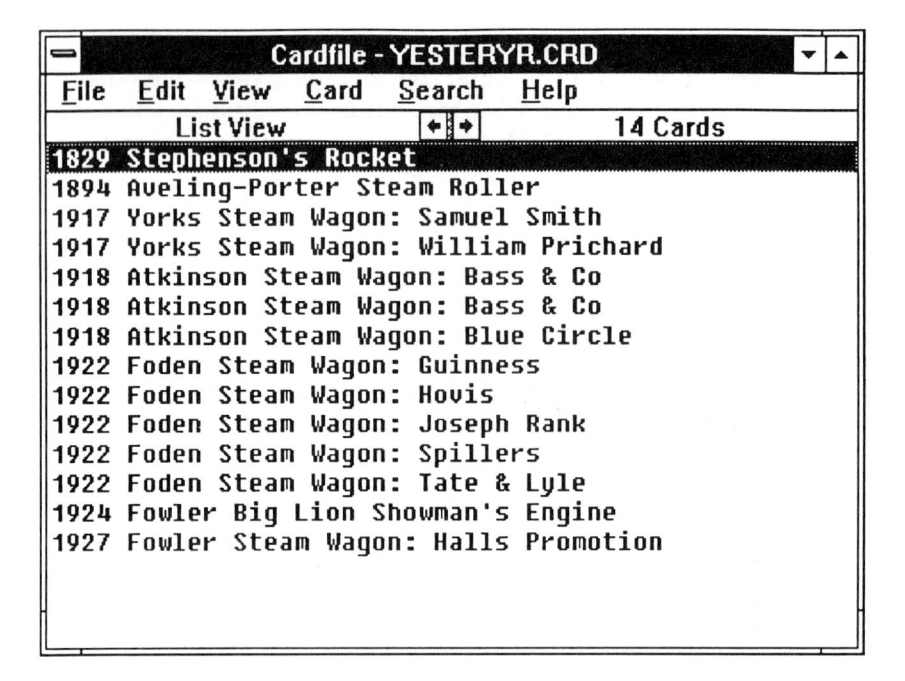

```
┌─────────────────────────────────────────────────┐
│ ═  │        Cardfile - YESTERYR.CRD      │ ▼ ▲ │
│ File  Edit  View  Card  Search  Help            │
│         List View      ← →        14 Cards      │
│ 1829 Stephenson's Rocket                        │
│ 1894 Aveling-Porter Steam Roller                │
│ 1917 Yorks Steam Wagon: Samuel Smith            │
│ 1917 Yorks Steam Wagon: William Prichard        │
│ 1918 Atkinson Steam Wagon: Bass & Co            │
│ 1918 Atkinson Steam Wagon: Bass & Co            │
│ 1918 Atkinson Steam Wagon: Blue Circle          │
│ 1922 Foden Steam Wagon: Guinness                │
│ 1922 Foden Steam Wagon: Hovis                   │
│ 1922 Foden Steam Wagon: Joseph Rank             │
│ 1922 Foden Steam Wagon: Spillers                │
│ 1922 Foden Steam Wagon: Tate & Lyle             │
│ 1924 Fowler Big Lion Showman's Engine           │
│ 1927 Fowler Steam Wagon: Halls Promotion        │
│                                                 │
└─────────────────────────────────────────────────┘
```

Cardfile List

12) Open the **File** menu a third time and click on **Print All**. You cannot select Print because it is grey, i.e. inoperable, and not available for printing the List format. The file will be sent to the printer. As it is, a message box appears telling you that it is being printed. Just leave this alone and it will vanish in a few seconds. Very shortly, the exact time depends on how large your file is, the list will be printed out for you. At the top of the page is the filename and each separate page has the correct page number on it.

13) Okay, time to print the cards. Change to the Card view by pressing **Alt-V C** and then press **Alt-F A** to print all the cards - use the same printer and file information as before. If you select Print then only the card at the front of the stack is printed. Again a message box appears telling you the file is being printed. This time your printout will contain a number of boxes, each one representing a single card.

Depending on the page size you should get between four and six cards on a page - all down one side only. This is one of the annoying foibles about Cardfile, even though there is enough room on a page for the cards to be printed two abreast it insists on printing then in a single column. Even if you reduce all the margins to zero and leave out both the header and footer you still only get one column - at least on an A4 sheet which is what I use!

Page Setup Dialogue Box

Cardfile Summary

- Cardfile is a simple flat database which uses small index cards to hold and sort information.

- The cards are sorted automatically into alphanumeric order, numbers take precedence over letters which come before symbols.

- The print out can be either a list of the Index lines or as representations of the cards - but the latter wastes paper.

- Within its limitations, Cardfile is a nice, easy-to-use program that is ideal as an introduction to simple databases. But is a great shame that you cannot use different sized cards.

Cardfile Keyboard Summary

Alt-Backspace	Undo last text action.
Alt-C A	Add new card to stack.
Alt-C D	Delete card from front of stack.
Alt-C P	Duplicate current card.
Alt-C T	Activate Autodial.
Alt-E C	Copy selected data to Clipboard.
Alt-E E	Allow the pasting of graphics.
Alt-E I	Edit Index line of current card.
Alt-E P	Insert Clipboard contents at cursor position.
Alt-E R	Restore current card to original state - providing it has not been moved.
Alt-E T	Allow the pasting of text.
Alt-E T	Cut selected data to Clipboard.
Alt-E U	Undo last text action.
Alt-Esc	Activate next program without using Task Switching.
Alt-F A	Save the current file to a new filename.
Alt-F L	Print all the cards or the List of Index lines.
Alt-F M	Load an existing file and add it to the current one.
Alt-F N	Create a new cardfile.
Alt-F O	Load a previously saved file from disk.
Alt-F P	Print current card, i.e. the one at the front, only.
Alt-F R	Select a printer to be used.
Alt-F S	Save current file to filename shown on the Title Bar.
Alt-F T	Activate Page Setting dialogue box.
Alt-F X	Terminate Cardfile and return to Program Manager.
Alt-F4	Terminate program and return to Program Manager.
Alt-S F	Find text on cards that matches user input.
Alt-S G	Move to a specific card, based on Index line match.
Alt-S N	Find next occurrence of text on cards.
Alt-Space C	Terminate program and return to Program Manager.
Alt-Space M	Move current icon or window against the background.
Alt-Space N	Minimise window, i.e. reduce it to an icon.
Alt-Space R	Restore icon to a window of former size and shape.
Alt-Space S	Resize or reshape the current window.
Alt-Space W	Activate Task Switching dialogue box.
Alt-Space X	Maximise window, i.e. make the window fill the entire screen.
Alt-V C	Shows cardfile as Cards.
Alt-V L	Show only the Index lines of current file.
Ctrl-Esc	Activate Task Switching dialogue box.
Ctrl-Ins	Copy selected data to Clipboard.
F1	Activate Help Main Index.

F3	Find next occurrence of user input text.
F4	Jump directly to a specific card that matches user input.
F5	Activate Autodial.
F6	Edit Index line of current card.
F7	Add new card to stack.
Shift-Del	Copy selected data from card to Clipboard and then delete it from the card.
Shift-Ins	Insert Clipboard contents at cursor position.
&C	Centre the text within the margins of printout.
&D	Print the current system date with file contents.
&F	Include the filename of the printed file. - this is the default header.
&L	Left justify the text.
&P	Include page numbers - this is the default footer.
&R	Right justify the text.
&T	Include the current system time.

Clock

The Windows Clock is just that, a timepiece that appears in a window. You can select to have either an Analogue or a Digital clock. Either way the window can be resized as much as you like. If the Clock is reduced to an icon it still appears as if it was in a window and so you can see the time which is very handy. The Clock has only one menu and that controls the appearance of the clock.

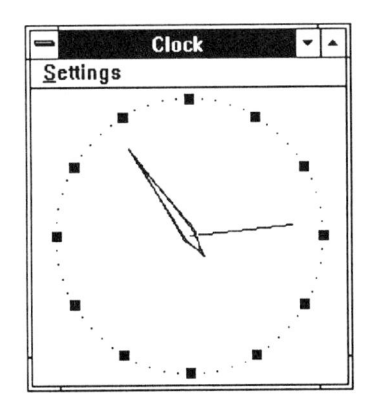

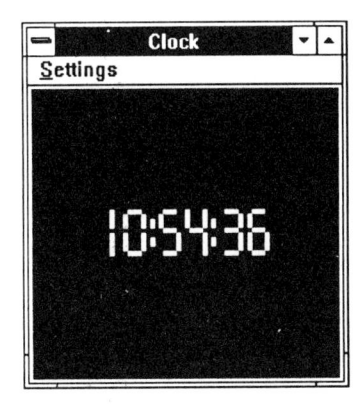

Clock - Analogue and Digital

Chapter 13
Games people play

Windows comes complete with two simple but compulsive games. The first, Reversi, is a computer version of a Japanese game called Othello, the second is Solitaire, a card game known in the U.K as Patience. Both are good - but Solitaire in particular is the most compulsive computer game I have ever played and the fact that I lose more often that I win doesn't matter.

When you installed Windows, the Setup program created a separate group called Games to contain these two programs - as much as anything to show you an example of how groups operate. Personally I have long since moved them into the Accessories group and deleted the original Games group. However, you may have chosen not to do this, and it doesn't really matter what group they are in. Anyway, we're going to look at the two games in this chapter and see what they are about.

Reversi

This is a fairly modern game, it was invented either in Japan or in China - depending on which version of the myth you subscribe to, and it lends itself well to being played on the computer. The object of the game is simply to end up with more of your coloured counters on the board than the computer has of its colour. Your counters are Red, white on monochrome monitor, and the computer's are Blue, black on monochrome. To run the game double click on the program icon.

The board is divided into 64 equal squares, in an 8 by 8 grid, and at the start of the game there are four counters, two for each player, positioned in the centre of this board. You can resize the program window, even to the extent of maximising it and the game board and counters will be stretched accordingly - although the board will never completely fill the window, it always has a large amount of background area around it. Equally as you shrink the Reversi window, the board changes to accommodate the new size.

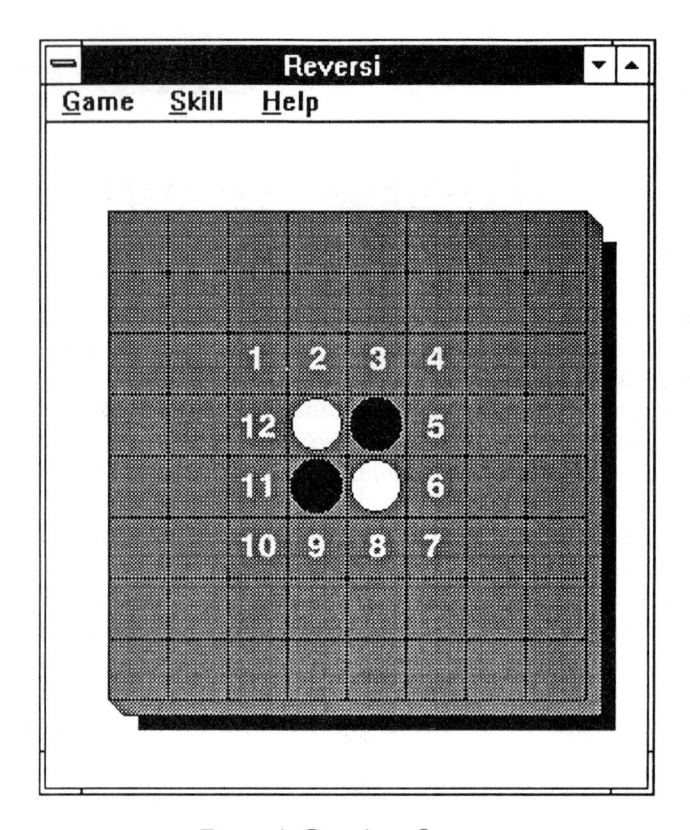

Reversi Opening Screen
(Note, the numbers have been added by me - they are not part of the normal board.)

Players, actually you and the computer - there is no provision for playing against another human player - take it in turn to move and each player must make a valid move if such a possible move exists. A valid move is one where you ensnare any number of your opponent's counters between two of yours. Thus in the illustration above, the only places that Red (White) can move are the squares numbered 3, 5, 9 and 11 because these are the only squares that trap the Blue (Black) counters. Counters can be trapped either vertically, horizontally, diagonally or a combination of all three. When a counter, or a number of counters, is entrapped in this way it is turned over and so becomes the opposite colour. In the board game the counters are coloured white on one side and black on the other. At the end of the game, the player with the most counters in their colour showing is the winner.

Simple? Don't you believe it! Reversi could almost have been designed and created to run on a computer. The game play is purely mathematical and computers have no equal when it comes to number crunching. The machine will beat the pants off you 99.9% of the time. On those very rare occasions when you do win it is liable to be more by skill and good judgment than by luck. Reversi is one game that has little or no element of luck in it - especially when you are playing against the computer because the computer doesn't make mistakes. Having said that though the fun comes in trying to beat the machine.

The fastest way to play the game is with the mouse. Whenever you move the cursor onto a valid square the cursor becomes a cross, otherwise it remains an arrowhead signifying an invalid move. To place a counter on a valid square, just click the mouse button and the counter appears. Then the computer makes its move. At times it seems that even before you have released the button the computer has responded and it's your go again, especially at the Beginner and Novice levels.

The program provides three menus; Games, Skill and Help. The Help menu will provide you with very brief instructions on playing the game and nothing else - it will not provide you with any tips or game plan ideas. The **Skills** menu is used to select a level of play for yourself and this affects how fast the computer responds when making its move. There are four levels of skill:

>**Beginner**, the simplest and the default, it provides the fastest game.
>
>**Novice** is almost as fast.
>
>Select **Expert** and things begin to slow down. The computer takes longer to make its move.
>
>**Master** is the slowest game pace. As each piece is placed so the next play take longer and longer. By the time you get near the end of the game the computer is literally taking minutes to move.

You can change skill level as you go through the game, every move if you wanted to, but you invariably lose when you do this.

The **Game** menu provides four commands:

>**Hint** which allows you to get a helping hand from the computer. By selecting this command the computer will position the cursor in that square of the board which is the optimum position for you to

win that round. This does not necessarily mean you will win the whole game - just that one placement. In Reversi fortunes change with every counter placement.

Pass allows you to miss a go. You can only do this when there is no valid square for you to place a counter on. If you can go then you must is the rule. When you do reach an impasse you have to select Pass so that the computer gets an extra go.

New terminates the current game and/or begins a new game with the four counters back in the centre of the board.

Exit terminates Reversi.

A tip: The computer always tries to get diagonal lines because these provide the most useful ways of trapping the opponent pieces. The four corner squares are the most valuable to any player.

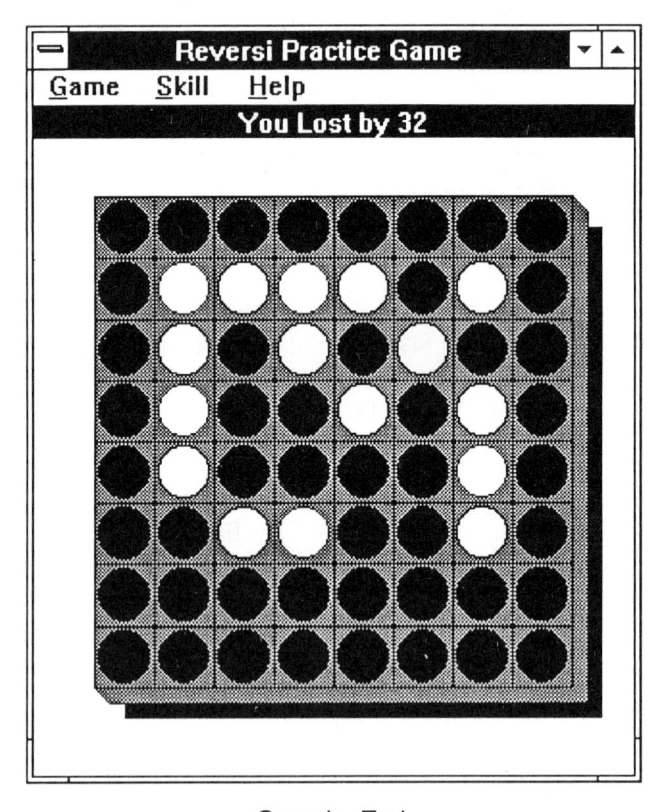

Game's End

Reversi Summary

- Reversi is very addictive but the computer invariably wins and ultimately this decreases the pleasure of the game.

- To play the game - take your time, have patience and look carefully before you move.

Reversi Keyboard Summary

Alt-Esc	Activate next program without using Task Switching.
Alt-F4	Terminate program and return to Program Manager.
Alt-G H	Get a hint from the computer.
Alt-G N	Start a new game.
Alt-G P	Miss a go - only if there is no valid move possible.
Alt-G X	Terminate the program.
Alt-S B	Set Beginner skill level.
Alt-S E	Set Expert game level.
Alt-S M	Set Master game level.
Alt-S N	Set Novice level.
Alt-Space C	Terminate program and return to Program Manager.
Alt-Space M	Move current icon or window against the background.
Alt-Space N	Minimise window, i.e. reduce it to an icon.
Alt-Space R	Restore icon to a window or former size and shape.
Alt-Space S	Resize or reshape the current window.
Alt-Space W	Activate Task Switching dialogue box.
Alt-Space X	Maximise window to fill the entire screen.
Ctrl-Esc	Activate Task Switching dialogue box.
Cursor keys	Move cursor in specific direction.
Enter	Place counter at cursor position.
F1	Activate Help Main Index.

Solitaire

Solitaire is a computer rendition of a popular card game, which in the U.K is called Patience. (In the U.K. Solitaire is a single player game played with little pegs or marbles on a slotted board.) The basic rules of the game are very simple, you have to place cards of decreasing value and of the opposite colour on the existing ones, e.g. you can place the Six of Hearts or the Six of Diamonds onto the Seven of Clubs or the Seven of Spades. In this computer game there is an added element - you have to assemble all the cards of the same suit into four stacks to win the game.

To run the program double click on the Solitaire icon, which looks like a pack of cards, in the Accessories group of Program Manager. You can run the game directly from MS-DOS by entering **WIN SOL**, which will invoke Windows and then automatically load Solitaire for you. I suggest that you maximise the Solitaire window because you will need a lot of space. When you resize the window the cards themselves do not change size and so in a small window you cannot see them all.

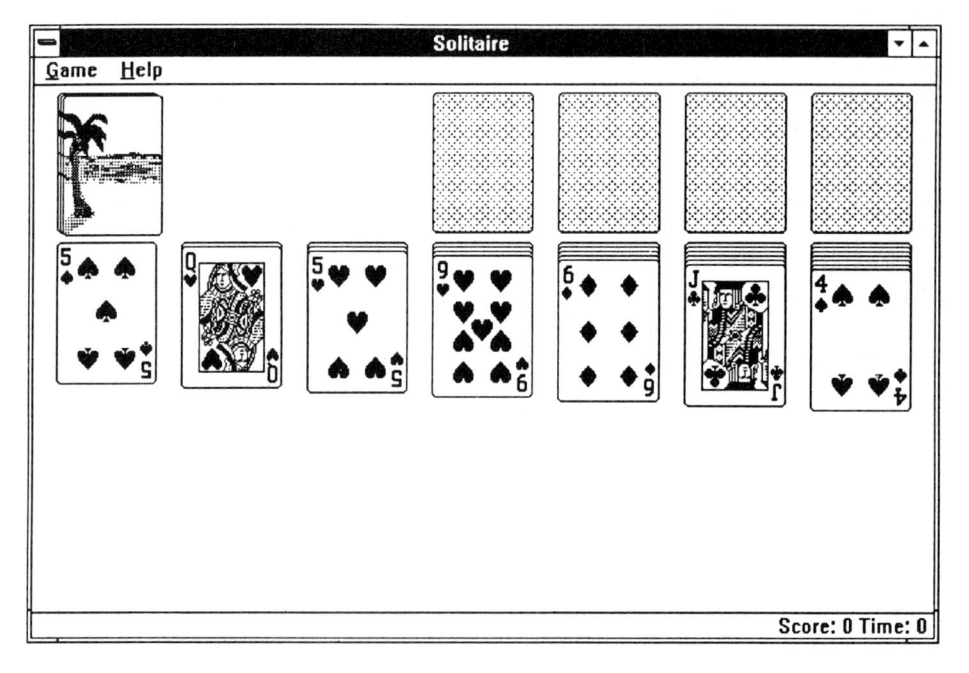

Solitaire Opening Screen

Please excuse the quality of the illustrations in this section but the Solitaire game in monochrome is truly appalling. The game has got to be played in colour or you are likely to strain your eyes. The game playing window consists of three areas:

> In the top left hand corner is the pack of unused cards. It is from this that you draw cards for placing, either individually or in threes.
>
> The main playing area consists of rows of cards. From left to right, the sequence runs like this: first a single card, face up; second pile, one card face down and one face up; third pile, three cards, two face down and one face up; fourth pile, four cards, three face down, top card face up; fifth pile, five cards, four face down, the top one face up; sixth pile, six cards, five obscured and one visible; seventh pile, seven cards, six face down, the top one face up.
>
> Above and to the right of the main area are four markers, these are used to place the cards in their correct suits. You must place an Ace first and then the Two, the Three and so on. You are not allowed mix cards of different suits here, i.e. each pile must be of a single suit only.

The program provides only two menus, the first labelled Game, which contains the following. There is also a Help menu but many of the details it gives you are wrong, especially about scoring!

> **Deal** which starts a new game by dealing the cards again.
>
> **Undo** allows you to cancel the move you have just made, at a price of losing points if you are playing the Standard scoring game.
>
> **Deck** allows you to select a new pattern for the back of the cards; there are a total of 12 possible graphics.
>
> **Options** which brings up a dialogue box that allows you to set various parameters for the game.

Playing the game

The game as it appears is ready to play, but before we get into that let's look at some of the options available to you. Open the **Game** menu and click on **Options,** or press **Alt-G O.** This will bring up the Options dialogue box.

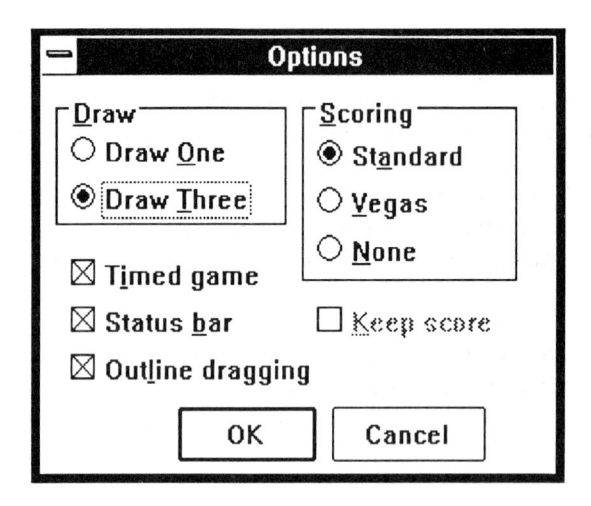

Options Dialogue Box

Draw One allows you to turn over one card at a time from the unused deck. Personally I consider this to be cheating as it makes the game too easy!

Draw Three turns the unused deck over in groups of three. This is the default option, shown by having a blob in the box beside it.

Timed Game means that the computer keeps a record of how fast or slow you play. The time, in seconds, will be displayed at the extreme right hand corner of the Status Bar along the bottom of the window. You can only get a bonus if you are using a timed game.

Status Bar is a toggle that turns the Status bar on or off. By default it is on. Besides you want to see what you running score is, don't you?

Outline Dragging means that when you bring a card that will fit over another one, the card it will fit with turns into inverse video. This is very useful because as soon as the target card is shown in this way you can release the card you are moving and it fits itself onto the pile of cards.

Keep Score only applies to Vegas scoring and it makes a running total of your losses.

Scoring

The Scoring is a bit complex! Basically you can have No score or one of two types of scoring. Don't change the scoring type, or any of the boxed options, during a game or it automatically restarts.

Vegas is based on money. Every time you start a new game it costs you $52. Why 52? I don't know, that's just the way it is and never having been to Las Vegas I don't know any different - maybe that's the minimum bet at the casinos. Anyway, you get $5 back for every card that you place into the suit packs, i.e. the ones at the top right hand corner of the screen. But there is a drawback. You are only allowed to turn the cards in the unused deck over a maximum of three times. After that a large red X appears where the deck should be. The odds on you completing the game this fast have got to be very high but by all means try it. It's not real money after all.

Standard scoring is based on points. You amass points for the following:

> For every card from the unused deck that is placed onto one of the seven sequences on the main playing area you get 5 points.

> For every card that is placed onto the suit stacks, at the top right of the screen, you get 10 points.

> Move a card from one sequence to another and you get 5 points. For example moving the Five of Hearts in one sequence to the Six of Clubs in another will get you 5 points.

> Turn over the card that is face down on one of the sequences, e.g. as a result of moving the Five of Hearts above, and you get 5 points.

If you manage to completely build the four suit piles, from Ace to King, and you are playing a timed game then you will get a huge bonus based on the time that it has taken you. I've never worked out exactly how this is worked out but completing the game in less than 150 seconds will get you a bonus of around 4,000 points.

On top of that you get a wonderful display of cascading cards when you complete the game. This is the most spectacular effect I have ever seen on a standard PC monitor, leaving aside things like animated cartoons. The speed and clarity with which the monitor display is updated is phenomenal.

You lose points for doing any of these:

Using Undo will cost you 2 points, sometimes, plus any points you got as a result of the previous action. For instance, if you placed a card on one of the sequences you would get 5 points. If you then undo it you lose 7 points, the 2 for using Undo and the 5 you got for placing the card in the first place. However, if you use Undo to reverse an action that cost you points then you get the points back again.

In a Timed game you lose 2 points for every 10 seconds of play as the clock records the next multiple of ten. Thus as the clock switches from 29 to 30 seconds you lose 2 points.

You are allowed to turn all the cards in the unused deck over three times without incurring any penalty. But turn them over a fourth time and you lose 20 points, and you lose another 20 points every time after that.

No matter how many points you lose you cannot end up with a negative score when using Standard Scoring. The highest score that I know of to date is 7,175 points. (Scored by my friend Pat Bitten - my friends and I indulge in friendly rivalry!)

Let's Play

Having sorted out the scoring and set your preferences, try a **Timed Game** with **Standard Scoring** and allowing **Outline Dragging**. First choose a different deck backing. By default the program uses the Robot but you can change this to any of the other eleven choices.

Open the **Game** menu again and click on **Deck** or press **Alt-G D** and this brings up the dialogue box containing the twelve decks. The current backing will have a black border around it. (The backing I've chosen, the Desert Island Beach, is the only one that shows up with any clarity on a monochrome screen!)

Reading them from left to right, top to bottom they are:

    a) A geometric pattern in red and blue.

    b) A geometric pattern in yellow and green.

    c) Four red and white fish against a cyan background.

    d) Three red and white fish on a blue background.

    e) Oak leaves and acorns on a black background.

    f) Oak leaves and acorns on a blue background.

    g) A little Robot. His dial moves and his lights flash once you start playing. He's cute!

    h) Dark Red Roses and leaves. Extremely well drawn.

    i) A Conch shell on a multicoloured background. Very pretty.

    j) A Dark and forbidding castle surrounded by flying bats, whose wings flap.

    k) A Desert Island Beach with a palm tree and sun. After a while a face appears on the sun and it sticks its tongue out at you before disappearing again! I wouldn't mind the beach but I can do without that.

    l) A Card sharp's arm, once you begin playing the odd Ace appears out of his cuff now and again.

I cannot provide an illustration for these because the majority of the backings come out as black on a monochrome screen. The graphics on these cards in colour are superb and whoever designed them deserves some kind of award, the roses in particular are fantastic. To change to a different deck you click on the one you want and then click on **OK**. You cannot select a new deck by double clicking on it unfortunately, nor is there any provision for using your own graphics as deck backing.

Right, having got all that done, let's play a game.

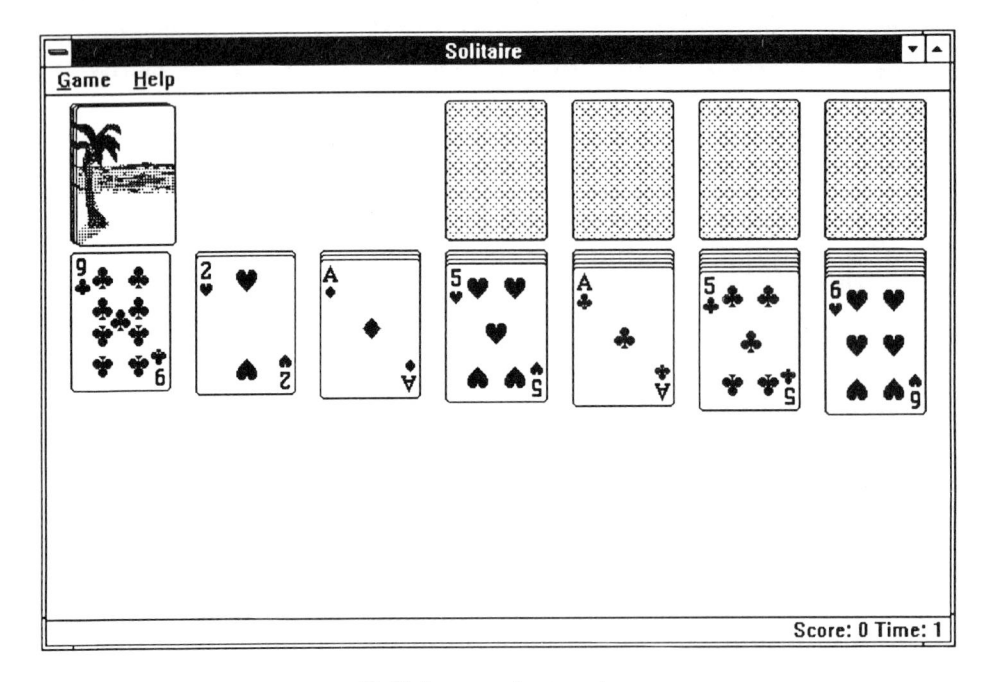

Solitaire ready to play

The Ace of Diamonds and the Ace of Clubs can be moved onto the suit stacks. You can either click and drag each one into position, one of the hatched areas will become inverse video as you get near it or you can double click on each one and it will be transported automatically. Once they are out of the way click once on each of the two face down cards that are revealed. (As it happens in this case, both were Aces and so they were moved up to the top as well and then the face down cards revealed again.) The Five of Clubs can be moved sideways onto the Six of Hearts, revealing another card, click on that to reveal it and we now have 60 points already. With the Ace of Hearts in position at the top, you can double click on the Two of Hearts and that will be moved up to cover it and you get another 10 points plus an additional 5 for turned up the revealed card. Now there are no more matches and so you have to turn over the first three cards of the unused deck. Click on this once and three cards are revealed, cascaded so you can see all three like this:

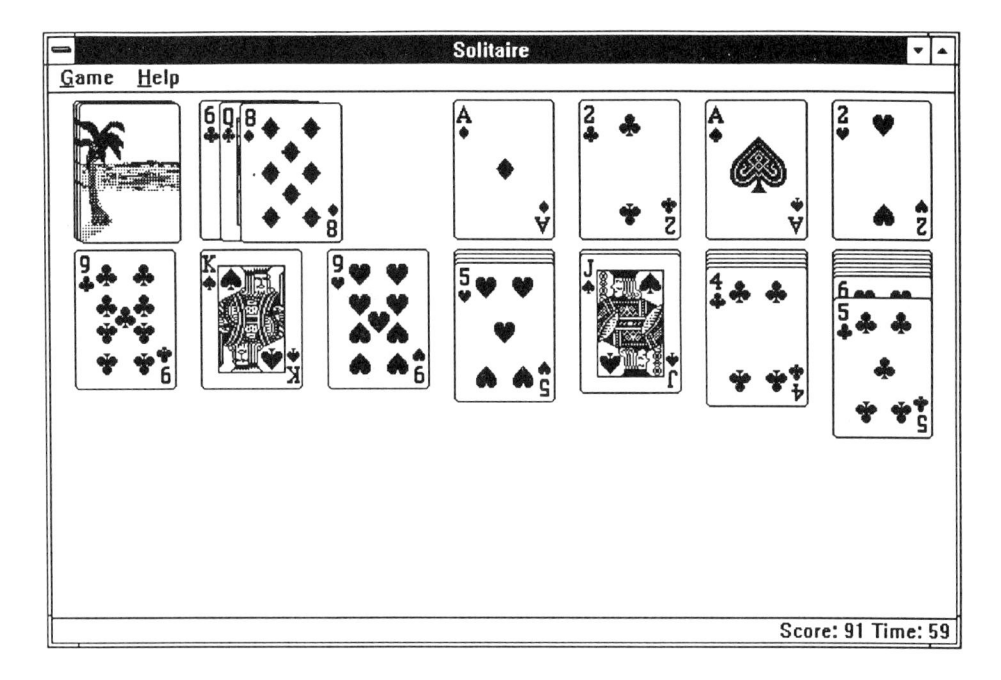

Into the Game

The Eight of diamonds, the top of the three, will go onto the Nine of Clubs - scoring another 5 Points. (By the way the score on the illustration above doesn't match because I'm writing this in real time, switching from Windows to WordStar and back again using **Alt-Esc**, and the game clock keeps running so losing me points. You can stop the clock at any time by reducing the Solitaire window to an icon.)

After further playing all the cards from one sequence had been moved to other sequences, leaving a gap. Into this you can only place a King, either from the unused deck or by moving one from another sequence.

Once all the cards in the unused deck have been turned over, a circle is revealed where the deck used to lie. Click on this and the unused deck is replaced, face down, and you can draw from it again - or you can combine both actions by double clicking on the circle. Off you go again, taking any drawn cards that fit and placing them on the sequences, moving sequences sideways until either you cannot place any more cards or you win the game. As you go along any card that will fit onto the suit packs, e.g. the Three of Hearts, can be placed into position either by dragging or by double clicking.

I've just played the above game out and was unable to complete it. The result looks like this and as you can see all the cards could not be turned over - in other words I didn't win.

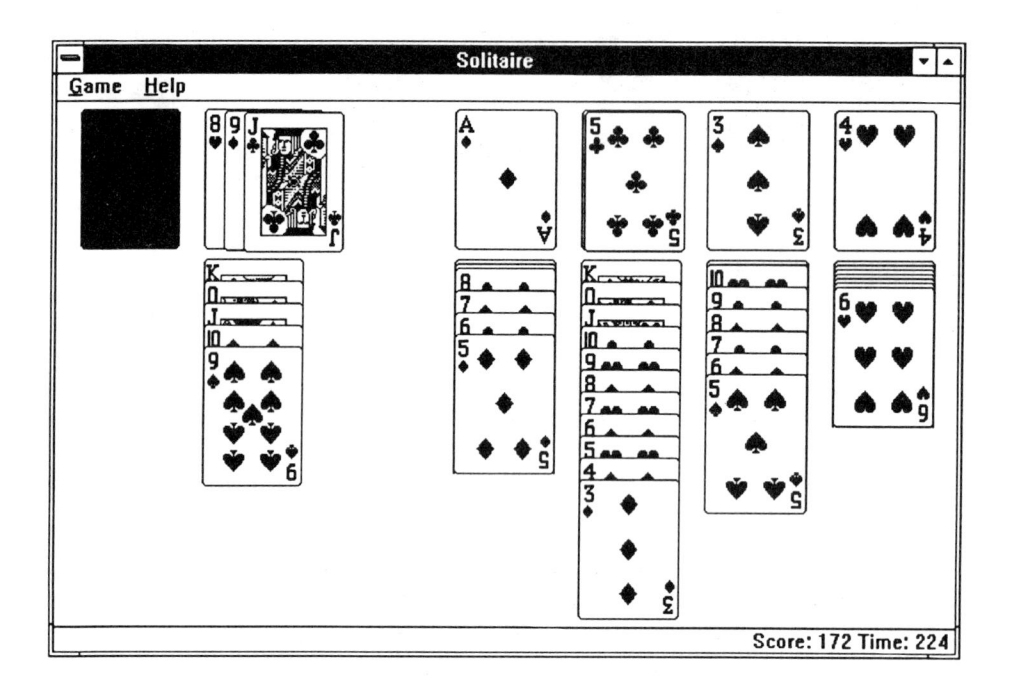

End of the Game

Solitaire Summary

- Solitaire is the most compulsive and addictive game I have ever encountered on a computer. It is much better than any such program that runs under MS-DOS.

- To obtain a bonus you must be playing a Standard Scoring, Timed game. The highest score known of to date is 7,175.

- The scoring is complex and the information given in the Help menu about it is incorrect.

- The graphical cascade when you win a game is one of the most spectacular screen effects you will ever see.

- A quibble! The card shuffling routine is not quite right and so you can end up with the sequences showing all the Twos one beside the other and the Aces all being in the sequence cards. Or you can end up with all the revealed cards being the same suit. This has never happened in real life, playing the game with actual cards, but still....

Solitaire Keyboard Summary

Alt-Esc	Activate next program without using Task Switching.
Alt-F4	Terminate program and return to Program Manager.
Alt-G C	Select a new backing for the deck from the dialogue box.
Alt-G D	Start a new game.
Alt-G O	Open the Options dialogue box and set game parameters.
Alt-G U	Undo last operation.
Alt-G X	Terminate Solitaire and return to Program Manager.
Alt-Space C	Terminate program and return to Program Manager.
Alt-Space M	Move current icon or window against the background.
Alt-Space N	Minimise window, i.e. reduce it to an icon.
Alt-Space R	Restore icon to a window of former size and shape.
Alt-Space S	Resize or reshape the current window.
Alt-Space W	Activate Task Switching dialogue box.
Alt-Space X	Maximise window, i.e. make the window fill the entire screen, somthing that you will need to do.
Ctrl-Esc	Activate Task Switching dialogue box.
F1	Activate Help Main Index.

Chapter 14

Notepad

What is it?

Notepad is a pure ASCII text editor that will allow you to create and/or modify simple text files. It is not, and doesn't pretend to be, a word processor but it is perfect for creating short notes. For instance I use it to record the Solitaire high scores. You can also use the program to create quite long documents and then paste the entire text into the Clipboard ready to go into another program. In fact much of this chapter was created that way, I wrote the bulk of the chapter in Notepad, because it was easier to do that than switch between Windows and WordStar all the time, and then pasted the resulting file directly into WordStar. That's the advantage of Windows 3. In reality the Notepad is not really suitable for doing this, because the text it produces is pure ASCII and this causes problems with WordStar, but it does give a good example of Notepad's capabilities.

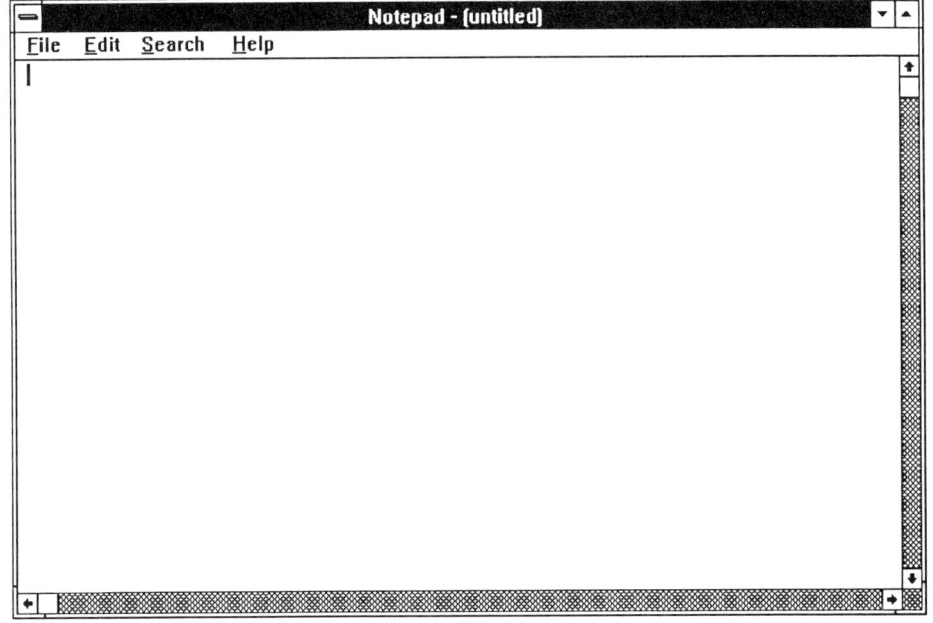

Notepad Opening Screen

I don't know of any other program, with the possible exception of Sidekick, that is as easy to use when it comes to dealing with pure ASCII files. Notepad will allow you to create an ASCII file of up to about 21 Kb, based on using the Laser computer with 2 Mb of RAM, although the actual file size depends on the amount of memory you have available. As with all Windows applications memory allocations are the limiting factor.

To run the program select the Notepad icon, it looks just like one, in the Accessories group window and then press **Enter**, or double click on the icon.

When the Notepad window appears it is fairly small. Along the top of the window are the usual Title Bar and Menu Bar and down each side of the main window area are the scroll bars. The reason for the scroll bars is very simple, Notepad uses pure ASCII and therefore it has no need of a word wrap at the end of a line of text - although you can produce an artificial one for the sake of clarity if you wish.

The Notepad **File** menu provides the following commands:

> **New** which allows you to start a new document. If you have made changes to the current one then you will be prompted about saving the changes before the new one is created.
>
> **Open** allows you to load a previously saved document. The dialogue box allows you to select any pure ASCII file from anywhere on your hard disks.
>
> **Save** is used to quickly write the current file to an existing filename. If you use this command with a new file you will be prompted to supply a filename first.
>
> **Save As** allows you to save the current file to a new filename. By default the program will always place your saved files into the Windows sub-directory.
>
> **Print** allows you to produce a hard copy of your file, including any details that have been set by the next command.
>
> **Page Setup** is used to include specific information on a print out and to set the page margins.
>
> **Printer Setup** is used to select which printer you wish to use for printing.

Exit terminates the program and returns you to the Program Manager.

The **Edit** menu gives you access to the Clipboard plus some other actions provided by the following commands:

Undo cancels the last action, e.g. if you have deleted some text accidentally press **Alt-Backspace** and it reappears.

Cut copies selected text to the Clipboard and then deletes it from the original card.

Copy simply copies the selected text to the Clipboard but leaves it in place on the screen.

Paste places whatever is in the Clipboard at the current cursor position. You can only paste text into a Notepad file.

Select All allows you to highlight all the characters, including blank lines, that are in the current notepad file, ready for use with the Clipboard or to be deleted.

Time/Date inserts the current time and date into the document at the current cursor position. The command can be shortcut by pressing **F5**.

Word Wrap turns off the bottom scroll bar so that any text you enter remains visible within the current sized window. If you do not use this option then any text you enter will lie on one line, until you press **Enter**, and this can extend way beyond the right hand border of the window.

The **Search** menu deals with finding strings of text using **Find** and **Find Next**. The Search facility in Notepad can be case sensitive, i.e. the text must match the letter type, although by default it is turned off.

You can move around the text using the cursor keys in the same way that they are used in Windows Write, although you have less options:

Home takes you to the beginning of the current displayed line.
End moves the cursor to the end of the line.
Ctrl-Home takes you directly to the beginning of the file.

Ctrl-End takes you directly to the end of the file.
Up, **Down**, **Left** and **Right** all move the cursor in the corresponding direction.

Exercise 14.1
Using the program

As promised at the beginning of the book, we're going to use Notepad to play around with the CONFIG.SYS and AUTOEXEC.BAT files of your computer. Almost by necessity these are likely to be different to mine, but as we are talking about principles rather than specifics, this does not matter.

1) The Notepad window is an odd size, it would be better if it was larger. Also because the CONFIG.SYS file uses short lines we can turn on the Word Wrap.

Press **Alt-Space W** and the Task Switching dialogue box appears. Use **Tab** to move the selector to **Tile** and then press **Enter**. The window expands to fill the available space but still leaves the Program Manager icon visible at the bottom of the screen. If you have not previously shrunk the Program Manager to an icon, using **Minimise on Use** in its Options menu, then the Notepad window will expand to fill the entire screen.

To turn on the Word Wrap press **Alt-E W**. The bottom scroll bar vanishes.

1) Click on the **Control Box** at the extreme top left hand corner of the window and then on **Switch To**. Click on **Tile** at the bottom of the dialogue box and Notepad window will be resized.

Click on **Edit** in the Notepad window and then on **Word Wrap** and the bottom scroll bar disappears.

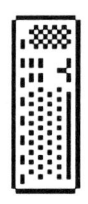

2) Load your CONFIG.SYS file into the Notepad. To do this press **Alt-F O** and a dialogue box appears. By default Notepad always logs onto the Windows directory and you need to change this so you are in the Root of Drive-C.

Press **Tab** twice to move the selector, the grey dotted outline, to the Directories box. Press **Space** to highlight the [..] entry and then press **Enter**. You should now be in the Root directory and the highlighter is back in the top box which says *.TXT. Type **CONFIG.SYS** - it will automatically replace the highlighted characters - press **Enter** and your CONFIG.SYS will be loaded into the Notepad.

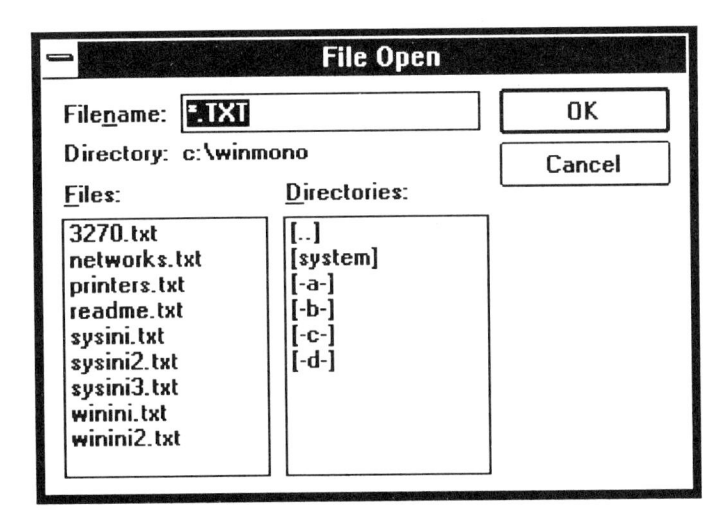

```
┌─────────────────────────────────────────────┐
│ ▬                  File Open                │
│ File name: [*.TXT    ]        ┌──── OK ────┐│
│ Directory: c:\winmono         └────────────┘│
│ Files:        Directories:    ┌── Cancel ──┐│
│ ┌──────────┐  ┌──────────┐    └────────────┘│
│ │3270.txt  │  │[..]      │                  │
│ │networks.txt│[system]   │                  │
│ │printers.txt│[-a-]      │                  │
│ │readme.txt│ │[-b-]      │                  │
│ │sysini.txt│ │[-c-]      │                  │
│ │sysini2.txt│ │[-d-]     │                  │
│ │sysini3.txt│ │          │                  │
│ │winini.txt│ │           │                  │
│ │winini2.txt│ │          │                  │
│ └──────────┘ └───────────┘                  │
└─────────────────────────────────────────────┘
```

Open File Dialogue Box

2) Open the **File** menu and then click on **Open** and the dialogue box appears. Double click on [..] in the Directories box and the program immediately logs on to the Root of Drive-C. (If you are logged onto another drive you will also have to double click on C in the Directories box.) Enter **CONFIG.SYS** and the file will be loaded as shown on the next page.

This file is the one from the Laser 80386 machine because that is the machine I use most often. The line of black squares along the bottom of the text are false characters that Windows doesn't know what to do with. Although Notepad is ASCII based it is limited in the number of characters it can display, to the original 127 ASCII characters, i.e. you cannot have any Extended ASCII characters. These characters are actually superfluous so let's get rid of them.

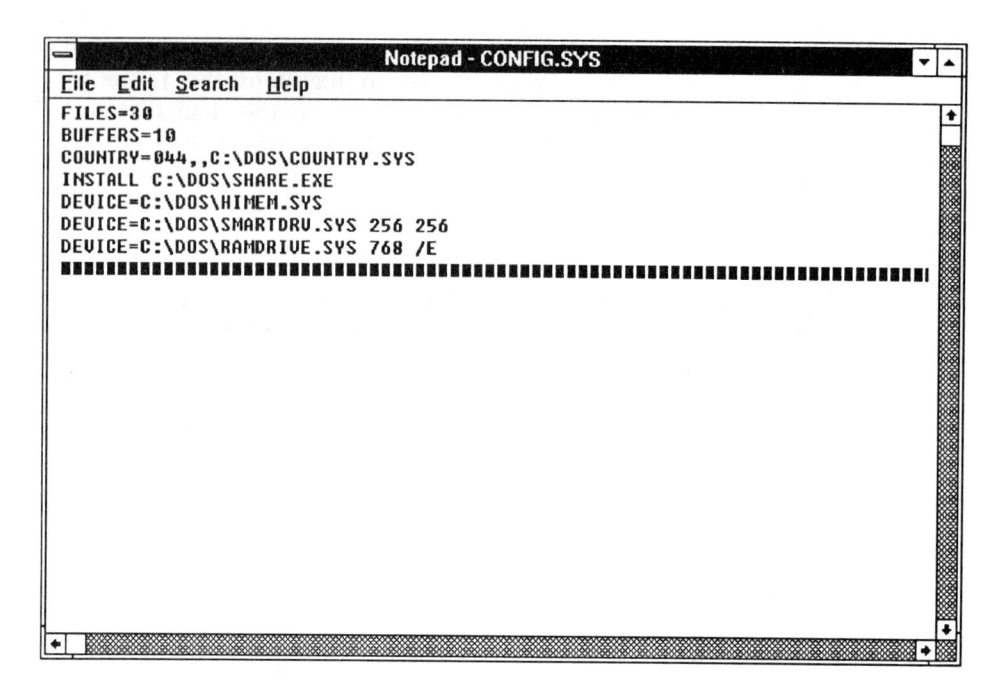

```
┌─────────────────────────── Notepad - CONFIG.SYS ───────────────────▼─▲─┐
│ File  Edit  Search  Help                                                │
│ FILES=30                                                              ▲│
│ BUFFERS=10                                                             │
│ COUNTRY=044,,C:\DOS\COUNTRY.SYS                                        │
│ INSTALL C:\DOS\SHARE.EXE                                               │
│ DEVICE=C:\DOS\HIMEM.SYS                                                │
│ DEVICE=C:\DOS\SMARTDRV.SYS 256 256                                     │
│ DEVICE=C:\DOS\RAMDRIVE.SYS 768 /E                                      │
│ ████████████████████████████████████████████████████████████████████████│
│                                                                        │
```

CONFIG.SYS Loaded

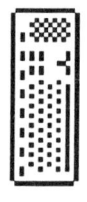

3) Move the cursor down to the bottom line by pressing **Down** until you reach the line. Then press **Del** until you have removed all the black squares.

3) Double click on the line of squares and the whole line is highlighted. Press **Del** to remove it. This double click to select a word is a facility that is built into many Windows-based programs. When you double click on a word, all the characters of that word plus its trailing space are highlighted. In this case the entire line of black squares constitutes a single word and you can select it in a single action.

You can now modify your CONFIG.SYS any way that you want. For example, suppose you wanted to increase the number of buffers to 30.

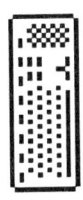

4) Press **Ctrl-Home** to send the cursor back to the beginning of the file. Press **Down** and then **End** to move to the end of the second line. Press **Left** once, to move the cursor to the 1, then **Del** to delete it. Press **3** and that's the new number in place.

4) Double click on the **10** at the end of the Buffers line, it will be highlighted, and then type **30** which overprints the highlighted characters.

5) Having changed the file it now needs to be saved. Press **Ctrl-S** and the file you have just modified will overwrite the original. (Don't forget that the changes won't come into effect until you reboot the computer.)

WIN.INI

The WIN.INI file is another pure ASCII file. It is stored in the Windows directory and it controls various aspects of the Windows programs. If the WIN.INI is damaged then you may well have to reinstall Windows all over again. Let's have a look at it. (Again, the file illustrated below is the one from the Laser 80386 and it will contain things that yours may not.) Rather than make an exercise of this, because any changes you might want to make are purely personal, I'm just going to cover the broad outlines of the file. If you want to make changes then do so in the same way as in the exercise above.

Press **Alt-F O** to open the loading dialogue box. If you have continued from the previous exercise then you will still be logged onto the Root directory of Drive-C and so you will have to log onto the Windows directory of whatever drive you have the program installed on. Notepad always looks for, and displays, those files that have a TXT extension - the default extension shown in the top box. Click on this to highlight it and then Enter **WIN.INI** to load the file. It is a large file even if you have no other Windows-based programs installed.

For the sake of clarity I have included the full file below, because it will not fit into a single Notepad window, and we'll look at each part of it in turn. The file contents are shown in Helvetica type to differentiate them from the body text of the book. Normally all the WIN.INI parts follow directly on from one another, separated by single blank lines. Each division of the WIN.INI file is headed by a title contained in square brackets, these are essential and should not be removed. Within the file there may be comments, denoted by a semi-colon (;), that are purely for your information. They are similar to REM statements in batch files and are in themselves acted upon.

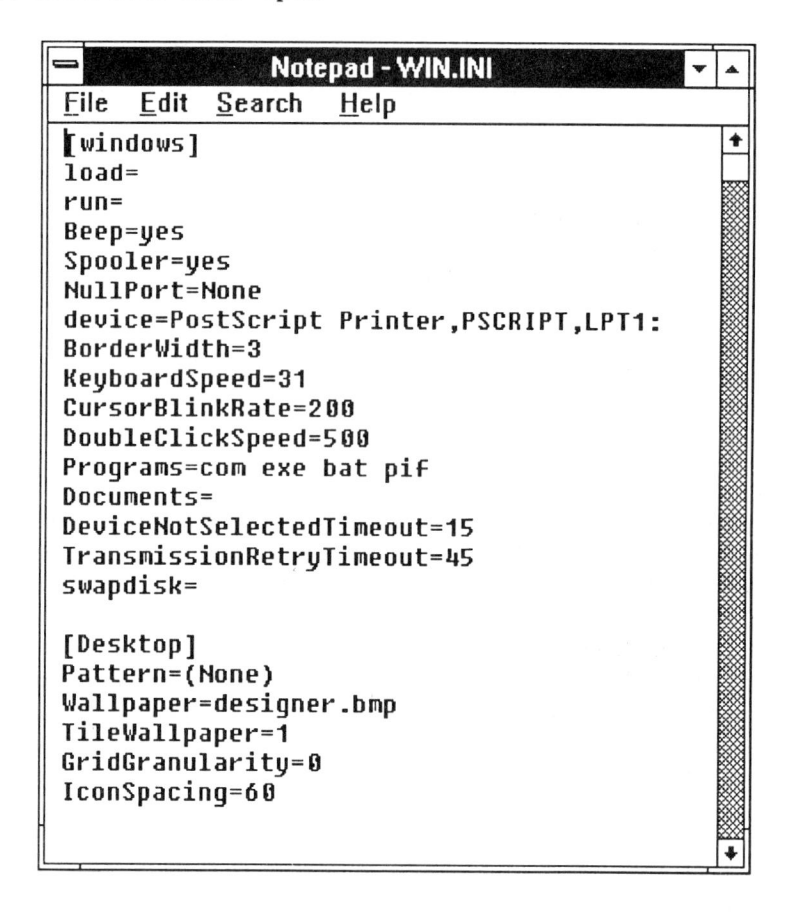

```
Notepad - WIN.INI
File  Edit  Search  Help
[windows]
load=
run=
Beep=yes
Spooler=yes
NullPort=None
device=PostScript Printer,PSCRIPT,LPT1:
BorderWidth=3
KeyboardSpeed=31
CursorBlinkRate=200
DoubleClickSpeed=500
Programs=com exe bat pif
Documents=
DeviceNotSelectedTimeout=15
TransmissionRetryTimeout=45
swapdisk=

[Desktop]
Pattern=(None)
Wallpaper=designer.bmp
TileWallpaper=1
GridGranularity=0
IconSpacing=60
```

The WIN.INI File

[windows]
load=
run=
Beep=yes
Spooler=yes
NullPort=None
device=PostScript   Printer,PSCRIPT,LPT1:

```
BorderWidth=3
KeyboardSpeed=31
CursorBlinkRate=200
DoubleClickSpeed=500
Programs=com exe bat pif
Documents=
DeviceNotSelectedTimeout=15
TransmissionRetryTimeout=45
swapdisk=
```

The **[windows]** section of the file contains basic details of what runs where, when and how. When you make changes in the Control Panel it is this part of the file that is changed.

load will open any mentioned program name and load it as an icon. Thus if the line said **load= SOL** then the Solitaire program would be loaded as an icon, which would be placed on the bottom of the screen. The Program Manager is still loaded as normal. Theoretically you could load every Windows program as an icon in this way, just by including their names, and if necessary their full paths, on this line.

run means just that. Any program name that is mentioned on this line will be loaded automatically as a full windowed application whenever you run Windows. The Program Manager will still be run as normal but then the named program will be run as well. For example, if you add **SOL** to the end of this line then the Solitaire program will be run, as a windowed application, every time you run Windows. You can include a range of programs in this way but each one must be separated by a space. For example to run Solitaire, Notepad, Calendar and Clock the line would read **run= SOL NOTEPAD CAL CLOCK**. Each of these programs will then be run, in a separate window, automatically.

Beep is just that. If the line says yes then the warning beep is active, if it says no then it is turned off.

Nullport in this case does not exist and so the line says None. If you have a device loaded here then the line will contains details of that device.

device contains the name of the active devices that have been configured, in this case the PostScript printer. You can have a number of device lines, each containing something different.

Borderwidth, KeyboardSpeed, CursorBlink Rate and **DoubleClickSpeed** show the numerical values for the those parts of the Control Panel you have set using the visual aids in that program. You can change them directly here by changing the values but you may find you get some very odd effects if you do so. Any changes you make cannot be seen until you reboot Windows.

Programs tells Windows what file extensions it should consider to be programs and therefore runnable. In this case it includes standard programs, batch files and PIF files. (See the next chapter for details of these.) Windows then considers any file with one of these extensions to be a program which can be run in a window.

Documents refers to those files which have been Associated with programs.

DeviceNotSelectedTimeout and **TransmissionRetry Timeout** are the settings that have been made in the Control Panel again and they tell you how much time the Print Manager will use before prompting you with an error message.

swapdisk is rarely used, it is the equivalent of the MS-DOS command TEMP, and basically it allows you to specify which drive will be used for the storage of termporary files. Normally this line is blank in the file because by default Windows will always try to use Drive-C. However if you have a large Ramdrive and you want to use that instead of the hard disk then you should specify the drive letter here.

I suggest that you don't change any of these settings, other than the first two. By all means add a program name to either of the first two lines if you wish but the other settings are best made using the Control Panel.

```
[Desktop]
Pattern=(None)
Wallpaper=designer.bmp
TileWallpaper=1
GridGranularity=0
IconSpacing=60
```

The **[desktop]** part of the file shows those settings that you have made in the Desktop element of the Control Panel. In this case there is no pattern in force and the wallpaper is a graphic called Designer which is tiled. If the graphic was centralised then the setting on the tiled line would be 0. The other settings are taken directly from the Control Panel. You can change the wallpaper by simply changing the graphic file name, provided that you have such a graphic in the Windows directory.

```
[Extensions]
smm=c:\amipro\amipro.exe    ^.smm
sam=c:\amipro\amipro.exe    ^.sam
doc=winword.exe  ^.doc
dot=winword.exe  ^.dot
cal=calendar.exe  ^.cal
crd=cardfile.exe  ^.crd
trm=terminal.exe  ^.trm
txt=notepad.exe  ^.txt
ini=notepad.exe  ^.ini
pcx=pbrush.exe  ^.pcx
bmp=PBRUSH.EXE    ^.BMP
wri=write.exe  ^.wri
rec=recorder.exe  ^.rec
PM3=PM.EXE  ^.PM3
PT3=PM.EXE  ^.PT3
MM3=MONEY.EXE  ^.MM3
cdr=c:\windows\corel\coreldrw.exe    ^.cdr
```

[extensions] is just that: a list of those file extensions which will be used by various programs. It is this section that allows you to save a file to disk by just giving a filename without an extension because Windows looks through this list to find the appropriate extension for you. Note that some of the programs mentioned, e.g. PageMaker, have two possible extensions listed and this implies that when you save a file you can select the extension you want to use. However, this applies only to those programs that are configured to allow this.

```
[intl]
sCountry=United  Kingdom
iCountry=44
iDate=1
iTime=1
iTLZero=0
iCurrency=0
iCurrDigits=2
```

```
iNegCurr=0
iLzero=1
iDigits=2
iMeasure=0
s1159=
s2359=
sCurrency=#
sThousand=,
sDecimal=.
sDate=/
sTime=:
sList=,
sShortDate=dd/MM/yyyy
sLongDate=dddd' 'dd' 'MMMM' 'yyyy
```

[intl] refers to the International settings made on the Control Panel. For some of the settings code digits are used, e.g. **Date=1** means that the date is displayed as dd/mm/yy. Again you should only change these in the Control Panel or you can get into an awful muddle.

```
[ports]
LPT1:=
LPT2:=
LPT3:=
COM1:=9600,n,8,1
COM2:=9600,n,8,1
COM3:=9600,n,8,1
COM4:=9600,n,8,1
EPT:=
FILE:=
LPT1.OS2=
LPT2.OS2=
```

[ports] are just that, a list of the various ports that Windows can use and their settings. It is not a list of the ports on your machine. For example on the Laser, to which this file applies, there is only one serial port, COM1, and yet the list above contains four. Again the settings come from the Control Panel.

[Windows Help]
Maximized=0
Xl=29
Yu=0
Xr=610
Yd=418

This section applies only to the Windows Help programs. As you change the appearance of the Help window so the values given here are changed.

[fonts]
Symbol 8,10,12,14,18,24 (VGA res)=SYMBOLE.FON
Helv 8,10,12,14,18,24 (VGA res)=HELVE.FON
Tms Rmn 8,10,12,14,18,24 (VGA res)=TMSRE.FON
Roman (All res)=ROMAN.FON
Script (All res)=SCRIPT.FON
Modern (All res)=MODERN.FON
Courier 10,12,15 (VGA res)=COURE.FON

[fonts] tells you what typefaces and fonts are loaded onto your system and ready for use. If you had deleted a font in the Control Panel then its name would not be here in this list.

[PostScript,LPT1]
device=2
feed1=9
feed15=9
orient=1

This section is concerned with the type of PostScript printer that is installed and how it is configured. Because the printer is the active one it is shown linked to the LPT1 port on the line in brackets.

[HPPCL,None]
paper=1
prtresfac=0
duplex=0

HPPCL is an acronym that means Hewlett-Packard Printer Control Language and it refers to an ordinary laser printer. In this case the printer has been installed but only for use when necessary and so it is not shown linked to a particular port. Instead it says None which means that the printer would have to be fully configured before use.

```
[PrinterPorts]
PostScript   Printer=PSCRIPT,LPT1:,15,45
PCL / HP LaserJet=HPPCL,None,15,45

[devices]
PostScript   Printer=PSCRIPT,LPT1:
PCL / HP LaserJet=HPPCL,None
```

Both of the above refer to the printers, how they are configured and to what ports they are connected. Windows tends to be fail safe and so you will find that the printers and their ports are mentioned a number of times.

```
[Solitaire]
Options=79
Back=9
```

The numeric codes here refer to the options that have been set and what deck is being used by Solitaire. The Back numbers don't seem to follow any particular pattern, 9 for example is the Desert Island but this is number 11 on the dialogue box.

```
[colors]
Background=128 255 255
AppWorkspace=0 255 255
Window=255 255 255
WindowText=0 0 0
Menu=255 255 0
MenuText=0 0 0
ActiveTitle=0 255 0
InactiveTitle=255 0 0
TitleText=0 0 0
ActiveBorder=128 255 0
InactiveBorder=255 0 0
```

```
WindowFrame=0 0 0
Scrollbar=2 14 238
```

This section contains a list of the settings for the three colour guns, Red, Blue and Green, and thus the colours they produce, for each of the elements of the Colour display. Three zeros is black, three 255's is white. You can change the colours here by modifying the numbers, but as you cannot see the results until you reboot Windows it is hardly worth it.

```
[Clock]
iFormat=0
```

What type of clock display do you want? 0 is digital and 1 is analogue.

```
[Paintbrush]
width=640
height=480
clear=COLOR
```

This contains the default settings for Windows Paintbrush, the screen size in pixels and the default palette to be used.

```
[PageMaker]
Defaults=C:\PM\PM.CNF
```

This section tells Windows where to find the PageMaker default file that contains information about the various elements of the program. This section only appears if you have installed PageMaker.

```
[spooler]
priority=medium
inactivealert=flash
DisplaySize=yes
DisplayTime=yes
```

[spooler] contains a list of the settings that you have used for the Print Manager. The settings are self-explanatory.

    [SciCalc]
    layout=1

Which calculator will you use? 0 is the standard one and 1 is the scientific one.

    [MSWrite]
    Backup=0
    Font1=Palatino,16,0
    Font2=AvantGarde,32,0
    Font3=Courier,48,0
    Font4=Bookman,16,0
    Font5=Helv,32,0

The above is a list of the default settings for Windows Write: the backup facility is either on or off, and what fonts were used the last time you ran the program.

    [Terminal]
    Port=None

The setting being used for the Terminal program.

    [HPPCL,LPT1]
    FontSummary=C:\WINDOWS\FSLPT1.PCL

More information about the PCL printer.

    [PMExports]

    [PMFilters]

    [AmiPro]

[AmiVISD]

[CORELDrwFonts]

[CORELDrivers]

[CDrawConfig]

[CDrawImportFilters]

[CDrawExportFilters]

[CDrawHPGLPenColor]

[CorelTrace]

All of the above refer to those Windows programs which have been installed and are ready for use in Windows. They are PageMaker, Ami Professional, Corel Draw and Corel Trace. Under each heading there is a long list of details and information, which I have deleted or this chapter would be huge. Any Windows program that is installed on your computer must produce such a file, or a number of such files, to work properly.

Having loaded and examined the WIN.INI file I suggest that you save it to the disk under a new name so that you have a backup copy of it. Press **Alt-F A** to bring up the Save As dialogue box. Use any filename you wish and this time include an extension. Don't use WIN.OLD because when you install new Windows-based program their setup routines takes the original WIN.INI and usually renames it WIN.OLD, although you could use WININI.OLD.

If you have made changes to the file then you will need to save it as WIN.INI, overwriting the original file, and then reboot windows, i.e. terminate it and then reload it, so that your changes come into effect.

Exercise 14.2
Logging your files

Notepad provides a facility that will allow you to add the current system time and date to your file. Just press **F5** and the time and date are inserted at the cursor position. However you can do more than just that with this facility.

1) Run the Notepad as usual and start with a new file.

2) With the cursor at the very start of the file type **.LOG** - you must use upper case letters.

3) Save the file under any name you wish. Hereafter whenever you open this file Windows will add the current system time and date to the end of the file. In this way you can keep a record of when various files were opened and modified last.

Do not use this facility on any systems file, e.g. the CONFIG.SYS or the Windows INI files.

Summary

- Notepad is a pure ASCII text editor that will allow you to create files containing up to a maximum of 50,000 characters. However this maximum depends on the amount of free memory you have available.

- Notepad allows you to created automatically logged files.

Keyboard Summary

Alt-E C	Copy selected text to Clipboard.
Alt-E D	Insert system time and date at cursor position.
Alt-E P	Paste Clipboard contents into document at cursor position.
Alt-E S	Select all the text in the current document.

Alt-E T	Cut selected text into Clipboard.
Alt-E U	Undo last action.
Alt-E W	Toggle word wrapping.
Alt-Esc	Activate next program without using Task Switching.
Alt-F A	Save the current file to a new filename.
Alt-F N	Start a new file.
Alt-F O	Open an existing ASCII file.
Alt-F P	Print the current document.
Alt-F R	Select a printer.
Alt-F S	Save the current file to the name shown on the Title Bar.
Alt-F T	Select Header and Footer information to be included on the printout.
Alt-F X	Terminate Notepad and return to Program Manager.
Alt-F4	Terminate program and return to Program Manager.
Alt-S F	Activate text finding.
Alt-S N	Find next occurrence of search string.
Alt-Space C	Terminate program and return to Program Manager.
Alt-Space M	Move current icon or window against the background.
Alt-Space N	Minimise window, i.e. reduce it to an icon.
Alt-Space R	Restore icon to a window or former size and shape.
Alt-Space S	Resize or reshape the current window.
Alt-Space W	Activate Task Switching dialogue box.
Alt-Space X	Maximise window, i.e. make the window fill the entire screen area.
Ctrl-Esc	Activate Task Switching dialogue box.
Ctrl-Ins	Copy selected text to Clipboard.
Del	Delete selected text.
F1	Activate Help Main Index.
F3	Find next occurrence of search string.
F5	Insert system time and date at cursor position.
Shift-Del	Cut selected text to Clipboard.
Shift-Ins	Paste Clipboard into document at cursor position.

Chapter 15

Further Accessories

PIF Editor

The PIF Editor is the program that allows you to create or modify Program Information Files. These are special files that Windows creates when you set up applications in Windows Setup, about MS-DOS Programs that lay down the various parameters that will be used by the program when it is run in the Windows environment. Whenever you try to run an MS-DOS program, Windows looks for the corresponding PIF file. The name of the PIF will usually match the name of the program, e.g. the one for WordStar is called W0.PIF. If Windows cannot find the PIF for a particular program it will then try to run the MS-DOS using standard default settings. These may or may not work, depending on the program involved, but in general they will do so. You can even run a program directly by selecting its PIF because the file contains the full details of the program, where it is stored, how much memory it needs, etc.

So if Windows creates the PIF for an application why bother changing it? In actuality you are unlikely ever to need to do so but suppose you had two versions of the same program, e.g. you have WordStar configured for standard use as WS.EXE and you also have the program installed to use the VGA 50-line display as 50.EXE. The Setup is limited in the number of programs it can identify and therefore set up for you, and so it is likely that it will find WS.EXE but not 50.EXE. Because you want to be able to run both from Windows you can load the WS.EXE PIF and change it so that the program involved is 50.EXE and thus create the second PIF from the first. Or you might have reorganised your disk and changed the locations of some programs. The PIF contains the full path details of each file and so you would have to change these or the program will not run and all you will get is an error message.

The important point to realise is that Windows only creates a PIF file for an MS-DOS program. Windows-based programs don't need them because their details are included in the WIN.INI file, see the previous chapter for details.

To run the PIF Editor select the icon, it looks like a luggage label, and press Enter or double click on it. The PIF Editor supplies two menus, plus Help. The first, File, allows you to create a new file, open an existing one and then save the result. The Mode menu allows you to switch between the two modes, Standard and 386-Enhanced, because the Program Information Files under the two modes are slightly different. Let's examine the Standard mode file first.

PIF Editor Standard Mode

The first line contains the full name and path of the program concerned - in this case WS.EXE which is stored in the WS6 directory of Drive-C. This is a vital piece of information because without it Windows does not know what program you want or where to find it.

The next line is the title that will be applied to the program, either as the Title Bar of a windowed program or as the Icon name. You can make this anything you wish. If you leave this line blank then Windows will use the program's title as the name.

The third line is used to contain any **optional parameters** that you would normally use if you ran the program directly from MS-DOS. In this case there are none but the option is provided in case there are some. For example, to run PC-Outline without the title screen appearing you use the parameter /Q. To run PC-Outline from windows you could include this parameter on this line. If you wanted Windows to prompt you to provide the characters, because there are a number of possibles and you are not sure which one you will be using at any one time, then place a question mark in this line. Then whenever you start the program, Windows provides a prompt that allows you to enter the parameter you want on that occasion. Equally you could leave this line blank and then run the program by selecting Run from the File menu of Program manager and appending any parameters at that time.

Start-up Directory is used to tell Windows what directory to log onto when the program is run. In this case it will log onto the WS6 directory because WordStar uses a lot of overlay files and these must be available by being logged onto the directory that contains them. As it happens in this case it is superfluous because the WS6 directory is included on the MS-DOS PATH. Because running any MS-DOS program necessitates returning to MS-DOS to do so, the PATH is fully operational. (You actually open the MS-DOS window to run MS-DOS programs - or rather Windows does it for you.)

The **Video Mode** tells Windows how the program uses the monitor display and thus how much memory is needed to hold the monitor image. This is necessary because when you switch from the application back to Windows and then out again, Windows needs to be able to restore the MS-DOS programs screen to the state it was in before you switched. It achieves this by saving the display in memory and thus the type of display being used affects how much memory is needed for this. This is why, by the way, that I cannot print from WordStar when running under Windows. The memory to hold the screen image comes out of the amount of memory allocated to the program and thus there is not enough left to access the printer properly.

The **Text mode** uses the least amount of memory, while Graphic/Multiple Text is a RAM hog. However, if you are using a program that uses this latter mode then you must tell Windows so otherwise you will not be able to properly switch between MS-DOS and Windows. If you are using the wrong mode then you may find that you cannot switch at all and the only solution will be to terminate the program completely - which defeats the object of the exercise.

Memory Requirements is the absolute minimum amount of RAM that must be available before Windows will try to run the program. It is not the amount of memory allocated to the program because Windows will give the program all the free memory available. Hence, increasing this amount in the WordStar PIF will not, for example, help my problem with printing. If there is less memory available than is mentioned in this box then Windows will not run the program, instead it produces an error message. The only way you can find out how much memory the program requires as a minimum is by guessing! Granted the program documentation should tell you but the figures given in the manual will be estimates not actual requirements. You could try running with the default amount of RAM, i.e. 128 Kb, and then increasing this until the error message no longer appears, but this does not always work because Windows automatically gives the program all the free memory that is available.

XMS Memory refers to Extended Memory, based on the LIM Standard. As it happens there are very few MS-DOS programs which can use Extended memory and so you will rarely have to change the default settings here.

Directly Modifies is precisely what it says, the settings here tell Windows that the program concerned will be changing the selected element of the computer system and using them in such a way that they cannot be shared with other programs. This really only matters if you are running programs concurrently. If the program changes the keyboard in this way then you will be unable to switch to Windows from the program and your only way back is to terminate the application.

If you select **No Screen Exchange** then you reduce the amount of memory required but you will be unable to copy information from the application into the Clipboard.

Prevent Program Switch does just that, it stops you switching from the application back to Windows. This frees memory but also defeats the object of running the program from Windows in the first place.

Close Window on Exit does just that. It particularly applies when you are running the MS-DOS program in a window under 386-Enhanced mode.

Reserve Shortcut Keys tells Windows that the selected keys will be used by the application and thus they will not have the effects that they usually have in Windows itself.

PIF Editor Enhanced Mode

The first few lines of this are identical to the Standard Mode Editor, it is only at the bottom of the box that there are any changes. The first option is the **Display Usage**. Under this you can use either **Full Screen**, which is the only mode available for MS-DOS programs under Windows in Standard and Real Modes, or **Windowed**. If you select Windowed then the program will be run in a window as if it were a Windows-based program - with all the advantages that brings.

Execution refers to the way that the program will be run and how it will cooperate with other programs. Under 386-Enhanced mode you can have multiple MS-DOS programs all running concurrently in their own windows but you have to sort out which has priority over what. If you click on **Background** then the program involved has low priority and so the system resources are available for other programs. Selecting **Exclusive** has the opposite effect, it means that the program gets first priority on any resource that it wants.

Windows 3 - A User's Guide

The Enhanced mode PIF Editor is actually in two halves and it is the first that is shown above. To get the next half you click on **Advanced** and you get this:

```
┌─ Advanced Options ──────────────────────────────────┐
│ ┌─Multitasking Options─────────────────────┐ ┌────┐ │
│ │ Background Priority: [50]  Foreground    │ │ OK │ │
│ │                      Priority: [100]     │ └────┘ │
│ │           ☐ Detect Idle Time             │ ┌──────┐│
│ └──────────────────────────────────────────┘ │Cancel││
│ ┌─Memory Options──────────────────────────────────┐ │
│ │ EMS Memory:  KB Required [0]  KB Limit [1024] ☐ Locked │
│ │ XMS Memory:  KB Required [0]  KB Limit [1024] ☐ Locked │
│ │      ☒ Uses High Memory Area    ☐ Lock Application Memory │
│ └─────────────────────────────────────────────────┘ │
│ ┌─Display Options─────────────────────────────────┐ │
│ │ Video Memory:  ○ Text  ○ Low Graphics  ● High Graphics │
│ │ Monitor Ports: ☐ Text  ☐ Low Graphics  ☐ High Graphics │
│ │     ☐ Emulate Text Mode    ☐ Retain Video Memory │
│ └─────────────────────────────────────────────────┘ │
│ ┌─Other Options───────────────────────────────────┐ │
│ │ ☒ Allow Fast Paste        ☐ Allow Close When Active │
│ │ Reserve Shortcut Keys: ☐ Alt+Tab  ☐ Alt+Esc  ☐ Ctrl+Esc │
│ │                        ☐ PrtSc   ☐ Alt+PrtSc ☐ Alt+Space│
│ │                        ☐ Alt+Enter                      │
│ │ Application Shortcut Key: [None]                        │
│ └─────────────────────────────────────────────────┘ │
└─────────────────────────────────────────────────────┘
```

Advanced Features

The advanced features allow you to further customise the PIF to take advantage of the system resources and to target which resources go to what program. In the normal course of events you are unlikely to need to change these settings but if you want to play with them, here, very briefly, is what they all mean.

> **Multitasking Priority** determines how much processor time will be allocated to the program. In each box you can specify a value in the range 0 to 10,000 although the default values are shown above. The values refer to the amount of time that each program will be able to use before the chip is switched to the next program and so on.

Memory Options refers to the amount of memory that the program will receive and use. Windows uses Extended memory but most MS-DOS programs can only use Expanded memory and so Windows simulates Expanded memory from the Extended memory for the applications to use. Again the values in the boxes are minimum not absolutes.

Display Options handles how the application appears on screen, in much the same way as it does the Standard PIF Editor.

Other Options sets the reserved keys, fast paste mode and allows you to close windows without having to terminate the MS-DOS first.

PIF Editor Summary

- The PIF Editor is a tool that allows you to create or modify Program Information Files which are then used to run MS-DOS programs in the Windows environment.

- Program Information Files will be created automatically for you when you use Windows Setup to setup applications and you should not then need to change them.

PIF Editor Keyboard Summary

Alt-Esc	Activate next program without using Task Switching.
Alt-F A	Save the macro file to a new filename.
Alt-F M	Merge two macro files into one.
Alt-F N	Start a new file.
Alt-F O	Open a previously saved file.
Alt-F S	Save the macro file to the existing filename.
Alt-F X	Terminate the Recorder program.
Alt-F4	Terminate PIF Editor and return to Program Manager.
Alt-M 3	Create 386-Enhanced mode PIF.
Alt-M S	Create Standard mode PIF.
Alt-Space C	Terminate program and return to Program Manager.
Alt-Space M	Move current icon or window against the background.
Alt-Space N	Minimise window, i.e. reduce it to an icon.

Alt-Space R	Restore icon to a window or former size and shape.
Alt-Space S	Resize or reshape the current window.
Alt-Space W	Activate Task Switching dialogue box.
Alt-Space X	Maximise window, i.e. make the window fill the entire screen.
Ctrl-Esc	Activate Task Switching dialogue box.
F1	Activate Help Main Index.

Recorder

The Recorder is a new program: prior to Windows 3 it did not exist. The program allows you to create macros, i.e. strings of actions, that can then be played back later. For example, suppose you wanted to run a program, minimise Program Manager, maximise the program window and then load a specific file into that program. If you do this only once or twice a week then you are just as well off doing it by hand, but if you were going to use these actions half a dozen times a day, then it becomes worth while creating a macro for the actions. The macro can then be run using either the menu or a combination of keystrokes and this makes life much easier.

The important point about macros is that they are only worth while creating if the sequence of actions is always going to be the same. If you wanted to run a program and then load different files into it each time, it would not be worth creating a macro because it is unlikely to save you any time and effort. It is only when the sequence of keystrokes and mouse actions becomes long winded but always remains the same that it is worth using the Recorder.

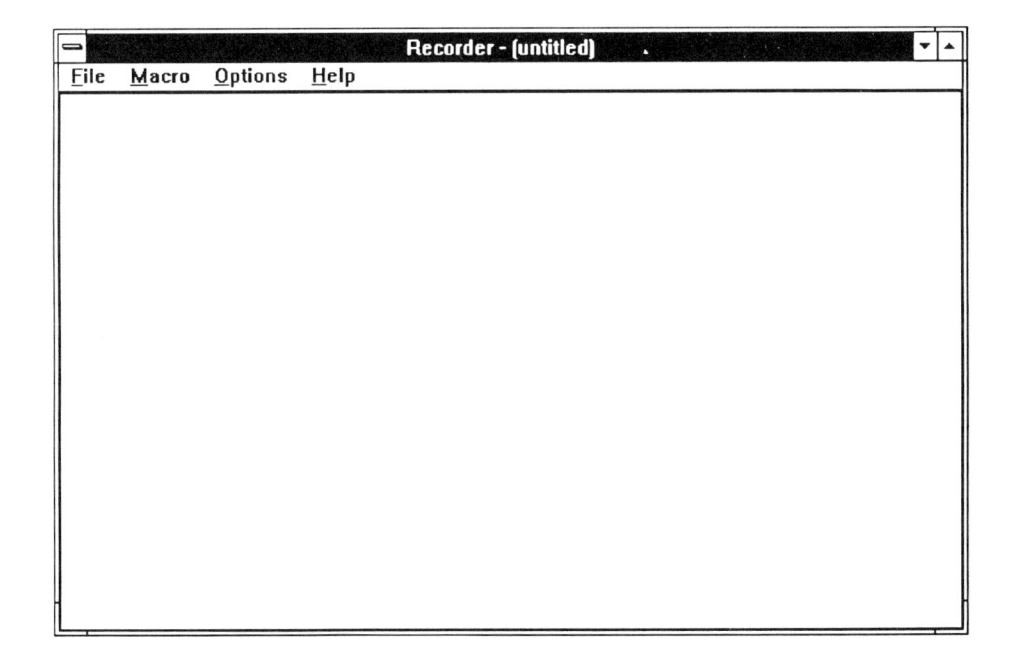

Recorder

The program provides three menus, plus Help. The **File** menu has the usual commands; **New, Open, Save, Save As, Merge** and **Exit**. All of which we have covered for other programs so we won't bother doing so again.

The **Macro** menu is the one that allows you to use macros and it contains the following commands:

> **Run** which allows you to run the selected macro. Within the main screen area will be a list of available macros, once you have created them, and these can then be selected and run using this command.
>
> **Record** is the command that allows you to create the macro in the first place, see below for details.
>
> **Delete** removes the selected macro from the on-screen list.
>
> **Properties** brings up the dialogue box that has been used to record the macro in the first place.

The **Options** menu allows you to set which actions within the macro will be allowed. The menu contains four commands: the first three are toggles and the last a dialogue box.

> **Control+Break Checking** allows you to suspend the macro if this command is turned on, which it normally is. Pressing Ctrl-Break or Ctrl-C will stop the recording of or the playing back of a macro.
>
> **Shortcut Keys** allows you to assign a key combination to a macro so that the recorded sequence can be played back using those keys.
>
> **Minimise on Use** shrinks the Recorder window to an icon every time you access a macro from it.
>
> **Preferences** brings up a dialogue box that allows you to set the defaults that will be presented every time you begin to record a macro.

Macro Tips

1) Try to avoid using the mouse. The Recorder is capable of including the mouse actions in any macro you create but it copies the mouse actions exactly. Thus if you used the mouse to click on a menu, for example, it will record it. But if when you run the macro the window, and thus the menu bar, is in a different position then the macro cannot perform correctly, i.e. it will try to access a menu that is not in the position it should be in. This will bring up an error message and terminate the macro.

2) Work with a clear screen. Close down, or reduce to icons, any applications that will not be included in the macro.

3) Use keystrokes to access menu commands. This is really an adjunct to the tip above but it is important. The keyboard shortcuts work much better in macros than mouse actions do.

4) Only use macros on the system they were created on. Because the Recorder takes its information from one system, the macro can then only be run without any problems on that system. Trying to use the macro on another system, e.g. one with a different monitor, will cause problems and possibly hangups.

Creating a macro

To create a macro you run the Recorder program and then select **Record** from the **Macro** menu. This will bring up a dialogue box, shown on the next page, that allows you to set your preferences for the macro.

The first line can contain up to 40 characters, including spaces, as the name for your macro.

Shortcut Key allows you to select a key combination that will be used to run the macro. Once the keys are assigned they will appear on the Macro name line above. You do not have to use a shortcut key sequence if you would prefer to run the macro from the menu.

```
┌─────────────────────────────────────────────────┐
│ ─              Default Preferences              │
│  ┌Playback──────────────────────┐               │
│   To:    │Same Application │▼│     ┌────────┐   │
│                                    │   OK   │   │
│   Speed: │Fast             │▼│     └────────┘   │
│                                    ┌────────┐   │
│                                    │ Cancel │   │
│   Record Mouse:  │Clicks + Drags│▼│ └────────┘   │
│                                                  │
│   Relative to:   │Window        │▼│              │
│                                                  │
└─────────────────────────────────────────────────┘
```

Macro Preferences

Playback tells the Recorder that the macro you are creating is either for a specific application or it can be applied to any program. The speed with which the macro is replayed can be either at the speed you created it, or Fast which will speed up your creation keystrokes and make them as fast as the computer can operate.

Record Mouse allows you to include mouse actions in the macro. This is not recommended, see above, but you have the option of doing so if you wish.

Once you have set your preferences you then select **Record** from the **Macro** menu and Recorder will be reduced to an icon, providing you have not changed the **Minimise on Use** toggle, and then it flashes while it records your actions. When you have reached the end of the actions, clicking on the **Recorder** icon brings up a dialogue box, opposite, asking if you want to save the macro as it exists so far, whether you want to continue recording or cancel the recording completely.

Select whichever option you wish. Pressing **Enter** accepts the first default choice. Having saved the macro you can run it from the Recorder window or by using the hot keys you selected. The macro you have just created is stored in a file and this has to be saved too, otherwise it will be only be active while you are running the program at present.

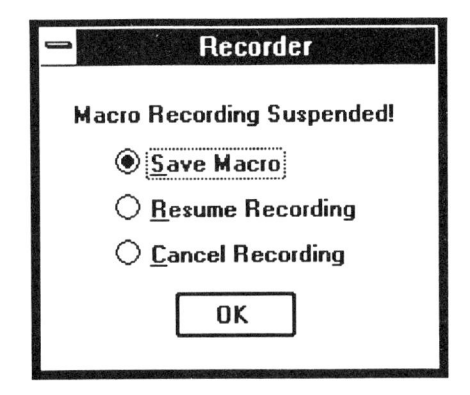

Macro End Dialogue Box

Summary

- Recorder is a a program that allows you to create macros.
- The uses of the program are limited by your actions.

Recorder Keyboard Summary

Alt-Esc	Activate next program without using Task Switching.
Alt-F A	Save the macro file to a new filename.
Alt-F M	Merge two macro files into one.
Alt-F N	Start a new file.
Alt-F O	Open a previously saved file.
Alt-F S	Save the macro file to the existing filename.
Alt-F X	Terminate the Recorder program.
Alt-F4	Terminate program and return to Program Manager.
Alt-M C	Begin recording a macro.
Alt-M D	Delete a macro from the file.
Alt-M P	Show details of selected macro.
Alt-M R	Run the selected macro.
Alt-O C	Toggle Ctrl-Break checking.
Alt-O M	Toggle Recorder minimise on use setting.
Alt-O P	Set new default preferences.
Alt-O S	Toggle use of shortcut keys.

Alt-Space C	Terminate program and return to Program Manager.
Alt-Space M	Move current icon or window against the background.
Alt-Space N	Minimise window, i.e. reduce it to an icon.
Alt-Space R	Restore icon to a window of former size and shape.
Alt-Space S	Resize or reshape the current window.
Alt-Space W	Activate Task Switching dialogue box.
Alt-Space X	Maximise window.
Ctrl-Esc	Activate Task Switching dialogue box.
F1	Activate Help Main Index.

Terminal

Terminal is a communications linking program. It will allow you to connect your computer to others over the telephone land lines and exchange information with them. In fact, the program will allow you to communicate with any other computer, that also has such a program, anywhere in the world. If it can be reached by telephone it can be reached by your machine. This process is known as Electronic Mail.

E-mail is the name given to the transmission of documents across the telephone network system. It incorporates communicating from one computer to another and accessing large databases on mainframe machines. For instance, in the U.K. you can use Telecom Gold to run checks on a number of companies because their end of year accounts are available for examination. However the real benefit of E-mail is that it allows the transmission of textual documents rather than just words, thus you can send contracts, bills of sale and what have you from one person to another. To transmit illustrations you need to use a Fax which is related but different to E-mail, although this is changing and some programs will allow you to transmit graphics as well as text. E-mail is a vital component in something that has been the dream of the computer industry since the days of Alan Turing - the Disseminated Office.

Basically the idea is that people will work wherever they wish, in their homes, on their boats, on a train, wherever they happen to be, and then transmit the results of their labours to a central point, for onward processing, probably by another computer. In the early days of computing when the machines were giant brontosaurus-like boxes that, like the dinosaurs, needed special environments to exist and work properly, the dream seemed to be far in the future and almost unattainable - but read some 1950's science fiction and you'll see what I mean. However with the development of the transistor and then the silicon chip and the resultant decrease in size, coupled with an increase in power and capabilities, the dream has gradually become more and more attainable.

The Disseminated Office is dependent on four basic factors. Firstly, computers that have sufficient power and storage to allow people to work effectively with the relevant data. They must be cheap enough and versatile enough to warrant the expense, and they must be small enough to fit comfortably into the average home and/or be carried about. Modern PC's meet all these requirements. It is now possible to get all the power (and much more) of the mainframes of even ten years ago into a plastic case no larger than a couple of shoe boxes. You can even carry them around and work with them on the train or in the middle of nowhere - until the battery runs out that is.

The second requirement for the dream to become reality is a decent communications network that will allow the transmission of data, quickly, efficiently and faultlessly, from the user's computer to the central point - and preferably at a low cost. Modern telephone lines, and their connections to satellites, provide this, even if the cost of phone calls seems to be going up all the time. Thus there is now the second element of the equation for the electronic office.

The third factor is an interface between the user's computer and the telephone network, after all it's a bit pointless having the first two elements if they cannot be connected together. This interface consists of a modem, a simple bit of gadgetry that allows data to be sent down the wire, and the necessary software to link the two main elements. Modems are getting to be smaller and more dynamic - once they were just as ponderous as computers. These days you can get a highly efficient modem, with many more capabilities than its earlier cousins, that fits on a single half card and occupies a single slot in the computer. You can even get one now that is not much bigger than a telephone socket itself.

The final piece of equipment is the software to provide a user-friendly interface between the various elements. This has been improving in leaps and bounds, and the range of possible software is huge - from Shareware products to Commercial programs in all shapes and sizes. The one in Windows is called Terminal.

In actuality there is probably another element that must be taken into account - the willingness, confidence and discipline of people to work at home. There is not much point in having all the technology if the people concerned are unable, for whatever reason, to use it! Working at home requires a rigid discipline, much more so than working in a specific office, and if you cannot develop the right approach then you are wasting your time. Coupled to this is the accommodating approach of the company concerned, if they are unwilling to allow you to work at home then having all the technology in the world is not going to make a blind bit of difference. However the dream lives on and gradually it comes closer and closer to reality. Who knows but in another ten years time it may well be an actuality and we'll all wonder what people ever did before hand.

Before you can use Terminal you must have the necessary hardware, specifically you have got to have a modem. You can also use the program to communicate between two machines in the same building, not to be confused with a network where the computers share resources, using a null modem cable. The cables, whichever one you are using, require that you plug them into a serial port and so you must have one of them free. Once you've got that, you're all set. Boot up Windows and load the Terminal program.

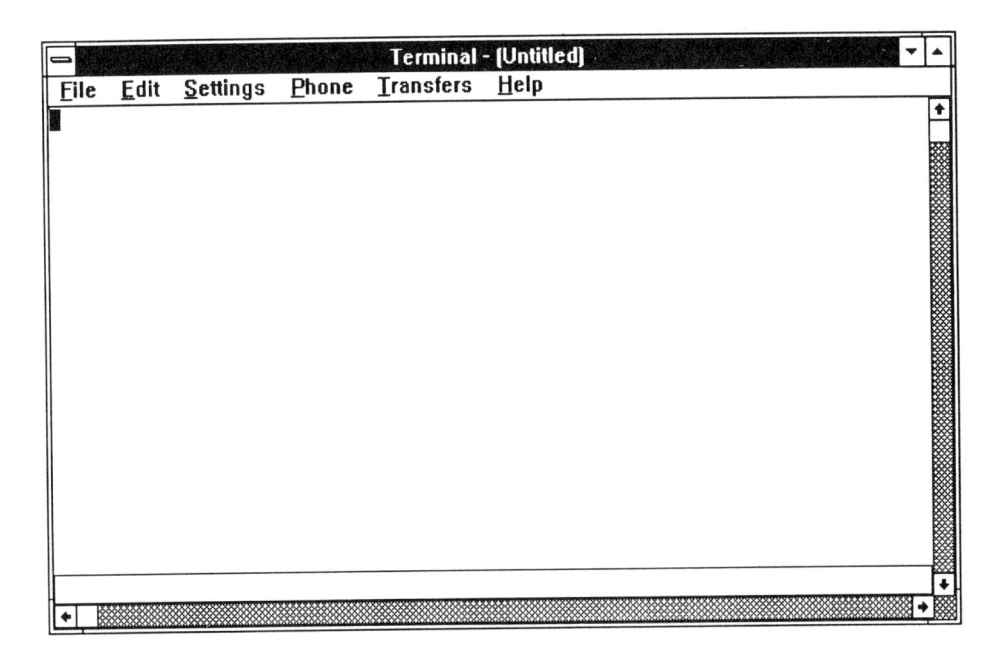

Terminal Main Screen

Window Layout

The window has the usual layout, Control Box, Title Bar, Minimise and Maximise buttons and the Menu Bar, but the bulk of the window is just blank. This is the buffer area and we'll come to that in a minute or three. Terminal provides five menus, plus Help.

The **File** menu contains the usual commands, **New, Open, Save, Save As** and **Exit** plus **Printer Setup** which is the same as in Cardfile and Notepad.

The **Edit** menu provides **Copy** and **Paste** - but no Cut command. It also has the following:

Send copies the selected text to the remote computer.

Select All allows you to select all the text in the buffer area in one operation.

Clear Buffer deletes everything from the buffer area and leaves it blank.

The **Settings** menu contains eleven commands, the first eight invoking dialogue boxes while the last three are toggles.

```
Phone Number...
Terminal Emulation...
Terminal Preferences...
Function Keys...
Text Transfers...
Binary Transfers...
Communications...
Modem Commands...
Printer Echo
Timer Mode
Show Function Keys
```

Settings menu

Phone Number allows you to enter a number that the program will dial. You can separate the digits using hyphens or brackets, they will be ignored by the program. However, if you use commas then there will be a delay of two seconds for each command included. Thus the number 3,,4,578 will cause the program to dial 3, wait four seconds, dial 4, wait 2 seconds and then dial 578.

Terminal Emulation allows you to select one of three terminal types. Whichever you select will affect how your computer system then operates.

Terminal Preferences determines how the program performs when you are using it. You can select a terminal mode, the number of columns, the type of cursor, the font to be used, what language is being used and the number of lines for the buffer.

Function Keys allows you to define the function keys so that they perform macro actions. The functions are already defined to some extent by Windows, e.g. **F1** activates Help, and so you should be careful about any redefining you do.

Text Transfers allows you to set the options for the sending of text, while Binary Transfers does the same for Binary files.

Communications sets the various parameters. You must set these before you begin any file transference.

Modem Commands allows you to specify the settings that are in accordance with the modem you are using.

Printer Echo is a toggle and it allows you send any incoming information to the printer and the screen.

Timer Mode is another toggle that displays an elapsed time clock at the lower right hand corner of the Terminal window.

Show function keys does just that.

The Phone menu contains two commands, **Dial** and **Hangup**. Both of which do exactly what they say they do.

The **Transfers** menu controls the sending and receiving of information and the commands it contains are self-explanatory.

```
Send Text File...
Receive Text File...
View Text File...

Send Binary File...
Receive Binary File...

Pause
Resume
Stop
```

Transfers Menu

Terminal Summary

- Terminal is a program that will allow you to link your computer to another, either over the public telephone lines or within the same office.

- To use the program you require additional hardware, other than the basic computer system

Terminal Keyboard Summary

Key	Action
Alt-E A	Select all the text in the buffer.
Alt-E C	Copy selected text to Clipboard.
Alt-E E	Clear all buffer contents.
Alt-E N	Send selected text.
Alt-E P	Paste Clipboard contents into file.
Alt-Esc	Activate next program without using Task Switching.
Alt-F A	Save the current file to a new filename.
Alt-F N	Start a new file.
Alt-F O	Load a previously saved file into the buffer.
Alt-F R	Select and setup the printer to be used.
Alt-F S	Save the current file to the filename shown on the Title Bar.
Alt-F X	Terminate the Terminal program.
Alt-F4	Terminate program and return to Program Manager.
Alt-P D	Dial programmed number.
Alt-P H	Cease dialling.
Alt-S B	Set binary transfer protocol.
Alt-S C	Set Communications options.
Alt-S D	Customise modem settings.
Alt-S E	Toggle printer echo.
Alt-S K	Show function keys.
Alt-S N	Open Phone Number dialogue box.
Alt-S P	Set Terminal preferences.
Alt-S T	Pop up Terminal Emulation dialogue box.
Alt-S T	Toggle delayed timer activation.
Alt-S X	Set Text transfer protocol.
Alt-Space C	Terminate program and return to Program Manager.
Alt-Space M	Move current icon or window against the background.
Alt-Space N	Minimise window, i.e. reduce it to an icon.
Alt-Space R	Restore icon to a window or former size and shape.

Alt-Space S	Resize or reshape the current window.
Alt-Space W	Activate Task Switching dialogue box.
Alt-Space X	Maximise window.
Alt-T B	Send binary file.
Alt-T E	Resume after pause.
Alt-T F	Receive binary file.
Alt-T O	Cancel sending or receiving.
Alt-T P	Pause sending or receiving.
Alt-T R	Receive text file.
Alt-T S	Send text file.
Alt-T V	View text file.
Ctrl-Esc	Activate Task Switching dialogue box.
Ctrl-Ins	Copy selected text to the Clipboard.
Ctrl-Shift-Ins	Send selected text.
F1	Activate Help Main Index.
Shift-Ins	Paste Clipboard contents into file.

Chapter 16
Problems in Windows

What problems?

This chapter is entitled Problems in Windows rather than Problems with Windows because as far as can be ascertained there are no real problems with Windows 3. The program is definitely the best ever and Microsoft have gone to considerable pains to make it as error free as possible. There are, obviously, a couple of minor teething troubles but the program is remarkably bug free. Most of the problems you will encounter are not the fault of Windows at all, rather they are machine problems caused by BIOS faults and interrupt clashes. In such cases it would be unfair, not to say unwarranted, to lay the blame for the problems at Microsoft's door.

The major problem that you will encounter with Windows 3 is lack of memory. The program is designed to make use of Conventional and Extended memory, it does not interface with Expanded memory, and it can use both of these very efficiently. However, it has to be said that Windows 3 is RAM hungry and you will soon find minor niggles arising due to lack of memory. The answer to the problem is to increase the amount of extended memory your computer has. If you boost your RAM to around 8 Mb you will have no problems at all with Windows 3.

> Windows 3 will run Real Mode on any machine, regardless of its chip, disk drives and the amount of RAM available. This mode is almost identical to that used by all previous versions of Windows and it is this that you should use for any Windows-based program that was designed for versions of Windows earlier than 3.0.

> Standard Mode is the default mode that Windows 3 will always try to run in on any machine. When you run Windows it automatically checks the system resources to try and run in Standard mode, and only if it finds more resources than it needs will it boot in 386-Enhanced mode. To run in Standard mode you must have a minimum of 2 Mb of free RAM available, any less than that and you cannot use this mode and you will have to use Real Mode. By itself Windows 3 cannot automatically run in Real Mode - you must supply a parameter for it to do so by entering WIN/R.

386-Enhanced mode will be used if you have 4 Mb of free RAM or more and you are using an 80386SX chip or better. You can force the program to run in this mode with less than 4 Mb of memory, providing you have at least 2 Mb free, by entering win/3. However, if you do so you will find that the program actually runs slower than if it was in Standard Mode. There are few benefits to be gained from using 386-Enhanced mode, unless you are using a lot of MS-DOS programs and you want then to run concurrently. You cannot use 386-Enhanced mode on an 80286 chip or earlier.

Earlier Versions

If you want to use any Windows-based program that was designed and written for Windows/286 with Windows 3 then you should use Real Mode. If you don't then funny things happen, especially to the screen display. When you try to use a program from an earlier version of Windows with Windows 3 you will get an message box warning you of the consequences. All Windows programs carry an identifying mark within the code that allows Windows 3 to know when you are trying to use old software.

Using old version software can have the following effects:

> The screen display becomes corrupted. This is the most likely problem to occur. You may get superfluous characters appearing along the Title Bar or the selector command is not refreshed properly or the colours are incorrect.

> Without warning Windows crashes and returns you to the system prompt. If this happens then you have probably encountered an interrupt clash. The two programs, your application and Windows have both tried to use the same device at the same time. The result is that Windows 3 crashes out, taking the application with it. If this occurs then you are likely to find a large number of unassigned clusters on your hard disk. Use Norton Disk Doctor or something similar to fix and then erase them.

> The machine hangs up completely, locking the keyboard and so forcing you to use the reset button or the On/Off switch. Any work that was in progress prior to the crash is now lost and, again, you will find large numbers of unattached clusters on your hard disk.

The moral of the story is if you are going to use old version software then run Windows 3 in Real Mode only.

MS-DOS Programs

One of the major advances in Windows 3 is the ability to run MS-DOS programs from within the Windows environment but this can cause problems. Any problems that you encounter as a result of this are likely to be caused by your hardware rather than Windows. The problems you might encounter are:

System Hangup which can occur without warning. This has happened a number of times in the course of writing this book. I have used WordStar 6 from within Windows for the bulk of this book and on no less than a dozen occasions the machine has hung up completely. Every time it did so, WordStar was in the process of doing a spelling check - which is something that uses a lot of memory! Fortunately I have learned to save any work I am doing very often and so the hangup did not cause any great loss but it is annoying. The problem only occurred on the Laser 386 which leads me to suppose that the fault is machine specific.

Once back at MS-DOS you cannot return to Windows. Normally whenever you use an MS-DOS program you also have access to any MS-DOS window that such a program contains. For example, I can run WordStar from Windows and then use WordStar's own MS-DOS window to get back to the system prompt. On more than one occasion I then found I couldn't get back to Windows. Mind you, the fault was mine because I know you shouldn't have a number of programs all trying to use the memory at the same time. The only answer when this occurred was to reboot the machine.

TSR programs do not work. Windows is a special environment that is graphical in nature. Most memory resident software is not. In addition Windows is a memory hog and so that limits the amount of RAM available for TSR programs. At the end of the day you have to decide whether you want to use Windows or use your TSR programs.

You get a memory shortage message. When running some MS-DOS programs you may encounter a lack of memory to perform certain actions, like my being unable to print from WordStar. Your only recourse is to close down any Windows applications that you have running, either as a window or as an icon, in the hope that this will free enough RAM for your needs. If the problem persists then you will have to run the program from the system prompt instead of the Windows environment.

In 386-Enhanced mode only, you may find that everything on screen suddenly vanishes. This is caused by the MS-DOS program suddenly using another video mode but its PIF only specifies one type of display, e.g. Text instead of Graphics. You can fix this problem by terminating the MS-DOS program and then editing the Program Information File using the PIF editor.

Increasing performance

There are a number of things you can do to increase your system resources and/or enhancing those resources so that Windows 3 runs better. Most of these have already been covered in this book but here is a brief summary of them and a few others.

Extra RAM

If you can afford it, it is well worth your while increasing the amount of Extended memory. The extra RAM will increase the speed at which Windows works and it has a dramatic affect on the system resources available. Ideally you want to have around 8 Mb of RAM, any more is superfluous as far as Windows is concerned. However, it must be Extended memory not Expanded because Windows cannot work with the latter.

Free memory

You should disable and/or remove any TSR programs that you would normally be using if you want to run Windows 3 for a large amount of your working day. The more memory that Windows has access to the better.

Tidy Disk

Before running Windows 3 you should ensure that all the files on your hard disk are contiguous. Run a utility program like Norton

Speed Disk or PC Tools Compress. Thereafter when you are using Windows it will work more efficiently because any files it produces will automatically be contiguous.

Free Disk capacity

Windows 3 will generate a number of temporary files in the process of running, not counting those files that you create yourself and then store on the disk. It is in your interests therefore to have as much free space as possible before you start. Ideally you want to have at least 2 Mb free - although you can get by with only half of this. How you create free capacity is up to you: archive your files; delete unwanted files; remove programs and data you no longer use or need.

Swapfile

Windows 3 runs faster and more efficiently if you have a permanent swapfile for it to use - although only when running in 386-Enhanced mode. The swapfile is not vital because Windows can create a temporary one as necessary but a permanent swapfile, being completely contiguous, is much better. The problem with a permanent swapfile is that it resides on your disk even when Windows is not running and disk space tends to be at a premium on any system.

By the way, don't set up a permanent swapfile if you are using a Novell network. There is a minor incompatibility between Windows 3 and Novell that causes all the network nodes to try and access the swapfile, which will be on the server, at the same time. Instead let Windows create temporary swapfiles as necessary - that cures the problem.

Ramdrives

A Ramdrive is a great deal faster than even the fastest hard disk and if you have the memory available it is well worth creating one to use with Windows 3. Then use the Ramdrive as temporary storage, using **SET TEMP=[drive]** in your AUTOEXEC.BAT. This will greatly enhance Windows' performance. Unfortunately there is a minimum limit that such a Ramdrive can be to work effectively - it must be at least 2 Mb and preferably more. We're back to memory again!

It may also be worth saving all your work to the Ramdrive but remember that in the event of a system crash you will lose the contents of this. The result is that the possibility of losing a day's work far outweighs the advantages that might be gained from using the Ramdrive as file storage.

General Problems

Windows 3 is remarkably free from bugs and problems - far more so than any other program with a x.0 version number that I have ever seen. To date there have been no major problems uncovered, either by end users or by other software companies. The only real problem that has been pointed out is the one about swapfiles and Novell network mentioned above. The result is that the only problems you are likely to encounter are those created by specific machines rather than Windows itself.

Windows 3 is designed, as are all MS-DOS programs, to work on an IBM computer - after all they invented the PC in the first place. However, very few people actually use IBM machines because they tend to be expensive, slow and under-specified when compared to alternative manufacturer's machines. The result is that you will have either a PC-clone or a PC-compatible machine.

> A Clone is a machine that is identical to the IBM one, it uses the same interrupts, the same chip configuration and so on so that it performs in exactly the same way as the IBM machine would - although it may be faster and have more resources. Running Windows 3 on any clone should not therefore cause any problems.

> A Compatible machine is one that is similar but not identical to the IBM one. Such machines use different interrupts; they may use different chips; they will certainly use different controllers and their system resources usually far outstrip those of the IBM machines. The result is that you may encounter errors - after all the majority of computer systems around the World are compatibles not clones. Most compatibles will not cause any problems but you may find the occasional one.

Here's an example. On the Samsung 286 Windows refuses to show the floppy disk drive! It does find and display Drive-C and Drive-D, both of which are 20 Mb hard disks, and Drive-E, the 320 Kb Ramdrive, but it refuses to log with Drive-A. Neither in File Manager or in the list boxes of any Windows application program does Drive-A appear. The drive still exists because you can load files from it by using the drive letter and then the filename, e.g. A:\ELEPHANT.BMP allows me to load the graphic into Paintbrush, but the drive does not appear in the list box. It's very odd and there is no apparent reason for it to do this. Fortunately I rarely want to load things from Drive-A in any case but what would I do if I did?

Appendix 1
The Intel 8000 Series

Many of the problems, and all of the advantages, of the IBM PC and compatibles are caused directly by the chip at the heart of the machine. Because each chip in the 8000 series is compatible with all the preceding generations of chips it means that any new chip is automatically handicapped before the computer manufacturers even start to create a new machine. At the same time hardly any software producer bothers to write programs that can take advantage of the capabilities of the newer chips and so everything is reduced to its minimum level with the result that the chips rarely, if ever, run at their most productive.

8086

This is the first chip in the series and it was developed by Intel in 1976. It possesses a 16-bit data bus and can address up to 1 Mb of RAM using a 20-bit address bus. It will run in one mode only - Real Mode.

8088

This is really a cut-down version of the 8086 and it was introduced in 1978. IBM used this chip as the base of the original PC - they used this one rather than the 8086 because it was cheaper and they thought that people would be disinclined to buy the more powerful and faster 8086. (In fact the original IBM PC, named the Model 5150-001 retailed at just $1,355 in 1979.)

The 8088 has the same internal architecture as the 8086 but it has only got an 8-bit data bus. This means that it is much slower in accessing data from disk or memory. Again though it can address up to 1 Mb of RAM using a 20-bit address bus. Like its predecessor it runs in only one mode - Real Mode.

Apart from the differences in the data bus size there is no real difference between the 8088 and the 8086, in fact the chips are virtually identical. However the larger bus on the 8086 means that it does tend to run slightly faster because it can read and write the data faster. The original PC used an 8088 running at 4.77 MHz, i.e. it could perform just under 5,000,000 operations per second, and this speed is used as the base measure against which all other chips are matched. It is still possible to purchase 8088 chips, they are very cheap and so they allow the construction of very basic, low level and low price machines. However the technology of the rest of the peripheral devices used in today's computers means that the 8088, or the 8086, actually act as a brake on the speed with which the computer can operate.

80186

This was introduced in 1982 and it is really just an enhanced version of the 8086. It has a 16-bit data bus and can address 1 Mb of RAM using a 20-bit address bus. It runs at a faster speed, normally around 10 MHz although it is possible to get chips with a speed of 16 MHz. It primary claim to fame is that it includes an on-board clock. Due to its internal architecture it can operate 25% faster than the 8086 even when running at the same speed. There is also a cut down version of this chip, the 80188. However neither of these was taken up by the computer industry as a whole, a few machines based on the 80186 were developed but they soon faded away. However the 80186 is making somewhat of a comeback today as an embedded controller on the EISA and MCA add-on cards.

80286

The 80286, launched in 1981, is special in a number of ways. The chip possesses a 16-bit data bus, and can address up to 16 Mb of RAM using a 24-bit address bus, finally it has a built in real time clock. It is fully compatible with the earlier chips in the series and so any software written for the 8088 or the 8086 will run on an 80286. In order to do so the 80286 operates in two different modes - Real, which is identical to the 8086 and 8088, and Protected, which is specific to the 80286.

The 80286 was a major step forward because it brought an enormous amount of power and processing capability to the PC, so much so that the industry invented a new term of computers built around the chip - AT, short for Advanced Technology. The take-up of the chip has been enormous, so much so that it has supplanted the 8086 as the most common chip and a base level AT has become the most common entry level machine in the marketplace - although this is beginning to change.

Theoretically the 80286 is capable of multitasking, i.e. doing two or more things at the same time independently of each other. The problem is that the multitasking part does not work as well as had been expected. In order to run the normal MS-DOS based programs the chip had to be in real mode but the multitasking meant that the chip had to switch into Protected mode. Unfortunately if you switch the chip in this way the system crashes and needs to be rebooted. OS/2 was originally written to take account of this fact but the problems it created have led Microsoft to specify that in future to run OS/2 the user must have an 80386 based machine.

The result of all this is that the 80286 is used as a fast 8086 and nobody really bothers with the multitasking ability. As such the chip can return very a impressive performance. Typically the 80286 will operate at two and a half times the speed of an 8086 when running identical software at the same clock speed, or 12 times faster than the original PC. (Curiously enough it can also run faster than a 25 MHz 80386 or produce speeds comparable with a 25 MHz 80486!) The fastest 80286 available from Intel is 12 MHz, although other chip manufacturers do provide faster versions. It is estimated that 40% of all the PC's and AT's sold in the past 12 months, i.e. to January 1990, were based around the 80286 chip.

80386

If the 80286 was a major step forward then the 80386 was a giant leap. A full 32-bit chip, it uses a 32-bit data bus, is capable of addressing a massive 4,096 Mb of RAM using a 32-bit address bus and it is also capable of true multitasking. Launched in 1985 but not commercially available in a computer until late 1986, the chip has a real time clock, which means that it is not dependent on the time in the battery backed RAM. Like the 80286 it can operate in Real or Protected Mode, however it can also use a third mode - Virtual Real.

The 80386 is produced exclusively by Intel. Prior to its introduction Intel had been prepared to allow other chip manufacturers to produce the 8000 series under licence but not when it came to the 80386. (Not that this will make a great deal of difference because clone manufacturers will simply reverse engineer the chip. In other words they will strip it layer by layer until they know what it contains and then build their own versions of the chip from the ground up.)

The major difference between the 80286 and the 80386 is that the latter can multitask correctly. It can switch from one mode to the other without having to be rebooted. One major problem is its compatibility with the rest of the 8000 series. As a result of this, the chip cannot run standard MS-DOS software in Real mode, at the same speed, any faster than an 80286 can - in fact sometimes it will be slower than its earlier cousin!

80386 Modes

Real Mode forces the chip to operate in an identical way, albeit faster, than the original 8086 chip. In fact it makes the chip operate as an 80286. This means that it can run standard MS-DOS software without any modifications to the programs. Any program running in real mode can only access 1 Mb of RAM.

Protected Mode is fully compatible with the 80286 Protected Mode.

Virtual Real Mode is brand new. It allows the chip to run with program memory protection but it simulates the Real Mode of the 8086. When in this mode the chip can perform genuine multitasking. Each standard MS-DOS program operates independently of the others and each is allocated its own 1 Mb chunk of the available RAM. In essence this means that you can have a number of programs all running on the same machine, in tandem with and yet separate from each other, i.e. you can apparently have multiple PC's on the same machine. Note however that if the machine only possess 1 Mb of RAM then the multitasking will be severely limited or even nonexistent. In a sense the amount of RAM available will have a direct bearing on the number of programs that can be multitasked as each one will require 1 Mb for its own use. Thus if you have 4 Mb you can have 4 programs running simultaneously, 8 Mb gives you 8 and so on.

80386SX

Because the 80386 was so expensive, although it is much less so now due to market forces, and also because it had capabilities that could not be fully utilised Intel produced a cut down version of the chip, the 80386SX. This chip bears the same relationship to the 80386 as the 8088 does to the 8086 - i.e. it has much of the same internal architecture but its links with the rest of the machine are limited. The 80386SX has a 16-bit data bus, making data handling slower, and a 24-bit address bus which limits its maximum RAM usage to 16 Mb. However internally it can produce the same processing speeds as the 80386.

Due to its low price, machines based around this chip are fast becoming the entry level systems and are displacing the 80286 machines.

80486

This chip will run 40% faster than the 80386 at the same clock speed with the result that a 25 MHz 80486 is faster than a 33 MHz 80386. In addition it has a built in co-processor. Prior to this chip if you wanted to do a large amount of number crunching you had to purchase and fit a co-processor chip, designated by a 7 rather than a 6 at the end of the chip number, e.g. 80287 or 80387. However the 80486 has the co-processor already on board and so there is no need to fit additional chips.

As yet, March 1990, there are very few 80486 based machines available and the few that are around are pitched at the high end of the market as Network Servers and the like. However it is likely that within 12 months such machines will have established themselves as the de facto standard of mid-level machines.

Appendix 2
ANSI Character Set

The Windows ANSI character set is similar to but different from the IBM ASCII characters. A full list of the charcaters is given below. To use any of the characters, not available from the standard keyboard, you press and hold **Alt** while typing 0 (zero) followed by the three digit number of the character you require, on the numeric keypad. You must use this rather then standard number keys at the top of the keyboard. If you omit the leading 0 then you will get the ASCII character for that code instead of the ANSI one. Be warned, the majority of printers do not support either the ANSI Character set or the IBM Extended ASCII one and so your printed document is liable to be different to the on screen one - hence the use of graphics here to show the characters.

001	▌	002		003	▌	004	▌	005	▌	006	▌
007	▌	008	▌	009		010		011		012	
013		014	▌	015	▌	016	▌	017	▌	018	▌
019	▌	020	▌	021		022	▌	023	▌	024	▌
025	▌	026	▌	027	▌	028	▌	029	▌	030	▌
031		032		033	!	034	"	035	#	036	$
037	%	038	&	039	'	040	(	041	)	042	*
043	+	044	,	045	-	046	.	047	/	048	0
049	1	050	2	051	3	052	4	053	5	054	6
055	7	056	8	057	9	058	:	059	;	060	<
061	=	062	>	063	?	064	@	065	A	066	B
067	C	068	D	069	E	070	F	071	G	072	H
073	I	074	J	075	K	076	L	077	M	078	N
079	O	080	P	081	Q	082	R	083	S	084	T
085	U	086	V	087	W	088	X	089	Y	090	Z
091	[	092	\	093	]	094	^	095	_	096	`
097	a	098	b	099	c	100	d	101	e	102	y
103	g	104	h	105	i	106	j	107	k	108	l
109	m	110	n	111	o	112	p	113	q	114	r
115	s	116	t	117	u	118	v	119	w	120	x
121	y	122	z	123	{	124			125	}	126	~

127	∎	128	∎	129	∎	130		131	∎	132	∎
133	∎	134	∎	135	∎	136	∎	137	∎	138	∎
139	∎	140	∎	141	∎	142	∎	143	∎	144	∎
145	´	146	´	147	∎	148	∎	149	∎	150	∎
151	∎	152	∎	153	∎	154	∎	155	∎	156	∎
157	∎	158	∎	159	∎	160		161	¡	162	¢
163	£	164	¤	165	¥	166	¦	167	§	168	¨
169	©	170	ª	171	«	172	¬	173	-	174	®
175	¯	176	°	177	±	178	²	179	³	180	´
181	µ	182		183	·	184	¸	185	¹	186	º
187	»	188	¼	189	½	190	¾	191	¿	192	À
193	Á	194	Â	195	Ã	196	Ä	197	Å	198	Æ
199	Ç	200	È	201	É	202	Ê	203	Ë	204	Ì
205	Í	206	Î	207	Ï	208	Ð	209	Ñ	210	Ò
211	Ó	212	Ô	213	Õ	214	Ö	215	×	216	Þ
217	Ù	218	Ú	219	Û	220	Ü	221	Ý	222	Þ
223	ß	224	à	225	á	226	â	227	ã	228	ä
229	å	230	æ	231	ç	232	è	233	é	234	ê
235	ë	236	ì	237	í	238	î	239	ï	240	ð
241	ñ	242	ò	243	ê	244	ô	245	õ	246	ö
247	÷	248	ø	249	ù	250	ú	251	û	252	ü
253	ý	254	þ	255	ÿ						

Glossary

The following is a list of those words and phrases used throughout this book which may require clarification.

386-Enhanced Mode
That mode which allows Windows 3 to take advantage of the Virtual Real mode of the 80386 and 80386SX microchips. Using this mode the program and the chip can perform true multi-tasking concurrency.

Accelerator board
An add-on card that is used to replace the CPU and which causes the machine to run faster.

Access
Specifically the ability to find and retrieve data from a storage medium.

Access Time
The time taken for the information to be found on the disk once you ask the computer to load a particular file or string of data. The time is usually measured in milliseconds and the faster it is the quicker the computer can manipulate the data. There are a wide range of programs available that will measure the access time for you. Access time becomes especially important when using disk intensive software such as DTP programs or relational databases.

Accuracy
A measure of the distortion of the data. 100% accuracy means that the data has been accessed, read and transmitted correctly without any deformation or corruption.

Active
The selected icon or window to which the next mouse or keyboard action will apply. When an icon has been selected its title appears in inverse video. When a window is selected the Title Bar of that window will undergo a colour change, assuming that you are not using the same colours for active and inactive windows.

Actuator
A device that moves the disk drive head assembly across the platters.

Address bus
An electrical conductor that is used to carry the data from the address within the processor to the rest of the system. The address bus is usually referred to as so many bits, i.e. 24-bit address bus. The higher the number of bits that can be carried the faster the machine will operate.

Add-on
Usually a card which is used to enhance the performance of a machine by providing a facility which is not built into the motherboard. Typical examples include Fax Cards, Additional Serial Ports and Video Adaptors.

Adobe
The originators of the PostScript page description language.

Alphanumeric
A character which is either a letter or a number.

ANSI Character
That set of characters supported by the American National Standards Institute. It contains 256 characters, some of which are radically different to the ASCII character set. All Windows-based programs use the ANSI character set.

Apple
The major competitor against IBM for the desktop computer market. Apple pre-date the launch of the IBM PC and the company was founded by Steve Jobs. Apple machines are notoriously expensive and, until recently, were considered far superior to the IBM compatible machines for producing graphics. However with the advent of VGA graphics this latter point is now debatable.

Application Program
Any program that does a specific task, e.g. word processing, rather than one which is concerned with the environment of the machine, i.e. an operating system.

Architecture
In essence the design of something. Thus one can talk of the System Architecture, meaning the chips and components that make up the system.

Archive
A method of compacting data and/or program files so that they consume much less disk space.

Archive Bit
That bit in a file attribute byte that sets the archive attribute. If the bit is set to On then the file is deemed to be new and will be backed up by the MS-DOS BACKUP command. If the bit is Off the file will not be backed up. The archive bit is also used by the majority of backup utility programs.

ASCII
It was decided in the distant past of computing that there should be a recognised standard for all text files so that every one would adopt the same procedure, thus making commands like TYPE work universally. Rather than create a brand new standard it was decided to use an existing one - that which was originally used for the transmission of messages on teletype machines. ASCII stands for the American Standard Code for Information Interchange and it defines a series of unique codes for 128 characters. Thus each individual letter, whether upper or lower case, numerals and certain control codes have a separate code.

Later it was decided that 128 characters were not enough and the codes were extended to 256. Unfortunately, these are not standardised and so the characters in IBM-Extended ASCII, used on all computers, are different from those in the Epson-Extended ASCII character set which are used by printers.

ASCII character
Any 1-byte character from the original ASCII character set. There are only 128 of these because they were originally defined using on 7 bits and this is the maximum number that can be contained in 7 binary digits. The 8th. bit was used for special purposes.

Associate

A command available in the File Manager that allows you to identify a file extension as being bound to a particular application. Thereafter the program can be invoked by double clicking on a filename bearing the associated extension.

AT

Abbreviation for Advanced Technology. The third 'generation' personal computer which evolved from the PC and the XT. The most notable features of an AT are:

a) based on an 80286 or 80386 microchip,
b) generally hard disk fitted as standard,
c) high capacity floppy disk drives,
d) 16-bit slots, and
e) the ability to address and use sizable amounts of RAM.

AT's are fast becoming the standard machines used by most businesses, commercial organisations and, although less rapidly, as personal computers. Over the past year they have also become noticeably less expensive until the price difference between an XT and an AT can be as little as #200 - a very small price to pay for the increased performance.

Attribute Byte

A single byte of information that is held in the directory entry of a disk and which relates to a given file. It describes the various attributes of that file. Some of these, such as Read-Only and Archive, can be changed using the ATTRIB command while others can only be altered by utility programs such as PC Tools or Norton Utilities.

Attributes

A set of bits giving details of a file's status. There are four possible attributes; Archive, Read Only, Hidden and System.

a) When any file is created or modified it will have the Archive attribute turned on. This is so that programs which produce backups, including the MS-DOS BACKUP, know which files to include in their operation. Normally after the files have been backed up the Archive bit will be turned off. The bit can be changed using the MS-DOS ATTRIB command.

b) Any file that is Read Only cannot be modified or deleted, though it may be backed up if it has it Archive attribute turned on. The bit can be changed using the MS-DOS ATTRIB command.

c) Hidden files cannot be seen in the normal course of events, though they are still present and can be used. The only way to change this attribute is through using a program such as Norton Utilities or PC Tools - the bit cannot be changed from MS-DOS but it can be in Windows.

d) System files are exactly what they say they are. Again this attribute can only be changed by a utility program or by Windows but not from MS-DOS.

AUX
Refers to an Auxiliary device, specifically the serial port and the device connected to it. The word is one of those reserved by MS-DOS and cannot be used as a filename or as a directory name.

Auxiliary Storage
Any storage device that is not a main storage device, e.g. a tape streamer.

Background
The main screen area against and on which all windows appear.

Backup
1) The process of making a duplicate copy of a file on another disk so as to protect yourself from its loss in case of damage to the original disk. Backups can be something as simple as copying the file to another disk, using the BACKUP command, or any purpose written program that will do this for you.

2) The disk, normally a floppy, that contains the backup copies of files.

3) The MS-DOS external command which is used to create contingency copies of files so that data loss as a result of a disk head crash is minimised. To be of any real use the command must be used regularly. The files backed up can only be replaced using the RESTORE command.

Backup disk
The disks used to store the backed up copies of files, they can be either floppy disks or another hard disk.

BAS
A reserved word which cannot be used for naming files or directories. Normally BAS is used as an extension by any program which is written in Basic.

Basic
An acronym for Beginner's All Purpose Symbolic Instruction Code. A programming language that is probably the most common on personal computers. It is typified by using commands which are close to common English and thus it is 'easy' to learn and understand. There are many varieties of BASIC available and they are not fully compatible but they all share the same common format.

BAT
The file extension given to Batch files and as such this is a word that is reserved by MS-DOS for its own purposes.

Batch file
Any pure ASCII file created by the user that is used to run a series of commands. Batch files can be extremely powerful in their effects but they are simple to construct. All batch files must have the extension BAT - which is also a reserved word. Batch files are an integral part of using a computer and hard disk. Every PC will normally contain at least two batch files, the AUTOEXEC.BAT and CONFIG.SYS. The latter is not normally known as a batch file but in reality that is what it is and both of these files will serve as an introduction to the subject. A batch file is simply a sequence of instructions, written in ASCII, such that those commands it contains will be operated or activated in serial order. They can range from the very simple to the exceedingly complex, but regardless of their complexity they are one of the most powerful tools you can use on a hard disk. Batch files are quintessentially mini-programs and as with any program they have their own specialised commands and rules of operation. In addition to using batch file specific commands you can also include the names of any program, with or without additional parameters, that is accessible to the batch file on the disk.

Binary digit
Either a 0 or a 1.

Binary File
A file contains characters in computer readable form, as opposed to human readable.

Bit
The acronym for Binary Digit, i.e. it must be a 1 or 0. The smallest possible unit that the computer can work with.

Bit-mapped graphic
Any graphic created in a paint-type program where the image is composed of a series of dots, usually with a specified number of dots per inch. Such a graphic can be imported directly into PageMaker, or most other DTP programs, provided that it conforms to one of the available filters, and will produce a quality printed image.

Bold
Any text which appears in bold is darker than normal and so it stands out more. For example the various headings on this page are in bold.

Boot
To load any program into the computer. More usually, as in boot up the computer, it means turning on the power so the machine performs the POST and then loads the operating system. A boot operation in this instance may be either cold, i.e. switching the whole machine on after it has been off for some time, or warm, i.e. pressing Ctrl-Alt-Del. Both methods load or reload the operating system.

Boot Record
A one-sector record which is on every disk that informs the operating system about the disk concerned and the files it contains. The boot record is always the very first sector on a disk and hence it is the one most likely to be damaged. Any disk without a boot sector cannot be used and will produce an error message. Equally if the boot sector is damaged then the disk becomes unusable. Occasionally reformatting can repair the damage but any data held on the disk will be lost as a result.

Boot strap
The terms comes from the expression "Pulling yourself up by your own boot straps." Quite simply it means that an internal action brings about the desired result, e.g. a computer becomes operable as a result of its own built in commands.

Boot up
Providing the computer with power so that it will operate.

Buffer
A predefined area of the computer memory in the RAM that is used as temporary storage to hold data before it is transferred from the application to the disk. The number of buffers to be used is set in the CONFIG.SYS file although there is a certain minimum that you must use.

BUFFERS
An MS-DOS command. When you read information from the disk it is not sent directly to the application as you might expect, instead it is moved into an area of the RAM called a Buffer. This is because the amount of data in the Sector being read might not be complete, for example it may have an overspill into the next sector. The reason for using the Buffers command is that it dramatically increases the speed with which the computer can access data - it can be as much as 100 times faster than a pure disk read operation. The reason is that the RAM, where the data is now held, is purely electronic in operation and therefore ultra-fast when compared to a electron-mechanical disk. In essence the BUFFERS command acts as a poor computer's disk cache.

Bus
A pathway through which power, data or other signals can travel.

Byte
Normally, a collection of 8 Bits which is the minimum space required to define a single character. The Byte forms the basis of all subsequent capacity measurement of both disks and the computer memory.

Cache
A special area of the RAM that is used to store information. Its purpose is to speed up the computer's operation. The reason for

using a Cache is that the chips at the heart of the machine have become too fast for the peripherals and so the Cache is used to try and compensate for this deficiency.

Capacity
The measure of the amount that can be stored on something, e.g. the capacity of a hard disk refers to the total available space. As the unit is used so the free capacity decreases.

Caps
Abbreviation for Capitals, i.e. Upper Case letters.

Card
A piece of plastic material on to which electronic components have been embedded such that they form an electric circuit. Cards come in various sizes, normally half size or full size, and they fit into the expansion slots within the computer's system unit.

Cascade
To arrange windows and/or sub-windows so that they overlap each other yet allow the Title Bar of each one to be visible.

Cassettes
A small self-contained plastic box containing two reels of magnetic tape - invented by Philips. The original PC used cassette tapes as its storage medium but these were quickly superseded by floppy disks.

CD-Disc
A 12 cm plastic disk coated with aluminium, containing a single spiral track on each side. The track is read by a laser. CD-Discs produce very high quality sound - but you have to have high quality speakers to notice the difference.

CD-ROM
A variation of the CD-Disc. Invented jointly by Philips and Sony as a publishing medium for the computer industry. A single CD-ROM can hold up to 640 Megabytes of data on a track that can be as much as 3 miles long and which contains over 3 billion pits. There are more than 1,000,000 CD-ROM users worldwide and the technology is becoming cheaper and more accessible every day.

Central Processing Unit

The heart of the microchip. The CPU manipulates bits and so processes instructions.

CGA

Acronym for Colour Graphics Adaptor. This is the lowest quality colour monitor you can buy - although they are now becoming fairly rare - they tend to be rather hard on the eyes. It can display the same number of lines and characters as the Hercules but the quality of the display is much poorer. The CGA monitor can display colour graphics at a resolution of 320 pixels by 200 but you are limited to use four, very poor, colours. It can also be used in monochrome mode, i.e. using greyscales, which increases the resolution to 640 by 200.

Character Set

A range of characters that make up a single group.

1) On a PC the ASCII Character Set contains 127 symbols, letters and numbers which are common to all PC's. The Extended ASCII set contains an additional 127 characters.

2) Within a Typeface there is also a specific Character set, i.e. that with Zapf Dingbats is different to that in Times Roman.

Characters Per Inch

Literally the number of characters that can be printed within one inch across the width of the paper. Also called Pitch. The higher the CPI number the tighter the characters will be printed and thus the less easy to read they will be. Normal printing is between 10 and 12 CPI.

Characters per second

The speed with which an impact printer can operate. Because the printer is basically mechanically operated there is a limit to the number of characters that can be produced within a given time.

Chip

Contraction of Microchip. Another name for Integrated Circuit. The name arises from the 'chip' of silicon which contains the IC. Normally the chip is set into a plastic or ceramic carrier that will allow it to be handled safely.

Clicking

Pushing a mouse button once and then releasing it. Windows uses a click to identify something. Compare Double Clicking and Dragging.

Clip Art

A collection of prepared illustrations, either monochrome or full colour, in various topics, elements of which can be incorporated into DTP documents or used individually. Some Clip Art is Copyright and so permission to use it is required, while the majority is copyright free. Originally distributed on floppy disks, Clip Art is one of the major forms of publication found on CD-ROM.

Clipboard

The Windows program that allows you to transfer data within a program or to other programs. The Clipboard is activated via the Edit menu.

Clock

A wafer of quartz embedded in silicon that is capable of producing extremely accurate signals. These are then used as the timing or regulating mechanism within the computer.

CLOCK

A window program that produces an analogue or digital representation of the current system time.

Cluster

Data storage is allocated in Clusters, each of which contains a number of Sectors. The number of Sectors per Cluster will depend on the type of disk and the type of computer being used. For example, a 360 Kb 5.25" floppy disk uses 2 Sectors making a Cluster 1,024 bytes, while a 1.2 Mb 5.25" disk uses only 1 Sector per Cluster.

Cold Boot

The process of supplying the computer with power by turning on the mains switch, i.e. the machine has been turned off and all drives have been allowed to come to rest before it is turned on again, e.g. the next day. Occasionally a complete system crash will necessitate a cold boot rather than a warm reboot.

COM
A word reserved by MS-DOS for its own purposes and which cannot therefore be used for naming files or directories.

1) Refers to the communications serial port, it will usually have a number attached, e.g. COM1 or COM2.

2) The extension for certain programs.

Command
The issuing of an order to the operating system. It can be something as simple as entering a program name or it can be a long string of commands and parameters to produce a particular effect.

Comms
Contraction of Communications, it refers to the use of two or more computers linked together over the phone lines, via modems, so that they can send messages to and receive messages from each other.

Computer
A collection of electronic, mechanical and electro-mechanical devices connected together in such a way that they function as a single entity. A super fast idiot savant.

CON
A word reserved by MS-DOS for its own purposes and which cannot therefore be used for naming files or directories. It refers to the Keyboard and monitor and is short for Console.

Configuration
The 'shape' imposed on a computer so that it performs in a certain fashion.

Configuration file
The file that imposes the configuration onto the computer, e.g. CONFIG.SYS. It also refers to the file kept by application programs that sets the basic parameters by which the program operates.

Console

Refers to the Keyboard and the Monitor. The word is a hangover from the early days of computing when the only means of giving commands to the computer was via a typewriter.

Contiguous

Literally the word means touching or joined together. When data is stored on a disk it is placed in the first available space. Thus if you had a file which was 8 Kb the operating system will try to put it into the first blank area of the disk it can find. However if the space is only 2 Kb then only part of the file can be placed there and the operating system puts the rest elsewhere. This process continues until all the file has been written to the disk. Of necessity this means that the file is scattered all over the place - such a file is non-contiguous.

On the other hand the file being written may be placed into an area where the whole file can be kept together. Such a file is said to be contiguous. Files which are contiguous can be accessed much faster than scattered ones and thus the operation of the program using the files will be speeded up. A number of utility programs, notably Norton Utilities and PC Tools, will allow you to make all the files on your disk contiguous. These utilities should, ideally, be run on a daily basis.

Conventional Memory

That first 640 Kb of the computer RAM.

Cookies

The name given to the coated discs of plastic which will become floppy disks through further treatment.

Corel Draw

An object orientated graphic program that runs under Windows. Version 1.2 has been released to take advantage of the abilities of Windows 3.

Copy

To duplicate the selected data into the Clipboard ready for transferring elsewhere, either within the same program or to another program.

Co-processor

An additional chip which can be inserted into the computer and which is designed specifically to handle mathematical functions - one area that normal Intel chips are poor in. A co-processor is only necessary if you are using programs which use a large amount of mathematical operations, e.g. very large spreadsheets or CAD.

CPI

Acronym for Characters Per Inch - the number of symbols that can be printed within one inch across the width of the paper.

CPS

1) Acronym for Characters per second - a measure of the speed at which impact printers operate.

2) In Physics and electronics, acronym for Cycles per second. Usually referred to as Hertz (Hz).

CPU

Acronym for Central Processing Unit - the heart of the computer. The CPU may contain anything up to 1,000,000 transistors. The 80486 contains three times that many.

CP/M

Acronym for Control Program for Microprocessors. The 8-Bit operating system that was used for the vast majority of desk top and home computers in the 1970's.

Crash

A disaster. Usually caused by a malfunction, either within the application program or, more rarely within the operating system that causes the system to come to a halt. Generally a warm reboot will correct the problem but any work in process at the time of the crash will be lost. Occasionally a complete cold boot will be necessary to remove the cause of the fault.

Cursor

The thin flashing line on the screen at which position the characters will appear. Within Windows the cursor can appear as a white arrowhead, a black arrow head or a vertical line, depending on the application.

Cursor Keys
The keys, either on the numeric keypad on a PC or as separate keys on an AT, which control the movement of the cursor.

Cut
To replicate selected data in the Clipboard, ready for replacing elsewhere, and then delete it from the original application.

Data File
The result of work in an application program. Any file created by that application is a data file.

Default
Literally that which exists. The defaults are those settings that you made, or the program makers set, the last time you used the program. In most programs the defaults can be changed.

Desk Top Publishing
The process of using a computer and software to create text and graphics which can then be imported into a special program, such as PageMaker, and composed to produce either finished documents or Camera Ready Artwork. The term was invented by Paul Brainerd, the creator of PageMaker.

Desktop
That part of the Control Panel program that allows you to apply patterns to the background.

Dialogue Box
A pop up box that allows you to make selections of the default status of something. For example, when loading a file Windows defaults to its own directory but you can change this within the dialogue box that appears.

Directory
A special kind of file that is created by you, or by an installation program, on a hard disk to hold related files. You can also have directories on a floppy disk but they are rarely used.

Disk

A contraction of Diskette hence the use of the letter k instead of a c. Even the Oxford English Dictionary, the epitome of lexicography, uses this spelling.

Double Click

Usually, to press the left hand mouse button twice in rapid succession without moving the mouse in the process. The exception being if you are left handed and have reversed the mouse buttons in which case you double click the right hand button.

Drag

To click on an object and then, while still holding down the mouse button, move that object or part of that object around the screen.

Drives

On every computer the disk drives are always allocated upper case letters in the following order. By default MS-DOS can only handle five drives unless you use the LASTDRIVE command in your CONFIG.SYS.

A - The first floppy drive

B - The second floppy drive. This may not be present on your machine, in which case the A-Drive functions as both A and B.

C - The primary partition on a hard disk, i.e. the first hard disk drive.

D - The second hard disk drive or secondary partition.

E - The next drive or partition.

Drop Shadow

An enhancement to a graphic that creates an apparent shadow behind it and so makes the graphic much more dynamic. Drop shadows need not be black, they can be any colour or density.

EGA

Enhanced Graphics Adaptor. This will display the same number of lines and characters as the previous two and the characters will be very nearly as good as those on a Hercules monitor. When it comes to colour EGA monitors will allow you to display different ranges, from 16 colours at a resolution of 640 by 350 pixels down to 320 pixels by 200 using 4 colours. Running the monitor in monochrome mode will allow you a resolution of 720 pixels by 350 and 16 greyscales.

EMS Memory

A form of expanded memory that conforms to the Lotus-Intel-Microsoft standard.

EPT Port

A port that requires an add-on card to be fitted to the computer. Used by only a very limited number of peripherals.

Expanded Memory

Additional memory, over and above the Conventional Memory, that is available to application programs. Expanded memory cannot be used by Windows 3.

Extended Memory

Additional memory, over and above the Conventional memory, that is added to the computer system - usually by inserting extra chips. Standard MS-DOS programs normally cannot use Extended memory but under Windows 3 the environment allows this to happen.

Extension

The three character suffix of a filename. Normally an extension is used to identify the type of file to which it refers, e.g. DOC or TXT is normally applied to pure ASCII files.

Filenames

On any computer running under the MS-DOS Operating system you can define a filename using up to 8 characters, plus an additional 3 for an extension. If you try to use more than 8 then the extra is simply ignored. You should always try to name your files so that they are instantly recognisable - not just by you but by any other person who may have to use your computer.

For instance you could decide to just number all your files, starting at 00000001 and progressing from there. As you create a new file you simply increase the number. In this way you could create a total of nearly ten million filenames. However there are two major problems with using such a system.

1) You need to be able to remember which file is which. In fact you would probably have to keep a log of the file names and their contents in order to be able to use such a system. The trouble with this is that if you lose the log you will have real problems.

2) Under MS-DOS there is a limit to the number of files you can have on a disk. On a hard disk the maximum number of files you can have in the Root directory is 512. On a floppy disk the limit can be as low as 128. There is a way around the limit - use sub-directories, but even that does not answer the first problem.

The best way to name files is using alphabetical characters in such a way that the names reflect the file's contents. Thus if you write a letter to me, for example, you could call the file LETTERMH, LET-MH or MIKELET. Note that in each case you cannot use blank spaces - the filename must be continuous. Thus LET-MH, LET_MH, LETMH and LET'MH would all be valid while LET MH is not. Similarly a full stop is used to separate the filename from its extension. So if you were to save the file as LET.MH when you then used DIR it would show, for example, LET   MH 1024 12-01-90 2:59a.

When you first acquire a computer or begin using one the 8 characters seems a lot but as you create more and more files you begin to find that this is rather limiting and you have to become more creative in your choice and use of filenames. At the end of the day what you call your files is very much a matter of personal preferences, likes and dislikes. There is no right or wrong way - you can even use the numerical sequence mentioned above - simply use whichever is easiest for you. However you should avoid giving any of your files the same name as program files or this will cause problems.

Files

Files are one of the fundamental parts of the computer system. Any computer consists of two basic parts, Hardware, which are those items you can physically see and touch, and Software, the program, data and associated files that you cannot see other than via the computer. So what exactly is a file? Basically a file, regardless of its type, is simply a collection of instructions or information that the computer can operate with. The former are known as programs while the latter are data files.

Program files are generally specific to the type of computer you are using. For instance, you cannot use a program that was written on a MAC on an IBM-compatible machine or vice versa - except in very special circumstances. The same normally applies to data files, they tend to be distinctive to the machine although it is much easier to transport data across machines and it is fairly common practise, for example, to translate data from an IBM-compatible machine to a Mac or vice versa.

Aside from the program files, which we have already covered, there are three types of data file.

> The first are system files. These are ASCII files, that is they are written by the user directly from the keyboard and all they contain are alphanumeric characters.

> The second type are document files, these include all the files created by word processors, spreadsheets, databases and what-have-you. Normally such files contain ASCII characters along with a number of control codes that make them specific to the application that produced them. However, a number of application programs are now capable of importing files which were created by another program, e.g. you can import WordStar files into PageMaker - but not vice versa.

> The third type are graphic files. These generally contain no ASCII characters whatever and can normally only be viewed by the program which created them or a program which is capable of importing them.

All files are stored on the disk, whether hard or floppy, in a format that the computer can access and use. Whenever you write a file to the disk it will be processed by the System Program files and then passed to the drive controller which is actually responsible for writing the file onto the disk.

Floppy Disk

All floppy disks are made from basically the same non-woven polyester material. This is coated with a resin which contains ultrafine ferrous particles in the case of low density disks, or micro-fine cobalt compounds in the case of high density disks. The material, which is actually in huge rolls, is then baked in a thermostatically controlled oven so that the resin will bond correctly to it. Once the rolls have been allowed to cool the actual disks are stamped out and then placed into their protective sleeves. In the case of 5.25-inch disks the sleeve is a flexible PVC material, usually coloured black, while 3.5-inch disks are enclosed in rigid PVC envelopes that provide much better protection. Standard density 3.5-inch disks, i.e. 720 Kb, have blue sleeves while high density ones have black covers. All quality disks these days are verified individually, i.e. checked to ensure that the coating is of sufficient quality to meet the manufacturer's standards.

In order to use the disk for data storage it must first be formatted, preferably in your own machine, but you can buy preformatted disks. This process, which is carried out by one of the MS-DOS external commands, lays down a series of rings called Tracks on the disk. These rings have no visible existence - they are simply patterns of magnetism. The number of tracks will depend on the type of disk being used and, more importantly, on the disk drive being used. You should only ever use the correct density disk in the corresponding drive. Never format a standard density disk in a high capacity drive or vice versa. If you do so then the disk will contain a large number of errors and its life is shortened considerably. In addition you cannot then format that disk in the proper drive because of the quality and pattern of tracks that it contains. A 360 Kb disk has 40 Tracks laid down on it and they are 0.33 mm wide. 1.2 Mb disks have 80 Tracks and they are 0.16 mm wide. Both types of 3.5-inch disk have 80 Tracks and they are 0.115 mm wide. Note that the possible number of tracks, expressed in the TPI figure, is not actually used. In other words the used area of the disk is less than 1-inch wide!

Once the tracks are laid down the computer then divides these into sectors - arc shaped areas that form the basis of disk storage. Sectors are always 512 Bytes, regardless of the disk size or capacity. This is one of the very few true standards within the computer industry.

Font

The set of identical characters within a typeface. For example, Times Roman is the typeface but 12 Point, 12 Point Italic, 12 Point Bold and 12 Point Condensed are all fonts of that typeface.

Footer
Text that appears at the base of the printed page, e.g. a page number.

Foreground
That which is in front of the background, e.g. the active window.

Formatting
The process of making the disk usable by the computer. During the formatting process the computer lays down a series of tracks and sectors on the disk surface. These then form the basis of the storage thereafter.

Group
A collection of programs that bear some form of relationship to each other, e.g. Windows Accessories, Games or Windows Applications. Groups are user defined and therefore subject to change.

Hard disk
Hard disks are made of aluminium coated with a magnetisable material. The actual discs are then called Platters. These are stacked, one above the other, and fixed to a central core called a Spindle. The Read/Write Heads assembly is then put into place and the whole thing is enclosed in an airtight casing. When the hard disk is fitted to the computer it has to be connected via ribbon cables to a controller: that item of hardware which is responsible for actually operating the hard disk and accessing the data on it.

Unlike a floppy disk, a hard disk spins constantly while the computer has power. It rotates at, usually, 3,600 Rpm - a floppy on the other hand spins at around 360 Rpm - and it is easier to allow it to spin continuously rather than only on those occasions when you want to access it.

In many ways hard disks are very similar to floppy disks, i.e. they use the same method of formatting and assigning storage space, but they have three enormous advantages:

1) Their access time, i.e. the length of time it takes them to find and present any file, is dramatically faster than a floppy.

Typically a hard disk can have an access time of around 28 milliseconds compared to four times that for a floppy disk.

2) A hard disk has a much greater capacity and thus removes the need to constantly switch disks as you run a program. Modern software tends to be on the large side, e.g. a typical word processor might need a total of 3 Mb to hold all of its files, and using it on a floppy based machine is a chore rather than a pleasure. The 'standard' size for a hard disk at the time of writing is around 40 Mb, i.e. the equivalent of 116,500 standard 360 Kb floppy disks. However this standard hard disk continues to increase in capacity and by the end of 1990 the standard is likely to 70 Mb plus - well over 200,000 360 Kb floppies! And the capacity will, in all probability, continue to increase for the foreseeable future. (IBM have recently announced that they have managed to pack 1 Mb of data on to a square inch of disk surface. Granted they used very high quality disks and a special Read/Write Head assembly but nothing that cannot be readily mass produced. No matter how you look at it this is a phenomenal achievement!)

3) Dynamic storage abilities. A hard disk is much more than just a giant floppy disk. Using a hard disk is almost an art and you have to learn to use directories as an adjunct to your normal usage. Using these you can 'tune' your storage requirements to a very high degree and so create a much more intensive method of storing data. In addition you can get into the realms of partitions, logical drives and physical drives, all of which make using a computer more exciting and rewarding.

The difference between using floppy storage and hard disk storage is best illustrated by an analogy. Using the former is the equivalent of walking everywhere, whereas a hard disk machine is like driving a high performance car. But note that it can be a two edged sword - using a hard disk wrongly can get you into a terrible mess awfully quickly. But on the whole the advantages to using a hard disk far outweigh the disadvantages.

Header

Text which appears at the top of the printed page, e.g. a page number or section heading.

Hidden File
A file that is not shown when you use the MS-DOS DIR command. Windows can show hidden files if you allow it to.

High Capacity Disks
A floppy disk which uses a high grade coating and thus allows data to be packed more precisely onto the disk. Such a disk also requires a special disk drive to be fitted to the machine. You should not use ordinary disks as high capacity or vice versa.

Highlighted
An object that is highlighted has been selected, either by clicking on it or by using the cursor keys and the selector box to that object.

Icon
A graphical representation of something, e.g. a disk drive, a program or a document.

Inactive window
A window which is open but which is not currently being used. Normally the Title Bar of such a window is a different colour to that of an active window.

Keyboard
Nowadays there are two standards for keyboards. The first is the one fitted to the early Personal Computers. It generally has 86 or 88 keys and the Function Keys are arranged in two lines down the left hand side of the main keypad. You will find this keyboard fitted to the majority of those machines that use an 8088 or 8086 microchip. The second standard is the AT keyboard. This normally has 101 or 102 keys. The Function Keys are arranged in a line above the main keypad and it also has an extra set of cursor movement keys, independent of those on the Numeric Keypad.

Kilobyte
A multiple defined as 1,024 bytes, usually written as 1 Kb, i.e. the space necessary to store 1024 characters. The reason that the multiple is 1024 and not 1000 is because it is a function of binary notation and 1 Kb is 2exp10. The capacity of standard 5.25-inch disks is 360 Kb, while that of standard 3.5-inch disks is 720 Kb.

List Box

A pop-up box containing a list of items.

Logical Drive

When MS-DOS was originally created the standard amount of memory, i.e. RAM, was 64 Kb. Hard disk drives did not exist, except for main frame computers and these were huge and so not applicable to the new desktop machines. The result was that the original version of MS-DOS, i.e. Version 1.0, did not have the ability to communicate with and control hard disks. It was based primarily on tape drives, using cassette tapes as the main storage medium. Very quickly it was found that such storage, known as serial storage because the data is written or read in a linear sequence, was too slow for the new PC and so Microsoft upgraded the operating system to handle floppy disk storage.

For a number of years this was all that MS-DOS could handle and it was, apparently, sufficient. But then Shugart Associates created the first hard disk for the PC. By today's standards it was very small: 5 Mb was the maximum size available, but the advent of the drive meant that MS-DOS had to be upgraded again. Microsoft took the opportunity to rewrite major chunks of the operating system at the same time and the new version was 2.0. This allowed for control of hard disk drives but it imposed a maximum limit on the size they could be - 32 Mb. At the time this seemed to be a huge amount, after all it was six times the size of the drives currently available, and so everyone was happy.

But then, as generally happens, the technology involved in hard disks increased and the size of the drives available began to increase at a phenomenal rate. 10 Mb drives, then 20, 30, 40 and beyond appeared and were used. The 32 Mb limit that MS-DOS imposed became an obstacle to using the hard disk storage efficiently. A number of computer manufacturers got round the problem by tweaking MS-DOS in various ways but this was less than satisfactory. Eventually Microsoft upgraded MS-DOS dramatically, with Version 4.0, which removes the 32 Mb limit - but it took them a long time and versions of MS-DOS less than 4.0 are still used by the majority of computers.

So how do you get around the problem if you are using MS-DOS 3.2 or 3.3 and you have a 70 Mb drive? Quite simply you partition it into chunks of 32 Mb or less. Each partition then becomes a separate logical drive and is accordingly assigned its own drive designator letter. Thus if you have a 70 Mb drive you would have to divide it into three logical drives and then you would have Drive-C, Drive-D and Drive-E - but they are all part of the same physical drive. The MS-DOS program that allows you to do this is FDISK, which we will cover in detail later.

MS-DOS 4.0 removes the need to partition a drive in this way, but a case can still be made for such sub-division; however, it now becomes a matter of personal choice rather than of necessity. For instance, you could decide to place all your textual programs, e.g. word processor, text editor, etc., onto one logical drive, have all your graphic applications one another, and have all your accounts on a third. This would then allow you to categorise your programs and data files and ensure that they are all kept separate. Essentially what MS-DOS 4.0 does is allow you freedom of choice, as regards disk storage, for the first time.

Macro

A series of actions, e.g. keystrokes, recorded in some way that can then be activated so that the recorded actions are carried out as a single operation.

Maximise

To enlarge a window so that it fills the entire available area, e.g. the whole screen or the working area within a major window.

Megabyte

A multiple defined as 1,024 Kb or 1,048,576 bytes, usually written as 1 Mb, which is used to denote the capacity of high density disks and hard disks. Again the definition is a function of binary notation and 1 Mb is 2exp20. 5.25-inch high density floppy disks have a capacity of 1.2 Mb while high density 3.5-inch disks have a capacity of 1.44 Mb. The difference is due to the number of sectors and tracks.

Memory Resident Software

Software which has been loaded into the memory where it now resides awaiting activation. Most memory resident software will not work in the Windows environment. Also called TSR programs.

Menu

A pop-down box that contains a list of possible commands. Menu can be accessed either by clicking on them or by pressing **Alt** and the initial letter of the menu required.

Menu Bar

The second line on most Windows applications that contains a list of the keywords which will open the associated menus.

Minimise

To reduce a window to an icon.

Network

The process of connecting a number of computers together in such a way that they can share resources and information.

Parallel Port

A point from which information can be sent from the computer to another device, usually a printer.

Parameter

A condition added to a command. Parameters change the way in which the command operates.

Paste

To copy the contents of the Clipboard into another program at the current cursor position.

PC

This is an acronym for Personal Computer, i.e. a machine based on an 8088 or 8086 microchip without a hard disk drive. However throughout the book the term PC refers to the entire family of IBM compatible machines, including those using the 80286, 80386SX, 80386 and 80486 chips.

Physical drive

A physical drive is quite simply a drive you can see and/or touch and the phrase refers to the actual hardware. Note that the disk(s) are irrelevant - it is the drive unit itself which bears the nomenclature. Every computer will, of necessity, have at least one floppy disk drive, whether this is a 5.25-inch or 3.5-inch is irrelevant. Equally this drive will always be Drive-A. This is the first Physical Drive.

At the front of the majority of computers, including the new shape tower systems that are beginning to appear, there are usually a series of slots which house the drives. The number of slots depends on the total capacity of the carrier. The carrier is, generally, a moulded piece of plastic or metal into which the drives are secured. The carrier is sub-divided into lateral divisions which hold the drive units. Depending on the type of computer you have these drive slots will usually number between 3 and 6, i.e. you can install that many drives. The slots which are currently vacant will normally have some form of sealing strip across them. This serves two purposes; one, it prevents dust and larger pieces of dirt from getting into the guts of the machines, and two, it gives an indication of how many additional drives you can add to the machine.

PIF

Acronym for Program Information File. The set of parameters that Windows requires to run an MS-DOS.

Pitch

The method of measuring how many characters can be printed along the line. The value is based on the number of characters per inch, thus 10 Pitch means that a maximum of 10 characters can be printed on the page. The size of the characters you produce will depend on the type of printer that you are using. Dot Matrix printers, without exception, and Daisywheel printers to a lesser extent base their printed character size on Pitch. This is a measure of the number of characters which can be printed in 1-inch across the width of the paper. The Pitch size is actually the number of characters within that space and it is based on the letter O which is taken to be the average size of all the characters, which is why wider letters like W and M will sometimes impinge on the letters to either side of them in the printed text. Thus 10-Pitch means you can print ten characters to the inch, 12-Pitch is twelve per inch and so on. Therefore the higher the pitch value the smaller the characters, because you are printing more characters into the same space.

Pixel

The smallest part of the screen that can be individually illuminated. Also called picture elements or pels.

Point

Laser printers base the printed character size on Points. A point is One Seventy Second of an inch and it refers to the height of the character block. It also influences the width of the character but to a much lesser extent. Thus 12 Point means that the characters are $^{12}/_{72}$, or $^{1}/_{6}$, of an inch high and so you can print them 6 lines to an inch down the length of the paper - which is the normal default for most printers anyway. On the other hand 36 Point being $^{36}/_{72}$, or $^{1}/_{2}$, of an inch means that you can only print 2 lines to the inch down the paper. Therefore the higher the Point value the larger the characters and so you can print less of them into the same space.

Port

A connection on the computer via which information can be sent or received.

Print

To send data to a peripheral device that will produce a hard copy of the data, e.g. onto paper or film.

Print Queue

A list of files that are awaiting printing.

Printer

A peripheral device that produces hard copy of data.

Printer Driver

A file that supplies Windows, or any application program, with information about the printer and how to use it.

Protected Mode

The operating mode of a computer that allows it to address extended memory. Available on the 80286 and later chips.

RAM

Acronym for Random Access Memory. The memory with which the computer is supplied. RAM can be in one of three kinds:

a) Conventional Memory, that part up to the 640 Kb limit imposed by MS-DOS.

b) Extended Memory, that memory that exists over and above the 640 Kb limit imposed by MS-DOS.

c) Expanded Memory, additional memory that is usually supplied on an add-on board and which can be used by some programs - though not Windows 3.

Read Only File

Any file which has had its attributes changed so that you can open it but not make changes to it.

Real Mode

That mode of the Intel 8000 Series chips that emulates the 8088 and 8086 microchips. This is the only mode available for using Windows 3 on any computer that has less than 1 Mb of free RAM.

Reserved Characters

There are a number of words that are reserved by MS-DOS for its own purposes and so you cannot therefore use them for naming files either as a filename or as an extension. You are not given any choice about this and you will find that you have to use something else. Certainly you should never use any of these reserved words as extensions because they will interfere with the way that MS-DOS handles calls for commands.

The reserved words are:

AUX which is short for Auxiliary and it refers to the communications port into which you can connect a number of other devices, e.g. a modem.

BAS used as an extension this is normally used by any program which is written in Basic.

BAT this is used as an extension for batch files.

COM refers to the communications serial port, it will usually have a number attached, e.g. COM1, and it is also used as the extension for certain programs.

CON is short for Console and it refers to the keyboard and/or the monitor.

EXE used as an extension for executable files.

LPT refers to the line printer parallel ports.

PRN also refers to the printer.

SYS reserved name for system files.

In addition to these words you also cannot use certain characters, either in the filename or the extension. These characters are the first 32 ASCII characters plus the following:

" $ * + = [ ] : ; | \ < , > . ? /
and a blank space.

ROM

The acronym for Read Only Memory and that is exactly what it is. The ROM contains certain bits and pieces that the computer must have to operate correctly, such as the POST procedure, but which cannot be changed - hence the name.

Root Directory

The whole capacity of a drive. Normally the term is used to mean the highest directory level attainable on a hard disk. The Root is created whenever you format the disk. Thereafter other directories can be subtended from it.

Scroll

To page through a list.

Scroll Bars

Horizontal and Vertical bars on the base and the right hand side of a window that allow you to page through the contents of the window when there is too much data to be displayed on screen at any one time.

Sectors

Once the tracks have been laid down on the disk they are divided into arc shaped wedges - the sectors. It is the sector which forms the basis of disk storage. Different disks have a different number of sectors per track, the exact number depending on the capacity and size of the disk.

Serial Port

A connection on the computer via which data can be transmitted or received.

Standard Mode

That mode in which Windows 3 can utilise the Protected Mode of the Intel 80286 and beyond chips. This is the normal mode in which Windows will run. However, you must have at least 2 Mb of free RAM for it to do so. In Standard mode you can switch between Windows applications and MS-DOS programs.

Swapfile

A special file created for use with Windows running in 386-Enhanced mode only. It allows Windows to swap data to the disk when it starts running low on memory. You can create a permanent swapfile, which thereafter exists on your hard disk until removed, or you can allow Windows to create temporary swapfiles as necessary.

System prompt

Contrary to what many people think this is not the flashing cursor that appears on the screen - that is only one part of it. The system prompt shows you the drive you are logged onto, and possibly the sub-directory, followed by the cursor, e.g. C:>_ or A:>_. Throughout this book, except when stated otherwise, the system prompt refers to Drive-C because the vast majority of PC's today include a hard disk.

Tile

To display windows and/or sub-windows in such a way that each window occupies roughly the same amount of screen area without any overlapping.

Title Bar
The first line on any window. It contains the Control Box, the Title of the program, the Minimise and Maximise buttons.

TPI
Acronym for Tracks per inch, usually found on the label of a box of floppy disks. Standard capacity 5.25-inch disks for example are 40 TPI while high density 5.25-inch disks are 96 TPI.

Tracks
When a disk is formatted the computer lays down a series of circular tracks, on inside the other, on the disk. Note that the tracks are circular and not a spiral as on a record. A different number of tracks are laid down on the disks according to whether they are standard capacity, high density, 5.25-inch or 3.5-inch floppies. Hard disks are treated the same way but they have a far greater number of tracks than a floppy does.

TSR
Acronym for Terminate and Stay Resident. Another name for memory resident software.

VGA
Short for Video Graphics Array. This is the monitor type that has become the standard fitted to the majority of AT's and higher priced PC's. The VGA monitor will allow you to emulate all the previous types but you get a clarity, in colour, that matches Hercules. The standard VGA resolution is 640 pixels by 480 pixels using up to 16 colours but you can switch it to produce a resolution of 320 pixels by 200 and then use up to 64 colours at once. In monochrome mode you are limited to 64 greyscales.

Virtual Mode
That mode of the Intel 80386 and 80386SX chips which allow it to behave as if it were a number of distinct 8086 machines, the object being to allow true multi-tasking concurrency of applications.

Wallpaper
The use of a BMP graphic to produce a pretty picture on the background.

Wildcard characters

A wildcard is a character that can be used to replace any other character or sequence of characters when used in conjunction with certain MS-DOS commands, e.g. COPY or DEL. There are only two such characters but there effects are considerable.

> ? can be used to replace any single character. Thus if you had four files named MIKE.DOC, MIKE.TXT, MARY.TXT and MIKE.DOS and you wanted to copy the first and the last you would enter COPY MIKE.DO? and they would be copied while the second and third ones would not. The question mark replaces the final character. To copy only those files with a .TXT extension you could enter COPY ????.TXT. The question marks replace the first four characters.
>
> However instead of using a series of question marks you could use the second wildcard character, *. The asterisk is used to replace any sequence of characters. Thus to copy the files above you would enter COPY *.TXT. To copy all the files you would enter COPY .*.*.

Using the wildcards is something that takes practise, and they add a degree of power to the commands they can be used with. For instance entering DEL *.* can delete all the files in the current directory, although you will be prompted to confirm that this is what you want in this case. So the secret with the wildcards to be careful with them - used abusively they can do an awful lot of damage to your files.

Window

A rectangular area of the screen that is used to contain a program.

Windows 3

The greatest thing since the creation of MS-DOS and the original IBM PC! Well done, Microsoft.

Index

386-Enhanced Mode 37, 48, 51, 53, 61, 396, 411
8086 Chip 43, 403
8088 Chip 43, 403
80186 Chip 46, 404
80286 Chip 45, 56, 404
80286 Protected Mode 45
80386 Chip 46, 58, 405
80386 Modes 47, 406
80386SX Chip 48, 57, 406
80486 Chip 48, 59, 407
80586 Chip 49

A

Accelerator Board 411
Access 411
Access Time 411
Accuracy 411
Active 411
Actuator 411
Adding a printer 156
Adding Fonts 142
Adding Programs with File Manager 220
Adding Programs with Setup 182
Adding to Groups 99
Address Bus 412
Add-on 412
Adobe 411
Allen, Paul xxi
Alphanumeric 412
ALR .... xxviii, 36, 59
ANSI Character Set 408, 412
Apple 412
Application Program, definition of, ... xix, 412
Application Workspace 69
Applications, Adding 183
Applications, Setup 105, 183
Applications 38
Arche Technologies .... xxvii, 34, 57
Architecture 413
Archive 413

Archive Bit 413
Arrange Icons 117
ASCII 353, 413
Associate Command 198, 215, 414
ATTRIB 414
Attributes 414
AUTOEXEC.BAT .... xxii, 33
AUX 415
Auxiliary Storage 415

B

Background 415
Backup 413, 415
BAS 416
Basic 415
BAT 415
Batch File 415
Binary 415
Bit-Mapped Graphics 152, 249, 417
BMP Files 240, 259, 262
Boot, definition of, ... xviii, 417
Boot Record 417
Boot Strap 418
Border 68
Border Width 154
Browse Command 100
Buffer 418
Bus 418
Byte 418

C

Cache 418
Calculator 304
    Keyboard usage 304
Calendar 309
    Finding Dates 314
    Printing 319
    Saving 319
    Setting Alarms 316
    Menus 310
Capacity 419
Cardfile 323
    Cards 330

Index

List	328
Menus	324
New cards	328
Printing	332
Saving	331
Cascade Command	86, 116, 206
Cassettes	419
CD-ROM	419
CGA	420
Change Attributes Command	199, 216
Changing Drive	192
Character Set	420
Chip	420
CHKDSK	247
Clicking	421
Clipboard	239, 284, 421
Clip-Art	240, 276, 421
Clock	335, 421
Clock in WIN.INI	367
Clone	400
Closing Windows	69, 77, 81, 194
Cluster	421
Cold Boot	421
Color Schemes	129, 131, 133
Creating	134
Hue	136
Luminosity	136
Palette	129
Saturation	136
Saving	137
Colors in WIN.INI	366
COM	159, 421
Command	421
Communications	387
Compatible	400
Computer	421
CON	421
Configuration	421
Configuring a printer	159
CONFIG.SYS	xxii, 33
Connect Net Drive Command	201
Console	421
Contiguous	421
Control Box	68, 83

Control Box - Commands
- Close 69
- Maximise 68
- Minimise 68
- Move 68
- Restore 68
- Size 68
- Switch To 69

Control Panel 125
- 386-Enhanced 126, 174
- Color 125, 128
  - Color Palette 129
  - Color Scheme 129, 131
  - Color Scheme Designing 133
  - Creating Colors 134
  - Custom Colors 131, 135
    - Hue 136
    - Lum 136
    - Sat 136
  - Screen Element 131
- Date/Time 126, 174
- Desktop 125, 148
  - Border Width 154
  - Cursor Blink Rate 154
  - Pattern Designing 150
  - Pattern Selection 149
  - Sizing Grid 154
  - Wallpaper 152
- Fonts 125, 138
  - Adding and Removing 142
  - in Windows 141
  - Pitch and Point 139
- International 126, 165
  - Country 166
  - Currency Format 171
  - Date Format 170
  - Keyboard 169
  - Language 168
  - List Separator 169
  - Number Format 173
  - Time Format 172
- Keyboard 126, 174
- Mouse 125, 146
- Network 125, 155
- Ports 125, 144

Printers 126, 155
    Adding 156
    Configuring 159
    Options 164
        Handshake 164
        Header 164
        Job Timeout 164
        Margins 164
        Print to 164
    Sound 126, 174
Conventional Memory 51, 421
Cookies 423
Copy, definition of, ... xix, 423
Copy Diskette Command 200
Copying Files 206
Corel Draw 249, 267, 423
Country 166
CPI 420, 424
CPS 420, 424
CPU 420, 424
CP/M .... xxi, 424
Create Directory Command 199, 207
Creating Colors 134
Ctrl, definition of, ... xviii
Currency Format 171
Cursor 424
Cursor Blink Rate 154
Cursor Keys, definition of, ... xix, 425
Custom Colors 131, 135
Cut 425

D

Data File 425
Date Format 170
Default 425
Deleting Files 107, 212
Deleting Groups 98, 107, 112
Desktop 149, 425
    Border Width 154
    Cursor Blink Rate 154
    Pattern Designing 150
    Pattern Selection 149
    Sizing Grid 154
    Wallpaper 152

Desktop in WIN.INI 363
Devices in WIN.INI 366
Dialogue Boxes 71, 425
Digital Research xxi
DIR 62
Directories, Moving 222
Directory 425
Directory Tree 190, 192
Disconnect Net Drive Command 201
Disk 426
Disk Drives 49
DISKCOPY 200
DMDRV.BIN 29
Double Click 426
Double Click Speed 147
Drag 426
Drives 426
Drop Shadow 426
DTP 411, 425

E

EGA 426
EMS Memory 427
Enlarging Windows 75, 191
EPT Port 159, 427
ESDI, definition of, ... 50
Expanded Memory 52, 427
Extended Memory 52, 427
Extensions 427
Extensions in WIN.INI 363

F

File Icon Selection 102
File Manager 189
   Associate Command 198, 215
   Cascade Command 205
   Change Attributes Command 199, 216
   Close Command 197, 223
   Confirmation 204
   Connect Net Drive 201
   Copy Command 199, 206
   Copy Diskette 200
   Create Directory Command 199, 207

Index

Delete Command 199, 212
Deselect All Command 200
Disconnect Net Drive 201
Disk Menu 200
Exit Command 200
File Menu 196
Format Diskette 201, 218
Label Disk 200
Make System Disk 201
Maximise Command 197
Menus 196
   Control Box 196
      Minimise Command 197
      Move Command 197, 199
      Restore Command 196
      Size Command 197
      Switch To Command 197
   Disk 200
   File 196
      Next Command 197
      Open Command 198
      Print Command 198
      Rename Command 199, 213
      Run Command 198
      Search Command 199, 210
      Select All Command 200
      Sub-directories 193
   Options 204
      Minimise on Use 205
   Tree 201
   View 202
   Windows 205
      Refresh Command 205
      Tile Command 205
Filenames 427
Files 428
   Copying 206
   Deleting 107
   Moving 95
   Selecting 196
Floppy Disk 428
Fonts 430
   Adding 142
   Raster 141
   Removing 142

Vector 141
Fonts in Windows 141
Fonts in WIN.INI 365
Fonts in Write 290
Footer 431
Foreground 431
FORMAT 201
Format Diskette Command 201, 218, 431

G

Games, Reversi 337
Games, Solitaire 342
Gates, Bill xxi
Graphics, BMP Format 239, 240, 259, 262
Graphics, PCX Format 239, 240, 259, 262
Group, definition of, ... xix
Group Window 69, 81
Groups 89, 431
    Adding to 99
    Adding to using File Manager 220
    Adding using Setup 104
    Browse Command 100
    Deleting 98, 107, 112
    File Properties 102
    New 108
    Protecting 94
GUI, definition of, ... xiv

H

Handshake 164
Hard Disk, definition of, ... xviii
Hard Disks 44, 431
Header 164, 432
Help 62, 71, 119
    Commands 119
    Index 119
    Keyboard 119
    Procedures 119
    Using 119
Hidden File 433
High Capacity Disks 433
Highlighted 433
HIMEM.SYS 34

I

IBM AT	45, 414
IBM Model 5150-001	43
IBM PC	43, 436
IBM XT	44
ICL 1900	xiii
Iconising windows	74, 194
Icons	70, 118, 433
Arrange Command	117
definition of,	xix
Inactive window	433
Intel Corporation	43, 403
International	126, 165
Country	166
Currency Format	171
Date Format	170
Keyboard	169
Language	168
List Separator	169
Number Format	173
Time Format	172
International in WIN.INI	363

J

Job Timeout	164
Jobs, Steve	412

K

Keyboard	169, 174, 433
Kilobyte	433

L

LABEL	200
Label Disk Command	200
Language	168
Laser 386	xxviii, 35, 58, 229
Licence Agreement	30
List Box	434
Paging	192
List Separator	169
Logical drive	434

LPT 159

M

Macros 381, 435
Make System Disk Command 201
Margins 164
Maximise Command 68, 435
Maximise Switch 69
Maximising Windows 75, 191
Megabyte 435
Memory 34, 398, 421
    Conventional 51, 421
    EMS 427
Memory Resident Software 435
Menu, definition of, ... xix, 436
Menu Bar 69, 436
MFM, definition of, ... 49
Microsoft xxi
Minimise 436
Minimise Command 68
Minimise Switch 69
Minimising Windows 74
Modem 391
Modes, definition of, ... xx
Modes selection 62
Mouse, Swapping Buttons 147
Mouse Pointer 70
Mouse Tracking Speed 147
Move, definition of, ... xx
Move Command 68
Moving between windows 194
Moving directories 222
Moving Files 95
Moving Windows 72
MS-DOS Program Problems 397
MS-DOS Programs .... xx, 38
MS-DOS window 246
MS-DOS .... xiii, xviii, 53

N

Network 155, 436
New groups 108
Norton Speed Disk 63, 399

Index 455

Notepad 353
   Cursor Keys 355
   Menus 354
   Word Wrap 356
Number Format 173

O

Object orientated Graphics 249
OS/2 45

P

Paging List Boxes 192
Paintbrush 249
   Menus 257
      Edit 262
      File 257
      Font 266
      Options 269
      Pick 268, 276
      Size 266
      Style 266
      View 263
   Printing from 278
   Tools 271
   Zoom In 263
   Zoom Out 265
Paintbrush in WIN.INI 367
Parallel Port 436
Parameter 436
Paste 436
Pasting Data 242
Patterns, Designing 150
Patterns, Selection 149
PC Tools Compress 63, 399
PCL Printer 227
PCL Printer in WIN.INI 365
PCX Files 239, 240, 259, 262
Physical Drive 436
PIF 39, 437
PIF Editor 373
Pitch 437
Pitch and Point 139
Pixel 438

Point 438
Port 438
Ports in WIN.INI 364
PostScript 227, 412
PostScript in WIN.INI 365
Print 438
Print Manager 227
Print Manager in WIN.INI 367
    Menus - Options 233
    Menus - View 234
Print Queue 230, 438
Printer 438
Printer Driver 438
Printers 37, 155
    Adding 156
    Configuring 159
    Options 164
        Handshake 164
        Header 164
        Job Timeout 164
        Margins 164
        Print to 164
Printing 230
    from Calendar 319
    from Cardfile 332
    from File Manager 198
    from Windows 230
    from Write 298
Printing Problems 235
Problems 395
Program Information Files 373, 437
Program Manager 81
    Menus 112
        File Menu 113
            Copy 114
            Delete 114
            Exit 114
            Move 114
            New 113
            Open 113
            Properties 114
            Run 114
        Options Menu 115
            Auto Arrange 115
            Minimise on Use 115

Index   457

    Windows Menu 116
        Arrange Icons 116
        Cascade 116
        Tile 116
Programs,
    Adding with File Manager 220
    Adding with Setup 182
    Copying 109
    Moving 95
Protected Mode 438
Protecting Groups 94

Q

Q-DOS xxi

R

Ramdrive 62, 399
Random Access Memory 51
Raster Fonts 141
Read Only file 439
Real Mode 395, 439
Rearranging Group Contents 95
Rearranging Windows 89
Recorder 381
Registration Card 30
Removing Fonts 142
Rename Command 199
Renaming Files 213
Reserved Characters 439
Restore Command 68
Reversi 337
Reversi Menus 339
RLL, definition of, ... 50
ROM 440
Root Directory 440

S

Samsung .... xxvii, 34, 56, 228
Saving Colors 137
Scroll 440
Scroll Bars 70, 440
SCSI, definition of, ... 50

Seattle Computer Products xxi
Sectors 441
Selecting, definition of, ... xx
Selecting files 196
Serial Port 441
SETUP 31
    Adding Programs with 182
    Applications 105
Shugart Associates 45
Shugart Corporation 50
Size Command 68
Sizing Grid 154
Sizing Windows 76, 85
SMARTDRV.SYS .... xxiv, 29, 34
Solitaire 62, 228, 342
    Decks 347
    Menus 343
    Playing the game 344
    Scoring 345
Solitaire in WIN.INI 366
Standard Mode, definition of, ... xxiv
Standard Mode 37, 48, 52, 61, 395, 441
StarScript 38
ST-506/412 45
Swapfile, creation of 63
Swapfile 51, 62, 177, 399, 441
Swapping Mouse Buttons 147
Switch To Command 69, 200, 244
Switching Drive 192
SYS 201
System Messages 72
System Prompt 441
System Resources 229

T

Task Switching 69, 200, 244
Terminal 387
Terminal in WIN.INI 368
Text Mode 373
Tile Command 88, 116, 205, 441
Time Format 172, 442
Title Bar 69
TPI 442
Tracks 442

TSR 442

U
Using Windows 81

V
Vector Fonts 141
VGA 412, 442
Video Mode 375
Virtual Mode 442
VTEC xxviii

W
Wallpaper 152, 442
Wildcard Character 443
WIMP xiv
Window 443
Windows .... xviii, xxii
    Arrange Icons 244
    As Icons 194
    Cascading 116, 244
    Closing 77, 81
    Enlarging 191
    In use 81
    Layout 66
    Maximised 75
    Memory Resident 246
    Modes 62
    Moving 72
    Moving between 194
    Printing from 230
    Problems 395
    Tiling 244
    Using two versions 66
Windows 386-Enhanced Mode, definition of, ... xxiv
Windows 386-Enhanced Mode 37, 48, 51, 53
Windows Iconising 74
Windows in WIN.INI 360
Windows Real Mode, definition of, ... xxiv
Windows Real Mode 37, 48, 52, 61
Windows Setup 177
    Display 178

Keyboard 178
Mouse 178
Network 178
Windows Sizing 76, 85
Windows Standard Mode, definition of, ... **xxiv**
Windows Standard Mode 48, 52, 61
Windows Tile 116
Windows/286 .... 46, 126, 284, 396
WIN.INI 176, 359
WIN/2 62
WIN/3 62
WIN/R 62
WIN/S 62
WordStar 227, 229
Write 284
    Block usage 296
    Cursor Keys 293
    Fonts 290
    Formatting 285
    Graphics 297
    Printing 298
    Saving Files 289
    Tabs and Ruler 286
Write in WIN.INI 368
WYSIWYG 299

X

XMS Memory 376